Scribe Publications
KASZTNER'S TRAIN

Born Anna Szigethy in World War II Budapest, Anna Porter and her mother left Hungary for New Zealand in 1956 to escape the increasing Soviet presence.

Porter built a career in publishing that, by 1969, took her to Canada, where she joined McClelland & Stewart, rising to become president and publisher of Seal Books, a paperback publishing house co-owned by McClelland and Bantam Books.

In 1982, she left Seal Books to establish Key Porter Books where she continues as the publisher and chief executive officer.

In addition to publishing, Porter has authored three mystery novels. In recognition of her varied achievements, she was appointed an Officer of the Order of Canada in 1992.

KASZTNER'S TRAIN

the true story of an unknown hero of the Holocaust

Anna Porter

SCRIBE
Melbourne

Scribe Publications Pty Ltd
PO Box 523
Carlton North, Victoria, Australia, 3054
Email: info@scribepub.com.au

Published in Australia and New Zealand by Scribe 2008

First published in the UK by Constable, an imprint
of Constable & Robinson, 2008

Typeset by Westchester Book Group
Map by C. Stuart Daniel/Starshell Maps
Printed and bound in Australia by Griffin Press
Only wood grown from sustainable regrowth forests is used
in the manufacture of paper found in this book

National Library of Australia
Cataloguing-in-Publication data

Porter, Anna
Kasztner's train : the true story of an unknown hero
of the holocaust
Carlton North, Vic. : Scribe Publications, 2008

9781921372155 (pbk.)

Kasztner, Rezső Rudolf, 1906-1957; Holocaust, Jewish
(1939-1945) – Hungary; World War, 1939–1945 – Jews – Hungary.

940.5318092

www.scribepublications.com.au

This book is dedicated to the survivors
and the victims of the Holocaust in Hungary

Contents

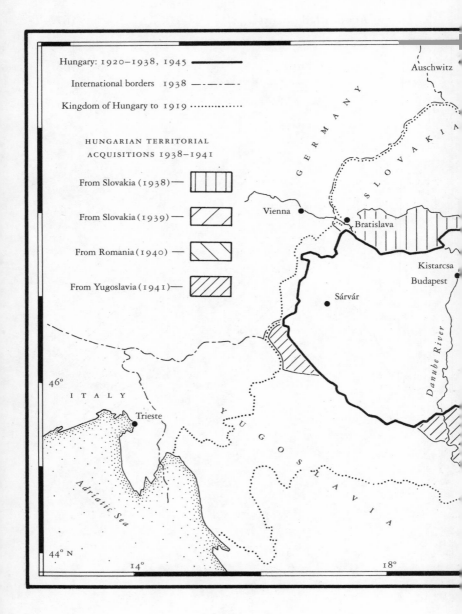

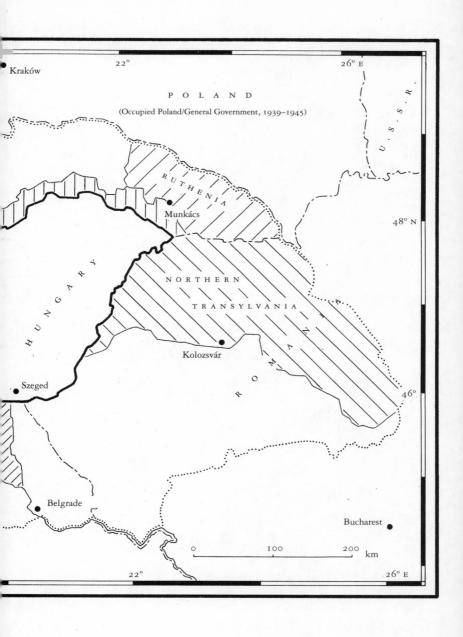

Kraków

P O L A N D

(Occupied Poland/General Government, 1939–1945)

22°

26° E

U
.
S
.
S
.
R
.

R U T H E N I A

Munkács

48° N

N O R T H E R N

T R A N S Y L V A N I A

R
O
M
A
N
I
A

H
U
N
G
A
R
Y

Kolozsvár

46°

Szeged

Belgrade

Bucharest

0   100   200   km

22°

26° E

Introduction

In the summer of 1944 in wartime Budapest, two men, a Nazi and a Jew, sat negotiating through a fog of cigarette smoke. One was notorious: Adolf Eichmann, architect of the Holocaust. The other was less well known: A Hungarian lawyer and journalist called Rudolf [Rezső] Kasztner... The topic of their discussion was a train to be filled with Jews.

Adam Lebor, "Eichmann's List: A Pact with the Devil," *The Independent*, August 23, 2000

The train would carry 1,684 passengers out of German-occupied wartime Hungary. They were a motley group: industrialists, intellectuals, and Orthodox rabbis, Zionists and anti-Zionists, Polish and Slovak refugees from pogroms and concentration camps, the oldest eighty-five, the youngest a month old. The wealthy Jews of Budapest paid an average of $1,500 for each family member to be included; the poor paid nothing. The selection process was arduous. Its memory is deeply distressing to those whose relatives did not survive the Holocaust.

It was a deal that would haunt Rezső Kasztner to the end of his life.

In addition to those on the train, Kasztner negotiated with Adolf Eichmann to keep twenty thousand Hungarian Jews alive—Eichmann called them "Kasztner's Jews" or "the Jews on ice"—for a deposit of approximately $100 a head. And in the final weeks of the war, Kasztner traveled to several concentration camps with ss

Lieutenant-Colonel Kurt Andreas Becher to try to prevent the murder of the surviving prisoners.

As he fought fearlessly for Jewish lives during the Holocaust, Kasztner met many of the now recognized heroes of wartime Europe, including Oskar Schindler, Raoul Wallenberg, and Carl Lutz. But his most fateful meetings were with Becher, Eichmann, and members of the ss Sonderkommando, whose chief purpose was to rob and murder all the Jews of Europe. These connections with high-ranking Nazis were to cost him his own life—and, for decades, his reputation.

I first heard of Rezső Kasztner in 1999 from Peter Munk, a Canadian businessman-entrepreneur. Munk's energy and charm are legendary, as are his successful business ventures. And he owes his life to Rezső Kasztner.

We sat in a dark room with leather furniture, Persian rugs, heavy silk drapes, paintings that looked old, and bronze statuettes that looked recent. There were some faded black-and-white prints on a low-slung coffee table. I noticed pictures of a five-story, white-painted brick house, a shaded garden with puffball flowers, and a small, slanting lawn. Then a picture of his grandfather, Gabriel Munk, in the garden, hand resting on a brass-handled walking cane, dressed in a three-piece suit, with a gold watch-chain and a white kerchief neatly triangled out of his top jacket pocket. Next, Peter's father, also with felt hat and walking cane, and Peter's stepmother—"a great beauty," as Peter said. Her face half in shadow, her chin raised, her short, flared dress a fashion statement of the early forties, she seems to be flirting with the photographer.

"I've been sorting some boxes," Peter said, almost apologetically. "I don't think about the past much, but we have to pack some of these old things . . ." He picked up another photograph, showing "the most elegant man I have ever known." In this picture Grandfather Gabriel is framed by an ornate doorway. He stands next to a slight woman whose hand rests on his forearm.

Gabriel Munk had purchased seats on the last train from Budapest transporting Jews not destined for the death camps. The train left

Budapest on July 1, 1944, three and a half months after the German occupation of Hungary, two and a half months after the first deportations of Hungary's Jews to Auschwitz-Birkenau.[1]

Munk showed me a photograph of gray and white people standing around a railway carriage. They seem aimless, as people often do when they are waiting. Some are lining up at metal steps, and one woman in a light, two-piece suit with padded shoulders and high-heeled shoes is looking back at the camera. A man in a long, belted raincoat is helping her up with one hand while holding her small valise in the other. In the background stands a German soldier, his rifle at ease. The woman is smiling.

It seems a very ordinary picture, except that this photograph was taken in the summer of 1944, at a time when Hungarian Jews were brutalized, robbed, beaten, and shot, and when many witnessed the slaughter of their children. It was the summer when 437,402 of them were packed into cattle cars destined for Auschwitz-Birkenau, where most of them were murdered.[2] At the time the photo was taken, Peter Munk's family was boarding a train toward the west.

It was Kasztner's train.

Like Peter Munk, I was born in Budapest. My early education about the war years, however, was somewhat different from his. Although mine was full of detail about the Soviet "liberation" of the country in 1945, it contained few references to the victims of the Hungarian Holocaust. Searching for Rezső Kasztner, I read all the books I could find that dealt with the years leading up to the war.

I met Erwin Schaeffer, Munk's business associate in Budapest, who took me to the Great Synagogue on Dohány Street and told me the story of how his father had been thrown off the Kasztner train and murdered by the Arrow Cross Party's thugs, the Hungarian Nazis who assumed power in October 1944. I visited libraries and archives in Budapest, New York, Washington, Tel Aviv, and Jerusalem. I read everything I could find about Kasztner, only to become more confused by the irreconcilably different versions of him presented in memoirs, documents, letters, and testimonials. Adolf

Eichmann described him as "an ice-cold lawyer" and talked of their mutual deals. Hansi Brand, Kasztner's lover, spoke of a "passionate believer in human values." Tomy Lapid, a former colleague, remembers his extraordinary facility with words and his devastating wit. American scriptwriter Ben Hecht saw him as a smug Nazi collaborator. Thousands owe their lives to Kasztner. But thousands still decry his "deal with the devil."

I listened to the stories of survivors. Some still remembered Rezső Kasztner, the brilliant raconteur, the idealistic Zionist, the humanist, the writer, the politician, the resourceful negotiator, the inveterate gambler, the romantic, the sarcastic critic of everyone less intelligent and less well informed. I met his daughter, Zsuzsi, who adored her father's warmth and humor. I had tea with Sári Reuveni, who said Kasztner could not have dealt with Eichmann without the support of Hansi Brand. "She was his soul," she mused, his partner in saving lives, his lover during the months of the German occupation of Hungary. I met Hansi's son Dani in Tel Aviv. He talked about his strong, spirited mother, who had hidden him during the siege of Budapest. He was proud of her fearlessness, her extraordinary empathy for others. We did not talk about Hansi's affair with Rezső.

In New York, Egon Mayer, a director at the Center for Jewish Studies at the City University of New York, collected a massive archive of Kasztner information. He had a special interest in the train: his parents were on it, and he was born six weeks after its second detachment of passengers arrived in Switzerland. It was Mayer who first told me that Kasztner had supplied the funds to feed and clothe Oskar Schindler's Jews.[3]

Schindler, I discovered, had gone to Budapest in 1942 to meet Kasztner. Both men had powerful egos; both believed they were the only ones who could outwit the Nazis. Schindler, the big-boned, rough-talking Sudeten German industrialist, and Kasztner, the soft-spoken Jewish intellectual, had not liked each other, but they shared a passionate belief that one man could make a difference. During subsequent meetings, exchanging letters, cash, and information, Schindler grew to admire Kasztner: "He was utterly fearless," he wrote in a postwar memoir, and "his actions remain unsurpassed."[4]

After the war, Schindler was recognized as a Righteous Gentile, supported by grateful survivors, celebrated, and lionized. Kasztner, in contrast, became a symbol of collaboration with the enemy.

The deals Kasztner made with the ss (Schutzstaffel), the Nazi Party's protection and security service, raise questions about moral choices, courage in dangerous circumstances, the nature of compromise and collaboration, and how far an individual should go to save other people. These questions are as valid now as they were in the 1940s. They continue to haunt the world today.

A NOTE TO THE READER

This is a work of popular history. I have done my best to be accurate but have allowed myself the leeway to reconstruct scenes and dialogue based on the diaries, notes, taped interviews, courtroom testimonies, pretrial interrogations, and memoirs—both written and oral—of the participants in Hungarian, English, German, and Hebrew. My primary sources are listed in the bibliography. Where I have attributed emotions or thoughts to people, I based these on published and unpublished sources. I interviewed more than seventy-five people—those who remembered most clearly are credited in the text, notes, and acknowledgments. Discerning the truth is never an exact science when relying on people's memories, but I have done my best to cross-reference wherever possible, and only when convinced of the credibility of the testimony did I use it. Is it possible that some of my judgments or reconstructions are mistaken? Of course. But I do not consider anything in this book to be simply speculative.

After all the reading, listening, and searching, I feel I have discovered the real Rezső Kasztner—an extraordinary man who played a high-stakes game of roulette with the devil. And won. In the only game he cared about, that of saving human lives, he achieved more in his way than any other individual in Nazi-occupied Europe.

In the end, all he lost was his own life. Kasztner would have considered that a small price to pay.

PART ONE

The Jewish Question

All that is necessary for the triumph of evil is that good men do nothing.

Edmund Burke[1]

Palestine is our ever-memorable historic home. The very name of Palestine would attract our people with a force of marvelous potency . . . We should there form a portion of a rampart of Europe against Asia, an outpost of civilization as opposed to barbarism. We should as a neutral State remain in contact with all Europe, which would have to guarantee our existence . . . We should form a guard of honor about these sanctuaries, answering for the fulfill-ment of this duty with our existence. This guard of honor would be the great symbol of the solution of the Jewish question after eighteen centuries of Jewish suffering.

Theodor Herzl, *The Jewish State*, 1896

Desperately Seeking Palestine

The ideals which characterized the great era of the individual,
such as humanism, justice, freedom and rationalism, will give way
to other slogans . . . and Judaism, which has been attached to these
ideals, will move on its road of agony.

Rezső Kasztner, *Új kelet*, June 28, 1940

Rezső Kasztner was born in 1906, in Kolozsvár, Hungary—soon to be Cluj, Romania, as the aftermath of the First World War divided and redivided the borderlands of the once powerful and widespread Austro-Hungarian Empire. This part of Transylvania had belonged, variously, to Romans, Saxons, Magyars (as Hungarians call themselves), and Romanians. Mindful of the surrounding history and their own Jewish ancestors, Rezső's parents blessed him with three names right from the start: Rudolf, with a nod to the German Saxons; Rezső, for the Magyars, and Israel, the name the biblical Jacob received when he fought the Dark Angel and won. It was a prophetic name for Rezső Kasztner, though he would have little time to savor his victory.

Kolozsvár, the largest city in Transylvania, has always had grand cultural and historical pretensions. In the shadow of the Carpathian Mountains that form Hungary's ancient protective border, Kolozsvár was cosmopolitan, its wealthy merchants reaching out east and west to fill the shops with Oriental silks and carpets, French and English antiques and formal wear, Belgian lace, Indian spices, and hand-crafted musical instruments from Russia. Its grand avenues, shaded by plane trees, featured the yellow stone houses of the rich. Its main square boasted the largest church in Transylvania. Built in the four-teenth century, the church's massive walls were used to display the flags of the local Catholic nobility who had paid for its construction. Outside, there was an imposing statue of Hungary's last Magyar king, Mátyás, his bronze horse trampling on Turkish flags, celebrat-ing his fifteenth-century victory over the invading Turks. Mátyás and his Black Knights were the embodiment of Magyar romantic pride, and the city of Kolozsvár was King Mátyás's birthplace.

Rezső grew up in a two-story brick house in the southern part of the city. His father, Yitzhak, a prosperous merchant, spent most of his days in the local synagogue, where he studied the Bible and debated various parts of the Talmud with other Jewish scholars. Rezső's more business-minded mother, Helen, ran the store. She was a born trader, an educated woman who aspired to a good life for her sons. Although she was religious, she decided to send all three of her boys to general high schools, where the curriculum was broad and included the study of languages. She recognized early that her youn-gest had the sharp mind, quick wit, and imagination to become more than a merchant. He was a slender boy with long, wavy, dark hair, the charming good looks of his mother, and his father's gift for intense concentration. By the time Rezső graduated from high school he spoke five languages—Hungarian, Romanian, French, German, and Latin.[1]

Helen Kasztner decided that Rezső would study to be a lawyer, but his passion was politics. He argued with his parents about the nature of Jewish privileges in Hungary, and he insisted that the Hungarian aristocracy, whose fancy carriages still pranced up and down Kolozsvár's streets, tolerated Jews only for their support against the other minorities in the country.[2] In 1900, non-Magyar speakers, including the Romanians of Transylvania, were 46 percent of the population. Jews helped to balance the vote in favor of the Magyar ruling aristocracy. The Kasztner family, along with most of the other Jews in the country, ignored the mild, fastidious, often jocular anti-Semitism of the ruling classes as well as the grimmer resentments of the disenfranchised poor. When others talked of the ancient bond between the Magyars and the Jews of Hungary, Rezső scoffed. The bond would last only so long as it was useful, he said. The rancor would remain.

Like most of the fifteen thousand Jews of Kolozsvár, Helen Kasztner had been a supporter of the 1914–18 war effort, a proud Hungarian citizen. There had never been any doubt that the Jews would volunteer for the army. They fought with uncommon valor by the side of other Hungarians, allied with the Kaiser's Germany. Even Field Marshall Archduke Joseph had expressed his appreciation of the empire's Jewish subjects. There were Jewish majors and colonels and a Jewish general. The National Rabbinical Association had called on its members to offer up prayers for an early victory. Rabbis gave their blessings to all those who fought, and they reminded their congregations of their patriotic duty to support the war effort. Rezső's father, who had studied at the Bratislava yeshiva, or religious school, volunteered for the Hungarian army, where he served as a chaplain.

Many Hungarian intellectuals argued that the war had been the Habsburgs' own personal conflict, that they had dragged Hungary along, and that it was all about territory. Archduke Ferdinand's untimely death at the hands of a Habsburg-hating Serb in 1914, while unfortunate, hardly seemed a clear cause for war.

Austria-Hungary lost the war, the House of Habsburg lost its centuries-old empire, and Charles, the last Habsburg emperor-king, was forced to abdicate. The government was in disarray, returning troops of the defeated Hungarian armies found a country in chaos, Romanian troops marched into historic Hungary from the east, the Czechs claimed new territories in the north, refugees from the provinces were arriving in carts and on foot, food was scarce, and strikes threatened to remove all semblance of order, while Charles had vacillated in appointing a new prime minister. Béla Kun, a former journalist who had just returned from the Soviet Union, formed the new Communist party, which promised land to the landless and work for the disarmed soldiers. Kun and his Communist reformers managed to grab control of the government with the aid of the mildly leftist Social Democrats. The short-lived Communist Republic confiscated property, abolished entitlements, nationalized industry, and hanged or shot real and imagined opponents. Kun imposed a range of reforms that echoed those of the Soviet commissars. After just four months (from March 21 to July 30, 1919), the Kun era ended with the arrival—on horseback—of Admiral Miklós Horthy, the former commander in chief of the unimpressive Austro-Hungarian fleet.[3]

For Hungary, the war ended with the June 1920 Treaty of Trianon, a sideshow to the grand Treaty of Versailles of 1919. Hungary was carved up by the victorious Allies, who donated two-thirds of its historic territory and three-fifths of its population to the surrounding countries. The package of punishments included the granting of Transylvania to the Romanians, whose delegation at the bargaining table had been ably assisted by a brilliant, beautiful, and selectively promiscuous queen, King Ferdinand's wife, Marie.[4] When all was done, Romania alone had gained more territory than was left of Hungary.

By the stroke of a pen, Transylvania became part of Romania, and Kolozsvár was now Cluj. To the Hungarians, the diminution of the country—the loss of Felvidék, or Upper Province, to the new republic of Czechoslovakia, of the Bácska area in the south to Yugoslavia, and of northern Transylvania to the Romanians—was unthinkable and unbearable. No other country had forfeited in such a spectacular way. The sheer magnitude of the loss has haunted Hungarians ever since. The additional 180 million crowns in war reparations barely registered in the minds of the thousands who demonstrated in rage and disbelief throughout Hungary. Their government appealed in vain to the newly minted League of Nations, to the winning nations of Britain, France, and the United States, and to the neutral powers; it gained no sympathy. Horthy declared himself Regent and promised to return Hungary to its former size. In response, Yugoslavia, Czechoslovakia, and Romania signed mutual defense treaties in case the Regent was serious about his intentions.

The postwar years were a desperate time for the poor: the peasants suffered extreme hardships, factory workers were forced to put in long hours, the homeless knew nothing but misery, and they all lacked food. In these terrible conditions, Horthy's new government was relieved to hit upon the perfect scapegoat for the country's ills— the Jews. With the rise in anti-Semitism in Germany and throughout eastern Europe, the Jews were a natural target. In Lithuania, Poland, and the Ukraine, there were murderous rampages against Jews. In Germany, Julius Streicher launched the Nazi newspaper *Der Stürmer* (The Stormer) in 1923 with the headline, "The Jews Are Our Misfortune."[5] The First Anti-Jewish Law, the Numerus Clausus Act, was introduced in Hungary as early as 1920, the first anti-Semitic legislation in twentieth-century Europe, and the fourteen-year-old Rezső saw it as an indication of the times. It limited the number of Jews at universities to the same small proportion, 6 percent, that they represented in the population at large. The "closed number" law proved to be only a mild rebuff to the success of Jewish students and was allowed to lapse eight years later, but many saw it as a harbinger of tougher laws to come.

Rezső declared himself a Zionist at age fifteen. For him, it was a romantic rather than a political notion. "Zion" was the biblical name of ancient Jerusalem, where King David had built the fortified temple that was later destroyed by the Romans. The fifteenth-century poet Yehuda Halevi was the first to apply the term to the people of the Diaspora. The idea that the Jews would, one day, return to their ancient lands in Palestine attracted Rezső even before he discovered the writings of Theodor Herzl. The Hungarian-born Herzl wrote of the ingrained, centuries-old anti-Semitism among Europeans and declared that he understood the reasons for it. Although Jews had endeavored to blend themselves into their surrounding communities while preserving the faith of their forefathers, they had not, he said, been permitted to do so. They had continued to be viewed as "aliens," as strangers. "Old prejudices against us lie deep . . . He who would have proof needs only to listen to the people where they speak with frankness . . . My happier co-religionists will not believe me till Jew-baiting teaches them the truth." Herzl in 1896 foretold the disasters of National Socialism under Adolf Hitler and warned his fellow Jews to found their own homeland before it was too late.[6]

In 1919, Britain was mandated by the League of Nations to administer and thus control Palestine. In 1920, following another resolution of the League, the British government agreed to the creation of a "national home for the Jewish people" in the mandate territory, as spelled out in the Balfour Declaration. The Yishuv, as the Jews already living in Palestine called themselves, would now be represented to both the British authorities and the rest of the world by a new organization, the Jewish Agency, which was composed of the various Zionist factions in the pre-1930s World Zionist Organization.

Rezső's older brother Gyula, whose enthusiasm for the land of Zion had inspired young Rezső, emigrated to Palestine in 1924 to work on a kibbutz in the Valley of Jezre'el. Eighteen-year-old Rezső would have accompanied him, but he had not yet finished high school. Instead, he joined a youth group, Barissia, whose Zionist student members were training to become citizens of Eretz Israel, the new Jewish homeland that would rise from the old in Palestine. Within a year, he emerged as the group's leader. For the evening sessions around the campfire, he prepared wildly impassioned speeches about the new promised land. The training was not much different from that familiar to Boy Scouts everywhere; they learned to be comfortable in the uncomfortable outdoors and, in addition, picked up a few Hebrew songs along with some scattered knowledge of Jewish history and basic agricultural techniques. In the new land there wouldn't be room for merchants or, for that matter, lawyers. Rezső was already a fine writer and a great debater. Even before he entered law school, he wrote articles for the Hungarian-language, Kolozsvár-based Jewish newspaper *Új Kelet* (New East), reporting on the development of British policies in Palestine.

Rezső was twenty-two when his father died in 1928. It was a

perfect death for a religious man: Yitzhak died as he read the Torah in the synagogue on the seventh day of Passover.[7] But for Rezső it meant he had to put off any ideas about emigrating. His mother needed him at home.

The only country willing to listen to the Hungarians' grief over their territorial losses was the other big loser under the Treaty of Versailles: Germany. Throughout the 1930s, as Hungary began to develop closer ties with Germany, discriminatory legislation against certain groups within Germany grew apace. In January 1933 Adolf Hitler, the leader of the National Socialist Party, or Nazi Party, was named chancellor by the addle-brained president of Germany, Field Marshal Paul von Hindenburg. In April, Hitler's National Socialists took over the Prussian Secret Police to establish the Secret State Police (the Geheime Staatspolizei, or Gestapo) and assumed the powers to arrest, interrogate, and imprison all those they considered enemies, without the benefit of legal process. Violent attacks on Jews, Communists, and rival right-wing party members were becoming the norm in German cities.

Rezső Kasztner had read Hitler's *Mein Kampf* (My Struggle) in its first German edition, long before it was published in Romanian. German newspapers, most of which were regularly available in Kolozsvár, hailed it as the brilliant work of a young genius who had a clear-eyed view of how best to solve Germany's postwar problems. Kasztner found it to be the incoherent ranting of a poorly educated man, full of hate and ambition. Hitler's one consistent thought was his identification of "the Jew" as the chief enemy of his *herrenvolk*, the Aryan master race. Like David Ben-Gurion,[8] the chairman of the Jewish Agency Executive in Palestine, Kasztner realized that if Hitler came to power, war was inevitable, and that the Jewish people would bear the burden of much of Hitler's war.

To anticipate where the Hungarians would stand, all he had to do was listen to the Magyars in Kolozsvár's coffeehouses along the renamed streets, read their imported newspapers, and tune in to their radio. The rallying cry of *Nem, nem, soha*, "No, no, never," had become the mantra of Hungarian politicians, who vowed never to accept the postwar settlement. Maps of historical Hungary, with its superimposed, dramatically reduced post-Trianon borders, decorated the walls in Hungarian schools. Even the youngest children were taught patriotic poems and songs about the return of the old territories. If Hitler went to war, Kasztner predicted in *Új Kelet*, Hungary would become Germany's ally, and Transylvania's Romanian adventure would prove short-lived.

After he graduated from law school, Kasztner joined the staff of *Új Kelet*. He was happy to start as a sports reporter, so long as he could write political commentary as well. He wrote about the Kun era's likely effects on Hungarian politics. Kun was from Kolozsvár, and some of his relatives still lived in the city. Unfortunately for all the Jews of Hungary, Béla Kun and many of his associates had been Jews. Traditional anti-Semites saw the whole Kun interregnum as a failed Jewish plot. The fact that many of Kun's victims had been wealthy Jews made no difference to those seeking someone to blame for the Communists' few months in power.

Kasztner was hired as an assistant to Dr. József Fischer,[9] a member of parliament, lawyer, and president of the Jewish Community of Kolozsvár. Fischer was one of the wealthiest citizens of the city. He was among the first to own a car; his family lived in a spacious villa with a range of housekeeping staff; he supported numerous charitable and cultural institutions, and, as a leading member of the National Jewish Party, he represented Romania's 700,000 Jews in Bucharest. A tall, patrician man with pale-blue eyes and a high forehead, he wore suits made to measure in Berlin or Budapest, handstitched shirts, and monogrammed gold cuff links. Fischer was respected in both Romanian and Hungarian society. He had noticed young Rezső Kasztner's articles in *Új Kelet* and encouraged him to continue his writing, even if his opinions drew few friends. Not only was Kasztner smarter and better read than others, but he also let everyone know that he was superior in wit and knowledge.

Fischer may have been the only other person whose intelligence the young man respected. Kasztner often dismissed people as stupid, incompetent, or intellectually cowardly. He was intolerant of his critics. "He had no sense of other people's sensitivities, or he didn't care whether he alienated his friends," said Dezsö Hermann, who went to law school with Rezső and, despite their ongoing battles, remained a lifelong friend.[10] Rezső's sarcastic retorts to those who disagreed with his views about Hungarian feudalism and the old ways were famous even at the University of Prague,[11] where his mother sent him to finish his studies. "He was a tough man to argue with," Hermann said. "Back then, in Kolozsvár, Jews kept their heads down. Not Rezső." Yet he was one of the few who could deal with the authorities as an equal.[12]

In local government, Kasztner was remembered as a "fixer," a man others trusted to solve their problems, but he was too smart to be much loved even by those he had helped. Still, he was sought out. The Jews of Kolozsvár needed someone like Kasztner to help them survive the difficult years after Transylvania was ceded to the Romanians. They and their ancestors had supported the Hungarians through several centuries. Now they were a minority within the Magyar-speaking minority. They endured not only the wild, enthusiastic nationalism of the newly jubilant Romanians but also the occasional virulent bouts of anti-Semitism by the Iron Guard, a fringe group of fascists whose main objective was to acquire Jewish property and destroy the Jewish presence in Romania.

Kasztner managed to keep in touch with bureaucrats and gentile functionaries of all political stripes. He knew whom to bribe and how much to offer, whom to flatter and how. He succeeded in securing interviews with leading politicians. Much to the consternation of his readers in Kolozsvár, he interviewed members of the Iron Guard, including dedicated anti-Semites who were keen to share their ideas. Even then, he thought it was wise to know the enemy.[13] In addition to his other languages, he spoke the form of courtly Romanian developed under Habsburg rule that endowed all men in authority with grandiose titles and employed an antiquated form of address that ordinary folk had never learned.

People consulted Kasztner about small problems, such as not being paid for goods delivered, and large problems, such as the time in 1938 when he persuaded a magistrate to release an elderly Jew charged with attacking two policemen. The beefy gendarmes couldn't refrain from laughing as they told their tale. The Jew, they said, had lunged at them with his cane. They failed to mention that they had pushed his wife off the sidewalk. Kasztner asked to have his client admitted to the courtroom. When the magistrate saw the frail old man, he knew the score. Yet, this being Romania in the thirties, everyone went on pretending. Kasztner knew how to play this game: he paid off the gendarmes, the charges were dropped, and the old man and his wife went home.[14]

Kasztner was outspoken, brash, unafraid. He could be seen striding toward government offices and into police headquarters, a pale, muscular, slender man, his dark hair swept back, his well-tailored black suit stark even during the summer heat, his tie loosened over his white shirt, the collar perfectly starched. He was confident, in a hurry, his briefcase casually swinging from one hand, the other ready to wave to all his acquaintances.

Given his quick rise in society, it was surprising that Kasztner did not leave behind his Zionism. For a Kolozsvár (Cluj) Jewish intellectual in the 1920s and '30s, being a Zionist was unfashionable. The idea of emigrating to Palestine, to live on communal farms and work in hardscrabble fields barely retrieved from the desert, did not appeal to people who had been part of Europe for centuries. Jews enjoyed public life, commerce, banking, the arts and sciences; some of them were noted writers, humorists, historians. They were simply not cut out for farming. Nor was Zionism popular among the religious Jews, who often sought Kasztner's assistance when dealing with the authorities. Most of them, like Rezső's father, did not believe Jews should return to their homeland until the Messiah came.

When the opportunity arose to join one of the Palestinian Jewish political parties planning to form a government once a new Jewish state was established, Kasztner chose the Ihud[15] (later known as the Mapai, or Labor Party). Its leaders, David Ben-Gurion and Chaim Weizmann, were renowned statesmen who had traveled in Europe and spoken at large gatherings of Zionists. József Fischer had met Ben-Gurion and sent financial support for the agricultural efforts near Haifa. He had also written to Weizmann,[16] who headed the

World Zionist Organization office in London, reporting on the situation of the Jews in Romania. Fischer encouraged Kasztner to be active in the politics of the Yishuv without losing interest in the politics of Romania and Hungary.

Kasztner's fortunes gained a brighter patina when he married Fischer's daughter, Elizabeth. Fischer had allowed his spacious living room to serve as a meeting place for Kasztner and his group of young Zionists. Elizabeth—her nickname was Bogyó, or "Flower Bud"—used to hide behind the banister of the receiving rooms, waiting to see Rezső, who was ten years older. He would arrive in his overly formal suits late in the evening, long past her bedtime. In her lacy white nightgown, she had looked every bit the angel in her father's gold-framed Titian adorning the wall. Rezső felt a generation away from the fragile eighteen-year-old girl who became his bride in 1934. A pretty brunette, with milky skin and dark, curly hair that she wore stylishly long, Bogyó was quiet and shy in public. The fact that he had known her since she was a child would influence their relationship in the coming years. He was intensely protective of her, and she admired him unconditionally.

Bogyó had their new apartment decorated with skill and taste, then settled into the social life of Kolozsvár. She had studied ancient history, and she left political science to Rezső. Yet she said once that not even after he had read *Mein Kampf* could Rezső imagine how the next few years would affect their lives—and Rezső was better informed than most people in Kolozsvár. When Hitler became chancellor, *Mein Kampf* sold more than a million copies, but the worst that Kasztner predicted was that Hitler would demand that all Jews leave the German territories.

Before the end of 1933, Jews in Germany were excluded from the universities and from most professions. On May 10, in the square next to the State Opera House in Berlin,[17] a massive bonfire, accompanied by a long, hysterical speech by the future propaganda minister, Josef Goebbels, incinerated thousands of books by Jewish authors deemed unfit for the new German ideology.

The September 1935 Nuremberg Laws, designed to protect "German blood and German honor," defined Jews as a race, not as adherents to a religion. Henceforth, a Jew was a person who had two or more Jewish grandparents. Jews were no longer German citizens, and marriages between Jews and Germans were expressly forbidden. The British and American press found the new laws barbaric, even though polite anti-Semitism was accepted in both countries.[18] The international community raised no voice of protest. Nor did any outside government interfere when, in defiance of the rules set out in the Versailles Treaty, German law forbade Jews from participating in trade and industry. As Kasztner saw it, the plans set out in *Mein Kampf* were inexorably being implemented.

By 1936 Hitler's anti-Jewish policies ensured that Jews in Germany had lost much of their economic power. They were selling their businesses and real estate to non-Jews at ludicrously low prices. The World Jewish Congress reported that Germany wanted all its Jews to disappear. Almost a quarter of a million of them were already fleeing, exchanging their possessions for slips of paper that allowed them out of Germany and gave them permission to enter Palestine. In Palestine, the Hebrew-language newspapers talked of deals between Nazi officials and Jewish leaders that allowed German Jews to transfer at least a portion of their wealth if they left for Palestine. The notion that Germans would systematically murder innocent people seemed far-fetched. József Fischer maintained that a civilized nation like Germany, the home of Beethoven, Schiller, Goethe, and Thomas Mann, would not, could not tolerate acts of murder. Germans had been one of the most cultured peoples of the world, he said, quite unlike those peasants to the east who habitually committed atrocities against their Jewish neighbors.

Alarmingly, 1936 also marked the beginning of widespread riots in Palestine by Arabs protesting against the influx of Jews. By the 1930s, about 400,000 Jews were living in Palestine, and their number rose as the German persecutions escalated. In the face of Arab opposition, the British began to vacillate between appeasing the Arabs and increased Jewish immigration. When Rezső's brother Gyula went to Kolozsvár to visit his family in late 1936, the picture he painted of his new homeland was anything but the bucolic scene his mother had imagined.[19] He had joined the Yishuv's underground army, the Haganah, as a small-arms instructor, to take part in the defense against Arab attacks on Jewish civilians. He anticipated that Britain would hesitate to live up to the promises of the Balfour Declaration.

In 1937 the Iron Guard bombed a Jewish theater during a performance in the Romanian city of Temesvár (Timisoara), a few hours' journey from Kolozsvár. There were anti-Jewish riots in Kishinev and Bucharest, where indulgent policemen looked on and chose not to interfere. The persecution of Jews continued in Poland and the Ukraine. By 1937, almost 400,000 Polish Jews had emigrated. Winston Churchill, in the British House of Commons, spoke of Europe "drifting steadily . . . towards some hideous catastrophe."[20]

On March 12, 1938, Germany occupied Austria in what Kolozsvár radio reported as a friendly, brotherly way, with cheering crowds welcoming the invading army. It was now the Austrian Jews' turn to prepare for the Nazis' expropriation policies. Over five hundred Jews committed suicide during the first few weeks of the Anschluss, the term by which the annexation of Austria became known. *Új Kelet* picked up the story from British newspapers about a family of six Jews in Vienna who, unable to face the fate of German Jews, chose instead to shoot themselves. Within a year, over 100,000 Austrian Jews had been "emigrated" by the well-oiled German state machinery. Some went to camps, some to Palestine, and others to the United States, Hungary, and other countries. Austrian villagers whose families had lived side by side with their Jewish neighbors for hundreds of years now proudly raised white flags declaring themselves *Judenfrei*—free of Jews.

In Nuremberg, a new exhibition opened under the title The Eternal Jew. It denounced Jews as a disease, a virus that infected Aryan races, and equated Judaism with Bolshevism. A film of the same title, featuring Jews as plague-carrying rats, went into production.

In 1938 President Franklin D. Roosevelt bowed to public pressure in the United States and called for an international conference to facilitate the emigration of refugees from Nazi-controlled Germany and Austria. As a result, in July that year, representatives from thirty-two countries met for nine days at the luxurious Royal Hotel at Évian-les-Bains on Lake Geneva. Most of the delegates availed themselves of the excellent sporting facilities offered by the hotel as they hiked, fished, golfed, swam, and played tennis.

Two weeks before the conference, sixteen thousand German Jews had been arrested and sent to concentration camps. The prison camps for Jews and those in opposition to the government were full: Dachau near Munich, Oranienburg near Berlin, Buchenwald near Weimar. In the Buchenwald camp a recorded voice announced over the loudspeaker every night: "Any Jew who wishes to hang himself is asked first to put a piece of paper in his mouth with his number on it, so that we may know who he is." Yet, as all the finely dressed gentlemen grandly assembled at the Évian Conference in France made sympathetic speeches to each other about the Jewish problem, immigration quotas at home stayed in place, and not one country offered asylum to the Jews of Europe. Later, those nations claimed they had had no idea how terrible the situation had become.

Canada had been reluctant even to attend the Évian Conference and, once there, committed to take only "certain classes of agriculturists." In practice, that meant no Jews. Brazil would accept only those who could show certificates of baptism. Australia agreed to accept up to fifteen thousand Jewish immigrants over the following three years, but its delegate explained: "As we have no real racial problems, we are not desirous of importing one." The British representative had similar concerns. Britain had already taken eight thousand, most of them children.

Only three small countries—Holland, Denmark, and the Dominican Republic—offered limited temporary asylum. The conference participants examined a proposal for a "large-scale settlement" in British Guiana that could accommodate up to 5,000 carefully selected "young people" at a cost of £600,000. Rhodesia could make room for up to 500 families over a "period of years." Ambassador Myron Taylor of the United States announced that his country's full quota of 27,730 German and Austrian immigrants would be admitted. It was a ridiculously low number from the nation that had called the conference, but U.S. State Department officials later made sure that the rules were applied so rigorously that even this quota would not be met; fewer than 15,000 managed to gain entry. At that time, about 625,000 Jews were under Nazi rule in Germany and Austria. When Germany invaded Poland, another 3.5 million were added. There were then about 780,000 Jews in Hungary, more than 800,000 in Romania, and hundreds of thousands in neighboring countries.

Having accomplished nothing, the delegates at the Évian Conference passed a unanimous resolution that they were "not willing to undertake any obligations toward financing involuntary immigration." For Kasztner, the conference confirmed his suspicions that, other than Palestine, there would be few safe havens for Europe's Jews. And even there, the doors were closing.

At the end of September 1938, Hitler won another major victory without bloodshed. He convinced the British, French, and Italian leaders of Germany's right to the Sudetenland portion of Czechoslovakia. The latter had mobilized its army after Hitler asserted this right, but a Munich gathering of "the great powers" accepted the reversion of Germany's agreements with the Czechs and its immediate occupation of the Sudetenland. The Czech government was not consulted and had little choice but to abide by the so-called Munich Agreement. On his return home, British prime minister Neville Chamberlain made his infamous announcement that he had achieved "peace with honour."

On November 9, a new wave of violence swept over Germany. During the night, 191 synagogues were burned down or destroyed with axes and hammers. Tombstones were uprooted, homes were smashed, shops were looted, and Jews found in the streets were beaten. The Nazis called it *Kristallnacht*—Crystal Night, or Night of Broken Glass. In response to this brutality, the British government organized a series of children's transports out of Germany. Almost ten thousand children were taken into temporary homes in Great Britain. Most of them would never see their parents again. Within three months, in one of his characteristically shrill speeches, Hitler declared that war would lead to the "annihilation of the Jewish race in Europe."[21]

On March 15, 1939, the German army occupied Bohemia and Moravia, the two western provinces of Czechoslovakia. In Hitler's view, this territory (including Czechoslovakia's capital, Prague) was part of the historical German Reich. Slovakia, which had been part of Hungary, thereupon seceded from Czechoslovakia and formed an independent nation under the protection of the Reich. It would now be governed by the fascist "People's Party," split between the clerical, fascist, ultranationalist faction of Josef Tiso, a Catholic priest, and the pro-Nazi group of Vojtech Tuka, who became the first prime minister. Both factions were enthusiastically and bitterly anti-Semitic.

The partition of Czechoslovakia was celebrated by the Romanian and the Hungarian press as a way to end Germany's search for *lebensraum,* or "living space," as outlined in *Mein Kampf,* providing new land and raw materials. Kasztner wrote in *Új Kelet* that he had foreseen it all: the acquisition of the Sudetenland was clearly outlined in *Mein Kampf* as a prerequisite to Hitler's vision of a vast, unified territory of German-speaking peoples. Hitler would be reaching out next to the more than 500,000 German speakers in Hungary. Meanwhile, like tossing a bone to a dog, he gave Hungary a chunk of Magyar-speaking Slovakia and Carpathian Ruthenia. Perhaps in gratitude for the gift, the Hungarian government enacted a stronger version of its lapsed First Anti-Jewish Law.

The Italians, encouraged by Hitler's success, invaded Albania. Benito Mussolini, the dictator of Italy whose ridiculous demeanor was fashioned after the rulers of ancient Rome, signed the pretentiously named Pact of Steel with Hitler in late May 1939.

Palestine had been the one sure destination for Jews fleeing from Europe, but, as German enthusiasm for Jewish emigration grew in the early years of the Reich, so did Arab resistance to Jewish immigration. The sporadic riots that began in Palestine in 1936 soon culminated in a full-scale Arab rebellion against British rule over Jewish immigration. About 600 Jews and some British soldiers were killed, and thousands more were wounded. The British government, determined to protect its access to the Suez Canal, "the jugular vein of the Empire,"[22] and to appease the Muslims in its colonies to the south, commissioned a White Paper on a new policy for Palestine. Its effect was to limit Jewish immigration to 12,000 people a year. Peace with the Arabs was of greater strategic importance to Britain than peace with the small number of Jews in Palestine or the powerless Jewish population of Europe. The British authorities soon amended the number to a maximum of 100,000 immigrants over five years, including refugees who arrived without appropriate entry certificates, but after 1941 Palestinian Arabs would have a veto over any further Jewish immigration.[23]

It was a pitifully small number seen from where Kasztner kept watch over the rising tides of anti-Semitism in Europe. "Perfidious Albion," he thundered in *Új Kelet*.[24] In exchange for political expediency, Britain had closed the door to the only land still open to the Jews. On May 19, Winston Churchill spoke in the House of Commons and accused his own country of setting aside "solemn engagements" for "the sake of a quiet life." Britain, he charged, had capitulated to threats from an Arab population that had been increasing at a rate faster than that of Jewish immigration. "We are now asked to submit to an agitation which is fed with foreign money and ceaselessly inflamed by Nazi and fascist propaganda."

Refugees from Poland, Slovakia, Austria, and other countries, with little more than the clothes on their backs, poured over the borders of both Hungary and Romania. There were no particular rules affecting the fleeing Jews, though some pedantic border guards insisted on hearing a recitation of the Lord's Prayer to test whether a person was a genuine refugee or just a Jew.

Despite specific government orders forbidding any aid for refugees, Kasztner set up an information center in Kolozsvár. He solicited help from local charitable organizations, seeking temporary accommodation and collecting clothing and food, but his main concern was to provide Jewish refugees with a safe destination. As a Zionist leader, he sent telegrams to the Jewish Agency's Labor Zionist leadership in Tel Aviv, asking for help and funds to buy passages on ships and to pay bribes to local officials. The Jewish Agency's staff were much more sympathetic to refugees than their British-authorized administrative functions allowed, but they could not issue more Palestinian entry visas than the imposed limits, and these were never enough. The solution, they agreed, was to encourage illegal immigration. The Agency's Executive had already set up an office in Geneva to monitor the situation in Europe, and Chaim Barlas,[25] head of its Immigration Department, moved to Switzerland to help with both legal and illegal immigrants. After the British White Paper, all Yishuv leaders supported illegal immigration, or *aliya bet*, as it became known.

To get people out of danger in Europe, the Jewish Agency paid the going rate for passage on forty-five ships between 1937 and 1939.[26] In 1939 alone, thirty ships, legal and illegal, sailed from Romanian Black Sea ports through the Bosphorus and on to Palestine.[27]

Ever the brilliant fixer, Kasztner obtained exit visas from the Romanian government even as Britain stepped up its efforts to persuade officials not to allow the departure of the overcrowded boats. Kasztner was certain that the British would allow the refugees to land once they arrived in Haifa's harbor. Of course officials and shipowners would have to be bribed, and ships in the Romanian port of Constanta were still willing to sell passage to Istanbul and thence to Palestine.

Refugees continued to set out down the Danube and from ports on the Black Sea, Bulgaria, Greece, and Turkey. As it happened, several thousand German Jews ended up in Shanghai, where no one had thought of setting immigration limits.

The German-Soviet Pact of August 1939 between Hitler and Russian leader Joseph Stalin turned out to be the prelude to the organized massacre of the Poles. Hitler cut off their escape route. It was a compromising agreement for Hungary, now leaning on German might for its territorial and industrial ambitions but historically allied with Poland. After much hand-wringing, the Hungarian government decided not to join in the attack on Poland and hoped that Hitler would be forgiving.

On September 1, 1939, German armies attacked Poland. The Luftwaffe, the German air force, dumped bombs on both military and civilian targets. The grotesque carnage left behind on the battlefield proved to the rest of Europe that old-fashioned warfare had no chance against German steel. Thousands of Poles joined the armies of refugees flooding over the borders into Romania and Hungary.

In defiance of the Treaty of Trianon, Hungary launched a massive re-armament program. The Romanians, expecting an attack, began to build new fortifications and increased their already significant armed presence on their western borders, including in the city of Kolozsvár. Their open hostility to the Hungarians in the region added fuel to the saber rattling on both sides. Hungary began to talk about liberating its fellow Magyars.

Britain and France, obliged through their mutual assistance treaties with Poland, declared war on Germany on Sunday, September 3. That day, close to midnight, the British Broadcasting Corporation (BBC) World Service reported that a German submarine, without warning or provocation, had torpedoed and sunk the British liner *Athenia*, which had been en route from Liverpool to Montreal. There were 1,400 passengers on board, and more than 100 perished. British parliamentarians were outraged, though the German naval commander later insisted it had been an innocent mistake. In fact, Germany was determined to disrupt British shipping lanes and had been building a range of submarines for that very purpose.

On September 21, Reinhard Heydrich, chief of the Reich Security Office, called all senior ss men in his special police force to a conference to tell them the process that had been decided on for eliminating Polish Jews. Given the very large number of about 3.5 million, German officers were to implement a staged plan, first to concentrate the Jews in designated areas in large cities, close to the railway lines; then to appoint Jewish councils made up of respected elders to ensure that German orders were followed, and finally to

confiscate all Jewish belongings and show no mercy when inflict-
ing pain.

With nothing more than words of comfort from the Allies,
Warsaw fell to the German forces on September 28. German army
recruits, "in the spirit of adventure,"[28] murdered Jews in their
homes, their synagogues, their villages, and on city streets. They
forced them to march naked through village squares, beat them with
bayonets and rifle butts, ordered old men to shave their beards, and
hanged the reluctant from lampposts when they disobeyed. They
shot thousands of Jews into open trenches, not even bothering to
cover the graves. The refugees told horrific stories of atrocities and
starvation in the labor camps, where German and Austrian intellectuals had been left to die. By the spring of 1940 there were more
than a hundred thousand refugees in Europe—and, increasingly,
fewer offers of employment for them, less food, and little shelter.

With each German victory—Norway and Denmark in April 1940;
Belgium and the Netherlands in May—the number of refugees grew,
as did the desperation of those who had seen inside the German
Reich.

On May 10, Germany launched its attack on France. As Europe
was overrun by the German armies, the fate of the Jews deteriorated,
inexorably, one step at a time.

Once the immigration quota for 1941 was filled, the British began
their blockade of Palestine, fearing an all-out Arab attack in the Middle East. Several ships carrying illegal immigrants were apprehended
by the Royal Navy. Conditions on others were so squalid that some
people who had escaped Nazi persecution at home now opted for suicide by water. The refugees who managed to reach Palestine were
herded into detention camps. Those with valid passports were sent
back to their countries of origin, where many were later murdered by
the Nazis. After arduous negotiations the year before with the governor of Mauritius, a few thousand had been sent there in late October
1940.

On one ship, the *Atlantic*, a group of Jewish saboteurs, members of the Haganah,[29] decided to disable the vessel in order to prevent the British from sending it out of Palestinian waters. Tragically, they caused an explosion that killed 260 people, many of them women and children. To make sure that would-be immigrants were aware of the dangers, the BBC reported the casualties, the deaths, and the redirecting of ships. Not wishing to incite British sympathy for the refugees, however, officials made sure that the details were only in broadcasts to the Balkans and eastern Europe.[30]

In the summer of 1940, Hitler, still enjoying a friendly alliance with Stalin, gave the USSR a couple of adjoining pieces of Romania: Bessarabia and northern Bukovina. In the wake of these losses, Marshal Ion Antonescu, who was sharing power with the violently fascist Iron Guard, gained control of the Romanian government. Unaccountably, Antonescu's regime blamed the Jews for the territorial losses. The objective may have been to provide the Iron Guard with an incentive—they could now rob the Jews—to continue its support of Antonescu's faction in parliament. Inevitably, pogroms followed throughout the countryside.

On June 14, 1940, the Eighteenth Army of the German Reich occupied the City of Light. Paris fell with barely a whimper, and the Nazi swastika was hoisted to the tip of the Eiffel Tower. In *Új Kelet*, Kasztner mourned the passing of an age—in fact, a whole civilization: "History likes to detach itself from its makers and run its own course," he wrote. "Who could imagine that the rule of common sense, freedom and democracy, the heritage of the French Revolution, would be swallowed up by the victory of a regime that negates all these values? . . . Once Paris fell . . . a page has turned in the history of France, Europe and humanity at large."

Delighted with his successes, Hitler ordered an all-out attack on Britain to begin in July. The "Blitz," an almost ceaseless bombardment of major British cities, lasted days at a time. The hunt for British ships in the North Atlantic, Hitler promised, would bring mastery of the oceans in only a few months. Germany, it seemed, was invincible.

It was time for the Hungarians to press their case. With the stroke of a pen, Hitler accomplished what the League of Nations had refused: on August 30, 1940, under German-Italian arbitration, he returned the northern half of Transylvania to Hungary. In return, the government of Prime Minister Pál Teleki agreed that Hungary's ethnic Germans—the Swabians—would have special privileges, including the right to an independent relationship with the Reich. As icing for the ethnic German cake, he also agreed to the recruitment of twenty thousand Swabian men into the Waffen-ss, the ss's own regular army units.

Hitler consolidated his power by signing the Tri-Power Pact with Italy and Japan on September 27, 1940. Hungary joined the pact on November 20. In Regent Horthy's opinion, the pact did not oblige the country to join Germany's war. The only requirement was for members to render assistance if one of the other partners was attacked.[31]

The Jews of Kolozsvár were jubilant to be Hungarians once more. Hungarian Jews had not suffered the kinds of random killings meted out to Jewish villagers in Romania, and there had been little Jewish emigration from Hungary. There, Jews still considered themselves part of the fabric of society. They were patriots. As the declaration of the Jewish Community of Pest expressed it in 1932: "Our course is the inseparably intertwined course of our Jewishness and our Hungarianness. This land, the Hungarian land, is our homeland. We watered this land with our blood and sweat and it is our useful work that brought to fruition the blessed fruits of legal equality. The storms of transitional times may shake or tear off the branches of the Hungarian tree of equality, but the tree itself cannot be toppled."[31]

Jewish ex-servicemen wore their First World War decorations with pride and remained devoted to Hungarian culture. Many Jews had become celebrated writers, artists, newspaper editors, doctors, lawyers, and intellectuals; they were busy rebuilding the economy, founding new industrial enterprises, developing exports and financial institutions. They took an active part in politics. Less than one-third of the Jews in Hungary considered themselves Orthodox, and most viewed themselves as Hungarians who, incidentally, professed the Jewish faith. The largest synagogue in Budapest had been built by the Neolog, or Conservative Jewish community. As some historians have claimed, even this nod to Judaism was superficial. The majority of Jews were indifferent to religion and merely observed traditions.

Most Jews remained adamantly unconcerned about the rise of anti-Semitism in Hungary. In 1938, when the Hungarian prime minister announced a program of rearmament, he argued that Hungary's military weakness was due to Jewish influence. The "Jewish question" and the "Jewish problem" were debated and reviewed in the press, as were a variety of options and solutions. Gains in popular acceptance and legal status were rapidly being lost in the wake of imposed restrictions on the percentage of Jewish children eligible for higher education, limited entry into the professions, and capped participation in government. But Hungarian Jews were not worried. These laws, they believed, were only temporary; they would be repealed as soon as Hitler was gone.

During the late 1930s, few thoughtful people took the extreme right seriously. Ferenc Szálasi, a fringe figure with a populist platform of land reform, incoherent patriotism, racist diatribes, anti-Trianon rages, and enthusiasm for the confiscation of Jewish property, was often heard at public rallies inciting his followers to acts of vandalism against Jews. A former army major and practicing spiritualist, Szálasi advocated the creation of a "Hungarist" state encompassing the lands in the Carpathian basin all the way to the Adriatic. He believed that the Bible was originally written in some early form of Hungarian and that Jesus was a Magyar. In the "Carpathian-Danubian Great Fatherland," the unifying language would be Hungarian. His Arrow Cross (Nyilaskeresztes, or Nyilas) Party adopted as its emblem the crossed-arrows design of an earlier Hungarian radical right-wing movement. The government declared his party illegal in February 1938, yet its ideas continued to attract Christian rightists of all parties. Thus, when his followers tossed hand grenades into the Dohány Street synagogue in Budapest, they received light sentences.

On March 5, 1938, the Prime Minister declared that Hungary was ready to deal with its "Jewish problem." This, as he and his supporters perceived, was undue influence in the economy, the press, theaters, and other cultural activities. Vocal opposition to these new measures from liberal parliamentarians, members of the Social Democratic Party, writ-ers, and famous musicians such as Zoltán Kodály and Béla Bartók went unheeded. The first Anti-Jewish law was passed by the Hungarian gov-ernment on June 28, 1938. The 1939 elections brought in a new gov-ernment, about 20 percent of its members radical right-wingers. It immediately passed the Second Anti-Jewish Law, which severely lim-ited the number of Jews who could work as doctors, engineers, pub-lishers, lawyers, or journalists. Henceforth, the number of Jews in the professions had strictly to reflect their proportion in the population. The same law reduced to no more than 20 percent the proportion of Jews in financial and commercial enterprises, in theater, film, and the press, and in businesses employing more than ten people.

This new legislation, adopted in May 1939, defined Jews as a race, along the lines of the Nuremberg Laws; prohibited Jews who were not yet citizens from obtaining citizenship or holding government positions, and provided for the retirement of all Jewish members of the judiciary. It re-established the original Numerus Clausus Act's restrictions in higher education. Article 239 provided for the forma-tion of the labor service system that would eventually force more than 150,000 Jewish men into military service, without guns, uni-forms, or rights, subjected to the whims of regular army command-ers. And, once Hungary reclaimed its Transylvanian territories, all these laws applied to the Jews of Kolozsvár, too.

By the end of 1940, most young Jewish men in Hungary were in labor battalions, and the young men of Kolozsvár were swiftly called up to join them. For a few months, Kasztner himself served in a labor battalion of mostly Jewish intellectuals, building military forti-fications in northern Transylvania, but he managed to negotiate a special dispensation for medical reasons and returned to Kolozsvár, where he continued to work on behalf of the refugees. He found that bribery was still effective with officials, and he managed to win simi-lar dispensations for other men. He obtained exemption cards for the sickly and for the sons of widows. He had connections on the black market, knew where to trade currencies, and kept abreast of the going rates for bribery. Few officials would turn down American dollars or Swiss francs. Local government functionaries, now responsible to Hungary, would still see Kasztner without an appointment. Secretaries to the new representatives treated him with deference. Typically, even after the authorities shut down all Jewish organizations in Kolozsvár, Kasztner was able to convince them that Zionist youth camps were actually sporting camps for youth about to emigrate—a grand idea for both the Hungarians and the Jews.

In January 1941, members of the Iron Guard launched a rebellion to overthrow Antonescu's Romanian government. Its ranks swelled by patriotic fervor and the hope for easy loot, the guards hunted for Jews in villages and small towns. Thousands, without food or water, were herded into boxcars that were left on sidings for days. In Bucharest, human bodies were hung on meat hooks and displayed in the windows of butcher shops. And, after March 1941, German troops were stationed in Romania, preparing for the invasion of the Soviet Union.

Still, although the new Hungarian laws affecting Transylvanian Jews were troubling, the Jewish community in Kolozsvár was relieved to be outside the jurisdiction of the Romanian mobs.

Perhaps in preparation for some friendly overtures toward the Allies, Prime Minister Pál Teleki signed "a treaty of peace and eternal friendship" with Yugoslavia in February. Many Hungarians thought it a hopeful sign, given the bellicose saber rattling of military leaders fixated on the reacquisition of Croatia to fulfill the dream of the former Greater Hungary.

Before assuming his lead role in the Hungarian political drama, Count Teleki had been a professor of geography at the University of Budapest, a nationalist, a member of the old-world gentry that had run the country for centuries. The joke doing the rounds in Kolozsvár cafés was that the old cartographer was so busy redrawing the map of Hungary and renaming its towns that he had no time for such basic matters of state as the natural flow of the rivers. The rivers, of course, had always run from Germany and from Russia. There was no hope for declaring a neutral position, and even less hope that Great Britain, the particular target of Teleki's fond aspirations, would support such a move.

A mild-mannered, vocal anti-Semite (he claimed he could "in eight or nine cases out of ten recognize the Jew"), Teleki particularly disliked the distinct traditions of eastern Jews, most of whom had come to Hungary over the previous two hundred years. He claimed to prefer the "assimilated," patriotic Jews of the big cities and to be relatively friendly toward them.

On April 6, 1941, using Hungary as its base of operations, the German army invaded Yugoslavia. Admiral Horthy, the Regent, though somewhat ambivalent about the action and concerned that it could affect his relations with Britain and the United States, acquiesced. It was, however, an act Count Teleki could not countenance, given his recently signed nonaggression treaty with the Yugoslav government. He committed suicide. In his parting note to Horthy, he wrote, "We have allied ourselves with scoundrels."

The Hungarian army crossed the border and joined the German attack. The reward: eleven thousand square miles of Hungary's former territory.

In early 1941, when the Hungarian government closed all Jewish newspapers, including *Új Kelet*, the thirty-six-year-old Kasztner decided to leave Kolozsvár and go to Budapest. Having lost his voice among his people, he was afraid he would also lose his status and influence. He needed a job, and he certainly did not want to accept support from his affluent father-in-law. Once he was established in the capital, they agreed, Bogyó would join him.

CHAPTER 2

The Gathering Storm

Probably in all 5703 years,[1] Jews have hardly had a time as tragic and hopeless as the one which they are undergoing now. One of the most tragic factors about the situation is that while singled out for martyrdom and suffering by their enemies, they seem to have been forgotten by the nations which claim to fight for the cause of humanity.

Senator William Langer,
Addressing the United States Senate, October 6, 1943

In the early spring of 1941, when Rezső Kasztner first went to Budapest, the city seemed deceptively friendly and rather grand. At this time of year the Danube is majestic; its swollen floods rush over the lower keys, and the sound of swirling waters overwhelms the chamber music coming from the musicians in the cafés along the Danube Corso, the main street along the Pest side of the river. Well-dressed couples strolled on the shaded boulevards, and Váci Street, which runs parallel with the Corso, was filled with shoppers. The women preened under their expensive parasols; the men pretended to read their newspapers. Flower vendors offered violets and carnations, the blossoms' strong bouquet mingling with the river's fishy smells. The massive Parliament Building—the largest in the world when it opened in 1902—with its gothic spires and voluminous baroque base, was still imposing enough to make a young man's ambitions soar. On the Buda side of the great river, the hills were covered in the light greens and yellows of the acacias. At the top of the hill, the Royal Palace gleamed almost white after the heavy rains.

The economy was booming, the theaters were playing Shakespeare, the stage at the Comedy Theater was taking risks with veiled references to the Nazis, and people were not afraid to laugh at Hitler jokes in revues at the jam-packed nightclubs. The opera season was in full swing with performances of Gounod's *Faust* and Mozart's *Così fan Tutte* and *The Marriage of Figaro*. The cafés and casinos were packed. Ordinary restaurants offered more interesting fare than even the best eateries in Kolozsvár. Here, it was easy to ignore the looming shadow of war. With the arrival of warm weather, people went boating on the Danube, the young filled the dance halls every night, and musicians played new, sad Hungarian love songs. At night, Pest lit up like a Christmas tree.

Jews were still an accepted presence in the city. Anti-Semitism appeared in the newspapers, in cartoons, and in quoted speeches from parliament, where there were regular discussions of "the Jewish problem," but it was well known that the right-wing press was paid by the Germans for its virulent attacks. The Social Democratic Party's *Népszava* (People's Voice) and the *Magyar Nemzet* (Hungarian Nation) provided more balanced reporting. Some accommodation was made after the latest round of anti-Jewish laws was announced, and they were more in name than in fact. Legal loopholes allowed most of the business empires to continue. Silent gentile partners were found for the country's ten largest industrial enterprises. All of them had been owned by Jews or, as in the case of most of the Weiss and Mauthner families, baptized Jews. The Weiss-Chorin-Kornfeld-Mauthner dynasties still controlled the Commercial Bank. Together with the Credit Bank, they held more than 50 percent of Hungary's industrial production. The Weiss-Chorin group also owned the Weiss-Manfred Works industrial complex and had controlling shares in machinery, food production, armaments manufacture, and textiles.[2] Ferenc Chorin, the head of the intermarried family group, was the most influential businessman in the country. Admiral Horthy had been wary of replacing the smart Jewish entrepreneurs who had helped rebuild Hungary after the war "with incompetent, vulgar and boorish elements ... Such a project requires at least one full generation,"[3] he told his Council of Ministers. While some of the ministers may have disagreed with the Regent's crude generalization about the arriviste gentile entrepreneurs who had been hoping to feast on the pickings from Jewish businesses, most of them agreed that the country's wealth had been in competent hands.

Although Protestant bishop László Ravasz's resounding radio sermons were heard all over the country on Sunday mornings, Kasztner found that they seemed less threatening here than in Kolozsvár. When the good pastor reached the inevitable anti-Semitic accusations in his lengthy orations, the big city did not appear to listen. Ravasz's obsession with the Jews killing Christ seemed more symbolic than real. Perhaps because Ravasz was from Transylvania, he was taken more seriously there.

Budapest was a cosmopolitan city. Kasztner was sure it would provide the assistance he sought for the refugees who were streaming over the borders. His letters home expressed guarded optimism about the possibility of employment and the new life that Bogyó would join him to share.

He rented a small, two-room flat in a pension on Váci Street near Vörösmarty Square and the legendary Gerbeaud Restaurant. The pension was in a lovely old building: the guest lounge had well-worn Turkish carpets, soft armchairs, and on the walls romantic paintings of prettified landscapes. In the large communal dining room, a gourmet cook served hearty Hungarian and German meals on white linen tablecloths that were changed every day. There was a cards room for gin rummy and bridge in the evenings, and the pension's owner, Elizabeth Zahler, played the piano and sang popular love songs on some evenings. She was a beautiful woman, an occasional actress, a recent divorcée. Her pretty teenage daughter, Eva, danced for the guests when she was in the mood. Rezső, who had an eye for attractive women, always listened to the singing with rapt attention.[4]

Eva Berg (née Zahler) remembers that her mother found Rezső fascinating. Here was a well-read, highly educated man who seemed delighted with Elizabeth's company and eager to tell her about politics and even to share his interest in Zionism, a subject about which she knew little. Elizabeth was impressed by his broad-ranging knowledge of Hitler's record and his predictions for the future of European Jewry. Budapest, he believed, would remain the safest place in eastern Europe, and he repeated what he had been saying in Kolozsvár: the spreading of this war to the Soviet Union was inevitable. A dictatorship of the right could not allow a dictatorship of the left to continue as an ally—indeed, to continue at all. For a few weeks while Bogyó was still in Kolozsvár, waiting for word from Rezső, he and Elizabeth met every day, talking, going for long walks along the Danube Corso. She showed him Buda, the Castle District, the grand old houses, the gardens around the Royal Palace, the lovely Coronation Church.

Elizabeth and her father, a highly respected surgeon, were already donors to charities supporting the refugees. From the time of his arrival in Budapest, Rezső was dogged in his pursuit of assistance for the thousands of people streaming into the city. He went to the offices of all the Jewish organizations—the Orthodox, the Conservative, the Zionists—and to the cultural societies and the charitable foundations.

Kasztner had a letter of introduction from József Fischer to Ottó Komoly, the president of the Budapest Zionist Association and author of two books about the future of the Jews. A heavyset man in his forties, Komoly was an engineer, a decorated war veteran, a reserve officer in the Hungarian army. He was socially well connected and a committed Hungarian patriot, despite his support for a Jewish homeland. "It is not a contradiction," he insisted. "There must be a Jewish homeland, but I am not likely to live there myself." In that, Komoly was prophetic. He had been introduced to Zionism by his father, a close friend of Theodor Herzl, but he had not applied for an entry visa to Palestine.

As the two men drank coffee in tiny, elegant Herendi cups, Komoly confided that he felt comfortable in Budapest, though he warned Kasztner that the time would come when no Jew would find comfort there. "Too many of us have been in the window of social life," he mused. "We have attracted the attention of other, less-fortunate segments of the population. A person is inclined to believe in the permanence of favorable conditions and is reluctant to pay attention to warning signs."[5] And that group, he thought, included himself.

Here, as in Kolozsvár, the Zionist movement had divided along the same lines as in Palestine and, eventually, as it would in Israel. On the left were the Ihud (later the Mapai), the Israeli Labor Party that had been running the Jewish Agency, in effect the government in Palestine; the socialist Hashomer Hatzair, a youth organization with small clubs (called "nests") throughout Europe; the Maccabee Hatzair, another socialist youth movement that had been organized at Jewish high schools in the late 1930s; and Dror (affiliated with the Ihud), which, with its leadership in Poland, had been active on Hungary's eastern borders, helping to bring across refugees from both Poland and Slovakia. On the right was Betar, the youth wing of the Revisionists, which, led by Vladimir (Zeev) Jabotinsky, a Russian Jew who had emigrated to Palestine, fought bitterly with the Mapai leadership. Jabotinsky fostered armed resistance to the British in Palestine and to the Germans in Europe (though he, too, became involved in deal-making to save lives). In addition the Klal, or general Zionists, tended to focus on emigration to Palestine, and the Mizrachi, the religious Zionists, saw themselves as the only intellectually qualified leaders of the Zionist movement. Despite all the alarming outside threats, the Zionists remained deeply divided along religious and political lines, each passionately opposed to the others' points of view.[6]

Komoly encouraged Kasztner to seek out Miklós (Moshe) Krausz, the Jewish Agency's man in Budapest. If Kasztner's refugees needed Palestine entry visas, Krausz was the one to see. He was the undisputed boss of the Palestine Office and a convinced Mizrachi. "It would be best," Komoly warned, "not to tell him of your own Labor sympathies."

The Palestine Office was on Erzsébet Boulevard, near the National Theater. When Kasztner arrived, he had to fight his way up the wide staircase through the scores of people who stood waiting, leaning against the wall, squeezed along the iron handrails, talking in Polish, Slovak, Croatian, or Yiddish.[7] He met a group of young Zionist pioneers, or *halutzim*,[8] from Slovakia, who wanted everyone to hear of the brutal deportations they had witnessed in their own country. When the roundups began, they said, the old and the families with young children were lined up, and they all did exactly what they were ordered to do. Only a few young people tried to escape: they had heard stories from the Polish refugees, and they suspected a fate that their parents refused to believe. They hid in closets, cellars, and lofts, or in bushes along the riverbanks. They found the Hungarian border during the night.

Kasztner talked to one young girl who was crying, her soiled handkerchief bunched into her mouth to quiet the sound. Her younger sister, ten years old, a dreamer, she said, had been caught just steps from the border and thrown into a waiting truck by Hlinka Guard militiamen—Slovak fascists. The older girl had promised their mother she would not let go of her sister's hand, but she had been so nervous that she needed to pee all the time, and she had to be alone when she did it, that's how shy she was. Suddenly there had been searchlights and dogs barking, men shouting, and her little sister's shrieks, "Run! Run!" Now the older sister wanted to know how such a little girl would find her way out of a Polish concentration camp. "Have you ever heard of Treblinka or Sobibór?" she asked. No one, so far, had come back from those places. And how would she explain to their mother that she had let go of her little sister's hand?

Upstairs, the large auditorium was jammed with noisy, desperate people, waiting, hoping to be on the lists of those who had been chosen for the few Palestine entry certificates that were still available. Would there be more certificates, Kasztner wondered, now that most of the Palestine offices in other countries had been closed? Was there still an office in Prague? The one in Warsaw, he knew, had been closed by the Germans. Surely the British would open the borders to Palestine now that Europe was in flames?

After two hours of waiting his turn in the line, Kasztner, ignoring protests by Krausz's busy secretaries, barged into the great man's office. He was greeted by a huge desk completely covered with piles of paper, letters spilling off the surface onto the floor, where hundreds of unopened envelopes lay in mountainous heaps. Boxes of papers lined the walls.[9]

Krausz, a thin, bespectacled, middle-aged man with an unusually large head balanced on a long neck, popped up from behind the desk, outraged at the unusual interruption. When Kasztner explained why he was there, Krausz said he was much too busy to discuss the problems of the Kolozsvár refugees. He had his own people to cope with; as Kasztner must have seen, there were more than a hundred of them on the stairs and more in the waiting rooms.[10] Surely he was aware of the difficulties, Krausz complained. "Once the British mandate certificates are in hand," he continued, "we need exit visas and official transit visas from neutral countries. Turkey will grant only forty to fifty a week. Yugoslavia has become impossible now that the partisans have made a few successful strikes against the Wehrmacht [the German army]. Italy refused."[11]

"Spain?" Kasztner inquired.

"None for now, but maybe they will once the new consul arrives."

When Kasztner asked about illegal immigration, Krausz countered angrily that nothing should be done to jeopardize the Agency's good relations with Britain and that the refugees would be processed strictly according to his instructions. Kasztner argued that there had been some contact between the Germans and the Revisionists and that the Ihud had been successful with a few shiploads of refugees— it was just a matter of funding the ships and bribing everyone along the way. Once the Jewish families reached Haifa, he was sure that the British would allow them to land.

Krausz was adamant that his office would abide by the rules. He had taken an instant dislike to the forceful, loud, and insistent Kasztner. He was used to the begging and cajoling of supplicants, not the aggressive, commanding tones of the young lawyer from Kolozsvár who thought he knew how to deal with functionaries. The dislike was mutual. Kasztner despised Krausz as a little man overly taken with the importance of his own position, one who paid more attention to bureaucratic minutiae than to the real plight of his people.

Kasztner offered to help with processing applications and seeking exit visas from the Hungarian government, an offer Krausz considered ludicrous. Later, when Kasztner urged him to include entire families in a single certificate, Krausz complained to his superiors. He was not going to bend the rules, he proclaimed righteously. He had held his position in the Palestine Office for several years, and in all that time he had kept the peace between the religious Mizrachi and the Hashomer Hatzair by fairly apportioning certificates between the two factions. He was not about to change how he handed out the documents. Until recently, he had been reasonably comfortable in rewarding those he agreed with and in denying those he disliked. Kasztner was going to be in the second category.

Having failed with Krausz, Kasztner spent hours in waiting rooms on the various levels of 12 Sip Street, the headquarters of the Neolog Jewish congregation in Budapest and of the National Bureau of Hungarian Jews, where a number of Jewish functionaries had their offices. Their Great Synagogue on Dohány Street, behind the faded-red brick office building, was one of the architectural wonders of the city. Leaders of the congregation were lawyers, bankers, industrialists, and members of parliament. Most of them had taken the position, publicly, that they were opposed to illegal immigration, and they parroted allegations made in the anti-Semitic press that some "eastern Jews" could be spies. They were adamant in their declarations of loyalty to the Hungarian nation and their refusal to be classified with Jews from other countries. Hungary was, after all, a German ally. And Germany was at war.

Samuel Stern, the head of the National Bureau of Hungarian Jews, had also been president of the Jewish Community of Pest for almost fifteen years. He was a *hofrat*, or court councillor (an honorary title awarded to those who had performed great deeds for the state), and a social friend of Horthy's. Stern's rank demanded that he be addressed as "Excellency." He had been head of the country's national food transportation company, which had distinguished itself by supplying the armed forces through the First World War and was still doing so. Though semiretired from office, he remained one of the country's most highly respected businessmen, and had been reluctant even to meet Kasztner. It was dangerous to associate with someone who might be helping enemy aliens enter Hungary illegally. Kasztner assumed he had been honored with an audience only as a result of a phone call by Ottó Komoly.

Contrary to his elevated status in society, Hofrat Samuel Stern was a surprisingly small, elderly, birdlike man. However, he had the proud demeanor of one used to exercising power and had a strong, decisive handshake, one he proffered readily once Kasztner stood directly before his wide oak desk. After the introductions, Stern stayed safely behind his papers, gilt-framed family photographs, and large array of fountain pens, most of which he had received as gifts from grateful customers and political friends. It was difficult to imagine, in this high-ceilinged room giving onto the airy, sun-streaked courtyard, that anyone in this country was endangered or that Jews belonging to respected associations in other parts of Europe had already been murdered with their families. Yet that was what Kasztner knew, or suspected, from the stories he had been told by the refugees.

Stern listened to Kasztner's report on the difficulties faced by the Jews who had managed to escape from Slovakia and Poland. Once he heard the appeal, he folded his pale, manicured hands and smiled. He said that he, too, had heard the stories. There were many such Jews in Budapest and in the provinces. But he was also sure that providing funds for "a few" might jeopardize the interests of the many. Hungary's Jews could not afford to be allied with the refugees, who were so different from them that they seemed to belong on another planet. Many of them still wore the distinctive fur-trimmed outfits of the backward, the uneducated, he said. They were leftovers from the fifteenth century. Hungarians had nothing in common with them.

To Kasztner's alarm, Stern said he was in general agreement with
the government's stance on the over-representation of Jews in certain
professions. It was unreasonable to expect, with only 6 percent of the
population, that Jews should make up 20 percent of the professions.
They held too many prominent positions, and they were too proud
of their accomplishments. "Vanity," he said, "too much vanity." He
echoed the attacks the daily press had made recently about Jews having become overly conspicuous in the intellectual life of the country.
The laws, as they had been imposed, were not "unreasonable,"
given that such a large proportion of millionaires in Budapest were
Jews. Certain exceptions to the new laws had already been granted,
and more, he knew, were on the way. Besides, he declared, the laws
were merely a sop to the Germans, a way for the government to
pacify its more powerful, belligerent neighbor.

Stern viewed the labor service imposed on able-bodied Jewish
men as a necessary evil. If Jews were not to be part of the regular
army, at least the labor brigades gave them a chance to help the
"homeland." It was honorable. Jews, who were only a segment of the
service, could prove themselves both reliable and hardworking.
Indeed, he noted, both he and his organization had helped collect
money and clothing for the men there.

When Kasztner mentioned the ghettos in Poland, Stern said he
could not imagine that such things could happen in Hungary, where
Jews were integrated into society at all levels, and they did not live in
isolation as so many of Poland's Jews did. As Hungarians, Jews
shared the goals of the majority for the well-being of the nation. It
was only their religion that was different. He was impatient with the
Zionist assertion that Jews should make their way to another
"homeland."

Before long, Stern's forbearance with Kasztner began to wear thin.
He stood up as soon as Kasztner began to talk about the unique
problems faced by Jews in Transylvania. For him, the meeting was
over.

Kasztner walked down the staircase, past the notice board
announcing that, in the evening, there would be a Mozart concert in
the auditorium with a visiting opera singer. Bizet's *Carmen* was

coming to the main stage of the Wesselényi Street Goldmark Hall,
Verdi's *Rigoletto* and *La Traviata* would be the main attraction the
following month, and there would be poetry recitals in the main hall
on Sip Street. Obviously the Jewish Community of Budapest was
not concerned about the fate of Jews elsewhere.[12]

Kasztner knew that the people at greatest risk in the city were the
refugees. Without official papers, they could be returned to
German-occupied areas. Though their numbers were not recorded,[13]
thousands were in refugee camps, and others seeking asylum in the
city were arriving every day: orphans whose parents had been taken
to concentration camps; families who had nowhere to hide and little
hope of getting help from the official Jewish organizations. Kasztner
was now gathering funds not only for people in Kolozsvár but also
for refugees in Budapest.

Kasztner found kindred spirits at the Bethlen Square Hungarian
Jewish Assistance building. Its large storerooms supplied clothing,
flour and margarine, dried fruit, and cans of vegetables to the
refugees and the poor of the city. Its free kitchen served daily
rations. This agency received funds from the American Joint Distribution Committee,[14] or "the Joint" as it was affectionately called,
and a great deal of help from the rich Jews of the city. Baroness
Edith Weiss, eldest daughter of the banker-industrialist Manfred
Weiss, volunteered there. As a member of one of the wealthiest families, she was used to privilege and comfort, to influence in government. Now she ran interference with the authorities and bargained
with tailors and dressmakers to provide winter coats for the men in
the labor battalions. Even in these difficult times she could open
doors in ministers' offices.[15]

In the courtyard of the Orthodox Jewish headquarters, a short
walk from Sip Street, Kasztner met Baron Fülöp von Freudiger, a
soft-spoken, patrician industrialist—the family owned several textile
factories—who was known for his generosity and his support for
charities. His group already ran a soup kitchen and food bank for
the refugees. He had little time for his visitor, or any Zionist, but he
encouraged Kasztner to come back over dinner when the refugee
halutzim gathered there to eat and talk. Freudiger's first impression of

Kasztner was of a young man too much in a hurry to listen to advice.

Ernő Szilágyi met Kasztner two or three months after the latter arrived in the capital in the spring of 1941. He thought that, already, Kasztner was on a personal mission to save people. The notion of becoming a leader, someone remembered later as a savior of Jews, had been on Kasztner's mind.[16] The two men met in a late-night café-cum-bar, a gathering place for both religious Zionists and the Hashomer Hatzair. Szilágyi, a scholar of Greek and Roman history, had taught at the university, where he garnered respect among his peers as a philosopher and as an expert on the Bible. Though he was a dreamer, he had been able to reach an agreement with Krausz to supply the youth wing of his Hashomer faction with a share of the much-sought-after Palestine certificates.

Germany broke its alliance and launched its attack on the Soviet Union on June 22, 1941. Special killing squads, Einsatzgruppen, followed the German army and organized local collaborators to assist in the systematic mass murder of the Jewish populations in the territories they passed through—Latvia, Lithuania, Estonia, and the Ukraine.

On June 26, after unmarked planes bombed the city of Kassa,[17] Hungary followed suit and declared war on the Soviet Union. The news blared through all the radios in Budapest, celebratory bands marched along the Great Boulevard, and six-foot placards everywhere called on young men to sign up for the battles to come. The right-wing political parties launched ferocious new attacks in their newspapers on Jewish industrialists and black marketers, and, without realizing the contradiction, they also attacked Jews as Bolshevik sympathizers and agitators.

After declaring war on the Soviet Union, Romanian armies occupied the territories they had earlier reluctantly ceded to the USSR at Hitler's insistence. Jews from the villages and towns of Bessarabia were driven hundreds of miles to the east. The sick, the elderly, the very young children, and others who could not keep pace were shot or beaten to death on the march. In the reconquered areas of

Bessarabia and Bukovina, where the majority of Romania's 800,000 Jews lived, 100,000 of them were murdered. The Germans agreed to send another 190,000 Jews into the conquered Ukraine, where they set up prison camps in the area near the River Bug. Most of the inmates froze or starved to death.

On February 16, 1941, the *New York Times* ran an advertisement over Ben Hecht's byline: "FOR SALE to Humanity, 70,000 Jews, guaranteed human beings at $50 a piece." Hecht was alluding to a purported Romanian offer to let Jews go to Palestine. "Romania is tired of killing Jews," he went on. "It has killed one hundred thousand in two years . . ."

Refugees from Romania and the Ukraine were now streaming across the Hungarian borders, recounting atrocities in the Ukraine that amounted to mass murder. The Einsatzgruppen forced women and children to dig ditches and undress, then shot and threw them into the mass graves. They covered the bodies—some of them still alive—with lime, repeating the process until whole villages were emptied of Jews.

Bogyó arrived in Budapest in late July 1941. Rezső felt that it was safer there than in Kolozsvár, and Budapest was farther from the Soviet border. There had been little change in Budapest after war was declared. As more German officers crowded into the city to enjoy their leave, hotels and restaurants flourished and even the lesser-known bands had the opportunity to play the maudlin tunes that Germans liked. "Lili Marlene" and "Gloomy Sunday" were such favorites that no orchestra along the Danube Corso could avoid playing them every hour.

Rezső had urged his father-in-law to move from Kolozsvár with the whole extended family but failed to persuade him. Although József Fischer had lost his law practice, he was still confident that, ultimately, reason would prevail, and as the president of the Jewish community in the city, he felt responsible for those who trusted him. There had been speculation that the Romanian government would be willing to sell a portion of the Jews it had deported to Transnistria for some kind of gain. And Chaim Weizmann, president of the World Zionist Organization, had petitioned the British to allocate all the remaining certificates from the quota set for emigration to Palestine for use by the persecuted Romanian Jews.[18]

Bogyó settled into the Váci Street pension with a trunk full of her treasured belongings: her Limoges china, a heavy silver service and coffee set, hem-stitched linen tablecloths, a couple of her favorite paintings in gold-leaf frames, a small bronze statue of a dancing girl. She tried to re-create some of the coziness she had known, though she did not feel that this busy city could ever be home.[19] With Rezső out the door at dawn and away until dark every day, she stayed in bed until noon, wrote long letters to her parents, read voraciously, and tried not to feel lonely.

Ottó Komoly introduced Rezső Kasztner to another key figure in the effort to help the refugees. Sam Springmann, a diminutive, balding, talkative man in his midthirties had, like Kasztner, been involved with the Zionist movement since his teens. Amiable and slightly disheveled in appearance, he was a diamond dealer, watchmaker, and jeweler. He and his parents had arrived from Poland after the First World War. His father was a war veteran, and Sam had been support-ing the family since he was a boy. He made unique, diamond-studded brooches for wealthy clients, including the Mauthner girls and other members of the Chorin, Kornfeld, and Weiss families.[20] All the money he made went to his relatives and friends in Poland. He told heartrending tales about the Lodz ghetto, where his relatives were incarcerated—or had been, when he had last heard from them. But that was six months earlier, and his most recent letter had come back unopened. The courier he had paid (a member of the German Abwehr, or military intelligence service) could not find Springmann's relatives.[21]

Springmann's method was to bribe a variety of people—but mostly German officers—to carry messages and food packages to Lodz and other ghettos in Poland. Since April, the ghetto had been sealed. No Jew could get out without German authorization, he explained, and no one was authorized to leave unless he had work in one of the German-run factories. This winter would be terrible in Lodz. There was never enough food or clothing, and the children were dying.

When Springmann received a postcard from Istanbul in August 1941 with the words "regards from your cousin in Palestine" written on the back, he immediately understood that the Jewish Agency was seeking a contact in Budapest.[22] He began to send regular messages to Istanbul, he told Kasztner, and the Yishuv responded with some funds—though never sufficient. A few of the young halutzim had volunteered to cross the border into Poland with false passports, to carry supplies to the ghetto. But no one could ever be sure whether they would make it back.

Though he still had a rough Polish accent, Springmann traveled on a Hungarian passport. He had been able to find a pleasant flat in the city through the Polish government-in-exile, which was still favored by the Hungarians. The Poles in that group found his courier and news services more reliable than their own, and their officials supplied him with funds for their colleagues who were still in Poland. Curiously, some of the Abwehr agents were willing to deliver packages to resistance members in Poland, and they were able to get into some concentration camps where former Polish officers were held.

Springmann introduced Kasztner to Joel Brand, and joked that, as left-leaning Zionists and members of the Ihud, they were likely to end up in Palestine, so they might as well organize a political party in Budapest. Brand, too, was involved in helping fugitives, and Springmann had a name for their enterprise: *tiyul*, or excursion. The ultimate tiyul was, of course, the one that would take the refugees to Palestine or another country willing to accept them. Now, however, they needed accommodation in Budapest.

Brand, who had been born in Transylvania but educated in Erfurt, Germany, spoke passable Hungarian with a heavy German accent. He was broad-beamed, with a ruddy complexion and an easy smile, his reddish-brown, curly hair flopping over his forehead. About the same age as Kasztner, he had lived a more adventurous life. In his late teens, he had joined the Communist Party, and for a while had been a sailor in the Americas, and had traveled to the United States, the Bahamas, Japan, the South Sea islands, and all over Southeast Asia. He gave the impression that he had been an agent for the Communists, and had served time in a German jail for his political affiliations, being expelled from Germany after a battle between the Communists and Hitler's "Brownshirts," the Nazi Party militia. Briefly, Brand found work in Romania, but he had to leave after bragging about his Communist activities to a bar filled with Romanian security agents.[23] Fortunately, Transylvania had been Hungarian when Joel Brand was born, and that allowed him to keep his Hungarian citizenship and find work in Budapest. He had decided he wanted to leave Europe again and, in his efforts to obtain a highly prized Palestinian immigration certificate, he had taken crash courses in Zionism and agriculture.

Brand told Kasztner that he worked for his wife's gloves-manufacturing business as a sales representative, calling on shops throughout Hungary, Slovakia, and Romania. His father had founded the Budapest telephone company and, when Joel first arrived in the city, he had been able to work there. Now that sort of job had become impossible. Being a salesman provided him with an income and a chance to spend time in the coffeehouses, better restaurants, and old clubs where he had become a favored client. The people he met in these places brought him useful contacts. Joel loved to play cards, had a knack for poker, and often won in a single night more than his salary for the week. Besides, he said, much to his wife's surprise he had turned out to be exceptionally good at sales. He could also procure things that had become difficult to buy. He could still find silk stockings and extra-fine flour for cakes; he could connect you to the right supplier for filter-tipped cigarettes, Parisian scented soap, and delicate lipstick colors.

Kasztner's conversation, unlike Brand's, was about politics. He had been fascinated by the German-Soviet Pact of August 1939. Assuming rightly that Brand hadn't read *Mein Kampf*, Kasztner was pleased to give his summary of its five hundred pages. He had not only read the original edition but could now make comparisons between it and the newly expanded German best-seller. He claimed that Stalin, like Brand, could not have read the book and was therefore equally ignorant of Hitler's ideas. Had Stalin read it, perhaps he would not have signed the pact. Kasztner talked about the price Hungary would pay in armed assistance to the Germans for the regained territories in Upper Province, the Bácska, and Transylvania.

Despite his initial irritation with Kasztner's intellectual swagger, Brand invited him to dine at the Mátyáspince, an expensive, old-world restaurant where the headwaiter knew which table Brand liked and which waitress he favored. Kasztner, who tended to be private about his personal life and careful about what he said when he met people for the first time, was amazed at Brand's fast-talking, open ways. As he listened to Brand's patter, he realized that his companion knew people on the fringes of society—some of whom could be very useful for saving lives. Brand, like Sam Springmann, used extensive connections among agents in the intelligence services—several Hungarian agents in addition to the Germans—to smuggle Jews out of Poland and Slovakia. Ottó Komoly had asked him to help send documents across the borders. "The only Zionist organization left in eastern Europe is the one in Budapest," Brand told Kasztner. "Believe me, despite everything, Ottó is still an influential man."

By late September 1941, most young Jewish men in Hungary were in labor service, and young non-Jewish men were in the army. When Brand asked Kasztner how he had avoided the service, his answer was less than honest. Kasztner said he had done his time and was on leave. Brand was proud of having successfully evaded labor service. In 1941 it was still possible to buy the necessary medical certificate, he said. He confessed with a laugh that he had been diagnosed as diabetic.

Joel Brand remembered Rezső Kasztner from that first meeting as an intense, rather overbearing man who liked to dominate the conversation. Kasztner was restless, impatient, barely listening to what someone else had to say. But Brand, too, was intensely interested in helping other people, and those were times when it was hard to find men like that.

A few days later, Brand took Kasztner home to meet his wife. "You'll want to meet the boss," he said. Other than his doing a reasonable job of sales, she made no demands on him, he told Kasztner. He was free to enjoy life as he chose—no questions asked, no need to go home for supper. It had been an arranged marriage, a marriage of mutual convenience. Hansi Hartmann had wanted to go to Palestine, and he had been sure he could get a visa both for himself and for his wife. Brand, in turn, had wanted a job while they waited.

Hansi Brand had learned how to make knitted and leather gloves from her aunt, an enterprising woman with no children of her own. Hansi's parents had provided the money to start the small business. Now, ten or twelve women worked for her at any one time, taking home leather bits and patterns, then returning with sewn gloves. The fashion for mixed leather-and-knit gloves had helped expand her business. Recently she had added men's socks and women's stockings. No one went hungry while in her employ, and the business was thriving. The Palestine entry certificate had not arrived, but the Brands could afford to put the journey off.

Their apartment was pleasantly furnished: parquet floor with colorful rugs, lamps with hand-painted shades, a long wooden table with a few framed photos, deep armchairs—a place designed for comfort. When the two men arrived, she was sorting clothes from a shipping crate onto the floor of the dining room.[24] Hansi, Joel explained, was setting aside garments for new arrivals. They were expecting a group of refugees from Poland.

She was pretty in a dark, mid-European way, well-proportioned, round-hipped, big-breasted, long-legged, and she wore a loose-fitting, light-blue summer dress with a row of pearl buttons decorously closed all the way to her neck. Rezső had a strange feeling that they had met before, as though he had known her but half forgotten. He followed her with his eyes as she stood and stretched, then she disappeared into the kitchen for coffee and cakes.

Joel had told her about him, she said when she returned and curled into the armchair by the standing lamp—about his hopes for finding ways through Joel's connections to rescue people. She had dark, expressive eyes and a warm smile, lively, welcoming, not the busy businesswoman he had expected.

She had paid a man named József Krem, a Hungarian army intelligence officer and part-time smuggler, to bring a family of Slovaks safely across the border. Krem had been one of Joel's coffeehouse finds, an inveterate gambler, always in debt, a man few would have trusted to deliver on promises. But she had trusted him, and her faith had really paid off when her sister and brother-in-law were arrested in July 1941. On orders from the government, Jews who could not prove they were Hungarian citizens were driven across the border into occupied Polish Galicia and turned over to the Germans. Many of them were refugees from Poland and the Ukraine, but some, like Hansi's sister, were Hungarians who had not bothered to get citizenship papers because their families had lived in the same area for centuries. These people were now driven into Poland at the rate of about a thousand every day and handed over to the Germans. Hansi had paid Krem what he demanded to rescue her sister and husband, not once but three times, and he kept returning empty-handed. Kamenetz-Podolsk in the Ukraine, where they were, was difficult to reach, and there German Einsatzgruppen were everywhere, trigger-happy, indoctrinated young men who seemed to enjoy shooting people.

When Krem finally arrived in the village, he found mass confusion; it seemed impossible to locate these two people when he was armed with nothing but a name and a couple of tiny black-and-white photographs. But on his last return trip, just a day before a massacre fated to occur there, Krem had found Hansi's sister and her husband. Few others of the eighteen thousand people who ended up near Kamenetz-Podolsk survived. On August 27 and 28, Krem told the Brands, they were machine-gunned in rows, one hundred at a time, and stacked into shallow graves.

Joel, then, offered Krem's services to other families who wanted to send letters and packages into the Polish ghettos, find relatives in Austria, or buy information about people in concentration camps. And through Krem, the Brands met other individuals with similar skills.

Joel's smuggling even extended to bringing home men from the labor service. There were thousands on the Soviet front, and they all needed news from home, medicines, and extra food rations. "It was often necessary for me to go into the enemy camp to rescue men who were in danger," Brand wrote later, "and I then had to join in drinking bouts with the enemy's agents. Sometimes this made me sick, but when my nerves failed, Komoly reassured me."[25]

On his second visit to the Brands' apartment, Rezső was surprised to find Hansi with a baby on her lap and a toddler playing on the floor nearby. The toddler was chubby, with tiny tufts of red hair like Joel's.

"I thought you said this was a business arrangement," Rezső said when he and Joel were alone again.

"This one," Joel acknowledged with a laugh, "has an upside."

CHAPTER 3

A Question of Honor, Law, and Justice

Though times had changed considerably since I had been aide-de-camp to His Majesty Emperor Francis Joseph, my concepts of honour, law and justice . . . had not altered . . . It was not my task to stand in judgement of the man who had shown nothing but goodwill towards Hungary.

Miklós Horthy, Writing About Adolf Hitler in *Memoirs*[1]

We stumbled into world history . . .

Joel Brand[2]

Hungary's third Anti-Jewish Law, of August 1941, prohibited marriage between Jews and non-Jews. Its punitive provisions were explained by declaring that mixed marriages were harmful to the "national soul." It went on to say: "They brought into a position of influence that Jewish spirit whose harmful effect we have seen. There is no doubt about the failure of the experiment in assimilation. We now want to exchange this for disassimilation."[3]

The new law allowed for just a few exceptions. A person was not considered to be Jewish, for example, if both his parents were Christians at the time of his birth and if he was, therefore, "born" a Christian or was converted before the age of seven. This loophole allowed many members of the country's establishment the chance to have themselves classified as bona fide Christians, thus saving them the embarrassment of having to declare their marriages to non-Jews invalid.

* * *

In October 1941 Rezső Kasztner was present at a meeting of Jewish leaders, a dinner at the elegant Corso-Pension Restaurant in Pest. It was attended by a few members and former members of the Hungarian and Romanian parliaments, including former members of the Hungarian upper house. "My aim," Kasztner recalled, "was to save Jewish lives, help the refugees, and prepare for the self-defense of the Hungarian Jews."[4] Yet no one he met that night was willing to contemplate that Hungarian Jews might need to be defended. Even without that message, however, Kasztner would not have been a popular presence at such a gathering. He was too brash, too persistent, too "country" by Budapest standards. He was also unknown. He lacked refinement, patience, respect for opposing opinions, never mind respect for his social superiors. Kasztner was not the sort of man who recognized anyone as his superior.[5]

As Kasztner had already learned from Samuel Stern, the educated, politically astute, influential members of the Jewish community thought they belonged to this land and its causes as much as any of their Christian neighbors did. Having fought alongside them in the last war, proud of their decorated war heroes, many of them continued to take the position that they were opposed to illegal immigration and refused to be classified with Jews from the east. Hungary was, after all, at war with some of those countries.

Over dinner, Kasztner told the assembled leaders of the dispossession of German and Austrian Jews, of the mass executions in the Ukraine and the Baltic States, of the gassing trucks, of the massacre near Kamenetz-Podolsk. They did not believe him.

He talked about the Iron Guard in Romania attacking Jewish homes and burning farms; of the grotesque display of the dead in butcher-shop windows in Bucharest; of the rapid spread of violent anti-Semitism, the stench of dead bodies in side-tracked wagons in the countryside; of public hangings and shootings in the streets. The diners who had heard of the murders shook their heads in disgust. Most of those killed, they thought, had been from the east, too easily identified by their long black coats and traditional black hats. They would not accept that the Hungarian government had sanctioned the murders at Kamenetz-Podolsk.

When Kasztner recalled the skepticism of the assembled Jewish bankers and industrialists, their reluctance to consider the possibility that Jews were being murdered in Europe for no reason other than that they were Jews, he realized that they would remain passive if they found themselves faced with German death squads. The Hungarian Arrow Cross Party held parades in Budapest, demanding that the government take more decisive action against the Jews, yet most Jews remained unprepared for a future that would rob them of their dignity.

Still, the Budapest Va'ada Ezra w' Hazalah (Aid and Rescue Committee) was born, at least in theory, at the Corso-Pension Restaurant that night, though several more months and Ottó Komoly's personal involvement were needed for it to become official. In his own way, Komoly had been working to help refugees for more than a year now. He used his connections with the public service, Jewish members of parliament (in those days there were still a few), and a handful of other sympathetic parliamentarians, including Endre Bajcsy-Zsilinszky. In the 1920s, Bajcsy-Zsilinszky had been a founding member of a party whose chief platform was the defense of the "Hungarian race," but he had aged well. A decade later he had started his own anti-Nazi newspaper, *Szabadság* (Liberty). He had joined with the Social Democrats to fight fascists and defend the rights of all citizens, irrespective of race. He was the man to whom Joel Brand had gone when he first learned of the mass killings in Kamenetz-Podolsk, and he had raised the matter in parliament and demanded an explanation from the perpetrators.

Komoly's influence and Kasztner's continued petitions helped to finally mobilize antifascist members of parliament to hold a mass rally on March 15, 1942, at the historic Petőfi Monument in Budapest, overlooking the Danube. Sándor Petőfi, a much-loved poet of romantic and patriotic verse, had died a martyr's death during the Hungarian uprising of 1848 against the Habsburg Empire. His statue was symbolic of the free spirit of the country and its independence from Germany.

Komoly also knew the editors of all the liberal newspapers, and he frequently lunched with the editor of the Social Democrats' *Népszava*. Komoly had remained friendly with Samuel Stern and his group of influential Jewish leaders; Stern and his friends still enjoyed the Regent's company. Without Komoly, as Brand recalled, the Va'ada would have lacked the authority to act in the name of the Jewish community. Komoly's presence lent the Aid and Rescue Committee an air of respectability.[6]

Great Britain declared war on Hungary on December 7, 1941, the same day that the Japanese attacked the United States Navy fleet in Pearl Harbor and brought the United States into the war in the Pacific. Then Hitler, tied to Japan through the Tri-Power Pact, declared war on the United States on December 11. The next day, the American ambassador departed from Budapest, as the United States no longer considered Hungary an independent nation, though it did not formally declare war on Hungary until the following June.

By Christmas that year the German attack on the Soviet Union had ground to a halt near Moscow. The mighty panzer divisions were now fighting defensive battles against the Soviet armies, as the infamous Russian winter overtook Hitler's generals. The formerly invincible German military might was stretched on two fronts, and a powerful new player, the United States, had been forced into the war. Once again, Hungary had allied itself with Germany—and its fate was tied to that of the Third Reich.

In Budapest, where such details of the war news were not readily available, people tuned in to the BBC and continued to hope that the war would soon be over.

In January 1942, Hungarian military units executed more than 3,000 civilians in the recently occupied part of Yugoslavia, including 140 children who, according to one of the commanding officers, "could grow up to be enemies." Joel Brand found out from one of his contacts that close to a third of those murdered had been Jews. The thin pretext that they were likely to have joined the Serb partisans was no more than a nod to the government authorities who had demanded an explanation. After a military tribunal apportioned blame, all the commanders of the infamous campaign found refuge in Germany.

The flood of refugees into Hungary now included Jews from the Délvidék, or "southern lands," as Hungarians referred to those parts of Hungary that had been awarded to Yugoslavia by the Treaty of Trianon. The new arrivals had terrible tales of mass executions: people had been shoved into the icy waters of the Danube. The men in charge of this so-called military expedition continued the killings even after they received orders to stop.

The Brands' apartment remained the first address known to the refugees. Soon it was filled with stunned escapees who wanted someone to hear what they had endured. For a few days, Hansi and the children went to the Majestic Hotel on Swabian Hill, in Buda, allowing them a place to rest while Joel looked for more permanent accommodation for the displaced. To escape the crowded apartment, Hansi often booked rooms in the Majestic. Her younger son, Dani, suffered from asthma, and the fresh air in Buda made it easier for him to breathe.[7]

Hansi frequently handed over her own clothes and money to families arriving from the bloody streets of Poland, Slovakia, and, now, Yugoslavia. Hundreds of refugees remembered her from those days. She let the women pick what they liked from her own clothes closet, fed them, and occasionally looked after their children while they hunted for work, treating them like family. Joel, meanwhile, worked with a group of young halutzim, preparing fake documents.

By late 1942 the Va'ada was launched and Kasztner was appointed as chief executive. Joel insisted, somewhat petulantly, that the idea for the Aid and Rescue Committee had really been Hansi's; though she wasn't interested in a formal role, she had been helping refugees long before Rezső arrived in the city.

Kasztner's appointment meant that he could now present himself at the offices of influential people as head of an organization. Joel recalled that Kasztner visited the Italian minister of foreign affairs, Count Ciano, at his mansion in the Buda Hills to ask him to intervene with the Germans on behalf of the Croatian Jews. Brand thought that Kasztner's spirited presentation of the "terrible plight of the Jews" probably motivated the Italians to send forty children to Budapest in Italian army cars.[8]

In the wake of the atrocities in Yugoslavia, Moshe Schweiger, a businessman in his midthirties, arrived in Budapest. He immediately joined the Aid and Rescue Committee to help teach Polish and Slovak refugees rudimentary Hungarian, enough to answer simple questions if they were stopped by the police and questioned about their papers. Schweiger, a longtime member of the Hashomer Hatzair ("the Marxists," as Hansi called them), brought news of large-scale deportations from the Croatian countryside, where women and children had been shoved into cattle cars. His contacts in Italy had news of the ghettos in the north. The Italians, he said, had not been as cooperative as the Croats in rounding up Jews, so the Nazis tried to whisk Italian Jews out of the country during the night. Some of the trains from Italy would have to cut through Hungary. Schweiger asked his new friends to help prepare food and water for them.

Despite the growing list of horrors, the rivalries continued among the different Jewish groups in Budapest and were reflected in the Aid and Rescue Committee. Ernő Szilágyi joined the committee to gain an advantage for his own left-wing Zionist group, intellectual young lads who lionized him and gathered around him in the evenings to hear about Maimonides and Ovid, Aeschylus and King David. Other young people from the various Zionist youth factions also joined. When they got into arguments late at night, Kasztner and Brand told them it was now more important to work together for the cause than to try to uncover which of them held the keys to the future of Eretz, the new Jewish homeland.

The Jewish Agency's first recognition of the systematic extermination of Europe's Jews was published in Jewish newspapers in Palestine in November 1942. Even then, the facts of the indiscriminate murder of whole populations seemed incredible. After the Agency Executive set up its own Relief and Rescue Committee in Istanbul, it sent a cable to contacts in Budapest, asking that a similar committee be established there—only to find one was already in place under Kasztner's direction. His was a full-time job, supported from funds that the American Joint Distribution Committee and the Jewish Agency sent to Budapest. The Istanbul group then began to send additional financial assistance to fund the bribes needed for a host of officials, border guards, policemen, and German agents.

A practical woman with a head for business, Hansi became the heart of the fledgling Rescue Committee. From the start, she had offered to do the paperwork, to keep track of donations, to organize. She had also expanded her own shop to create more work for refugees, supplying sewing machines to the women she employed, deducting their costs from the piecework. The continuing popularity of the new style of leather-and-knit gloves allowed her to rent a small factory building on the outskirts of Pest where she could employ even more women.

Rezső often drove Hansi to the Majestic Hotel when she was living there, sometimes staying on for long walks in the garden or a cool beer in the shade of the lush chestnut trees. She confided that she had met Joel through a friend in the Hashomer Hatzair; she had not belonged to the leftist movement but found their social events attractive, and she did want to emigrate to Palestine. In 1935 she had wanted a valid certificate, and Joel had needed a job. He was sure he would have his entry permit in a few months and, like all permits in those days, it would allow him to take his wife. Friends had initially picked another man for her, but she thought him repugnant. Joel, if nothing else, was great company.[9]

An arranged marriage, Joel had told Rezső, a business arrangement. But now there were the boys, and Joel doted on them.

Hansi, too, described her marriage as a practical arrangement. She was sure Joel did not love her, nor did she expect him to. Gossips were glad to tell of his latest flirtations and occasional entanglements. He loved the cafés, the restaurants and bars, the nightlife of the casinos, the plush private clubs. He was a gambler—and so were the Germans stationed in Budapest. Joel always made sure that he lost just the right amount. He spent some of his nights with women who also consorted with German spies. You never knew, he had told her, what you might discover from a night with the right woman.

Rezső found it all incomprehensible. He would watch Hansi as she walked around the apartment, her every movement graceful. He was drawn to her, and he knew that she was attracted to him.

Bogyó saw too little of Rezső during the two years before the German occupation of Hungary in 1944. He left early and returned home late, if at all. Often he called the pension just to reassure her that he was still at work and she should not wait up for him. She had wanted a child, but Rezső insisted Jewish children should not be born into a world like this.[10] Yet he was attracted to a woman with two children.

Already, Rezső had seen something in Hansi that he needed. Like him, she could hide her fear and live in the moment. Together they visited the wealthy Jews in the city, collecting funds and clothing.

Kasztner tried, in vain, to get financial help from the left-leaning Christians, Socialists, Communists, and newspapermen with known sympathies for the underdog. He dictated long letters to the Jewish Agency, asking for more Palestine visas, including information that Brand's and Sam Springmann's couriers had brought back from other countries. Some had heard of a killing camp in Chelmno, about fifty miles from Lodz in Poland, and of the mobile gassing trucks in the Ukraine; others knew of the killings at Majdanek,

Treblinka, and Belzec in Poland. On March 2, 1942, some five thousand Jews were machine-gunned into a pit near the town of Minsk in Russia. Babies were thrown into the hole alive and left to suffocate, covered by the bodies of their parents. Two boys who had survived the Kamenetz-Podolsk massacre were picked up by Ottó Komoly from the stairwell of the Palestine Office. The older one, aged fourteen, had been in the fields with the men when the transports of Hungarian and Polish Jews arrived. The boys had seen their family slaughtered. The little one could only nod his head when his brother told their story; he could not speak.

Joel Brand was the main contact with the halutzim arriving from Slovakia, where deportations had begun on March 26, 1942, with a transport of girls sixteen and older.[11] Joel took the young men home for evening meals and set them up with Christian birth certificates and military service release papers. Among them was Peretz Révész, a skinny young Slovak Jew with almost orange hair, a sideways smile, and bruises all over his body. Beaten by the police after he was arrested lurking near the Palestine Office with no identity papers, Peretz had escaped from the police sergeant on their way to the internment camp—he thought the sergeant had let him run.[12]

Peretz became one of the regular members of the Rescue Committee in Budapest. He was brilliant at discovering new paths across borders, one time bringing the full complement of children from a Jewish orphanage over from Slovakia without losing a single child in the dark.[13]

Joel bought a small printing press to produce fake identity papers. Fortunately, most of the documents did not require photographs, so he and his halutzim helpers changed names, inserted new dates, and restamped the papers with a handmade stamp whose imprint resembled the smudged marks of the government. When demand became so great that one small press could not keep up, Hansi took a chance and hired gentile printers. Costs, of course, escalated with the number of refugees. Peretz and Kasztner visited cemeteries for likely Hungarian-sounding names to use on the new identity papers. By then, the effort to send all these illegal emigrants to Palestine had become known as the Tiyul Department—the Excursion

Department—and it was run by Joel.

The Rescue Committee sent regular shipments of food to Vienna for Jews who had gone into hiding after the Anschluss. Ironically, their courier for these trips was the driver of a delivery van belonging to the Nazi Party newspaper *Völkischer Beobachter* (People's Observer). In Vienna, the food was distributed by a non-Jewish woman whom Joel Brand gratefully acknowledged in his memoirs.

Sam Springmann was responsible for the committee's financial affairs and for developing useful contacts with Abwehr men and Hungarian spies who could be bribed and trusted. As couriers, they often carried significant sums of cash. One of his first was an Abwehr major, Jozsi (Josko) Winninger, a rotund, amiable man popular with women who was also a devoted gambler. He traveled the Turkey-Slovakia-Hungary route. Frequently, only a portion of the money he carried arrived at its destination, but both Ehud Avriel, one of the Agency's men in Istanbul, and Springmann were afraid to ask him to return the missing funds. Fritz Laufer, Erich Popescu, and Bandi Grosz all played significant roles as double and even triple agents.

Fritz Laufer, a.k.a. Karl Heinz, a heavyset man with sandy-red hair, sallow complexion, and glasses, had the uncanny ability to blend into a crowd. This characteristic had been useful for his early life as a petty criminal, but now he worked for the Germans in Yugoslavia and Prague while pretending to work for Czech Intelligence. He also took assignments from the British, who hoped to recruit him as a full-time operative in the east. At times he ran errands for Springmann, bringing dollars from "the Joint" in Istanbul or delivering packages to concentration camps in Slovakia and Poland. Occasionally he would bring someone out of jail, but he was expensive and unpredictable. Jozsi Winninger warned Joel that Laufer was dangerous.

Laufer had, apparently, done some jobs for Freddy Schwartz, a.k.a. "Dogwood," the highly intelligent, multilingual head of the American Office of Strategic Services (OSS), otherwise known as American Intelligence. Educated in both philosophy and psychology, a perfect combination for a spymaster in troubled times, Schwartz had handpicked his men from among the ready coterie of other nations' spies and named each one after a flower. Laufer's code name was "Iris." Some of Laufer's former oss and Abwehr colleagues had been betrayed and executed by the Sicher-heitsdienst (the Reich Security Office, or sd). Winninger reasoned that if he knew that much about Laufer, so did the ss.

According to Joel Brand, Springmann had met Erich Popescu at the French Embassy—both of them were used by the French for information gathering. Popescu, a.k.a. Erich Wehner, Werner, or Wenda, was an Abwehr spy who also worked for the Romanians and the Hungarians. He proved his reliability to Springmann by delivering, intact, a small package of diamonds to one of his Polish contacts. Popescu met the Jewish Agency's Teddy Kollek (later, mayor of Jerusalem) through Dogwood shortly after Kollek arrived in Istanbul. Dogwood had been keen to establish closer relations with Kollek because he found the information from the beleaguered Jews of Europe more reliable than his own agents' work. In early 1943 Kollek set up an office in Istanbul to organize a network of spies who could bring news to and deliver financial help from the Yishuv.

Gyorgy or Andy Grosz, a.k.a. Andor or Andre Gyorgy, André Giorgi, Bandi, and Antal, was short and ugly, with protruding teeth, bandy legs, and a thatch of red, curly hair. His nickname was "Little One," the reverse of his name "Grosz," which means "big" in both Yiddish and German. He was, as Brand and Springmann knew, a triple, perhaps quadruple agent with several jail sentences, in a range of countries, hanging over his head. Here, he worked for both the Hungarians and the Germans. He had frequently been used by the Hungarian government to reach Dogwood with the message that the Hungarians were ready to negotiate a separate peace. Because all sides assumed he was their man, Grosz, half Jewish, traveled more or less freely across borders. Dogwood, optimistic that Grosz, too, would become an oss agent, had code-named him "Trillium." Like Laufer, Grosz had a reputation for being dangerous to cross. When he decided that a particular agent was becoming too greedy or slicing off too much of the well-paid work, he alerted whomever he was working for at the time that the agent was a courier for the Jews. That kind of information could have the man demoted, moved, jailed, or executed.

Both Springmann and Kasztner thought it vital to inform the Jewish Agency's people in Istanbul of the full impact of Germany's war on the Jews of Europe. It was heartrending to realize how little of the truth was known. Through 1939 and 1940, for example, the Mapai's Central Committee did not once put the subject on its meeting agenda.[14]

Kasztner continued to focus on his political contacts, working to gain sympathy for renewed emigration to Palestine even as Britain kept the borders closed. Jewish emigration had not been expressly forbidden by ss Reichsführer Heinrich Himmler until late October 1941. Now, a year later, there was still hope that refugees could slip through the German dragnet in exchange for bribes, and, if the Hungarians allowed free passage for ships down the Danube, there was a chance of finding a boat in one of the Black Sea ports.

The Jewish Agency in Palestine issued its own statement condemning Britain's "breach of faith" with the Jewish people: "It is in the darkest hour of Jewish history that the British government proposes to deprive Jews of their last hope and close the road back to their Homeland." Britain did not budge—in fact, because some Zionist leaders continued to support illegal immigration, it tightened the conditions for emigration to Palestine and declared that, thenceforth, all illegal immigrants would be carefully deducted from the overall "legal" totals. At the same time, Britain demanded that neutral nations, such as Portugal and Turkey, deny Jews transit to Palestine and that ships stop delivering them to any port close to Palestine. The Foreign Office began to seek other settlement opportunities for refugees in Australasia, Africa, and South America, without success.

"There is strong evidence to suggest," Ottó Komoly told Kasztner, "that the British would rather see us all perish than grant one more visa for that benighted land. It's a protectorate only because they want to protect it from us."

Not until the case of the ss *Struma*, however, did British policy toward Jewish refugees receive worldwide attention. An old, marginally refurbished, British-built yacht, the *Struma* had set out from Constanta in Romania in December 1941 with 769 Jewish refugees on board. The Greek shipowner had sold tickets for the voyage at exorbitant prices, aware that few ships would risk the voyage and that, for most of the passengers, the *Struma* offered the last chance to survive. The vessel arrived at Istanbul with a broken engine, the passengers crowded together with barely enough room to sit and no fresh water, food, sanitation, or medicine for the ailing children or those suffering from dysentery.

The ship remained in Istanbul for two months. No one was allowed to leave or to board, though the Jewish Agency did succeed in distributing small amounts of food and water. The British government had prevailed on the Turks to block the *Struma*'s entry and to prevent its leaving for Palestine. There was some discussion of lifting the women and children off the ship, followed by more discussion and exchange of cables among the Foreign Office, the Turks, the Jewish Agency, and the governments of the United States, Romania, and the Reich. Eventually, the ship was towed out of the harbor, whereupon an explosion ripped open the hull, and the ship sank. One person survived.

To this day, no one knows for sure whom to blame for the disaster, but whether the destruction of the *Struma* was accomplished by a bomb on board or a Soviet torpedo, as later claimed, all those familiar with the story at the time laid the blame squarely on Britain's intransigence. On walls all over the Jewish areas of Palestine, posters appeared bearing the photograph of Sir Harold MacMichael and the words: "Known as High Commissioner for Palestine, WANTED FOR THE MURDER of 800 refugees."

In the early summer of 1942, Baron Fülöp von Freudiger of the Budapest Orthodox Jewish congregation received a letter from a little-known Orthodox rabbi named Michael Dov Weissmandel, in Bratislava, Slovakia. It was a cry for help, mostly financial, but also for advice on how to deal with the Joint and the Jewish Agency on the survival of the remaining Jews of Slovakia. The Germans had already taken 52,000 Slovak Jews. Rabbi Weissmandel and a woman called Gizi Fleischmann had founded the Bratislava Working Group, an offshoot of the local Jewish Council, whose sole purpose was to save the remaining Jews in Slovakia.

It was an unusual alliance. Gizi Fleischmann was the leader of the local branch of the Women's Zionist Organization, and both her daughters had already left for Palestine. She was a Slovak representative for the Joint and had been entrusted by the Jewish Agency with the task of creating a Slovak Aid and Rescue Committee. Rabbi Weissmandel, in contrast, was the son-in-law of the spiritual leader of the ultra-Orthodox, anti-Zionist rabbi of the Slovakian town of Nitra, Shmuel David Ungar.

Rabbi Weissmandel claimed that he had come up with the idea of bribing the Germans. For each Jew transported out of the country, the Slovak government had paid the Germans five hundred reichsmarks.[15] Perhaps the Nazis would accept a larger sum to leave the Jews at home. Weissmandel said that he and his group had met with Germans not all of whom were equally committed to what the Nazis called the "dejewification" of Europe. Some, perhaps even one at the top, could be bribed, and the process had been started with a down payment of $25,000 (they had received the total sum from a local Jewish businessman) and an indication that they were not acting on their own but were part of a larger "World Jewry." Weissmandel had used notepaper with a Swiss hotel's letterhead to write himself a formal letter in the name of his invented "rabbis of the world" and had authorized himself to act on their behalf. The Nazi officer had fallen for the fake letter immediately. It fitted his worldview.

Weissmandel believed that a deal, perhaps a series of deals, could be made if sufficient funds were found. With one down payment and promises of more to come, he thought they had succeeded in halting the deportations temporarily, but another $25,000 was urgently required.

In subsequent meetings with this Nazi officer, a man called Wisliceny, the Working Group had realized that its experience could be extended to other countries in Europe. Weissmandel called it "the Europa Plan." He and Gizi Fleischmann believed that further deportations of Jews in Europe could be stopped.

In answer to Freudiger's question about what sums would be involved, Fleischmann wrote that the whole Europa Plan would cost only $3 million, and then many remaining Jewish lives would be spared.[16] The plan, unfortunately, would not apply to Polish and German Jews.

When Freudiger showed the letters—written in archaic Hebrew—to Kasztner and Brand, they were unconvinced: Hitler would not tolerate any Jews in Europe, they said. But Kasztner agreed that perhaps fewer barriers would be put in the way of Jewish emigration, provided it was paid for and fast. The rabbi's Europa Plan, after all, sounded very much like the Europa Plan devised by Reichsmarschall Hermann Göring, which had earlier allowed large-scale emigration from Germany until it encountered stiff opposition from the Arabs and the harsh quotas of the British. A grand gesture—and $3 million was certainly grand—would reinforce German belief in the power of worldwide Jewry, its financial clout, its solidarity. With German armies stalled in the east by Stalin's Bolsheviks, it would be very useful if the Nazis thought of Jews as instruments of capitalism rather than Communism.

Gizi Fleischmann had written to Saly Mayer, the Swiss representative of the Joint, and to Nathan Schwalb, the European representative of the Hechalutz, the international Zionist youth movement that prepared its members for life in the settlements in Palestine; she begged them to put the case to their superiors in the United States and Palestine. If the money could not be ready in a few weeks, she warned, the plan would die. She believed that the German officer they were dealing with was a strict adherent to timelines. He had told them that he was taking the proposal to Himmler and would talk with the Working Group again in a few weeks. He had also told them that permission from the Slovak government would be needed to allow the Jews to remain in the country. That, Weissmandel and Fleischmann believed, would require additional bribes for government officials.

Fleischmann and Weissmandel used Springmann's "reliable" courier service to send their messages to the Jewish Agency's Rescue Committee in Istanbul. The man who brought them money and letters of encouragement from the Yishuv was Jozsi Winninger, who doubled as the Abwehr's agent and, when it served his purpose, passed copies of useful information to his German handlers.

To raise this large a sum of money, Weissmandel and Fleischmann warned, all Jewish groups in Palestine and the United States and Britain would need to be involved. The Bratislava Working Group hoped that the Hungarians would contribute.

In December 1942, Sam Springmann received a card from the Jewish Agency office in Istanbul telling him that a former Austrian dentist turned German officer named Rudolf Sedlaczek would be visiting Budapest and suggesting he be made welcome.[17] The card, one of the Agency's coded messages, made it clear that Sedlaczek was a "friend." Springmann had already met Sedlaczek, and he knew that he was, indeed, a "friend," a man who traveled regularly between Vienna, Kraków, and Budapest and was willing to carry in his false-bottomed suitcases large sums of money that would be used in local bribes. In addition to his sporadic dental activities, Sedlaczek, like Jozsi Winninger and Fritz Laufer, worked for the Abwehr. He was also a courier for the Zionists, and he had been sent to gather hard information on what had been happening to the Jews of Europe. Dr. Sedlaczek had visited Kraków recently and had heard news about the systematic extermination of Jews in Poland. This information was so startling that he had decided the Jewish Agency's people, the Rescue Committee in Budapest, had to hear it firsthand from his own source.

Sedlaczek told Springmann that the committee should prepare to receive a German visitor by the name of Oskar Schindler who would tell them, directly, about those regions of eastern Europe occupied by the Wehrmacht. An industrialist, Schindler had been allotted a large number of Jews for slave labor in his Kraków factory, one he had acquired through "Aryanization." He had shown himself to be a decent employer and had been helpful in delivering letters and parcels to Polish Jews in concentration camps. He had fed and clothed his workers, using the thousands of reichsmarks that had been delivered to him by couriers of the Jewish Agency and the Joint, but he needed more cash for this enterprise. Taking money across the borders had become too dangerous for Dr. Sedlaczek.

Schindler endured two days of uncomfortable travel in a freight car otherwise filled with Nazi Party newspapers to reach Budapest, and he was not in a good humor when Springmann and Kasztner met him at the Hotel Pannonia in Pest.[18] Kasztner would remember Oskar Schindler as a huge man, almost threatening with his massive bulk, pacing from the window and back, drinking occasionally from his flask of brandy, and talking about conditions for Jews in the General Government—the German term for the part of Poland not absorbed into the Reich. He talked of the atrocities in Kraków and the remaining ghetto, the terrible hunger in Lodz, and the freight trains leaving Warsaw full of Jews whose final destination was not labor camps as they had assumed, but *vernichtungslager*—extermination camps. In the midst of this stupid war, he said, the Nazis were using the railway system, expensive engineering, and an untold number of guards and bureaucrats whose sole purpose was to apply hitherto untried scientific methods in murdering large numbers of people. These new camps were run by the ss Economic Office at Oranienburg. People would be reduced to usable by-products—clothes, jewelry, toys, hair. Once inmates were in these camps, there was no chance of reaching them, no hope of rescue.

Kasztner and Springmann had heard of such camps, but Schindler's account was the first confirmation they had of their existence. They had known of atrocities, but their general assumption had been that the people in the camps were used for slave labor.

"Is it still possible," Kasztner asked Schindler, "to get some small comfort, letters, and food to people in these camps?"

Schindler said his experience proved that most of the guards were corruptible, but the committee would be wasting its resources sending food to the extermination camps. There were, however, still several work camps—some for women only—where food would be useful. He asked about their couriers and what the going rates were. When Springmann told him about Bandi Grosz and Jozsi Winninger, Schindler seemed amused. He had seen both men deliver

packages to his own workforce of Jews in his factory in Plaszów, on
the outskirts of Kraków. He paid the ss just five zloty a day for his
"slaves." Given the terrible conditions in the Kraków ghetto, he
thought he was helping by increasing his workforce to the maximum.
But he was concerned that even his own workers would be transported to one of these extermination camps while he was away in
Budapest. The ss seemed to be bent on eliminating the ghetto.

The priority, Schindler told them, had to be finding escape routes,
not sending packages of food. Hans Frank, who was the German
governor general of the General Government, he said, had been
open about his mission: "As far as the Jews are concerned, I want to
tell you quite frankly that they must be done away with one way or
another . . . I must ask you to rid yourselves of all feeling of pity. We
must annihilate the Jews." Otherwise, Schindler said, Frank was a
perfectly reasonable fellow with a law degree, a love of literature and
music, the father of five children, a connoisseur of fine wine, and a
sportsman. "You would enjoy his company if you met him in other
circumstances," he told the horrified men in his hotel room. Two
days before, he and Frank had dined in the governor general's
residence, the old Royal Castle on Wawel Hill in Kraków, and had
talked about economics and the arts. Frank's wife was in Warsaw
with the children, and Frank was concerned that one of them had
the mumps and was running a high fever.

The three men discussed access roads from Poland into Slovakia
and Hungary. Schindler would later recall that Kasztner was extraordinarily well informed about ways to extract people from the
ghettos. He knew council members' names and also their likelihood
to cooperate with the German authorities. Indeed, his information
about where the weak guards were posted seemed impeccable.[19]

After some persuasion, Schindler agreed to travel to Istanbul to
personally deliver his information to the Zionist leaders there. It was
vital that all Jewish organizations be aware of the facts, to give them
the ammunition to effect changes in Western immigration laws,
loosen British resolve on Palestine, influence Western leaders to
interfere in Hungary, and help the ever-increasing number of
refugees. Kasztner did not really believe that adverse publicity would

deter the Germans from further atrocities, but public opinion might delay some of their plans, and any delay was good. With luck, the war could end before the annihilation of the Jews was realized.

Kasztner later admitted he had not felt comfortable in the big German's presence. Even if the man had sympathies for the Jews, he was still enriching himself by their slave labor, so his hands were far from clean. All three men repaired to the Gellért Hotel's famous restaurant overlooking the Danube, where Schindler ordered a Transylvanian platter of assorted meats and a full-bodied Hungarian red wine. Unlike Springmann and Kasztner, he was unconcerned that many of the patrons wore German uniforms and that several others in black-tie attire were Abwehr agents out for the night with their mistresses. He talked about conditions in the General Government, the difficulties in obtaining good food and quality wines, and the deprivations faced by those German entrepreneurs who were willing to work hard. He was pink-faced, animated, loud, except when he mentioned that he had been able to buy black-market bread and shoes for his workers with the money "your people" had sent him.

Back in Kasztner's pension, he and Springmann deliberated over how to remove Moshe Krausz from his position of control over the number of Palestine visas that were handed out and to whom. If they were in control, they knew they could combine several families on one permit, to expand the numbers allowed under the British rules, and they could add orphans to families with few children. By some means, they would have to try to send out more "illegals." If the ghettos were being emptied now, they would meet immediately with the halutz boys to run more rescue missions from Poland. They could try to contact the Yugoslav partisans to help spirit children across the border.

In December 1942, unbeknownst to Kasztner, Springmann, and the others in Budapest, most of the politicians in Europe already knew of the disaster befalling the Jews. During each of October and November, more than 300,000 Jews had been deported to Auschwitz, including 106,000 from Holland and 77,000 from France.[20] Newspapers in the United Kingdom and the United States, as well as in Tel Aviv, carried reports, some firsthand, from traveling diplomats, businessmen, and refugees that the Germans were systematically murdering the European Jews. But anyone who followed these news stories assumed that the Germans' resolve to annihilate the Jews would likely be slowed down by defeats on the battlefields.

As recently as November 24, Budapest-born Stephen Wise, one of the United States' most prominent Jewish leaders, and president of the American Jewish Congress, announced to a packed room of reporters what State Department sources had confirmed—that more than two million Jews had already been killed in Europe and that it was Nazi policy to exterminate them all. He informed reporters that Jews were being moved from all countries in Europe to mass-killing centers in Poland.[21]

In hindsight, it is surprising that the extermination camps were not anticipated. As early as July 1941, Göring had issued a directive "for the implementation of the Final Solution." Reinhard Heydrich, security chief of the ss and Hitler's volatile confidant, also known as "Hangman Heydrich" to his victims in the east, had boasted openly at the Wannsee Conference for senior ss and sd men in January 1942 that "in the Final Solution to the Jewish problem, there are about eleven million Jews involved." All eleven million would be selected for hard labor, and most would die "through natural diminution." The rest would be killed. He had singled out the 3.5 million Jews of Poland as the "greatest danger."

CHAPTER 4

The Politics of Genocide

The orchestra played "The Triumphal March" from Aida, *conducted by the former musical director of the Warsaw Philharmonic Orchestra. The prisoners were lined up ready for inspection. The guards stood at attention, their arms sharply pointed away from their bodies at a ninety-degree angle. First Lieutenant Rudolf Höss, the camp commandant, wore his best uniform, his boots polished to a fine gleam by his personal valet. Reichsführer Heinrich Himmler was visiting the Auschwitz concentration camp.*

It was July 17, 1942, four years after the Anschluss, two years after the gift of northern Transylvania to the Hungarians, a year after Hungary joined the Reich in the war against the Soviet Union. Nevertheless, the Reichsführer had things on his mind regarding Hungarians.

Deep in thought, with an expression of growing dissatisfaction on his puckered face, he inspected the overcrowded buildings, the primitive latrines, the hospital, the field where the Russian prisoners of war had been slaughtered, the spotlessly clean kitchens that cooked the thin broth the prisoners were fed each day. He observed

the arrival of a transport of Jews, the selection of the few deemed fit
for labor, the murder of the rest, the burning of the bodies in open
trenches. Though he said nothing about his dissatisfaction, Himm-
ler was disappointed with the rate of the killings.

In neighboring Birkenau (Auschwitz ii), he ordered the build-
ing of modern concrete gas chambers and large, efficient cremato-
ria.

O skar Schindler's firsthand information was a warning that
the use of extermination camps could spread to the whole
Jewish population of Poland and Slovakia, but Rezső Kasztner and the Aid and Rescue Committee still hoped that the ghettos
would remain as sources for local labor. They knew of several camps,
such as Dachau and Bergen-Belsen, where the treatment, though
harsh, could be relieved by a supply of food parcels, clothing, and
bribes. The committee had managed to stay in sporadic touch with
Jewish leaders in the ghettos, and Sam Springmann had sent food
packages to the Warsaw and Lodz ghettos. The couriers reported the
starvation and the rounding up of work gangs, but not the extermination camps.

The committee believed that some 25,000 Jews were still alive in
Slovakia, and the Yishuv had started collecting funds for that desperate
idea of buying Jewish lives, the Europa Plan. As for the Slovak
Jews who had already been deported, Gizi Fleischmann and Rabbi
Weissmandel believed that many of them were still in labor camps.

As Schindler's story circulated to the different Jewish groups in
Budapest, it initiated an immediate if limited response. Fülöp von
Freudiger called for more generous donations to help Orthodox Jews
in Poland. Joel Brand asked the halutz groups to organize more tiyul
missions for illegal emigration, and Hansi Brand stepped up her
clothing and food collection drives. To the Polish halutzim,
Schindler's news was no surprise. They had been spreading information about mass murder already.[1] Whole camps dedicated to killing
did not seem far-fetched to young people who had seen the ss
murder babies in front of their mothers.

Samuel Stern remained confident that these terrible stories were isolated incidents. His group was busy providing financial help for recently impoverished professionals. The exclusionary laws had taken their toll on the middle class—lawyers, doctors, civil servants—who could no longer work in their professions. Stern did not wish to discuss horror stories about murder. Scientifically regulated extermination facilities were impossible to imagine. "In the months to come, we may be left without our money and comforts, but we shall survive," he told Kasztner when they met in the stairwell of Stern's Sip Street office building. The very idea of the *vernichtungslager*, of extermination, seemed improbable. Why would the Germans sacrifice men, transportation, and scarce resources to murder unarmed civilians with no means to defend themselves?

The *Times* in London reported from Paris that four thousand Jewish children had been deported to a Nazi concentration camp. In the House of Commons, British prime minister Winston Churchill gave a scathing address that was broadcast by the BBC and heard throughout Budapest: "The most senseless of their offences . . . ," he said, was "the mass deportation of Jews from France, with the pitiful horrors attendant on the calculated and final scattering of families. This tragedy illustrates . . . the utter degradation of the Nazi nature and theme."

Meanwhile, Jewish organizations in Budapest continued to provide learned lectures in their well-appointed halls on every conceivable subject, except the one of greatest importance to their members—the ongoing fate of the Jews in Germany, Austria, Greece, France, and Poland and what that meant for Hungary.

Although Springmann's bribed Abwehr officers could still penetrate the ghettos and sometimes extract people for fake work details, none would venture into the strictly forbidden camps at Sobibór, Treblinka, or Auschwitz. There were now fewer ghettos than before, and their populations had dramatically decreased. It was as though two million Polish Jews had disappeared without a trace.

In January 1943 the Second Hungarian Army was destroyed in the battle of Voronezh. The losses were terrible: 40,000 dead, 35,000 wounded, 60,000 taken prisoner by the Soviets.[2] The news was played down by the media and the politicians. Only those who listened to the BBC's Hungarian broadcasts or to the Soviets' Kossuth Radio Service heard of the disaster. The Germans' defeat by the Red Army at the Don River that same month was handled with equally cavalier disregard for the truth.

The Sixth Army had been ordered by Hitler to "stand fast" at Stalingrad no matter what the sacrifices as winter set in and the German forces were encircled by Soviet troops; the casualties at the end of this longest battle of the war amounted to about a quarter of a million German soldiers. No word of that defeat reached Budapest. Instead, Reichsmarschall Hermann Göring delivered entirely false information in a broadcast heard throughout the country. "In spite of everything," he claimed, "Germany's ultimate victory was decided."[3] It was small comfort for the ninety thousand frostbitten German prisoners, only five thousand of whom were to survive Soviet captivity in Siberia.

Under Miklós Kállay, prime minister since March 1942, Hungary's industries continued to thrive. The German army needed raw materials, the mines were busy, agricultural production was in high gear, and the manufacture of armaments, military uniforms, and buttons kept most people employed and earning reasonable salaries. The Hungarian government, with Horthy's full approval, sent agents to Istanbul to try to talk with the British and the American Office of Strategic Services (OSS) about the guarantees it would need if Hungary were to withdraw from the war. Moreover, Kállay's personal resistance to any further anti-Jewish laws lent credence to Samuel Stern's theory that "it cannot happen here."

By the summer of 1943, rumors were circulating in Budapest's cafés of an armistice agreement with Britain and the United States. There was talk that Kállay's emissaries had visited the capitals of neutral countries, shopping for acceptable terms. In desperation, Kállay himself went to see the dictator Benito Mussolini in Rome to propose a new alliance of Italy, Hungary, Romania, and Greece to stand firm against Hitler's further belligerence. Mussolini declined.[4]

Back at home, the politically astute Ottó Komoly realized that the Germans would soon have to terminate all these breakaway plans. Hitler would not allow a defection at such a critical time in the war.

Samuel Stern knew in advance about the Regent's meeting in late April 1943 with Hitler. He had been at Horthy's official residence, Buda Castle,[5] playing cards, when the call came from Hitler's headquarters inviting Horthy to Schloss Klessheim. Earlier that evening, Horthy had made jokes about the Führer's declamatory talk, his uncultured German, his strange way of marching up and down when he was in a fit of rage. But when the time came, Horthy had been too frightened to decline the invitation.[6] Hitler ranted about Kállay's clumsy overtures to the British. As a show of loyalty, he demanded another Hungarian army at the front. Horthy stood his ground. He would not agree to sending Hungarian forces to the Balkans, nor to further extreme measures against the Jews. Hitler, his hands clutched behind his back, screamed and marched. Horthy wondered whether the Führer was affected by some ailment that forced him to hold down his hand—he knew Hitler had come under the care of a doctor who insisted on a diet of strange pills.

They somehow got through the formal dinner that followed, and, by the time Horthy left, he was convinced that, for once, he had outsmarted Hitler. Germany could not afford to have an enemy on its borders. Josef Goebbels, Hitler's propaganda minister, also attended the dinner, but he had a different impression; he wrote in his diary that Horthy's "humanitarian attitude" regarding "the Jewish question" convinced the Führer that "all the rubbish of small nations still existing in Europe must be liquidated as fast as possible."[7]

Terrible stories were circulating in Budapest about the actions of Hungary's soldiers as they returned from the Soviet Union. Perhaps in response to the murderous carnage of their undefended retreat, they themselves had become inhuman. Disgusted young men on temporary furlough talked of hideous atrocities committed by the regular army corps. In late April 1943, retreating Hungarian soldiers in the Ukraine ordered eight hundred sick men from the Jewish labor force into a hospital shed and then set fire to it. Officers commanded the soldiers to shoot anyone who tried to escape from the flames.[8] Neither the Hungarian press nor the Hungarian Jewish newspaper reported these deaths. Nor had there been a mention of the routine murder of Jewish civilians behind German lines. Instead, the pro-Nazi press increased its vitriolic attacks on Jewish influence at home, persistently blaming food shortages on the Jews, who were falsely accused of hoarding lard, sugar, and flour, engaging in black-market activities, and reaping enormous war profits from the industries they controlled.

In the summer of 1943, Oskar Schindler returned for a second visit to Budapest, bringing letters to be forwarded to Istanbul for the Palestine relatives of "his" Jews. He offered to take return mail and food packages. He gave a detailed report on the situation in Poland as he knew it, the possibilities of rescue and escape from the ghettos, as well as new routes across the borders to Hungary that he believed were relatively safe for those who managed to escape from the ghettos. Kasztner, as Schindler recalled,[9] urged him to increase the number of Jews in a workers' "protected camp" close to his factory, and he was able to replenish the additional funds Schindler had advanced to hire more workers at his Plaszów facilities.[10]

In a letter she wrote to the Jewish Agency's Rescue Committee office in Istanbul on May 10, 1943, Gizi Fleischmann reported: "Over a million Jews have been resettled from Poland.[11] Hundreds of thousands have lost their lives due to starvation, disease, cold and many more have fallen victim to violence. The reports state that the corpses are used for chemical raw materials." On September 5, her letter to the American Joint Distribution Committee's representative in Geneva added: "We know today that Sobibór, Treblinka, Belzec and Auschwitz are annihilation camps."

Kasztner, Komoly, and their colleagues had seen copies of her letters, as had Samuel Stern. Baron Freudiger was in frequent touch with Rabbi Weissmandel, whose desperate cries for help from the rest of the world, demands that American and British Jews should express outrage, and calls for the Allies to bomb railway lines in Europe were even more persistent than hers.

In September 1943, Gizi Fleischmann traveled from Bratislava to Budapest, where she visited the offices of both Komoly and Kasztner, seeking help. Well-dressed, in her midforties, with auburn hair, she retained the appearance of the society woman she had been before the Nazi tragedy.

"Willy," as she called Dieter Wisliceny, the ss man in charge of deportations in Slovakia, had been ready to sell her one million Jews. If Saly Mayer of the Joint's office in Switzerland would only petition American Jews, she was sure these wealthy and influential people would pay the necessary funds, once they knew what was really happening in Europe. Yet the best that Mayer had offered was $2 million in a locked bank account, payable only after the end of the war. Wisliceny had scoffed at that offer, asking what use money would be to him after the war.

The grand Europa Plan might already be dead, she feared. All the Bratislava Working Group could still hope for was to save the remaining Slovak Jews. Saly Mayer had agreed to advance $100,000, but Wisliceny had specified $200,000, plus weekly installments.

Fleischmann said she had presented her case at a short meeting with Hofrat Stern and his "trusted advisers." Never in her life had she met with such colossal indifference, such lack of sympathy. They were not willing to share what funds they had, and they thought her allegations about the fate of Polish and Slovak Jews were preposterous. She also informed Kasztner that Wisliceny had told her about a visit he had made to Budapest. He had dined at the Golf Club on Swabian Hill with a senior functionary from the prime minister's office. They had discussed the extermination of the Hungarian Jews. Why, she asked, did the gentlemen upstairs think they would be spared?

After her visit, Kasztner again wrote to Nathan Schwalb of the Hechalutz, the international Zionist youth movement. He did not mince words. "The gas chambers in Poland have already consumed the bodies of more than half a million Jews. There are horrible, unbelievable photographs of starving children, of dead, emaciated bodies on the streets of the Warsaw ghetto," he told Schwalb.[12] The Va'ada, his Rescue Committee, urgently needed money for bribes and forged identity papers to help the young people out of the ghettos. There was still hope for some of them, but, in another year, there might be no one left to save in either Poland or Slovakia. The Joint had to raise more cash—and as much of it in U.S. funds and Swiss francs as possible. Other European currencies had become unreliable, and exchange rates were always pegged to black-market conversions.

To help Fleischmann, Kasztner collected $57,000, partly from the Joint's contribution to the Budapest Va'ada, but mostly from Freudiger's Orthodox membership, and he sent it to Bratislava with Bandi Grosz. After Grosz's commission as courier, there was still about $50,000 left. And that was the amount Fleischmann finally offered to Wisliceny in exchange for the remaining Slovak Jews.

Soon after this second payment, deportations in Slovakia stopped. It seemed that Wisliceny was a man of his word.

Many theories have been suggested to explain these events. The papal ambassador in Slovakia had intervened with the mostly Catholic government to urge the end of the deportations. President Josef Tiso had not agreed to the murder of Slovak Jews, only to their deportation, and he was raising concerns with Wisliceny, who reported to his superior, Lieutenant Colonel Adolf Eichmann, that the Slovak prime minister, Vojtech Tuka, had demanded that a Slovak government delegation be allowed to visit the Slovak Jews' labor camp.[13] Eichmann thought that could prove tricky, as most of the Slovak Jews were already dead. And Wisliceny soon left for Salonica and Greece to implement the deportation plans there. Whether the bribes contributed to the two-year hiatus in murdering Slovak Jews is still—more than sixty years later—in dispute. There is no doubt, however, that Gizi Fleischmann and Rabbi Weissmandel believed their bribes had stopped the deportations.

News of the ghetto rebellion in Warsaw in April–May 1943 was never reported by Budapest radio; there was no mention in the

Jewish newspapers of the house-to-house battles of the last Jews in the Polish capital. The rest—about 350,000—had been taken to extermination camps. Blindly optimistic, Zionist offices in Istanbul were still estimating almost half a million Jews remained in the ghetto. Springmann's Abwehr men had not been allowed in for months. Only the BBC's newscasts provided some day-to-day commentary on the Jews' heroic resistance. The unequal battle had lasted more than four weeks. Some evenings, Rezső and Bogyó Kasztner stayed by their radio for hours, waiting for news about the ghetto. Typically, the BBC suggested that there had been active assistance by the British, even though none had been offered.

Shortly before he committed suicide in London, Samuel Zygelbojm, a former leader of the Jewish Socialist Party in Poland and a member of the Polish government-in-exile, wrote a letter:

> With these, my last words, I address myself to you, the Polish government, the Polish people, the Allied governments and their people, and to the conscience of the world.
>
> News recently received from Poland informs us that the Germans are exterminating with unheard of savagery the remaining Jews in that country. Behind the walls of the ghetto is taking place today the last act of a tragedy which has no parallel in the history of the human race. The responsibility for this crime rests above all on the murderers themselves, but falls indirectly upon the whole human race, on the Allies and their governments, who have taken no firm steps to put a stop to these crimes. By their indifference to the killing of millions of hapless men, the massacre of women and children, these countries have become accomplices of the assassins.
>
> Furthermore, I must state that the Polish government . . . has not taken adequate measures to counter this atrocity which is taking place in Poland.

Of the three and a half million Polish Jews (to whom must be added the seven hundred thousand deported from the other countries) in April 1943, there remained alive not more than three hundred thousand . . . And the extermination continues.

I cannot remain silent . . .

Let my death be an energetic cry of protest against the indifference of the world . . .

The letter was transmitted to the British and American governments, but neither increased its national quotas for refugee Jews. Nor would Britain open the doors to Palestine, the only place willing to accommodate those who were able to escape.

On May 16, members of the Hungarian Rescue Committee gathered around their radios and toasted the Warsaw ghetto's last heroic stand.

On June 11, Reichsführer ss Himmler ordered the liquidation of all Polish ghettos.

On July 10, British, Canadian, and American troops landed on the southern shores of Sicily. If Italy extracted itself from its Axis alliance with Germany and Japan, Jozsi Winninger told Joel Brand, the Führer would have Mussolini's head, served with garnish, on a platter.

The German armies marched into Italy from the north and went south to confront the Allied forces. Moving behind the lines, the ss began to round up and deport the remaining Jews that the Italians had been reluctant to isolate.

Bogyó found the apartment in the Váci Street pension too small, the neighborhood too crowded. When her father went to Budapest to check that she was well cared for, he did not like the place any more than his daughter did. It was a large and confusing city. He dined with his son-in-law in the confines of the pension's low-slung dining room. In Kolozsvár, he said, there were still ways to circumvent the anti-Jewish laws. For the right consideration, officials were still willing to look the other way. "If we keep our heads down, we can survive this war," he said. He was concerned that Rezső's activities with the Rescue Committee would land him in trouble with the authorities. "It is important to remember that our prime objective is to survive the war."

Elizabeth Zahler, the couple's landlady, remained bubbly and optimistic despite what they called "the times." They would change soon, she often assured Bogyó. The papers would tire of the subject, and Horthy would not, could not remain indifferent about the mistreatment of the Jews. He had Jewish friends. One of his doctors was Jewish. His son's new wife was at least partly Jewish.

"It's a kind of madness that comes over otherwise normal people from time to time," Rezső said. "Afterward, there will be learned treatises and explanations, there will be university studies of when and how it began and ended, but it will end."

Bogyó was not reassured. She had become afraid to walk in the Váci Street area, where a number of the finer stores were owned by Jews. She felt people were staring at her.

She planned her days around lunch with Elizabeth and maybe a short walk with her along the Corso. The fall of 1943 was spectacular with its bright colors: the old chestnut trees along the Danube turning crimson and rich sienna browns, the screaming yellows of the acacias, the bronze birches, the oranges of the dogwood trees rising up Gellért Hill, crowning its head with the dark leaves of the beeches. Musicians still played in the outdoor cafés; young women paraded their winter furs. Late in the evenings there was frost in the air.

On October 4, 1943, at a meeting of ss generals in Poznan, Heinrich Himmler boasted that only his ss could have carried out the "action" against the Jews. This steadfast killing spree, he said, was "a page of glory in its history which could never be truly appreciated." In a long, rambling speech, he identified the Jews as an implacable enemy of Germany and talked openly about "the extermination of the Jewish race." He was convinced, he announced, that the Jews both inside and outside the Reich had been conspiring against Hitler's regime and that they would continue to do so until they were finally silenced.

He praised the ss: "Most of you must know what it means when one hundred corpses are lying side by side, or five hundred, or one thousand. To have stuck it out and at the same time to have emained decent fellows, that is what has made us hard. This is a page of glory in our history . . . We have taken from them what wealth they had," but all of it, he insisted, had been and would be turned over to the Reich. He commended the honesty of his officers and men.

Himmler's speech was an exception to the rule. Reich officials had been instructed to keep the extermination camps a secret. At no time was anyone to say the words "murder" or "annihilation." Rather, the term was to be "special handling." "Gas" and "crematoria" were banned from official reports. Anyone found to have information about the systematic killing of people was charged with possession of *greuelmärchen*, "horror stories." The punishment for spreading such tales was execution.

Every ss guard and officer at Auschwitz had signed a pledge that he would not discuss with anyone, including his family or his coworkers, "anything dealing with the operation." They all understood "the top secrecy of all of the occurrences of the so-called Jewish Relocation."[14] Members of the ss who sought reassignment because they suffered from unusual stress would not be relieved. A number of former soldiers who had been assigned to extermination camps chose to commit suicide rather than face another day of killing.

But while the camps operated with brutal efficiency, Germany and its allies struggled in the various theaters of war. Mussolini, Hitler's stalwart Italian ally, had been ignominiously dismissed by King Victor Emmanuel in July 1943. In September the Italian divisions surrendered to the American Fifth Army, and Italy withdrew from the war. In November the Soviet armies took back Kiev and crossed into the prewar territory of Poland. Meanwhile, American and British planes were bombing German cities and selected industrial plants. After months of heavy fighting, marching up from the boot of Italy, the British finally took the Foggia airfields. From there, Allied bombers had even easier access to German cities. Field Marshal Erwin Rommel's prized Afrika Korps had been all but wiped out.

Despite mounting evidence of the persecution of Jews under the Third Reich, the British government adhered to its established limits on Jewish immigration, and neutral nations, such as Switzerland and Portugal, did not want more Jews crossing their borders. Both the United States and Britain tried to persuade Portugal to accept a sizable Jewish settlement in Angola, and they agreed to bribe the Dominican Republic with $3,000 a head, but neither of these measures could help to alleviate the magnitude of the problem.

Finally, in January 1944, by Executive Order 9417, the United States created the War Refugee Board, charged with taking "all measures within its power to rescue victims of enemy oppression who are in imminent danger of death and otherwise to afford such victims all possible relief and assistance consistent with the successful prosecution of the war." The board was to receive cooperation from all departments, including the State Department, whose officials strictly adhered to immigration rules. Visas were often denied on the grounds that the applicants had relatives in enemy countries, though most of those relatives were, of course, on their way to the gas chambers. Two affidavits of support and sponsorship from "reputable American citizens" had also to be attached to each application. It would have been difficult to invent a more restrictive set of rules.

A joke made the rounds in Budapest at the time: A Jew goes into the U.S. Consulate to ask for a visa. He is told to come back in 2003.

"In the morning," he asks, "or in the afternoon?"[15]

On January 24, 1944, the chief of the Hungarian general staff met with Field Marshal Wilhelm Keitel and suggested that Hungarian forces might withdraw from the Eastern Front. The Germans had been aware of Hungary's vacillations about the war, its fear of Allied attacks, and its appeal to the British not to bomb Hungary while it was reassessing its position. Several more Hungarian emissaries had approached both British and American agencies, including the oss in Turkey, and offered separate peace agreements. Prime Minister Kállay, whom Hitler had called "a swine," made other overtures toward the Allies. His definition of acceptable terms had loosened considerably since the beginning of his time in office.

Admiral Horthy followed suit within a month in a formal letter to Hitler. He suggested that Hungarian troops be withdrawn to aid in the defense of the Carpathians. The soldiers would perform better if they were defending their homeland, he said. He stressed his anxiety about Budapest, the "spiritual, political, economic" center of the country, and asked that German troops not be stationed near the capital "since it would attract heavy air-raids."[16]

Hitler thought Horthy's plan was as ridiculous as the Regent himself and on Friday, March 17, summoned him once again to Schloss Klessheim for a meeting next day. Horthy had well-founded misgivings. He had made it a rule not to set out on Fridays—an old superstition of his from seagoing days.

The Führer had known of Hungary's various withdrawal discussions and had some plans of his own for Horthy. He insisted that Jewish influence in Hungary had to cease. He told the Regent that the German army would occupy Hungary. If Horthy did not agree to the occupation and ordered his armies to resist, Germany would enlist the help of its surrounding allies in a joint attack. They would dismember Hungary and return it to its Trianon Treaty borders. Hard-won territories in Upper Province, Transylvania, and the south would be claimed by the Slovaks, the Romanians, and the Croats. Such talk was the stuff of Horthy's nightmares. As German foreign minister Joachim von Ribbentrop recalled, Horthy turned pale and recoiled at Hitler's words.[17]

Hitler offered only one alternative: an unopposed occupation of Hungary and the appointment of a German Reich plenipotentiary in charge of Hungarian affairs. Horthy could remain nominally in charge. He could keep his beloved title, "Regent." After that, it had been relatively easy to persuade Horthy to demand the immediate resignation of Miklós Kállay and to install a new prime minister more to Hitler's liking.

In the midst of the shouting and Hitler's threats, Horthy also consented to the delivery of 100,000 Jewish workers. They would be employed by the Todt Organization, a military engineering group absorbed into the armaments ministry under Albert Speer. Afterward, Döme Sztójay, then the Hungarian minister to Germany, suggested that the agreement could be stretched to include additional Jews and that he would promote some general action that deported an even larger number to whatever destination the Germans had in mind. Horthy later claimed this dimension was completely unknown to him or any member of his staff at the time.

Over the winter months of 1943–44, many of the labor service camps had become death sentences for the underfed and poorly clothed Jews. In some Hungarian army labor units the brutality meted out to Jews was comparable to Nazi tactics in occupied Poland. In one division, sergeants doused Jews with water and cheered as their victims turned into ice sculptures. In another encampment, officers ordered men in the work detail to climb trees and holler "I am a dirty Jew" as they leaped from branch to branch. They were used for target practice.

Of the fifty thousand men in the labor companies, only about seven thousand survived.

Randolph Braham, Distinguished Professor Emeritus of Political Science at City College and of the doctoral program at the Graduate Center of the City University of New York, is one of those survivors. He remembers marching in ragged clothes, in the rain, his unit "no longer human," sleeping as they marched. "Until then," he says, "I didn't know you could sleep and march at the same time." As they marched, they sometimes hummed an old Hungarian folksong with the refrain, *Kisangyalom, én igy nem birom tovább,* "My angel, I cannot bear this anymore."

CHAPTER 5

Budapest:
The Beginning of the End

When Heinrich Himmler visited Auschwitz-Birkenau again in 1943, he was able to inspect the realization of his plans. Commandant Rudolf Höss had arranged for a special transport of three thousand Jews to demonstrate the effectiveness of the new systems.

The train arrived, the wagons were emptied, those who were already dead and the bags they had hopefully carried were cleared out by the kapos, prisoners who did certain chores in return for more privileges, and the new arrivals were rushed toward the selection stand by stick-wielding SS guards. Only three were judged fit by the very businesslike SS officer and physician Dr. Josef Mengele. The rest were crowded into the new gas chambers; with their "Keep Clean" notices, they were designed to resemble showers. When the prisoners were pressed together so that no one could move in any direction, the guards threw in the babies and small children over the heads of the adults, then closed and sealed the doors.

About two hours later, when Reichsführer Himmler had finished his leisurely breakfast at Commandant Höss's villa, he

*returned to see the completion of the process. The ss men on the
flat roofs of the gas chamber put on their protective masks,
removed the lids from the camouflaged openings, and dropped in
the cyanide-based Zyklon B pellets.*

*Himmler was able to watch the last struggle through the obser-
vation windows: children clinging to their mothers, the hoarse
cries of the men still trying to open the sealed doors, the hopeless
screaming of those clawing for air in the airless chambers. When
everyone inside was dead, Höss demonstrated the new lifts that
removed the bodies, the quick, efficient work of the kapos in
removing gold teeth, hair (used as insulation on torpedo
warheads), a few baubles that had been hidden in crevices not
already searched, and the final trip to the recently completed
crematoria, containing fifteen ovens that could burn three bodies
each, at the same time and in less than twenty minutes.*

*The cremation capacity of the ovens had reached the initial goal
of 4,400 human bodies a day, or more than 120,000 people a
month.[1] Himmler was satisfied. Auschwitz-Birkenau was ready
for the Jews of Hungary.[2]*

O n March 13, 1944, six days before the German occupation
of Hungary, the Abwehr agent and sometime courier Jozsi
Winninger told Rezső Kasztner that, within a short time,
the German army would place control of the Jewish camps in the
hands of the Red Cross. The couriers would then, he said, be able to
take money directly into the Polish camps. The mere formality of a
$200,000 deposit in cash would be needed.[3]

The very next day, Winninger called Kasztner again.[4] He had been
able to improve his position in the Abwehr because of his dual roles:
he reported on the activities of the Rescue Committee to his bosses
while, at the same time, he served the Zionists by delivering letters and
food packages to work camps and carried official correspondence and
money from Istanbul to the Rescue Committee. Now he said he had
news for Kasztner and Joel Brand and wished to deliver it in person.

He suggested a restaurant on the Buda side of the river, a favorite of his boss, Dr. Josef Schmidt, who ran the Hungarian spy operation reporting to Abwehrstelle III F, the counterespionage unit of the Abwehr military district headquartered in Vienna. Brand had first met Schmidt at his own favorite Budapest spot: the Moulin Rouge nightclub. Kasztner found it amusing that the self-important Schmidt (whose doctorate was, at best, a curiosity) had been a newspaper hawker on the streets of Vienna only months before the Anschluss.

Kasztner and Brand arrived a few minutes before 8 PM. The restaurant, famous for its Viennese specialties, was full, the music muted, and the view over the Danube enchanting. Schmidt, balding, stout, red-faced, had already finished most of a bottle of Szekszárdi Vörös, a full-bodied Hungarian red wine, which he proceeded to compliment in courtly, overblown German, as if he were talking about the charms of a fleshy woman. He was affable, conciliatory, friendly, presenting himself as a reasonable man in an unreasonable world.

Winninger acted the part of the genial host. He recommended another Hungarian wine with the main course. He had, he said, taken the liberty of having it set aside already to breathe. In the two years Winninger had spent in Hungary, his girth had grown; his neck overflowed his impeccably ironed shirt collar, and his tie soon bore traces of the copious hors d'oeuvres the waiters deposited on the table.

Schmidt, as if indulging in dinnertime small talk, said the war effort would demand more and more of the German army, and the troops needed food and clothing, ammunition, and transport. It had been stupid of Regent Horthy to imagine he could pull Hungary out of the war at this time, when Germany needed support. Had he decided to do his little dance with Hitler before the Italians pulled out, there might have been a small chance the Führer would have overlooked the effrontery. Now he needed reliable forces to the east, and the only forces truly reliable were his own. Edmund Veesenmayer, the corpulent German envoy to Hungary, had been reporting to Hitler that, at best, Hungary was a hesitant and unreliable ally; at worst—and it seemed that the worst was happening on the Eastern

Front—Hungary was a liability. Veesenmayer viewed Horthy's effort to bring back what was left of the Hungarian armies as treasonous. At seventy-six, Horthy was befuddled by age, Schmidt said, and he would have to be swept aside.

Winninger added that Hitler had signed the orders for Operation Margarethe I, the invasion of Hungary, two days earlier. The order, issued to the commander of German forces in the southeast, meant the immediate deployment of troops along the Hungarian border. The German army would occupy Hungary within a few days.

"Wouldn't the Hungarians resist?" Brand asked.

Winninger laughed.

They could not, Schmidt replied. Most of their better units were still in the Ukraine, and the forces stationed closer to the capital were sympathetic to the Germans. Many of the senior officers were Swabians, Germans at heart. Prime Minister Kállay, like his predecessors, had thought that the Russians were the greater threat. Their participation in the Allied armies had prevented Kállay from negotiating an unconditional surrender. Now, it was much too late for that.

"Veesenmayer will be made Reich plenipotentiary, and Admiral Horthy's government will cooperate whether they like it or not," Winninger said. "Hungary will cease to be an independent country."

Brand and Kasztner stared at the two Abwehr men, both of whom had finished their sizable pork filets and their second bottle of red wine and were examining the dessert menu. Although the Va'ada leaders had grown used to expecting bad news, they were unable for a few moments to absorb the information they had just been given.

"What," Brand finally asked, "are their plans for the Jews?"

Winninger was sure that Jewish matters would be administered by the ss. The Führer was convinced that there was still too much Jewish influence in Horthy's Buda Castle. Two detachments each of ss and sd men would be arriving in Budapest. Himmler's deputy, Ernst Kaltenbrunner, who became security chief after Heydrich was assassinated, was already in the city. Lieutenant-Colonel Adolf Eichmann's special unit had been mobilized and would arrive in the capital a few days later. Neither Kasztner nor Brand needed to ask how

Eichmann's unit was "special."

What Winninger did not realize was that Himmler had already decided to dispense with the services of the Abwehr's intelligence network; soon both Winninger and Schmidt would be incarcerated. The Abwehr chief, Admiral Wilhelm Canaris, had been fired by Hitler in February, and the Abwehr was to be absorbed into the Security Service and the ss.

Winninger did, however, suggest that, when dealing with the ss, money and valuables might prove to be useful in exchange for something of no value: Jewish lives. That was the first mention of what became known as the "blood for goods" deal.

Kasztner immediately called Ottó Komoly to share the stunning information, and Brand raced home to warn the people they had been hiding. For this kind of emergency, Peretz Révész and the Polish halutzim had prepared "bunkers," camouflaged underground hiding places. They had not anticipated a German occupation, but they knew what to expect if the special commando came. Peretz thought of armed resistance, arguing that even if they all were killed, they should at least make it expensive for the Germans.

Moshe Schweiger, the man least likely to fill such a role,[5] had been picked by the Haganah[6] in Palestine as the most capable person to organize an attack on the German army. He told Kasztner that he had received his commission and instructions in a sealed envelope from Istanbul. In the event of a German invasion or an attempt to deport Hungary's Jews, he was immediately to form a military unit—"here, in Budapest. In full view of the security forces," he laughed. "They must be mad." Someone in the Haganah, he said, must have confused him with another man, one more inclined to suicide.

In the early afternoon, though, when they all gathered at the Pilvax Café, Schweiger was there studying an old copy of *The Science of Military Strategy*. He now revealed to the group that an expeditionary force of high-level Yishuv operatives, supported by the British army,[7] would be dropped into Hungary. He did not know when or how, but the committee needed to be ready and prepared to join the soldiers when they arrived.

Kasztner listed the weapons and ammunition they could round up. "A hundred and fifty pistols, forty hand grenades, three rifles of World War I vintage, some bags of ammunition. Perhaps we could add a few kitchen knives?" He started to laugh as he came to the end of the list. "Gallows humor," he said. "Shouldn't a man at the end of the rope be allowed a last laugh?"

Hansi suggested that the women, leaning from their balconies, could pour boiling oil over the tanks, a modern version of what the heroic women of Eger Castle in northern Hungary did when the occupying Turks advanced on their stronghold in an earlier century.[8] More practically, she moved the children to the Majestic Hotel. It offered reassuringly familiar surroundings, and some of their friends had rooms there, too. They would be safer there, she thought, than in the crowded apartment.

Komoly cabled the Jewish Agency's people in Istanbul and the Joint's men in Geneva to alert the British and the Americans that Hungary was in danger. The Americans' War Refugee Board had to be informed immediately, he said. He asked that Chaim Barlas, then the Jewish Agency's immigration officer in Istanbul, send more Palestine entry permits, more cash.

A Hungarian counterintelligence officer took a package to Istanbul for the Va'ada on March 17. It was written in Hebrew and contained some of the more nightmarish accounts of German atrocities against Jews in Poland. It also included the news of the imminent German invasion.

At a late-night meeting at Samuel Stern's home in Buda, everyone agreed to wait and see. They reviewed what they knew of the war. Their main source, the BBC, had been broadcasting hopeful news of British victories. The British and Americans had conquered southern Italy, and General Bernard Montgomery's forces were driving up the coast. The Italian army had given up on East Africa and Greece and had proved to be hopeless even on its own turf; on September 8, 1943, it had surrendered to the Allies. The ceaseless bombardment of German cities had reduced many of them to rubble, and no longer was there any doubt about Allied superiority in the air. In Cologne, for example, only the cathedral was spared. Hamburg and much of its population had been destroyed in a massive conflagration caused by intensive bombing. Darmstadt, Würzburg, and Kassel had been burned to the ground. The Royal Air Force had bombed Berlin in a daylight raid that showed its mastery of the skies over Germany. The Allies had bombed factories and railway lines, and Germany was running short of oil. The once mighty German air force, the Luftwaffe, according to the BBC was mighty no more. German submarines had been all but blown out of the oceans. In January, the Germans had abandoned their attack on Leningrad. More German soldiers had escaped from the horrors of the Soviet front, and dozens of deserters were hiding in Budapest. Some members of the Nazi Party's paramilitary youth group, Hitler Jugend, as young as sixteen, were now enrolled as fighting men.

Despite what the Abwehr men had said, the group meeting at Stern's house concluded that the Reich had greater problems than the Jews. If Horthy was still in power, Stern believed, they would still be safe. There must be no hint of disloyalty to Hungary. The Hungarians would not abandon their Jewish citizens. "We have lived here for a thousand years," he reminded his friends.

As for resistance, they would certainly all be murdered if they tried that route. In 1942 in Minsk, when the Jews organized resistance against continuing German occupation of the Belarusian city, the German army retaliated with a full-scale military attack and executed everybody.

A strange, fatalistic calm descended on the gathering.

PART TWO

The Kingdom
of the Night

From now on, the Gestapo ruled unhindered. They spied on the government, arrested every Hungarian who did not suit them, no matter how high their position and, by their presence, instilled fear in those who would have attempted to save the remnants of Hungarian sovereignty or protest against German orders. Concerning the Jewish question, the supreme, the absolute and unfettered will of the monster ruled ... the head of the Jewish command, Lieutenant-Colonel Adolf Eichmann.

Rezső Kasztner, *Der Kasztner-Bericht*

CHAPTER 6

The Occupation

It is easily said that we should have preferred to engage in a hope-
less struggle rather than to submit to Hitler's demands, and such a
view reads well on paper. In fact, it is errant nonsense. An indi-
vidual can commit suicide, a whole nation can not.

Miklós Horthy, *Memoirs*

On Sunday morning, March 19, 1944, the German army
marched into Budapest. By nine o'clock, most of the city
knew that the Germans had invaded, though Radio
Budapest kept broadcasting light music, a little Mozart, a few Strauss
selections, as if nothing had happened. There were no newspapers.
Only the BBC saw fit to announce the occupation of Hungary. SS
Colonel Dr. Edmund Veesenmayer, the former Reich minister to
Hungary, had been named Reich plenipotentiary. He ordered the
arrest of prominent intellectuals and public figures, left-leaning
members of parliament (at least one of whom resisted and was
wounded), journalists, writers, several industrialists, and hundreds of
Poles, French, and Slovaks. A group of forty Polish officers who had

been stationed in a house in Buda offered armed resistance. They were all shot. The Gestapo ransacked the offices of the Smallholders Party, the Social Democratic Party, the editorial offices of newspapers sympathetic to the democratic system, and of trade-union buildings. It occupied the airport and the railway stations.

The thunderous roll of long lines of tanks greeted late risers. Along the great Andrássy Avenue, a few enthusiastic citizens raised their arms in the Hitler salute, but most people stayed in their homes.

Hundreds were detained at railway stations for disobeying a new law, not yet announced, that required Jews to obtain written permission to travel. Some two hundred others were picked, at random, from the telephone book's listing of doctors and lawyers whose names looked to be Jewish.[1]

The Va'ada, the Aid and Rescue Committee, met that afternoon at the Café Parisette on the Duna Corso, where even that day Sunday strollers were enjoying the afternoon warmth. The committee members sat at Sam Springmann's usual table near the back of the stately café. The maître d' greeted them with customary deference, though Rezső Kasztner noticed that his hand shook when he placed the menu in front of him.

Hansi Brand, the first to arrive, had already unfurled an old newspaper and was reading about the rising prices, the black-market racketeers, the stockpiling of luxury goods by Jews—the usual pap—but there was no mention of the only news worth mentioning at press time: the German army's impending invasion of its ally. Joel Brand was slumped over his beer, suit rumpled, collar open, his hair unbrushed. The night before, he had been in one of his favorite clubs with a couple of Abwehr agents. He had arrived at the Majestic Hotel at 4 AM with Jozsi Winninger, grabbed the suitcase with cash from Istanbul intended for the refugees, and gone for coffee at the apartment Winninger had rented for "his" ballerina. He had "lent" Winninger some $8,000 in cash and a gold cigarette case to make sure the goods, and Joel himself, would remain safe. Brand was exhausted. He hadn't slept all night. He reported that Winninger had been very nervous and, when asked what would happen to the

Jews, had replied: "A fate worse than for the Polish Jews."[2]

Moshe Schweiger did not join the group—Ottó Komoly said he thought he had been arrested. Schweiger had called him the previous day about a message from Palestine: a small force of parachutists would arrive in the next few days to help the local Jewish community. Perhaps someone had overheard the conversation. Perhaps the Germans had known Schweiger was the official representative of the Haganah, the underground army of the Jews in Palestine. Sam Springmann had always suspected that the couriers shared with their Abwehr handlers most of the secret correspondence they carried for the Va'ada.

Springmann himself had disappeared. He had known he would be on the list of those to be arrested first. He told Kasztner: "They have me both ways. I am Polish and I am a Jew."

The Germans' sand-colored Mercedes cars had gone to the residence of Ferenc Chorin, the most powerful industrialist in Hungary, president of the Industrialists' Association, the wealthiest man in the country, a strong Hungarian patriot, and a friend of Regent Horthy. Chorin, as everyone knew, was a rum hand at bridge, a canny bidder, Horthy's favorite partner. Would they dare arrest him?[3] On the night just passed, there had been an elegant party at the Mauthner family's mansion, where all the guests had worn evening dress and their patriotic decorations, champagne flowed, and liveried waiters served fabulous delicacies on silver platters. Ferenc Chorin, Jenő Weiss, and Móric Kornfeld had all been there.[4]

André Biss, who had gone to the meeting with Hansi, could not believe that Chorin would have stayed in the country. He would, surely, have known of the German occupation long before anyone else did. Biss, a successful businessman, was a cousin of Joel Brand by marriage, and, through his Swabian mother, he had genuine *volksdeutsche* papers. As a fake German, he had kept his pottery and faience stove factory and even expanded it after other Jewish enterprises had been sold. Now he could afford to help Hansi Brand and the children.

The government of Miklós Kállay had been dissolved. The prime minister had fled to the Turkish legation and begged for asylum.

Most members of parliament had resigned. "They will be on their way to jail by now," Brand guessed—correctly, as it turned out, though several were taken to Germany instead.

Ottó Komoly said that the first priority must be the thousands of Jews with "unsettled citizenship," those who had arrived with no documents and were registered with the Central Authority for Alien Control, a notoriously unfriendly department of the Hungarian government with a one-policy-fits-all approach to handling Jewish refugees: intern them. Many had not yet been furnished with identity papers and were still at the mercy of the authorities. Others, who had not registered, were hiding, walking the streets, or lining up at the Jewish Agency's Palestine Office. They needed safe places to stay and a supply of food until the situation became clearer and they learned what their options were.

Biss knew a couple of reasonable policemen who might help bring people out of jails. The wily Peretz Révész had made friends with an expensive gendarme who could be trusted in exchange for the right amounts of money. Joel Brand offered to contact the halutz group at the Palestine Office. Kasztner raised, again, the possibility of armed resistance. They all knew the Germans would focus their attention on the Jews.

It was Hansi Brand who made the suggestion that they try the Bratislava Working Group's Europa Plan: negotiate to buy lives.[5] The Germans had shown in Slovakia that they loved bribes. If fighting with 150 handguns was futile, if there was not going to be a mass revolt of thirty Zionists and a few ragtag refugees with kitchen knives, they could at least give the Slovak scheme a chance. Kasztner immediately supported this idea and agreed to ask Jozsi Winninger to arrange a meeting with Dieter Wisliceny, Fleischmann's Nazi contact in Bratislava, if he was already in Budapest. Winninger would know where they stood with the ss.

At the end of the Va'ada gathering, they decided it was too risky to return to their own homes. The Brands and the Kasztners would go, by separate routes, to André Biss's apartment at 15 Semsey Andor Street, a fair distance from the center of Pest and in a safely gentile neighborhood. Hansi, ever the realist, had already moved the children there.

Rezső called Bogyó from the restaurant and urged her to go to Biss's place with everything she could carry of her personal belongings. She should use a streetcar; this service, after a short display of concern, had returned to its usual routes. He had told her of the coming invasion but had not said they might be forced to move. The speed with which the Germans took over had been astonishing.

Kasztner and Brand went to the Palestine Office, only to find it closed, two policemen posted outside, and the street deserted. Krausz had vanished. The pair stopped at the Kasztners' pension to make sure Bogyó had left, and they collected the leather suitcase full of reports from Palestine, notes from meetings of the Aid and Rescue Committee, and Gizi Fleischmann's and Rabbi Weissmandel's letters from Bratislava. Reviving the Europa Plan seemed the only hope now that the Germans had landed.

Regent Horthy, whose train had been held up near Vienna while the Germans occupied Hungary, announced a new government under the "protection of the Reich." Döme Sztójay was named prime minister. A devout follower of National Socialism, Sztójay was a vocal anti-Semite and an angry man—he seemed to have a grievance he had been nursing for years. He had few friends in parliament, but, while he was Hungary's minister in Berlin, he had formed close friendships with several high-ranking Nazis. The minister of the interior would be Andor Jaross, a strong rightist, another extreme anti-Semite, and an enthusiastic proponent of the National Socialist agenda. He had been a German informer during his tenure in the previous government. He picked, as his state secretaries, László Baky and László Endre.

Baky had served in the Hungarian military and the gendarmerie, from which he had retired (with the rank of major) in order to devote himself to politics. He had first joined Ferenc Szálasi's Arrow Cross Party in 1938, then switched to the Hungarian National Socialist Party and used its newspaper, *Magyarság* (The Hungarian), for his diatribes against the Jews. He had been an informant for the ss. From 1940 on he was, again, a member of the Arrow Cross. At a December meeting of the party, he said to Szálasi, "We are going to have some hangings, aren't we, Ferenc?" Baky was now the political state secretary to Jaross.

László Endre was another ardent anti-Semite. After his appointment to district magistrate in Gödöllő in 1921, he had initiated raids on Jewish businesses, banned local Jews from public baths, closed Jewish shops, and levied high fines on Jewish-run restaurants for minor infractions. At the time, his rulings were overturned and his behavior curbed by his bosses. Later, as subprefect of Pest County, he had had a free hand. On March 22, only three days after the German invasion, he issued nine anti-Jewish decrees. One of them denied Jews sugar and shortening; another ordered the confiscation of Jewish summer homes and the surrender of radios; yet another banned books by Jewish authors in libraries within his jurisdiction. Now he was appointed state secretary in charge of public administration.

German cars sped like angry wasps[6] from street to street, their back seats occupied by machine-gun-wielding ss men. They stopped in front of houses and apartment buildings, dragged people (some still in their pajamas) from their homes, and took them to the Buda jail or to the Astoria Hotel. Not long before, there had been spring dances in the ballroom of the stately, white Astoria; now the Gestapo had taken over all the floors. Prisoners were held in the basement. Their piercing screams kept pedestrians from the Astoria's sidewalks for the next year.

On the day of the German occupation, at four o'clock in the afternoon, two German cars stopped in front of the Jewish community's headquarters at 12 Sip Street. A young, uniformed ss man jumped out of the first car and ran to open the back door of the second. Two ss officers marched into the building. Both men, Captain Dieter Wisliceny and Lieutenant Colonel Hermann Krumey, were members of Adolf Eichmann's Sonderkommando, the Special Action Commando. They demanded to see the president of the Jewish community, but Samuel Stern was not there. They informed a terrified cultural secretary who had been filing papers in an upstairs office that they wished to have a meeting with the heads of all the Jewish organizations in the capital at 10 AM sharp the next day. "Everyone must come," they told her. "*Liberalen und Orthodoxen*," Krumey added, displaying his knowledge of Jewish affairs.[7]

Wisliceny was polite, but he left no doubt that attending this meeting was by command. Only thirty-two years old when he arrived in Budapest, he was chubby, pink-faced, generally cheerful. After the rigors of provincial Bratislava, he had been looking forward to spring in Budapest. He wore gold-framed spectacles that he pushed up on his head when he wanted to appear casual. Today was not one of those days.

Born in East Prussia, Wisliceny had studied history and theology in preparation for becoming a Protestant minister. Instead, at the age of twenty-two, he joined the ss. Two years later, in 1936, he found himself at Bureau II/112 of the Reich Security Main Office (the Reichssicherheits-hauptamt, or RSHA) in Berlin, specializing in "Jews." Adolf Eichmann worked in the next office and on the same files. As first sergeant, Wisliceny had outranked Eichmann, but their relationship was collegial: Wisliceny shared his daily reports on Jewish organizations around the world; Eichmann shared his reports on local groups. Books and diaries, circulars and lists, everything not of obvious value that the Gestapo had seized from Jews passed through Wisliceny's hands. He was convinced, back then, that the solution to the "Jewish problem" was to oblige all German Jews to leave the country, and therefore he advocated German support for the Zionists. He graduated to become Eichmann's eastern European envoy, a man fully versed in all the German tactics for assembling and deporting Jews. Wisliceny completed the deportations from Salonica and of most of the Jews from Slovakia. He had headed the Sonderkommando für Judenangelegenheiten, the Special Commando for Jewish Affairs, with distinction and had been promoted to his current rank.

Hermann Krumey was a pharmacist, then a district gymnastics superintendent, before joining the ss. He was thin and quiet, a man for detail, meticulous, always punctual, excellent at following instructions. Eichmann met him in 1938 in Austria. In 1939, Krumey was sent to Poznan to supervise the eviction of the Poles from the Warthe administrative district set up by the Germans. Later, he described his task as one of organizing "the transport by rail required to carry out the compulsory transfer . . . of those Poles evicted from their farms . . . My duties included negotiating with offices in the General Government about the destinations of the trains."[8] In 1942 he was responsible for the "special treatment"[9] of eighty-two orphans from Lidice, a Czech village among those chosen to pay after a pair of partisans attacked ss security chief Reinhard Heydrich in Prague in May, causing his death in June. The children lost their parents during the retaliatory execution of 340 inhabitants of the town, who were among 1,331 killed overall. Now Krumey was Eichmann's deputy in Hungary, a lieutenant colonel.

As soon as news of the proposed meeting spread, Jewish community leaders rushed to their telephones to try to contact members of parliament and those of their secretaries who had proved useful or sympathetic. Would they have to assemble for the Germans? they asked anxiously. Samuel Stern, who had played poker with Admiral Horthy only days before, now could not get a call back from his secretary. Endre Bajcsy-Zsilinszky, a liberal in Horthy's government, could not be reached. There were rumors (which turned out to be true) that he had resisted arrest, had been wounded in the ensuing gunfight, and had been dragged away by the ss.

At 6 AM on March 20, the day of the meeting, a message from Budapest's chief of police confirmed the order: "The Germans' commands must be obeyed."

The leaders of Budapest's Jewish community arrived early at 12 Sip Street. Kasztner was, of course, not among them. The men were formally dressed for the occasion. They climbed the fake marble staircase to the third floor and settled on the narrow wooden chairs in the great hall. The hall had always been used for formal events, concerts, book launches, invited speakers from other countries, and a few celebrations. Several of the leaders had brought their wives with them; some carried extra-warm overcoats and small suitcases of essentials in case they were to be deported immediately.

Wisliceny and Krumey drove up at ten sharp. They both wore their ss uniforms, with holstered handguns. They greeted everyone with a polite *guten morgen* and saluted their future victims. They sat on the podium, under the ornate chandelier, their backs to the massive, hand-carved marble menorah. Incongruously, on either side of the menorah a uniformed ss man stood guard with a machine gun held casually at waist level.

Wisliceny crossed his chubby legs with infinite decorum, gesticu-lated with his expensive-looking gold cigarette holder, and addressed Stern as "Herr Hofrat," inviting him to sit with them on the podium, as if this were an ordinary meeting where they might expect to be introduced as guest speakers. While they waited for a German-speaking stenographer to arrive, Wisliceny cracked jokes about there being no reason to prepare for the worst and how all the assembled leaders would be taking their wives and valises home again after the meeting. Krumey, lean and sallow-complexioned, bent forward look-ing at the floor or stared quietly, expressionless, at the crowd.[10]

Then Wisliceny opened the meeting with assurances that the occupation would not have to mean extra hardships for the Jews of Budapest. If they behaved responsibly, obeyed orders from the German high command, left their money in the banks, kept calm, and did not go into hiding, all would be well. No harm would come to any Jews in the city. He treated these men with respect, addressed individual Jewish leaders as "doctor"—and he lied.

Only the day before, however, his colleagues had occupied the homes of several wealthy Jews in Buda, appropriated a city syna-gogue to be used as stables for cavalry horses, and arrested hundreds of people, some of whom were now in the Astoria's basement or had been transferred to the larger prison facilities in Kistarcsa, near Budapest. The Sonderkommando had taken over the old Jewish Rabbinical Seminary on Rökk Szilárd Street. (Most of the students had already left in a hurry when they learned of the occupation, and the few who decided to stay were arrested.) The building was trans-formed into a prison for both Jewish and non-Jewish prisoners—

women on the second floor, men on the first. The Germans had also commandeered the old city prison in Buda and were prospecting for houses on Swabian Hill.

Wisliceny instructed the assembled Jews to establish a council whose orders would be obeyed, with no questions asked, by all the Jews in the country. The Germans needed a responsible body to work through, one that could present their "reasonable" requests in future. Members of the council would, they said, be issued with special Gestapo immunity certificates that would exempt them from any measures affecting other, "ordinary" Jews. The Central Jewish Council, as it would be constituted, would have "the right of absolute disposal over all Jewish spiritual and material wealth, and over all Jewish manpower." As many of those present knew from the Polish and Slovak refugees, the idea of a Jewish council was hardly new. It was a formula that Reinhard Heydrich had devised in 1939 as a first step to the "ultimate goal." It was specific about the functions and composition of the council, and Wisliceny and Krumey were not about to fiddle with a successful model.

The council members would all be "influential personalities." Their initial duty would be to prepare a census of all the Jews in the city and be accountable for the housing of those Jews as well as to compile a complete list of real estate owned by Jews and a list of the heads of all Jewish institutions. Wisliceny declared that henceforward all travel by Jews was forbidden except by special permit and that those found traveling without permission might be executed. Once the leaders had made a list of potential council members, they should submit it to Wisliceny for approval. The last remaining Jewish weekly newspaper could continue to be published, but it would, "naturally," have to be shown first to the Gestapo censors for approval. As a first task, the new council had to invite Jewish leaders from across the country to an information meeting to be held on March 28. Each leader would be issued a travel permit for this single occasion only, and would face dire, personal consequences should he fail to appear.

The Budapest Jewish leaders were impressed with the politeness and the respect Wisliceny and Krumey had shown them. They called their friends and relatives after the meeting to reassure them that, as usual, the horror stories had been exaggerated. These Germans, unlike the Hungarian Arrow Cross riffraff they had seen on the streets, were gentlemen.

The two ss officers repaired to the Astoria bar, equally satisfied with the results of the meeting. Their job, unbeknownst to the assembled Jewish leaders, was to annihilate every one of them as well as every other Jew in Hungary. They wished to do so expeditiously, cleanly, and without the unpleasantness of the Warsaw ghetto uprising. The plan called for calming Budapest Jews through regular communication with their Jewish Council.

Samuel Stern, who was already president of the Jewish Community of Pest and of the National Bureau of Hungarian Jews, set about nominating members of the Jewish Council. He would, of course, be president. Doctors Ernő Boda, Ernő Pető, Samu Csobádi, and Károly Wilhelm would represent the Neolog, or Reform, communities; Samuel Frankl and Baron Fülöp von Freudiger would represent the Orthodox; Dr. Nison Kahan would be the Zionist representative. Wisliceny accepted all eight names without question.

The only member of the Rescue Committee who had been invited to the meeting was Ottó Komoly. "You won't believe what one of them told me today," he said to Joel Brand about the leaders' reaction. "Zionist predictions have been wrong. Unfortunate things have happened in Poland, and in the east, but it will not be so bad here. All we have to do is make sure nobody undermines discipline."[11]

During the week following the German occupation, more than ten thousand people were arrested. About a third of them were Jews. After making the arrests, the Gestapo loaded documents and valuables, including furniture, paintings, and carpets, into trucks and transported them to Germany.

They arrested the leaders of the Polish community in exile. Some of them were shot where they were apprehended; others were taken to the prison in Buda, where they were tortured by both ss and Swabian guards. Prominent Hungarians who had voiced opposition to the war were also beaten in the Buda jail. The guards devised methods of sleep deprivation and personal humiliation that usually caused prisoners to reveal whatever and whomever they knew. One of the guards' favorite pastimes was to force naked prisoners to do frog jumps or make swimming motions on the stone floors while they hosed them down with cold water. The ss selected other prisoners for "protective custody" in Vienna. There the men were immediately separated from the women, and they were all questioned for several days while they were deprived of food and clothing. Then they were transported to Oberlanzendorf, a village not far from Vienna, where they were crowded into small, dank cells. After a few weeks in this prison, apart from their families, beaten and tortured by sadistic guards, several committed suicide. The local townspeople complained of the horrific noises, the shrieks and howls that interrupted their sleep during the night. Some of the prisoners were transported to larger prison camps in Germany and Poland.

Leaders of Jewish communities throughout Hungary followed the Budapest example and organized themselves into councils for the Nazis' convenience. Stern sent a telegram marked "Urgent" to all Jewish leaders, asking them to come to a meeting at 11 AM on March 28 at 12 Sip Street: "I expect your presence at this most important national meeting. If for some extraordinary reason you cannot be here, send a telegram by return with the name of your proposed substitute." He went on to alert all the recipients that the Budapest Jewish Council had been in meetings with the German command, which considered it of vital importance that there should be no panic. He sent each delegate a personal travel permit and warned that it could not be given to anyone other than the person named.

Members of the new Central Jewish Council rushed to comply with the Germans' every wish, just as other Jewish leaders had done in Poland and Slovakia, Latvia and Austria. Demands for goods and for services such as gardening or cellar-digging arrived daily, then several times a day. They were mindful of every detail on their lists: three hundred mattresses, six hundred blankets, plus gold watches, binoculars, silk stockings, boxes of chocolates, antique furniture, eighteenth-century paintings, all to be delivered to specified addresses. They vied with one another in their eagerness to provide faster, better goods, whatever luxuries the Germans desired, even their own villas in Buda and their summer houses on Lake Balaton. Orders for the evacuation of buildings, including places of worship, required by the Germans were met the same day. In response to a request by Otto Hunsche for a piano, they supplied eight instruments in all. The officer replied graciously, "But gentlemen, I just want to play a bit of music, I don't want to open a piano store."[12]

Adolf Eichmann's Sonderkommando had begun to implement the dejewification of Hungary.

CHAPTER 7

Obersturmbannführer
Adolf Eichmann

Heydrich sent for me. I reported. He said to me: "The Führer, well, emigration is . . ." He began with a little speech. And then: "The Führer has ordered physical extermination . . ."

[I]n the autumn of 1941, I was sent to Chelmno in Warthegau. I received orders from Müller to go to Linzmannstadt—now it's Lodz again—and report back to him on what was going on there. He didn't put it the same way as Heydrich . . . not as crassly. "An action against the Jews is underway there, Eichmann. Go take a look. Then report to me." . . . I saw a room about five times as big as this one. There were Jews in it. They had to undress, and then a sealed truck drove up. The doors were opened, the naked Jews had to get in. Then the doors were closed and the truck drove off . . . The whole time I was there I didn't look inside. I couldn't. What I heard was enough. The screaming and . . . I drove after the truck . . . The doors were opened and corpses [gassed by redirected exhaust fumes] were thrown out.

Adolf Eichmann[1]

S Lieutenant Colonel Adolf Eichmann arrived in Budapest in late March 1944. Although he regularly reported to the Gestapo's Major General Heinrich Müller, chief of Section IV of the Reich Security Main Office in Berlin, and in "more personal matters to Ernst Kaltenbrunner,"[2] who had taken over from the assassinated Heydrich as the chief of Reich security, Eichmann's assignment had come directly from Adolf Hitler.

Eichmann had been inspired by Hitler's rise to power for he, too, was of modest means, no family respectability, not much education, and, even worse, an Austrian. Although Eichmann was born in Germany, his family had moved to Linz in Austria and he and Hitler had attended the same junior school there. The son of an accountant, Eichmann had initially lacked both ambition and prospects. He had not finished school and had lost his first job as a salesman, but he lived modestly on his father's sufferance. Through the older man's contacts, he found a position as an oil and kerosene agent for Vacuum Oil.

Hearing Hitler's speeches on the radio changed his life. Eichmann went to a Nazi rally in Austria and was immediately caught up in the smart uniforms, the marching band, the loudspeakers, the salute to the leader, and the patriotic songs. He joined the Nazi Party a few months after Hitler took power in Germany. Eichmann had his uniform made when National Socialism was still outlawed in Austria.

After Hitler became chancellor in 1933, Eichmann returned to Germany and began to work his way up from a low-ranking SS operative to having ultimate control of one of the regime's key objectives—the deportation and extermination of the Jews of Europe. Little of his success came from diligent study, but he had the ability to grab opportunities that crossed his path. His first big break, as he saw it later, presented itself in 1934, when he was told to report to Second Lieutenant Leopold von Mildenstein at 102 Wilhelmstrasse in Berlin. Von Mildenstein ran the "Jews Section," or Section IV B4, in the Reich Security Main Office.

A fellow Austrian with an easy manner, von Mildenstein took an interest in teaching Eichmann the basics of his department. He told him that his first task was to read *The Jewish State* by Theodor Herzl.

Eichmann loved the book. He thought it gave him insight into the Jewish mind, and it also presented a possible solution to the "Jewish problem": emigration to Palestine. He had, finally, found his focus. He determined that he would become an authority on the Jews. After Herzl, he read Max Nordau and Moses Hess.[3] He wrote a paper on Herzl's ideas and on Zionist organizations. He learned the Hebrew alphabet, and, within a few months, he could read, albeit slowly, a Yiddish newspaper. He subscribed to *Haint* (Today), a Jewish periodical. He wanted to see who was writing about what aspects of Jewish life in the Reich. He wanted to understand what kind of people Jews were. He knew now how he would be promoted.

In 1937, after Austria was annexed by Germany, he received his first commission as second lieutenant—the task of ridding the country of its Jewish population. He established the Central Office for Jewish Emigration in Vienna. The plan was to deprive Jews of all their property and, in exchange, grant them exit permits. His Jewish and Hebrew studies were useful when he dealt with emissaries from various factions of the Jewish political leadership in Palestine. If the Jews were ready to brave the high seas on illegal ships, crossing British lines, Eichmann was ready to oblige. In just eighteen months, he "emigrated" more than 100,000 Jews. In 1938 he was promoted to first lieutenant and, a year later, to captain.

On September 27, 1939, still in his early thirties, he was given executive powers as part of the Reich Security Main Office's Bureau II. On "the Jewish question" he reported to Müller, the top man at the Gestapo, which also fell under the ss. The answer had been given with the Final Solution—a set of new orders clarified by ss chief Heinrich Himmler himself in April 1942. Eichmann had personally viewed the German Einsatzgruppen actions in the east and visited the Bergen-Belsen, Auschwitz, and Dachau camps. He had demanded, persistently, that all departing transports be completely filled with Jews and, even as the war raged on and the army needed urgent supplies, he had the authority to commandeer trains for the death chambers. By the time he arrived in Budapest, Eichmann had already sent a third of the Jews in France to the east in 380 trainloads, most of the Jews in Poland had been murdered, and the Jews of western Russia, the Ukraine, and Holland had been slaughtered. In his reports to Himmler, he had urged that more efficient means than shooting people into mass graves be found, not only because this method was slow but because it was hard for the men to kill naked women and children. These hundreds of thousands of women and small children might have reminded ss men of their own families. It was heartening, he said, to see how young men fresh out of school could cope with the dreadful task of murdering unarmed civilians. He had championed the establishment of efficient gassing stations in the east and of gas chambers elsewhere.

For their first few days in Budapest, Eichmann and his team occupied suites in the Astoria Hotel. Centrally located in Pest, facing a wide, four-cornered intersection, the hotel had been specially picked by "the Master," as Eichmann was known in Gestapo circles, as one easily defended, should defense become necessary, but also comfortable while planning the perfect job he had come to accomplish.

He arrived in Hungary with a small contingent of his men—all highly trained, experienced, and unlikely to go soft on their jobs or weaken when faced with difficulties. He brought along his best. Dieter Wisliceny and Hermann Krumey had both proved their effectiveness. Captain Alois Brunner, another Austrian, had been Eichmann's own secretary at the Central Office for Jewish Emigration in Vienna; he had been instrumental in the execution of the Nisko resettlement project under which thousands of Austrian and Czech Jews were shipped to and abandoned in Nisko in southeastern Poland, and he had earned Eichmann's praise for his help with the efficient deportation of French and Austrian Jews. To complete the team, ss captain Otto Hunsche was responsible for legal matters, and Captain Franz Novak was in charge of transportation.

A week after his arrival, Eichmann found more congenial offices in the Majestic Hotel on Swabian Hill. It was not only the name "Swabian" (German Hungarian) that attracted the Sonderkommando but also the pleasant location. A mile or so west of Buda, the hill offered long, tree-lined promenades, healthy mountain air, and a spectacular view over the countryside. The hotel and its adjunct, the Little Majestic, were old villas built by the very wealthy, offering comfort and privacy. For his home, Eichmann picked another hill-side villa with a magnificent view of the Danube; it belonged to a Jewish industrialist now interned in Kistarcsa.

Eichmann had been expecting some resistance from the new Hungarian authorities. Instead he was offered immediate, enthusiastic assistance. A week after he arrived, he asked for a conference with the two new state secretaries, László Endre and László Baky. It proved to be a friendly meeting, over bottles of wine and pretzels, in the Majestic's garden. Wisliceny, who had dined with Baky in Budapest before, made the introductions.

Eichmann informed the secretaries that he had orders directly from Himmler for the ghettoization and deportation of all Hungarian Jews. His statement received wholehearted support. Baky and Endre were eager to begin the task of concentrating the Jews the very next day. They offered immediately the 100,000-plus refugees without Hungarian citizenship papers, most of whom were already assembled in "appropriate" facilities. Eichmann, ever the practical man, declined. His transportation system would not be ready for another few days. At full capacity, it could handle only 12,000 people a day. Baky and Endre's proposal would put undue stress both on the gas chambers and the crematoria in Auschwitz.

A more gradual plan was agreed upon, and the men discussed the assistance that could be expected from the Hungarian gendarmerie, the disposition of exemptions, and the welcome possibility of Hungary's paying the fees for transport and guards, just as the Slovak government had done. They gave priority to all practical matters. Eichmann had arrived with a map of Hungary. Budapest's large, influential Jewish community would be last to be deported. The entire operation, Eichmann believed, could be accomplished by the end of June. The possibility of Jewish resistance was reviewed and dismissed by the state secretaries. The gendarmes were trained to keep order, and the remaining Jews were unarmed civilians, women with children, and old men—the young men were all serving in labor battalions.

For the sake of formalities, Eichmann asked that a member of the Hungarian government submit to him a request for the evacuation.

Eichmann, as Wisliceny recalled, was a stickler for the correct paperwork.[4]

Elated, Baky left for a meeting with Lieutenant Colonel László Ferenczy of the gendarmerie, whose assistance would be needed to execute the orders. Ferenczy commanded five thousand men who, he said, would not only be able but also eager to carry out the gathering of Jews into ghettos and their expulsion. Many of his men, he was proud to report, were of German (Swabian) origin and viewed Jews as enemy aliens. Wisliceny was appointed to liaise with the gendarmerie.

Many years later, in an interview with a Dutch journalist in Argentina, Eichmann recalled his meeting with Baky and Endre: "On that evening, the fate of the Jews of Hungary was sealed," he said.[5] The following evening, when Eichmann's senior staff visited the two secretaries at the County Hall, all that was left to determine were the details. The country was neatly divided into six ghettoization and deportation zones. Each zone would be handled separately and in an agreed order, beginning with Carpathian Ruthenia and Transylvania in the northeast,[6] and all communication between the zones would be cut off.

On March 22, Prime Minister Döme Sztójay informed the government that Dr. Veesenmayer, the Reich plenipotentiary, had insisted that Jews throughout the country wear a distinguishing yellow star. Regent Horthy, still smarting from his personal humiliation in the German takeover of power, asked that, in future, such "requests" not be presented to him. Later, when he spoke to Samuel Stern, he complained that his hands were tied—Veesenmayer had informed him that he would be excluded, in future, from all political decisions. He had, he felt, held out long enough on the Jewish question. The order would go into effect on April 5.[7] Naturally, he said, Stern and members of the council would be exempted, as would war invalids, decorated war heroes, and those who had converted to Christianity before August 1, 1919.[8]

The United States president, Franklin D. Roosevelt, issued a statement condemning Nazi atrocities and warning that "none who participate in these acts of savagery shall go unpunished."[9] But

Döme Sztójay expressed complete indifference to such warnings: "In the event of a German victory, such a warning would be of no interest," he said. ". . . In the event of defeat one's life would be at an end anyway."

At two o'clock that afternoon, Samuel Stern met Rezső Kasztner at the Budapest, the elegant, old-world café that Jews would soon be forbidden to enter. There were white tablecloths, wide-armed oak chairs, and an orchestra discreetly playing Strauss. Neither man would have aroused interest in this place. They were both well dressed: Stern in a gray suit with silk cravat, silk handkerchief peeking out of his pocket, signet ring on his finger; Kasztner in a casual dark-brown suit and white shirt.

Kasztner leaned toward the older man, his hands resting on the table. He pleaded as before: "The gentlemen in the Astoria know everything about us, sir—they know who we are and what we have been doing. They have had dealings with Zionists before, most recently in Bratislava. They are expecting to hear from us—in fact, they would be astonished if we did not try to make contact. They know we are tough bargainers and that we will try to save lives. They know we deliver on our promises."

Stern sipped his espresso. "We don't need help from Zionists," he said. "A few months, and the Germans will disappear."[10]

"Exactly," Kasztner replied. "But it's those few months we are talking about—how to survive those months. Don't imagine, sir, that those months will be uneventful. We know what they can do. You have heard from the refugees. You must know, as I know, that obeying every order, that delivering whatever they ask for, that begging and crying at their doorstep, is useless. We are looking for an alternative to committing suicide."

"We don't need advice from Zionists," Stern repeated.

Though Stern already knew the whole story, Kasztner persisted in telling him about Dr. Adam Czerniaków, the Warsaw engineer who was president of the Jewish Council there when almost 400,000 Jews were stuffed into the ghetto. Czerniaków had been eager to please the

Germans, fulfilling their every wish, responding to their calls, a good negotiator, a professional, "just like you, sir." Late one night, the Jewish Council was told to appear before the German commander. Word spread through the ghetto like wildfire. Nobody slept. In the crowded one-room apartments, children and adults stood by the windows, waiting, talking about what it was the Germans wanted this time. They were frightened, hungry, exhausted, beaten. During the night, the Gestapo came for the doctors, the lawyers, the other prominent Jews and their families and murdered them where they found them. At dawn, the militia arrived with dogs, hunted down more people, and packed them into waiting trucks.

The next morning, the German commander gave Dr. Czerniaków this order: "Seven thousand Jews to be ready for transport to Treblinka tomorrow morning. Seven thousand more the next day. Seven thousand the day after tomorrow." The first seven thousand had already been collected by the Ukrainian militia the night before. Czerniaków knew what Treblinka meant, as did everybody else in the ghetto. The next day, the Jewish Council had a new president. Czerniaków had killed himself.

"This, sir, is the Jewish Council," Kasztner said.

"I know the story," Stern said, his voice hard and decisive. "It has nothing to do with us. I have my contacts with the Hungarian government, and they are confident these are temporary measures. If we keep our heads down, we shall survive. And I have my own contacts with the Germans."

But Kasztner persisted: "Now I would like to tell you about the kind of contact Zionists in Bratislava had with the Germans."

"I know that story, too," Stern said, irritated. He had started to wave for the waiter to bring the bill.

"It is the Zionists they will wish to deal with, sir. As they did in Vienna and Berlin,[11] and Bratislava. And we are going to need money, sir, a lot of money, but more than that, we will need your trust. We must be able to represent you and the council when we go to meet Eichmann's men . . ."

Hofrat Stern had risen to his feet. He left some coins on the table for the waiter, looked at Kasztner with the kind of dismissive expression he had used with underlings at his company, nodded to say goodbye, and walked quickly to the door.

At dawn on March 27, Kasztner went to see Carl Lutz, the Swiss consul now occupying the former U.S. embassy in Szabadság (Liberty) Square. The Swiss represented U.S. interests in Hungary, just as they had represented German interests in the Middle East after Britain declared war on Germany. Lutz had done an exemplary job of ensuring the safety of German citizens and shipping them home from Palestine, unharmed. He had reason to expect full cooperation from Germans.

The vast area in front of the six-floor office building was filled with people clamoring to get inside. There were women with young children, and old men in their best suits, claiming to have American relatives; a couple sitting on the sidewalk wept as Kasztner pushed by them. He asked the consular employees barring the doors to announce him to Consul Lutz. He was expected.

He went upstairs, past the protesting secretary, and straight into Lutz's large, airy office.[12] Ottó Komoly and Moshe Krausz were already there, settled into two leather couches, Komoly studying a sheaf of papers, Krausz looking at his bitten nails and talking too fast. Their clothes were rumpled, their faces unshaved, in obvious contrast to Lutz, dapper in his off-white suit, clean-shaven, his hair still damp from his morning shower. He was a tall, thin man in his forties with wire-rimmed glasses, his brown hair receding from his forehead. He had been standing at the window, gazing at the dark hulk of the Stock Exchange Building across the wide expanse of the square. Constructed in the 1920s, it had once been the center of Pest's burgeoning business life, a meeting place for all those active in the postwar rebuilding of the country. It was closed now, the outside walls blackened with soot.

Lutz turned to welcome Kasztner. "Did they stop you at the corner?" he asked. About two dozen policemen were stationed at each of the entrances to the square. Near the Stock Exchange, he could see that some of the police had been joined by a group of teenage boys dressed in makeshift military garb with Arrow Cross armbands, all carrying weapons. One of them was holding an old man by his collar, shaking him and chatting and laughing with his friends while the man squirmed, his hand vainly reaching for the identity papers inside his jacket pocket. "No," Kasztner said. "But, unlike the man we are looking at, I'm not afraid."

He noticed that over the right pocket of his creased jacket Ottó Komoly wore his silver Military Service Cross–First Class, the medal Emperor Charles had personally pinned on his uniform when he thanked Komoly for his extraordinary bravery in battle during the First World War. It was the first time Kasztner had seen the medal. He hoped it would help Komoly with the young thugs, should they ask for his papers.

Krausz said his office had been ransacked that morning by Hungarian police, his secretary arrested, his papers, files, and lists carried away. He and his wife had waited in the café near the square until the consul's car drew up in front. He had not slept since the Germans arrived.

Lutz proposed that the Jewish Agency's Palestine Office be transferred into the legation, together with Krausz and his wife. Because the Swiss represented British interests in Hungary, it could be deemed perfectly natural for the office of the Palestine protectorate to be located in the Swiss Consulate. They would be safe, and he would see what he could do about getting some of the papers back. Meanwhile, Krausz should start working on new lists for the six hundred Palestinian permits he still had when Lutz last spoke with him.

"It won't be easy," Krausz complained. He no longer had the official stamp, nor the forms he was supposed to use for making the entrants legally acceptable. Besides, his secretary had been arrested.

Lutz said he would send one of his staff to retrieve the official stamp and the forms. Krausz estimated it would take weeks for him to re-create all the files he had lost.

Kasztner, suddenly furious, yelled at Krausz, calling him a fussy little cockroach. How could he worry about files and stamps at a time like this?

"Quiet!" Lutz interrupted. "There is no sense in fighting among yourselves." He sounded a lot more commanding than his immaculately tailored appearance suggested. He turned to Krausz: "We will set you up with an office in the basement where you can work uninterrupted and there is plenty of room for your staff." He promised to do his utmost to extract Krausz's secretary from prison.

Komoly suggested that Lutz rename the office the "Emigration Department." That, after all, was how it would be used.

Lutz replied that he would have to obtain approval from the Hungarian Ministry of Foreign Affairs, if it still existed. And he would present his credentials to Veesenmayer; the Reich plenipotentiary would surely extend the necessary courtesies.

Hungarian Radio had reported that Hungarian Jews could no longer emigrate, but Kasztner said this restriction couldn't apply to Jews who were citizens of other countries, nor to those who already held valid visas for Palestine. The obvious answer would be to find countries—such as Switzerland—to hand out citizenship to Jews.

Lutz promised he would talk to his superiors.

On March 28, as ordered by the Sonderkommando, leaders from the provincial Jewish communities assembled and waited for Lieutenant Hermann Krumey to give them his vague reassurances. It was the last meeting of Hungary's Jewish leaders.

Unlike Wisliceny, Krumey had no prepared speech. He preferred to respond to questions all too humbly asked, framed in educated but unpracticed German. In response to the request that the three thousand or more Jews who had been arrested at railway stations be returned to their families, Krumey muttered, ". . . aber ich bin noch nicht durchgekommen." For days afterward, while awaiting the release of these people, the leaders tried to guess what Krumey had meant by this laconic statement. "Durchgekommen" could mean "dealt with" or perhaps "looked into," or was it simply "arrived at"? Ernő Munkácsi, who took notes at the meeting, thought Krumey's behavior was perhaps affected by his belief that he was conducting a meeting with the soon-to-be-dead.

On March 31 Eichmann summoned the Central Jewish Council to his offices.[13] Several times on the drive up Swabian Hill, their cars were stopped by gendarmes demanding identification. Eichmann's men had surrounded the buildings—the Majestic and the Little Majestic—with three rings of barbed wire. Guard dogs patrolled the periphery. Armed sentries were stationed at the main entrance. The Majestic had been built into the hillside, with a concrete bridge connecting it to the road. To gain entry, visitors had to walk along the exposed bridge, open the main door to a short corridor, and announce themselves to the ss man in the newly installed guardroom to the side. Once they had been thoroughly searched and their papers checked, they were allowed to enter through a second set of heavy wooden doors, only to be confronted by another ss man for a second search before they were allowed to proceed.

Eichmann's office was on the second floor. László Baky had installed an office for himself on the third floor so that he and his staff could plan mass murder without interruption from other pressing matters.

Once members of the council were waved through by the guards, they were ushered into a room overlooking the gardens. There was only one chair in the room, its back to the picture window, a wide oak desk in front of the chair.

This time there was less politeness than at the first meeting at the Jewish Community Center on Sip Street. Eichmann, when he entered, hurried to the chair and sat down, crossed his legs, all the while looking at the assembled men with something like a smile on his face. He wore a gray ss uniform, a holstered handgun at his belt. He did not remove his cap. He was a thin man, pale, ordinary, much younger than the men he was smirking at.

Eichmann began by asserting that he was not in favor of executions except when Jews were linked with resistance movements. He was here to raise the output of the war industries. Jews, like everyone else in the Reich, would have to work. Council members, who enjoyed the rare privilege of not having to work themselves, would have to supply volunteers. He assured them he would ferret out all resisters, all who had something to hide. "Do you know what I am?" he shouted. "I am a bloodhound! All opposition will be broken. If you think of joining the partisans, I will have you slaughtered. I know you Jews. I know all about you. I have been dealing with Jewish affairs since 1934. If you behave quietly and work, you'll be able to keep your community and your institutions. But—and I am being frank with you here—where Jews opposed us, there *were* executions."

After the war, he told them, the Jews would be free again to do whatever they wanted. "We Germans will again become good-natured, as we were in the past."

He talked about his continued support for Jewish schools and a national Jewish newspaper, and his pledge to help the council raise the funds it would need to operate. "You are the council, you command," he said. As if it were a mere trifle, he mentioned that from five o'clock that afternoon, all Jews were to wear the yellow Star of David badges. "Not just your membership," he clarified. "I will make no distinction between religious Jews and the converts. As far as I'm concerned, a Jew is a Jew, whatever he calls himself." He saw the fashioning of the canary-yellow cloth badges as an opportunity for Jewish manufacturers—a bonanza in top-priced orders. "To be fair, you can't keep it as an exclusive business for Jews. Of course, we have to open up the bidding to gentiles." Eichmann chuckled at his joke with a loud, coughing sound that ended in a gurgle.

Samuel Stern found the chuckling more terrifying than Eichmann's shouting had been. When Stern pointed out that it would be impossible to have the stars manufactured by five o'clock, Eichmann said he would allow Jews to wear temporary versions for the first two days. After that, the measurements would have to be exactly as prescribed.[14]

He demanded four hundred volunteers for urgent work detail; he preferred volunteers, he stated, though he would order up four hundred able-bodied men if none volunteered.

When he deemed the meeting was over, Eichmann jumped to his feet and marched out of the room. The council was dismissed.

The members piled into the two cars they had arrived in and puzzled all the way back to Sip Street about what Eichmann had meant when he talked of his support, why he had not offered them seats, how they could apply for exemptions from wearing the badges, and where the Hungarian government was in this scheme of things.

Their fears were confirmed later the same day. The government issued several new decrees regarding Hungarian Jews: they were prohibited from employing non-Jews; they could no longer work as lawyers, journalists, or public servants, or in the theatrical and film arts; they were not allowed to own motor vehicles or to drive them, even if they belonged to someone else. Nor could they own motorbikes or bicycles. They were commanded to hand their radios and telephones in to the central authorities in charge of Jewish affairs; those who did not sell or surrender them immediately would be arrested. And they all had to wear the yellow Star of David, marking them clearly "for purposes of their differentiation."[15]

The next day, the government banned all Hungarians from listening to foreign radio stations. *Jud Süss* (The Jew Süss), an anti-Semitic 1940 propaganda film promoted by Reichsmarshall Hermann Göring, was playing to packed cinemas. It told the story of an eighteenth-century court Jew, named Süss, who plotted to seize power by the use of black magic, bribery, and lies. Süss was, like most of Budapest's Jews, assimilated into his gentile milieu—and all the more dangerous because of his social veneer.

Together with reports on the new laws, newspapers ran stories about *The Protocols of the Elders of Zion*, a volume first published in Russia in 1905 and mentioned admiringly by Hitler in *Mein Kampf. Protocols* purported to reveal a Jewish conspiracy for world domination. Years before *Mein Kampf* was published the work had been exposed as an anti-Semitic hoax, a piece of fiction that had plagiarized texts from several other nineteenth-century books. Yet now the newspapers described the "protocols" as though these old fabrications were true and had just been discovered.

On the morning of April 3, British and American aircraft bombed Budapest for the first time since the beginning of the war. Whole buildings collapsed along the main arteries into the city and in the Castle District of Buda. In response, Hungarian security police demanded that the Jewish Council provide five hundred apartments for Christians who had been affected by the raid. Those Jews moving out of their homes were to be concentrated in apartment buildings in an area between the National Theater and the Dohány Street synagogue. The Jewish Council was charged with arranging the relocations of the Jewish families. They would be given formal receipts for their belongings because they would not be able to carry everything with them in the two days the security police had given them to evacuate.

Stern was ordered to find five hundred high-profile hostages to be stationed near industrial and military installations. Peter Hain, the chief of Hungarian Intelligence, assumed that locating influential Jews there would prevent the Allies from bombing these targets. He seemed to be convinced that the Jews were in touch with their foreign co-religionists in the United States and Britain and that the location of these hostages would be passed on to the pilots, thereby keeping vital buildings safe.

Stern, who had been ill for the previous two days, rose from his bed to deliver his response to Hain: "In respect of your request for a list of hostages, I can offer only eight. All, including myself, are members of the Jewish Council."

Wisliceny told Hain to abandon the crazy plan. The Sonderkommando still needed the council to cooperate.

Two weeks after the invasion, the cold-storage rooms of hospitals and even the medical institute were packed with the corpses of suicides; outside storage facilities had to be assigned until next of kin came for the bodies. In some cases, husbands and wives killed themselves at the same time. The price of cyanide pills had gone up tenfold in the capital, and most stores had sold out of rat poisons.

On April 4, László Baky, two members of the Sonderkommando, two high-ranking officers of the Wehrmacht, and Lieutenant-Colonel László Ferenczy of the gendarmerie met to firm up plans for the ghettoization and deportation of the Jews of Hungary. All Jews, irrespective of sex, age, or illness, were to be concentrated in ghettos, and schedules would be set for their deportation to Poland. The few people who were still employed in factories engaged in war production or in mines were temporarily spared, but only until suitable replacements could be found for them.

Each regional office would be responsible for its own actions. "The rounding up of the Jews is to be carried out by the local police or by the Royal Hungarian Gendarmerie units," they ordered in a directive. ". . . If necessary, the police will assist the gendarmerie in urban districts by providing armed help."

It took until April 16 for the full directive and extensive explanations to be typed in multiple copies and sent to the local authorities—mayors, deputy mayors, prefects—but the ghettoization had already begun on April 7. The orders were marked "Secret," and they bore the signature of László Baky. "The Royal Hungarian government will cleanse the country of Jews within a short time," he declared. "I hereby order the cleansing to be conducted district by district. Jews are to be taken to designated collection camps regardless of gender and age."[16]

CHAPTER 8

In the Anteroom of Hell

*It is a shame to live. It is a shame to walk under the sun. It is a
shame to live.*

Sándor Márai, Hungarian novelist,
in a diary entry a few weeks after the German occupation

Jozsi Winninger, Josef Schmidt, and several other Abwehr men
had spent most of March being interrogated by the Gestapo.
They were accused of running errands for Jews, a charge they
freely admitted, and of spying for the British, a charge they fiercely
denied. What had, finally, emerged from their nights in the basement of the Astoria was that ss boss Heinrich Himmler no longer
trusted Admiral Wilhelm Canaris's men. He wanted control in his
own hands. However, both the ss and the sD seemed to be fascinated
by the Abwehr's dealings with the Zionists and decided they could
not dispense with these agents' services after all.

Winninger contacted Rezső Kasztner on the afternoon of his
release. "I guess," he said, "we are more valuable alive than dead." As
for the Zionists' wish to find some common ground with Adolf

Eichmann's men, his advice was to continue to use the Abwehr for alleviating suffering wherever money could do the job. He warned against direct contact with the Sonderkommando. However, if the Va'ada insisted and if they were willing to meet his financial terms, he could make the arrangements.

For several hours, the two men speculated on how best to open negotiations with Dieter Wisliceny and whether to admit that the now illegal Zionist organization knew of his dealings with Gizi Fleischmann and Rabbi Weissmandel to halt the deportations from Slovakia: Kasztner finally decided on a direct approach. He asked Winninger to inform Wisliceny that the Rescue Committee was ready to deal "in economic terms" with the Sonderkommando, in order to "mitigate the anti-Jewish decrees."[1]

Word came only four hours after Kasztner's request: Wisliceny was willing to meet the next day.

In the hours before the meeting, as Kasztner became more and more anxious, Hansi Brand tried to calm him by telling stories about simple-minded Germans and their gullibility, but also stressing that the Germans, too, were taking a chance—the only difference between them, really, was their motivation. They wanted money and valuables. The very fact that these Germans were corruptible, as the Abwehr's men had proved to be, meant there was a chance they would all survive.

Having grown up in Germany, Joel Brand had more experience dealing with the Germans and was more relaxed. His main concern was that their group could hardly claim to represent the Jews of Hungary, or even the Jews of Budapest. They still had no authorization from Samuel Stern, and, as Winninger had reported, Baron Fülöp von Freudiger had made his own approach already. He had gone to the Astoria, talked with Wisliceny, and successfully ransomed his brother for two large rubies in a chocolate box. Freudiger, as a member of the Central Jewish Council and head of the Orthodox community, at least had some standing in the eyes of the Germans. He had been present at the first meeting on Sip Street.

"Old fool," was Rezső's unkind observation. "Offering a few baubles will only muddy the water."

Kasztner knew he would have to cut a convincing figure as a powerful adversary, or as the representative of a powerful adversary. Rabbi Weissmandel had warned that "Willy" (a deceptively affectionate nickname for a Nazi murderer) was not interested in bribes from within the country. That was why, in Bratislava, Weissmandel had had to invent a representative of the "rabbis of the world" to make the deal. The Germans appeared to like the idea of dealing with a mythical "World Jewry" that could offer untold riches in exchange for Jewish lives. "In a game of chicken," Rezső told Hansi, "it is vital not to arrive on a platter."

At four o'clock in the afternoon on April 5, Rezső Kasztner and Joel Brand knocked on the door of Winninger's villa on Swabian Hill. The high-ceilinged rooms were inviting with their exotic carpets, oak antiques, and wall-hung prints of elegantly posed horses. The air was thick with cigarette smoke. Captain Erich Klausnitzer, in a blue-gray uniform, hands behind his back, stood at attention with his back to the windows. A former Abwehr man, he was now representing the SD and, specifically, Otto Klages, who held the same rank as Lieutenant Colonel Eichmann and reported to Major General Heinrich Müller on security matters. Dieter Wisliceny, his corpulent form comfortably folded into a leather club chair, received them with cordial nods. He neither stood up nor offered to shake hands.

Coffee was served in small, white, fragile espresso cups, accompanied by sugar cubes in a silver bowl, delicate silver tongs, and a silver creamer.

Kasztner introduced himself, as did Brand. Neither of them sought to sit down until Winninger pointed to a couple of wide-bottomed chairs in the middle of the room, indirectly facing the two Germans. There were two small, decorative tables, and a woman in a white apron was pouring coffee.

Once she had gone, Wisliceny smiled at the Zionists and acknowledged receiving their message. Then, as a means of establishing his credentials for the discussion to follow, he pointed to a small package on one of the tables. They were letters from Gizi Fleischmann and Rabbi Weissmandel. One, addressed to Baron Freudiger, informed him that, as a result of the payments, at least 25,000 Jews had escaped deportation. More foreign currency was expected from the American Joint Distribution Committee. Weissmandel still had hopes that all deportations, including that of the Hungarians, could be stopped for a payment of $3 million.

Wisliceny knew that Kasztner and Brand were already aware of these dealings. He himself had given the travel permit to Fleischmann for her visit to Budapest, and he knew that her letter referred to him as a gentleman whose word could be trusted. All correspondence from Bratislava had passed through his hands. He had also seen the letters to the Joint's Saly Mayer in Switzerland and knew that dealing with the Joint there had not been as productive as the Bratislava Working Group claimed. He was interested to see how the Budapest Jews would handle themselves.

Kasztner and Brand came straight to the point: What conditions would the Sonderkommando require in order to spare Jewish lives? Wisliceny responded with a laugh. All the Germans were here to ensure that Jewish influence in Hungary would end. "Obviously, Jews cannot hold any positions of power in the economic or political life of the country," he elaborated with the utmost politeness, as if discussing accepted facts. "We are not necessarily insisting on ghettos, but ghettos may be necessary in certain areas."

When Kasztner asked about the deportations, Wisliceny dismissed the question with a wave of his cigarette holder. "We are at war," he said. "We need to know where our enemies are."

Kasztner had kept his eyes on the other man's highly polished boots and looked up only when Wisliceny suggested the price: $2 million, with a "modest down payment" of $200,000 in pengős—the basic Hungarian currency from 1925 until 1946—within a week to demonstrate goodwill and mutual trust. In exchange, Wisliceny said, deportations could be prevented.

Kasztner and Brand persisted with questions about Nazi orders to assemble Jews into ghettos, as had been done in Slovakia, Greece, Poland, and elsewhere. Would there be any transportation of Jews to concentration camps in Poland, for example?

Wisliceny remained evasive. He did not mention the fact that he had already instructed the Hungarian government to have all Jews registered and that orders to assemble them in designated ghettos would go into effect within three days.

When the Zionists suggested that the down payment would be difficult to obtain from outside the country, given German barriers to couriers crossing borders, Wisliceny guffawed. "Dr. Kasztner, you have never had a problem with transportation before," he sneered. "You'll be sure to find a way."

Brand commented that the second payment of $1.8 million would have to be phased. Overseas financial sources would be looking for proof that the negotiations were actually helping the Jews. He suggested that, as a first step, the ss release the hostages from the Rökk Szilárd rabbinical seminary and stop the daily manhunts.

"Such things," Wisliceny smiled, "are the inevitable accompanying music of war—*nicht wahr* [right], Herr Brand?"

Klausnitzer chuckled at Wisliceny's little joke. Other than that, he made no sound during the meeting. Nor, unusually for him, did Winninger.

Kasztner insisted that the price Wisliceny quoted must include the guarantee that, even if deprived of their homes and their former businesses, the Jews of Hungary would be given subsistence—maybe in a ghetto, in fields, in work camps, but in Hungary. The price, he said, should cover—at least for the moment—whatever costs such lives would incur.

Wisliceny agreed that, no matter what, "the substance" of Jewish lives would be preserved. As to how and when, he had to refer final decisions to higher authorities in Berlin, but he was willing to say that there would be no deportations for the moment.

He did not agree to any interim releases of Jews already imprisoned, but he allowed that if the Allied Western powers wanted Jews, they could have them. "If we could rid ourselves of all Hungarian Jews in one sweep," he declared, "that would be of interest to the Reichsführer," Himmler.

As they were leaving the house, Winninger suggested that a 10 percent commission for himself and for his Abwehr boss Josef Schmidt might suffice for their part in setting up the deal.

Kasztner called on Ottó Komoly at his new Central Information Office on the third floor of the Sip Street building. He had jotted down notes from the meeting with Wisliceny, trying to see how much of the down payment they could hope to collect in Budapest. What had the fat man meant when he said "the substance" of Jewish life? And what had he really offered in exchange for the down payment?

Komoly told him he had heard at the council that one large contingent of Jews was to be sent to Germany right away. "It's not what you think," he tried to reassure Kasztner. "The admiral [Miklós Horthy] promised Hitler a hundred thousand Jewish workers, all able-bodied men, to be employed by the Todt Organization."

"To do what?"

"To work in airplane assembly plants. This makes sense when you see all the bombers here. You can imagine the destruction over there." Komoly said German industry, even airplane assembly plants, were in desperate need of workers.

Some of the men would be selected from the labor service units, others from the countryside. Perhaps some of the larger prisons outside Budapest, places like Kistarcsa and Sárvár, would disgorge their able-bodied Jews for work detail in Germany.

"And Horthy agreed?"

"He must have done. He is still maintaining his government's independence—at least the appearances are still in place."

Va'ada members, collectively, sent a cable to Chaim Barlas, now senior representative of the Jewish Agency in Istanbul, to say they had begun negotiations aimed at preventing deportation and "avoiding death," but that success depended on financial requirements they had no hope of meeting without help from the outside. They stressed the urgency of the matter and that delay could be catastrophic for almost one million souls, the last of Europe's Jewish communities.

Barlas in turn sent an urgent demand to the Jewish Agency for £100,000 for the purchase of a Turkish boat to take refugees to Palestine. The Joint had collected the equivalent of £315,000 in the United States, intended for rescue work. It had also allocated £20,000 a month to fund the use of the Yishuv's representatives in Europe.

Meanwhile, the news arriving from Kolozsvár, where the Kasztners' families still lived, was troubling: Jews would have to leave their homes and move to a single area of the city designated for Jews only. Later, they might be transported to Kenyérmező in western Hungary and be employed as agricultural workers. Families would stay together. Western Hungary, some people reasoned, would be safer than the east, where the advancing Soviet armies were bound to destroy whole towns. When the war was over, they reassured themselves, everyone would return.

"But it's only in the eastern provinces," Samuel Stern rationalized. "You can see from the papers that there are saboteurs in these areas, and we can't be sure that some of them are not working directly with the partisans. It makes sense for the nation to protect itself. And we can't be seen to be on the side of the partisans."

The Sip Street building was filled with people seeking news about relatives who had been arrested, lining up for new apartments after their own had been requisitioned for non-Jews, or seeking jobs—another newly announced law banned Jews from all white-collar jobs. The capital's most distinguished lawyers, bank presidents, and factory managers were offering to volunteer at Sip Street for part-time employment. An internationally celebrated opera singer and a dramatist were the doormen, attempting to control traffic in and out of the building.[2] The courtyards and corridors resembled an eastern market. An SS officer visiting Sip Street with new requisitions remarked to Ernő Munkácsi that it had been just like that in Lemberg and Warsaw—wild, loud activity at first, followed soon after by absolute silence.

On the side, the Gestapo sold certificates of immunity against some of the restrictions at prices few Jews could afford, but even these papers had expiry dates and could only be renewed for additional payments. In the streets, hundreds of police could demand to see identification, and any Jew found to have neither the star nor a valid immunity certificate was taken into custody. Children, if there was no place to leave them, were often jailed along with the parents.

Those Jews who survived the next few months always resented the special status they thought the members of the Budapest Jewish

Council enjoyed. However, although each member had been provided with a certificate that declared the bearer would not be classified as a Jew under the laws of Hungary and was excused from wearing the yellow star, these certificates also came with an expiry date, usually two weeks from the date of issue, and the council members had to submit to the humiliating experience of lining up for renewals at one of the Gestapo's offices. A few exemptions were still granted to veterans of the First World War and, through Wisliceny, to members of the Rescue Committee. Brand, Kasztner, and the young halutzim were still able to gather in the Va'ada's Information Office and Provinces Section to talk and make their plans.

Samuel Stern spent most of his days helping to satisfy the Germans' ongoing demands for more material goods. He sat or stood in waiting rooms, hoping for brief audiences with various members of Eichmann's staff so that he could plead for the release of leading members of his community. Captain Otto Hunsche, a sallow-complexioned, tight-lipped former lawyer, was the one who usually met Stern, always keeping him standing while he listed the council's complaints. "Herr Hofrat," Hunsche said one day, "you are always haranguing me with new requests." Surely Stern understood that many of those he was seeking to help had already been judged as collaborators with the enemy. Surely he understood what that meant in wartime? There would be no amnesty for any of them.

When Stern asked for one of his closest friends, a lawyer and member of the council, he noticed that Hunsche winced. "A member of the Judenrat [Jewish Council], you say, Herr Hofrat?" There was always a note of irony in Hunsche's voice, as though he wanted to make Stern understand how he felt about the respectful tone he had been ordered to take with the older man. "That is something entirely different. All members of the council are to be free to come and go as they please. He shall be released this afternoon. With the usual dispensation from the yellow star. Naturally."

Stern remembered Kasztner's story about Dr. Czerniaków of the Warsaw Judenrat, and he told Komoly that same evening that he would help to raise the funds for Wisliceny. And, he said, the Zionists could claim to speak for all the Jews—a considerable *volte face* for him. "I was aware of the race against time," Stern recalled later. "I anticipated that the war would end within months."[3]

Less than a week after the occupation, Kasztner was offered an opportunity to test his new status with the ss. Eva Zahler arrived to tell him that her mother had been taken by the Hungarian police.[4]

One of the sand-colored cars had arrived at the Váci Street pension, and the occupant demanded to see the proprietor. Elizabeth Zahler, dressed in her new blue-and-white spring suit, met them at the foot of the stairs. They ordered her to show them Kasztner's rooms. Two men searched every corner, emptied the drawers, ransacked the bed and the closet, broke the mirrors and one of Bogyó's Limoges vases, and confiscated the painting over the dressing table. They searched the two common rooms, including the piano. When they still found nothing, they put Elizabeth into the backseat of the car.

She had spent one night at the Rabbinical Seminary, trying to convince her interrogators that she had no idea where Kasztner had taken his papers or where he had gone. They transferred her to Kistarcsa. Eva had been down to the police station, asking about her mother, but no one seemed to know her whereabouts.

Kasztner decided to walk Eva home. He knew she had been followed—two men were waiting in the doorway of the next building, pretending to be deep in conversation—and that it might be dangerous for him to show concern for any individual who had been arrested. Yet a sign of fear now could lose the battle almost before it had begun, for the Germans would not accept his role as a representative of some grand Jewish power if he was cowed by the first scent of an overt personal threat.

He put his arm around Eva's shoulder and they walked to the Váci Street pension, never turning around to check for the men who were sure to be following. Using the phone in his old rooms, he called Dieter Wisliceny at the Astoria and left a message with his adjutant about Elizabeth Zahler, making sure the man understood his contention that some mistake had occurred. Perhaps the local police had been overzealous. Perhaps it was someone else they had been sent to collect. Then he strolled back to Sip Street, still not looking to see if he was being followed. He was certain the men shadowed him all the way, but they did not try to stop him.

The next morning, Eva's mother returned. She had been put on the train from Kistarcsa with an ss safe pass valid for trains and trams for one week. Bogyó, who did not have her own pass, ventured out of the apartment to visit Elizabeth. It was another warm day, smelling of fish and lilacs. The Danube had been rising with its spring floodwaters; boys were fishing off the embankment and flower sellers hawked their bouquets along Váci Street. The shops had their doors wide open, and the cafés already had their summer chairs out under big umbrellas. It was a day like any other spring day, except that April would never feel like this again. Bogyó felt that it was going to be her last spring in Budapest. The Germans would finish the job the puppet Hungarian government had begun.

She walked with her head down, her jacket pulled over her chest to cover the star. It was no use Ottó Komoly telling her to wear it with pride. She could see the expressions on people's faces when they looked at her and how quickly they averted their gaze.

She found Elizabeth saddened but still optimistic. She had not been hurt during the interrogations. Because she was no longer allowed to own a business, she had asked the manageress to buy the pension with a loan she provided. As soon as the Germans were gone, she would take it back.[5] She and Eva were going to move in with Elizabeth's parents.

It took five days and considerable pressure by both Stern and Freudiger to gather even three million pengős (about $90,000), just a portion of the down payment. Contrary to what the Germans wished to believe, none of it came from the Joint. There simply hadn't been time for the Jewish Agency and the Joint to react to the urgent requests. At the appointed hour, when Kasztner and Brand arrived at the Astoria Hotel bar to deliver the cash, Wisliceny was not there. Krumey said he had been transferred. In fact, as Kasztner discovered later, he had been sent to northeastern Hungary to supervise the gathering of Jews there into ghettos.

Hunsche joined Krumey for the delivery of the first portion of the down payment. Kasztner had been relieved to note that there were two of them. He and Brand had been concerned that the money might have been a personal rather than an official bribe. The bonbon-boxed jewels that Freudiger had given Wisliceny had certainly been of a personal nature. They now felt reassured that they were dealing with the ss hierarchy. However, Hunsche was incensed at the amount of money offered, questioning whether Kasztner's group could deliver the $2 million if it could not even raise the paltry down payment. "Perhaps," he said, "the Americans cared little for the Jews?"

The ss had to be convinced that, all appearances to the contrary, the Jews did influence Western policies. Astonishing as the myth of an all-powerful World Jewry seemed to Kasztner, it had remained one of the motivating assumptions of Germany's war. He pleaded for time, blaming the suspicions of the Allies and pointing out that such sensitive negotiations took longer in wartime. Both Great Britain and the United States had put in place new regulations regarding the movement of money, he said. The Joint and the Jewish Agency were completely supportive. They would find a way. "The money will be here," he asserted with conviction.

Then, while the two Germans absorbed this argument, Kasztner re-iterated what he had understood from the Wisliceny meeting: so long as negotiations continued in good faith on both sides, "the substance" was to be safe. There would be no deportations.

Krumey nodded, as if in agreement, but Hunsche insisted they would need "higher authority" to make any commitments. Besides, he scoffed, the full deposit had not been paid.

The Cultural Department of the government now issued a decree banning all books by Jewish authors, whether foreign or Hungarian. A few black-clad Arrow Cross youths burned piles of books in a public square.

By April 16, Jewish citizens were ordered to report all their property, along with its estimated values, to the State Financial Directorate. Special attention was to be paid to "luxury items" such as art, carpets, and silverware.[6] By order of Andor Jaross, the minister of the interior, Jews were to declare and deposit in the bank all their valuables, including monies and jewelry kept in safety boxes. Henceforth, Jews would be permitted to withdraw a maximum of only one thousand pengős a month from their accounts, barely a subsistence level. Jaross spoke openly of the confiscation of "Jewish wealth" and tried to make it sound natural. "It will be incorporated into the circulatory system of the economy," he noted.

"It's as if they have all become drunk from the smell of money," Kasztner said. "As if the arrival of the Germans has given [the Hungarian ministers] a last gulp to drown whatever sobriety, or sense of decency, had held them back before." Ottó Komoly's view was that the Hungarians were being thrown their own Jewish citizens' wealth in order to compensate them for the wagonloads of valuables the Germans were taking from them.

The concentration of Jews in Carpathian Ruthenia and northeastern Hungary (Zone I) was launched at a meeting with local officials in the city of Munkács. László Endre brought László Baky's exacting instructions and reviewed all the measures, including how to keep the local population in the dark about the fate of the Jews. To ensure that there would be no panic, the rounding up of the Jews into one confined area was to be classified as a security measure in a military operational area. The Russian front was moving closer, and Baky could count on Hungarians' fears of the Russians. To enhance their fears, he reminded them of the brief Bolshevik interregnum under Béla Kun in 1919.

The gathering together of Jews in Zone 1 began on Sunday, April 16. Locating the Jews was simple: two weeks earlier, local prefects had demanded lists of names and addresses from the Jewish councils. All Jews were to move to designated areas not yet described as ghettos. "There is no cause for concern," the Jewish Council of

Munkács assured the anxious people in its care. Strangely, the Neolog chief rabbi was still urging his congregation "to pray to God for yourself, your family, your children, but primarily and above all for your Hungarian Homeland."

At dawn, gendarmerie units fanned out over the towns and villages, woke up their fellow citizens, and told them they had a few minutes to pack. They were allowed to take only what they could carry. They were ordered into walled-in ghetto areas, mostly local factories, or brickworks. There was little food and barely enough space for each person to lie down. Where no suitable area existed, they were left in open fields without shelter or sanitary facilities, surrounded by hastily erected barbed-wire fences. In Munkács, one of Europe's foremost centers of Jewish learning, Orthodox Jews in full Hasidic garb were forced to destroy their own synagogue while gendarmes and Arrow Cross youths laughed and urged them on with sticks.

At first Kasztner believed that the delay in paying the full deposit had been responsible for the roundups. He blamed himself for not being persuasive enough when he had a rare chance to talk on the telephone with Saly Mayer of the Joint in Switzerland. Mayer had seemed unable to grasp the urgency, the desperation in Kasztner's voice.[7] The Gestapo had allowed the Sip Street center to keep its telephones, but they had installed listening devices on every one. All conversations were now in some kind of code, mixing ancient Hebrew with Yiddish words and inventing names for the Jewish Agency, the Joint, and the ss. Jews could not use public telephones, and there were daily reports of arrests for all infractions, no matter how minor. Using a public phone was considered major.

When Samuel Stern called with news that the full deposit had been collected, Kasztner almost cried.

Krumey and Hunsche accepted the next payment of 2.5 million pengős on April 21 in Winninger's house. However, they no longer pretended that there would be no ghettos. Despite the prohibition on travel and telephones, Krumey realized that Kasztner knew about this development. "Herr Obersturmbannführer," he said to Krumey, "there is no point in playing these games with us. A month ago, Captain Wisliceny announced in your presence that the Germans had no interest in deportations. Are you telling us that the Hungarian government is sending Jews to Germany against your express wishes?"[8] The Va'ada had made every effort to meet its end of the bargain, Kasztner said. Wisliceny had agreed to certain undertakings, including no ghettoization, no deportations.

Krumey responded that whatever deal the Va'ada had struck with Wisliceny, they had better discuss it with Wisliceny, and he was now in Kolozsvár.

If the ghettoization was in progress already, Kasztner persisted, how could the Germans deliver on the deal? Krumey announced that the Sonderkommando was willing to discuss the procedures for Jewish emigration as a gesture of goodwill, provided a neutral country was willing to accept the Jews.

Kasztner showed them Chaim Barlas's cable confirming that a ship in Constanta in Romania had been hired for six hundred Jewish families who had Palestine entry certificates.

"They cannot leave via Romania," Krumey said. "They would have to take a boat from here to Bratislava, then through Germany." The Hungarian government must not know that the ss was dealing with the Jews. Under no circumstances should Kasztner and his associates reveal to anyone the nature of these discussions. If they broke confidentiality, there would be dire consequences, not only for them but for all the remaining Jews. "These actions are a Reich secret," Hunsche stated. "If the Hungarians find out, the deal is off."

The next day, Krumey told Kasztner that they had received permission for the six hundred emigrants. He agreed to Kasztner's request that at least half of them could be from the provinces. However, Krumey used the word "person," not "family." Kasztner had been thinking of his own family in Kolozsvár.

In parting, Krumey said he could let another three hundred go for 100,000 additional pengős. He called it a "laughably small amount," claiming he had been offered much more by some Budapest Jews eager to emigrate.

Kasztner was able to get a travel pass for Kolozsvár. He wanted to see Wisliceny about the deal he believed they had made. "It's crazy," Hansi Brand told him, "to expect an ss officer to keep his word to a Jew." Neither did she believe Wisliceny about not deporting the Jews. "They have made conditions so tough for people that the deportations will seem like a relief. Death will seem like a relief."

Kasztner went anyway. To make sure he took no detours, the ss sent along Rudolf Sedlaczek, the double agent who had introduced Schindler to the Hungarians. Along the narrow highways they saw thousands of Jews, most of them walking with small bundles of their belongings, a few frail individuals jammed into ox-drawn carts. A gendarme followed behind each group, bayonet fixed to his rifle.

In Kolozsvár, too, gendarmes had already started moving Jews into the brick factory on the outskirts of the city. Kasztner found Wisliceny at the headquarters of the Hungarian security police. He had no problems gaining entry once he showed his identity card. He tried for a pleasant, friendly tone, reminding Wisliceny of what he had said about conserving "the substance" of Jewish life in Hungary and also about deportations. What was going on in Kolozsvár and the rest of Transylvania?

"My hands are tied. It's Eichmann's game," Wisliceny said. "He did not want any part of our discussions; perhaps he doesn't want me dealing with Zionists. He doesn't like me trying to make it easier for you Jews. I wear a uniform. I must follow orders."

"At least tell me the truth," Kasztner begged. "You owe me that much." Had Eichmann planned the deportation of all Jews or just a select number for work camps?

Wisliceny said he didn't know, but he promised to see Kasztner again in Budapest after he had spoken with Eichmann. In the meantime, Kasztner could prepare the list of just six hundred names—those he could save in return for the payments made.

"I made the decision," Kasztner wrote later, "that we must keep this vital link alive, that even this slender thread was more than the nothing our friends in the Jewish Council had been able to accomplish."[9]

When Kasztner spoke with his friends in Kolozsvár, some called

him an alarmist. They could not imagine that the Hungarian government would go along with atrocities. Resettlement, yes; deportation, impossible. Both Rezső's and Bogyó's families had been
paralyzed by fear and disbelief. Members of the local Jewish Council
had been left out of the first roundup, but the reprieve would last
only a few days. As head of the Kolozsvár council, József Fischer was
entrusted with the responsibility of providing food and medicines
for those already in the ghetto, where there was little food and no
adequate supply of water. He urgently needed money for bribes. The
center of the ghetto was the old brickworks, with long, covered
structures used for drying bricks, with open sides and walls only at
each end, a partial roof, no toilet facilities, and packed-earth floors
that turned into mud in the rain. They wondered whether they
would all be forced to assemble there, and for how long.

Fischer was still unwilling to believe in the extermination camps.
As for attempting to cross the border into Romania, only an idiot
would trust in Romanian goodwill. After all, they were the people
who had thought it a grand idea to hang Jewish bodies in butcher
shops.

Ernő Márton, the former editor of *Új Kelet*, took Kasztner aside.
Márton had studied maps of western Hungary and the only place
that sounded like Kenyérmező—where the Hungarian police had
mentioned they might settle—seemed too small to accommodate all
these people. Did Kasztner think they would be going to Poland?
Was there some truth to those far-fetched rumors about an extermination camp?

Kasztner said he believed his own sources were reliable. Perhaps
as many as three million Polish Jews had vanished. He was not sure
about extermination, but he was sure now that Hungary's Jews
were to be transported out of Hungary. Years later, Kasztner would
try to reconstruct those conversations in Kolozsvár in detail. Could
they really not have known what other Jews suspected or knew for
sure? But by then it was too late to change anything.

Márton and a few others escaped to Romania. The rest awaited
their turn to be ordered to the brickworks.[10]

CHAPTER 9

Bargaining with the Devil

He summoned me in order to propose a deal. He was prepared to sell a million Jews—"goods for blood," that was how he spoke at that time. Then he asked me a question . . . which sticks in my mind until today. He said: "Who do you want to have rescued—women able to bear children, males able to produce children, old people? Speak!"

Joel Brand, testifying at the trial of Adolf Eichmann

On April 25, ss Lieutenant Colonel Adolf Eichmann summoned Joel Brand to his office in the Majestic Hotel. The order was delivered by Jozsi Winninger. The former Abwehr agent was anxious, but he was also pleased that the ss still showed confidence in him. "The Abwehr is finished. And there is something going on between the sd and the ss," he confided to Kasztner. "It's at the highest level, and nothing to do with us here, but we live in times when suspicion is enough to convict."

"What does Eichmann want with Joel?" Kasztner asked.

Winninger said that Eichmann had decided to take over the

negotiations. "He's always dealt with Zionists. He used to sell the Revisionists [right-wing Zionists under Vladimir Jabotinsky's leadership] Jews from Austria. He was invited to Jerusalem by some other of your people—everyone wanted in on the act. I think Eichmann likes Zionists." Winninger laughed, "Doesn't everyone?"

"And why Brand and not me?" Kasztner asked, peeved at the perceived slight. "I am the executive director of the Va'ada, not Joel."

Winninger shrugged. "Eichmann picks his own men."

Hansi Brand, who also found it odd that Eichmann chose her husband, thought Eichmann must have seen the letters and the cash from Istanbul, all addressed to Brand for the tiyul, the "excursion" to Palestine. Winninger and Bandi Grosz, as double agents and couriers, would have shown the ss whatever they wanted to see. She made sure that Joel wore his best suit and his brown German-made felt hat. It's not going to impress them, she said—but the hat usually made Joel feel he was in charge.

Brand was meticulously searched at the entrance of the Majestic, then ushered upstairs by two gun-wielding ss men. Eichmann's large office on the second floor had a magnificent view over rolling, light-green chestnut trees, their white blossoms opening in the spring sunshine. As he entered, Brand noticed a few round-backed chairs, and a large walnut desk on which was a framed photograph of a dull-haired woman and two children.

Eichmann sat behind the desk, his back to the windows. He was a small man, with narrow shoulders slouched forward in his gray, tight-fitting ss officer's jacket, epaulets displaying a lieutenant colonel's four stars, a thick leather belt, light-brown hair cut short, large ears, a wide forehead, narrow lips, and flat, blue eyes, small for his long, pale face. His revolver and holster were on the table close to his right hand. His fingers were drumming impatiently. Thick smoke from his cigarettes fogged up the windows. Nothing about the scene had a sense of reality. It seemed to Brand that they were meeting in a dense blue cloud, that the men in the room were dissolving into the blue-and-white wallpaper that in the smoke appeared blue-gray. Two of the men wore ss uniforms; the others were in civilian clothes.

When Eichmann finally looked up, he tilted his head slightly to one side as if sizing up his prey. Then he smiled a sort of half smile and stunned Brand by announcing that he was a Zionist. "Have you," he demanded, "read · The Jewish State?" He glared at him. "Well? Have you?"

Brand didn't trust his own voice. He just nodded. Theodor Herzl's Zionist classic offered the only happy solution for the Jews: their own homeland. They needed a place where they could be safe from men like Adolf Eichmann.

Eichmann started pacing around the room—long, energetic, furious steps that brought him face-to-face with Brand. "I know all about you!" he shouted. "You know nothing about me." He stood, legs astride, hands on his hips. "I am in charge of the *Aktion*![1] In Poland, Czechoslovakia, Austria, it has been completed. Now, it's your turn."[2]

Brand noticed his own hands pumping the felt hat, twisting it into a damp knot. He could hear his own breathing.

"If you could make that decision about whom to save, Brand, who do you want to have rescued—women able to bear children, males able to produce children, old people?" Eichmann shouted. "Speak!" He spoke in short, sharp phrases, like bursts from a machine gun.

"I couldn't . . . ," Brand stammered.

"You what?"

"All of them," Brand thought he said, but he was never sure of the exact words in that room on that day.

Eichmann laughed. He then mentioned his possible interest in trucks. An exchange of useless Jews for something the Reich needed, he said. *Blut gegen waren*—"blood for goods." This was the second time Brand had heard that phrase. He was ready to offer money, foreign currency, gold, jewelry, the kind of deal that had interested Wisliceny, but Eichmann said he wanted foreign goods, war materials.

Hermann Krumey stepped out of the fog by the windows. The German war effort, he suggested, could use a variety of goods. Tools, leather, coffee, but they preferred trucks.[3] Perhaps, if the Zionists moved quickly, ten thousand trucks would suffice for one million lives. "Not a bad deal," he mused, "one hundred Jews for only one truck. One truck for every one hundred lives. A million Jews for ten thousand trucks—a great bargain, don't you think?"

"You have the contacts with the Joint and the Jewish Agency!" Eichmann shouted. "You tell them what a great deal the ss is offering."

When Brand protested that, even with his extensive contacts (though he really had none), trucks would be difficult because the Allies might think trucks were military equipment, Eichmann said he was prepared to be reasonable. He would personally undertake that the trucks would not be used on the Western Front. Only in the east—against the Soviets.

Brand promised that he would try to reach the Jewish Agency people.

"Turkey or Switzerland?" Krumey asked.

Brand said Turkey, because the money had come from the Jewish Agency's Rescue Committee in Istanbul in recent months. Encouraged by the calm that had descended on the room now that the blood-for-goods deal had been mentioned, Brand brought up the understanding he and Kasztner had had with Wisliceny. They had paid the required amounts, yet there were ghettos in Carpathian Ruthenia and in Transylvania.

"War zones!" Eichmann shouted. "We must clear the area of Communists and spies. Jews are Communists and spies."

"The children . . . ?"

"Don't talk to me about the children," Eichmann barked. "They stay with their families."

"It's the humane way," Krumey said. "And one more thing: remember that this offer is secret. Not one word to anyone who does not need to know. Understand?" The meeting was over.

Brand descended Swabian Hill on foot. He needed to think. The butcher of millions of Jews, the man whose name was cursed by the refugees, had just offered him a preposterous deal that he must know the Jewish Agency and the Joint couldn't accept. Or could they?

From the Buda side of the Danube, he took the streetcar to the stop closest to Sip Street. The building was filled with people shouting and arguing, crying, gesticulating, begging for explanations where there were none. A large family group returning from a funeral in the Rákoskeresztúri Cemetery, their friends, the rabbi, and the gravediggers had all been taken off the streetcar and sent to Kistarcsa.[4] Some halutzim were negotiating for a room of their own in Sip Street, and a group of women and children, camped in the courtyard overnight, had now moved in from the rain. Someone was screaming in the Housing Department; it had been hastily set up on orders from the Ministry of the Interior after the first demand for 500 apartments soon increased to 1,500 as the Allied bombing continued.

Ottó Komoly and Kasztner were in the Central Information Office, the room designated for the Zionists. "One more call for the council to empty Jewish apartments and we'll have to move to the country," Komoly said in a light tone. "There are accusations of favoritism. Bribery. Stern says the keys to the apartments must be turned over to the ministry by the morning."

Brand interrupted the conversation and told them about Eichmann's offer. They were all silent for a while, Kasztner clutching and releasing his fingers, Komoly pacing to the window and back.

"We must try to meet their terms," Kasztner said at last.

"Are you crazy?" Brand spluttered. "Where do we get the trucks? You're going to steal them from the Germans and give them back? They're the only people with trucks around here. Or haven't you noticed? We have nothing . . ."

"I didn't say we would meet their terms," Kasztner replied. "I said we must try to meet their terms. We have to play this hand as if we held a full house. It's our only hope."

Immediately, Komoly began to compose a letter to Chaim Barlas of the Jewish Agency's Rescue Committee in Istanbul, and another to Saly Mayer at the Joint in Geneva.

The Jewish Council had been busy with a multitude of German demands: five hundred typewriters, two freshly painted rabbit cages, five parakeets, one thousand sets of bedsheets and pillowcases, pillows and blankets. When Samuel Stern told Otto Hunsche that it would take a few days to assemble the sheets and blankets, he was given one day. "In twenty-four hours, we can empty your building and take everyone to Kistarcsa. Surely it is faster and easier for you to supply the sheets."

When the bed linen was late, the Germans occupied the Jewish Hospital, ordered the sick from their beds, piled the items they wanted in giant heaps on the floor, and demanded that they be laundered and delivered as planned in four hours, or they would intern the staff.

That afternoon, Stern himself was taken into custody. He was thrown into the back of a car and deposited in the Buda jail. His immunity certificate had run out, he was told. When he was released, he had to go up Swabian Hill and stand in line with all the others to obtain a new one. The Germans, Stern realized, were showing him that he had no power at all.[5]

Carl Lutz called on Prime Minister Döme Sztójay with a formal request from the Swiss Consulate, representing the British government in Hungary, that the people with Palestine certificates be allowed to leave now. The previous Hungarian government had approved the emigration of seven thousand children and young people, and he saw no reason why the new administration would not honor these obligations.[6] Sztójay said there was no reason why the unwanted Jews—mostly children—should not be allowed to leave, but he would need the agreement of Edmund Veesenmayer. Jewish affairs were now under the Reich's jurisdiction.

Veesenmayer, conscious of Lutz's help with German citizens caught in Palestine at the outbreak of war, received the Swiss consul with deference. Thousands of Germans trapped in enemy countries might, again, need Swiss help. Lutz noticed that Veesenmayer wore civilian clothes, perhaps feeling that his ss uniform might offend. He pumped the consul's hand energetically and offered champagne and hors d'oeuvres, but nothing concerning the Jews. They were Eichmann's department, he said. Not even he could interfere. It was a matter of protocol. As for Lutz, could he suggest to the Swiss Red Cross that they look into the Allied bombing of civilians in Germany? Women and children were suffering terrible hardships in the Reich. Had he seen the photographs of Hamburg?

Once back in the embassy, Lutz urged Moshe Krausz to increase the number of Palestinian visas he issued as the Jewish Agency's man in Budapest. Despite what Veesenmayer had said, Lutz was sure he would get the exit permits. The Germans owed him, and they knew it. Krausz was still persisting in typing every form personally, insisting that each visa was his responsibility, that he was the one who would be held accountable.

A day later, Lutz began to hand out Swiss immigration papers to Jews who had come to him for help. His office duly numbered each certificate, making sure that, no matter how many they handed out, the number at the top was always under the numeral "7000." For additional administrative assistance, he hired a bunch of new Swiss Immigration Department clerks: the young Slovak, Polish, and Hungarian halutzim who had sought refuge at the embassy. He gave them blank forms to fill out.

From the beginning, Lutz was skeptical about Joel Brand's assignment, knowing the ss could buy goods they wanted on the black market. Why would they ask a Jew, a former Communist, a sometime agent, to run such an errand? And if it wasn't trucks, what was it that Eichmann wanted? Lutz went to see Eichmann with a proposal he thought would be pleasing to a man who had earlier helped Jews emigrate from Austria and Germany.

Eichmann, however, said he would let the seven thousand go if, and only if, Lutz stopped interfering in the transport of all the others. The Swiss Consulate had become an embarrassment. He said he had driven by Szabadság Square several times in the preceding days and been affronted by the swarm of riffraff trying to gain entry to the embassy building. There were hundreds of Jews lining up outside, and the noise, the stench, was unbearable. He would, if necessary, have the place shut down so it could be cleaned.

When Lutz remained unfazed, Eichmann threatened to have him recalled. He had, Eichmann said, become much too involved in matters that should be of no interest to a neutral nation.

On April 27 the Central Jewish Council sent a long letter to Interior Minister Andor Jaross, asking him to intervene in the inhumane treatment of Jews in Carpathian Ruthenia and northern Transylvania. Since April 18, Jews had been living in overcrowded ghettos where they had little food. Their former homes had been robbed. The lack of clean water had caused outbreaks of typhoid.

In Nagyszöllős, Carpathian Ruthenia, eleven small communities—about fourteen thousand people in all—had been forced into an area around the synagogue that had accommodated four thousand before. Fourteen-year-old Suti Weisz (later, Yitzhak Livnat) and his family now shared their quarters with five other families. Their house on the Perényi baronial estate had been confiscated, as had all their possessions. When Suti's father said that the only gold he had ever owned had been buried with his wife, the gendarme assured him they would dig up the grave and remove it from her finger. Until the gendarmes threatened to arrest him for aiding Jews, Baron Perényi sent in wagonloads of potatoes, the only food the ghetto received over the first two weeks.

* * *

Rezső Kasztner and Joel Brand asked to see Dieter Wisliceny, but the captain had not yet returned to Budapest. "Have you called your friends yet?" Krumey asked.

"They won't give you war materials," Brand blurted out. "The whole thing is madness—"

"They are considering the matter," Kasztner interrupted. He knew that perception was key in this game they were playing. "What about the people in Carpathian Ruthenia?" he asked. He had heard horrific stories about the treatment of women and children. "What has happened to the agreement we reached with Wisliceny?" Krumey said he did not know "the details" of their deal with Wisliceny. And he certainly was not responsible for the way the Hungarian gendarmes handled their Jews.

The next day, when Wisliceny finally returned to Budapest, he held out no hope for Kasztner, but he did agree to see him.

On Melinda Street, almost at the top of Swabian Hill, Wisliceny lived in a large villa with glass all around the top floor.[7] At the entrance to the estate, visitors passed through a flower-laden gate and along a red stone pathway lined with chestnut trees, big green fronds of summer ferns, heavy-limbed walnut trees, and thickly planted rosebushes. In one far corner of the grounds, there was a gaily painted rabbit hutch with several white-tailed animals behind the bars. The cage was kept sparkling clean by a small, shy, balding man, a Jew whom Wisliceny had saved from a crowded ghetto, supplied with passes for his family of nine children, and sent on to Budapest with a letter of introduction to the Rescue Committee. This man, a simple small farmer and rabbit fancier from a Transylvanian village, served as his gardener as well. Wisliceny made the point to Kasztner that he had not forgotten how to be kind.

When Kasztner asked him about his promise of keeping "the substance" of the Jews in Hungary, Wisliceny explained that Eichmann would not hear of it. The deposits they had paid would perhaps buy the six hundred he had suggested earlier. The rest of the Jews would be deported.

CHAPTER 10

The Auschwitz Protocols

I shall never forgive . . .

Rudolf Vrba, *I Cannot Forgive*

Rudolf Vrba and Alfréd Wetzler escaped from the Auschwitz-Birkenau concentration camp on April 7, 1944. Commandant Rudolf Höss spared no effort to find them. That the escape succeeded was due to the fact that both men had been assigned to the Aufraumungskommando, the cleanup unit. Its job included removing the luggage and the corpses from the arriving boxcars, scrubbing the floors clean of blood, urine, and feces, and transporting the bags to the storage area. After each train's passengers had been murdered, these workers burned the bodies, cleared out and sifted the ashes, ground larger bone fragments in a mill, and packed the ash into bags marked "Fertilizer."

They carried the former passengers' bags to the "Kanada" storage area, so named by the prisoners because, for them, Canada represented a place of plenty.[1] The thirty-five "Kanada" buildings were, in fact, a place of plenty for the camp's officers, the guards, and the

Reich—a profit center that provided clothing, gold and valuables, hair, and children's toys.

It was a streamlined operation, completely routine. The steam engine pulled the train into the station. The doors of all the freight cars were unchained and opened at the same time. The deportees were ordered to leave their luggage and run down a wooden ramp, their way illuminated by closely spaced lampposts. Heavily armed ss men surrounded the new arrivals, most of whom had been traveling without food or water for several days, crowded eighty to one hundred in a wagon. They stumbled into the nightmarish light, stepping over the dead and the dying as they were hurried along with shouts, threats, and lashes from the bamboo canes. The selection process took less than a minute per person. Those deemed unfit for work were trucked—exactly one hundred to each truck—to Birkenau's gas chambers, a big improvement from when prisoners were gassed with truck exhaust fumes.

For both these young Slovak men, "Canada" provided the means of escape. They took civilian clothing and German money, then hid in a woodpile while the search of the surrounding countryside was at its height. Once the guards had given up, the pair crawled out under the two electrified barbed-wire fences. For a week they traveled at night, avoiding the local residents and hiding in barns or outbuildings during the day. When they reached Bratislava, they contacted the Jewish Council the next day. They told their incredible story, illustrated by drawings of the barracks, the gas chambers, and crematoria. They reported on the selection process that sent women and children directly from the trains to be gassed, on the desperate attempts of people to save themselves, on the collection of valuables, and on the systematic disposal of bodies.

In January 1944 Vrba had witnessed the building of two new crematoria and a new railway ramp that led directly to the gas chambers, bypassing the need for trucks. The purpose of the additional facilities, he had learned from one of the German kapos, or prisoner-guards, was to accommodate the arrival of a million Jews from Hungary. "We'll be eating fine Hungarian salami," the man had said, referring to food he hoped the prisoners would bring. He was tired of Polish food.[2]

Vrba's mother was still in her own home in Slovakia, one of the 25,000 Jews who had, so far, escaped deportation. She took care of her son while he recovered from his travels. Strangely, when she berated him about not sending postcards, he did not mention Auschwitz. Only twenty years old, Vrba was already a veteran of the most terrifying place on earth. He felt overwhelmed by the importance of his message to all surviving Jews, particularly the Hungarians: do not board the trains.

"The Auschwitz Protocols," as Vrba and Wetzler's report was labeled by the Bratislava Working Group, was translated into German and English within a couple of weeks. Then they tried to decide what to do with the information, knowing that anyone caught with the document—or its authors—would be executed.

On April 28, Eichmann summoned Joel Brand back to the Majestic Hotel.[3] Otto Klages, chief of the Budapest SD, was sitting at the table next to Eichmann. Klages was taller than Eichmann and an imposing figure in his gray uniform. They both greeted Brand with smiles and nods, as though they had been expecting a friend. Eichmann handed over a package of letters from Switzerland and a bag of money that Saly Mayer had sent for the tiyul effort organized by the Aid and Rescue Committee. It was an extraordinary situation: the most senior German in charge of murdering all the Jews was handing confiscated money to a Jew whose mission it was to rescue Jews from the Germans.

"You see, Brand, what a reasonable man I am?" Eichmann asked, his voice lowered in tune with his newly cordial stance. "We intercepted these packages at the border. The money is for your children's-relief work. I have nothing against your work for children. Some letters are in Hebrew, some in Yiddish, others in Hungarian. I don't have time to censor all this. Let me know if there is anything here that I should know about."

Brand was stunned.

Eichmann went on to say that he now had consent from Berlin

that he could continue these discussions. Had Brand received similar approval from his associates? He did not wait for a reply, continuing with a long speech on the desirability of new frontline trucks, fresh from the factory, with all the accessories and fully equipped. Abruptly, he looked at Brand, who had been standing all this time, silent, holding the bag of letters and money, and he asked, "So you want to have a million Jews?"

Brand stammered yes, he would like all the Jews.

"One million is all we are discussing now," Eichmann said, his voice rising, "and ten thousand trucks. Brand, you are getting a bargain." He had a list of additional goods he would consider. Coffee, soap, tea, cocoa, and, if they didn't have all the trucks ready at once, perhaps a slightly reduced number of trucks. "Remember," he insisted, "I can assure your Allies that they will not be used on the Western Front."

Klages suggested, jocularly, that they would stop the whole Aktion, the ghettoization and deportation of the Jews—if World Jewry had the trucks winterized. The German army, Brand thought, was settling in for a long campaign in the east.

Eichmann then suggested that, if Brand returned from his mission to Istanbul with an agreement in principle about the deal, he would bring 10 percent of the Jews on offer—"ten thousand of them, think about that, Brand!"—to the border. The exchange could start right away. "You see what a reasonable man I am, Brand?"

Encouraged by his surprisingly affable reception, Brand asked whether Eichmann could put a stop to the rounding up of Jews in the countryside. "Every day we are getting alarming reports about hunger and disease, dysentery, typhoid, pneumonia," he began. "The gendarmes are beating and torturing women and even children to make them confess where they have hidden some small objects of value, and dentists are pulling gold teeth from the mouths of old men—"

"Atrocity propaganda, Brand!" Eichmann shouted. And he advised his visitor not to bring up the subject again.

CHAPTER 11

The Reichsführer's
Most Obedient Servant

*There is no doubt that this [the murder of the Hungarian Jews]
is ... the greatest and most horrible crime ever committed in the
whole history of the world, and it has been done by scientific
machinery by nominally civilized men in the name of a great State
and one of the leading races of Europe.*
Winston Churchill, *Hansard*, June 26, 1944

Eichmann's last meeting with Joel Brand was attended by Fritz
Laufer, the former Abwehr agent, and ss Lieutenant Colonel
Kurt Andreas Becher. Brand did not know who Becher was,
but, later, he remembered him as tall, good-looking, youthful with
an unlined face, his light-brown hair smoothed back, wearing a well-
cut suit, leaning against the door frame as though he had come by
inadvertently.

Eichmann had been shouting at the top of his voice, ranting
about the duplicity of Jews and their associates and demanding that
the Zionists obtain the few items he wanted from their fellow Jews
worldwide. Becher had moved near the shaded window, his back

straight, shoulders tight. He said nothing during the entire tirade.

Becher was Heinrich Himmler's own man in Hungary. His official title was "chief of the economic staff of the field ss." He signed all his letters and cables to Himmler as *Reichsführers gehorsamster Becher*— "the Reichsführer's most obedient Becher." He was thirty-four years old.[1]

Becher had enjoyed the benefit of good, middle-class parents who had sent him to a fine school in Hamburg. After graduation, he became a diligent salesman in a Hamburg cereals and feedstuffs firm, but his life did not gain momentum until he and his own horse entered the ss cavalry in 1934. Two years later he joined the National Socialist Party. He took six weeks' infantry training in Oranienburg and rode into Poland in 1939 with an ss Death's Head Division squadron. He participated in a range of house-to-house searches and, more than likely, in a series of mass executions, serving with distinction under the command of Lieutenant General Hermann Fegelein, who reported to his superiors that Becher's squadron had been conscientious in executing its orders. Becher was then stationed in Warsaw, where he was promoted to second lieutenant. There are various accounts of what he did to earn this promotion, but Becher claimed later at Nuremberg that he had trouble remembering the details.

In May 1941 Becher's ss cavalry brigade came under ss Reichsführer Himmler's command. Ably led by Fegelein, its tasks included the "pacification and cleanup" of areas the Reich had acquired in its eastward push, ensuring that Jews were gathered in ghettos and that those who resisted were shot. Becher's squadron distinguished itself by conducting executions of civilians in the Pripet Marshes in Russia during the summer and fall of 1941. Himmler's specific orders had been to kill all Jewish men and drive the women and children into the marshes. In a dispatch to headquarters, one of the officers complained that the marshes had proved to be too shallow, so the survivors were herded into gassing trucks and, when dead, their bodies were driven to nearby ditches for burial. The idea was to spare German soldiers the horror of listening to the children's screams. Reports about the mass murders were disguised in military communiqués, as they were in most ss documents. Massacres were called "military action" or "heavy fighting," depending on the number of bodies. Becher had difficulty recalling these events, too, though he admitted there had been some "searching of houses for weapons."[2]

Eventually, Fegelein was able to report to Himmler that the area under his command had been completely "cleansed." More than fourteen thousand Jews, one thousand partisans, and seven hundred Soviet soldiers had been killed in the assignment. Becher said in his testimony after the war that he missed this action because he was suffering from a skin infection. Nevertheless, Becher received his first major commendation, judged to be of "leadership material," with "perfect racial features, polite, well brought up, fine mannered," a man of ambition "who set an outstanding example" for his men. He received the Iron Cross–Second Class and the Iron Cross–First Class for his part in the "cleansing" of the areas under Fegelein's command. From late 1942 to 1943, Becher's cavalry regiment took part in combat near the Dnieper River against the Soviet army.

Becher's remarkable rise in the ss landed him on Himmler's personal staff as a man who had earned praise not only for battling unarmed Jews in the field but also for his success in separating them from their valuables—all of which had been sent home to the Reich treasury. The sole shadow on his career had been a minor charge, soon dismissed, that he had used his authority to keep some valuables from the Warsaw ghetto.

Under direct orders from Himmler, he now displayed his abilities with a much bigger deal. He acquired for the ss all the horses of Baron Oppenheim, the most famous thoroughbred breeder in Germany. When at first the baron proved reluctant, Becher assured him that the ss "had other methods" than mere persuasion. Becher was proud that, once the deal was signed, the baron had full ss protection in exchange for his horse farm and that his brilliant financial advice had enabled the baron to circumvent the tax implications of the deal. Thanks to Becher, Baron Oppenheim kept both his life and a small portion of his former vast fortune.

The Oppenheim deal was a major career move for Becher, who

was then promoted to lieutenant colonel in January 1944. In a friendly letter, Himmler congratulated him on his diligent participation in "the unflinching struggle against a lower species."

It was not coincidental that Becher turned up at Klessheim Castle the day after Hitler's unpleasant meeting with Admiral Horthy on March 18. Himmler had plans for him in Hungary.

Becher arrived in Budapest in March 1944 as the Reichsführer's economic adviser. Formally, he was under the command of ss Lieutenant General Hans Jüttner, but he had a direct line to Himmler. He claimed that his only mission was to acquire twenty thousand horses and some equipment for the cavalry but, as Rezső Kasztner discovered, his mandate was much broader than that. He was to take a leadership role in the systematic looting of Hungary. To begin with, he planned to acquire for the ss the largest industrial concern in the country, the Weiss-Manfred Works, and most of the controlling families' wealth, including their sumptuous mansions on Andrássy Avenue. The acquisition process included the torture of the firm's senior managers and the head of the extended family, Ferenc Chorin.

Chorin and his brother-in-law, Móric Kornfeld, were able to evade capture in the first ss sweep and go into hiding in the Cistercian monastery the night before the Germans invaded because, late that Saturday night and an hour or so after the last guests had left the Mauthners' cocktail party, Prime Minister Kállay's secretary had phoned Chorin to warn him that columns of German tanks had crossed the western border.[3]

Chorin had been the chief executive of the family's most significant holdings—the armaments factories, the iron works, the aviation and engines factory; he was also a former vice president of the Hungarian Commercial Bank and a former president of the Hungarian Chamber of Commerce. In response to the anti-Jewish legislation enacted by the Hungarian government, he had transferred nominal control of the companies to various Aryan members of his family and sold minority shares to the government. William Billitz, his trusted senior executive, had taken over as president of the company. A nationalist, Chorin had not left the country in the years leading up to March 1944 because he was confident that Hungary would evade the Germans' worst excesses.

When Chorin and Kornfeld were discovered at the monastery, they were interrogated and beaten. Both men were kept standing for three days and four nights of ceaseless questioning. At the end of March they were transferred to the Oberlanzendorf prison in Austria, where the humiliations and beatings continued. Chorin's wife, captured with Chorin and taken to prison with him, had typhoid fever by the time Becher discovered their whereabouts. The slightly built, sixty-six-year-old Chorin was no longer recognizable. Gaunt, pale, his hair turned white, he suffered from severe dysentery and could walk only by holding on to the walls.

Becher obtained permission from the Berlin headquarters of the Gestapo to visit Chorin. By this time, he knew all about the Chorin-Kornfeld business empire from William Billitz, who was trying desperately to save his superiors' lives. Billitz had been at pains to explain the wealth and structure of the companies to Becher, including all the Hungarian holdings and the contractual international trading relationships. There were complex share structures that involved not only the Hungarian government but certain non-Jews whose loyalty Chorin commanded. Simply put, without Chorin, Becher would not be able to take over the Weiss-Manfred Works for the Reich.

Becher had the Chorins and Kornfelds transferred to Budapest, installed them in the library of the Andrássy Avenue building Chorin had recently owned, and urged Chorin to sign over his wealth, foreign currency holdings, and factories to the Reich, in exchange for the lives of his family and $600,000 of his multibillion-dollar wealth. When Chorin hesitated, Becher suggested that he and his family would have to be returned to Oberlanzendorf. "That was not a threat," Becher said later, but "simply a statement of the facts. If there was no deal to be made, I couldn't hold them any longer. I would have had no choice but to return them to the Gestapo."

Chorin complied. All sixty members of the Chorin, Weiss, and Kornfeld families signed the agreements, as required by law.

Himmler was pleased. Even Hitler, when notified, considered it a good transaction.

Later, when Brand asked Bandi Grosz about Becher, Grosz shrugged his shoulders. "One of Himmler's men," he told Brand. "No one you need to know." Brand had kept an eye on Fritz Laufer throughout the meeting, not only because he had earlier been warned not to trust him in his Abwehr capacity but also because Laufer now wore a German Security Service uniform. Laufer told the bewildered Brand that Grosz would be traveling with him for his meetings with the Jewish Agency people in Istanbul. He was an odd choice for such an important journey: as a petty criminal and a triple agent with a checkered history, he did not seem to be senior enough for such a mission.

The goods on Eichmann's list had become more specific: 110 tons of coffee, 200 tons of tea, two million pieces of soap. And, of course, the trucks. What could be fairer? Eichmann demanded. He would, of course, keep Brand's family hostage until he returned.

During this crucial time in Budapest, Rezső Kasztner was in Bratislava, Slovakia. He delivered badly needed American dollars to Gizi Fleischmann and a few letters to Slovak relatives from Palestine. The Jewish community was in relative safety because of Dieter Wisliceny's orders, Gizi told him, but she had to keep paying bribes to both the Slovaks and the ordinary Wehrmacht soldiers to look the other way. Rabbi Dov Weissmandel's Orthodox yeshiva was still attended by boys in full Hasidic garb. It had become an oasis, a secure, isolated spot for Slovak and Polish boys, a temporary haven for the halutzim. But a constant supply of cash was needed to keep the local authorities at bay.[4]

When Fleischmann spoke to Kasztner about the "Auschwitz Protocols," the report written by escapees Vrba and Wetzler, she presented the document in the context of what could, in these circumstances, be believed and what might be the product of the feverish imagination of young men who had faced the misery of a concentration camp. Unable to fully accept what Vrba and Wetzler had reported, she nonetheless handed the document to Kasztner. Her group had already given copies to the papal nuncio in Slovakia and to a couple of senior men in the government. She was certain the Slovaks believed what the German propaganda machine had told them: the Jews were safe in labor camps. Not even the most rabid anti-Semites among them would condone extermination.

Kasztner returned to Budapest with a copy of the protocols. He did not sleep that night. He and Hansi Brand read and reread the terrible account, its full meaning hard to absorb. A whole apparatus set up to destroy people was what Oskar Schindler had told them about, yet they had not imagined this fate for Hungarian Jewry. Kasztner recognized in himself the same intentional blindness he had abhorred in his colleagues, the fervent denial of unbearable reality.

Early the next day he went to Samuel Stern's home. Stern, still in his dressing gown, pale, stooped, so much older in appearance than the man Kasztner had met only three years before when he arrived in Budapest, had to sit down abruptly when he began to read the report. He decided that the first priority was to have a translation prepared. Perhaps the facts, as portrayed, would seem clearer in Hungarian. The detailed descriptions were too horrific, far-fetched, incredible. Stern was shaken, as he had been by the refugees' stories he had heard earlier, yet he still could not accept the possibility that innocent people were being killed in such a way. Surely his former colleagues on the Royal Council would have warned him.

That night at the Opera Café, Rezső and Hansi argued with Joel that Rezső would be better able to make the case to the Jewish Agency for Eichmann's deal; Rezső was, after all, already in touch with Chaim Weizmann, the head of the World Zionist Organization, and was himself a Zionist leader who had run training camps for young Zionists in Transylvania. The Vrba-Wetzler report meant that this journey to Istanbul might be the last chance they had to make the Jewish Agency, the Joint, and the War Refugee Board understand what was happening in Europe.

Joel remained adamant: he was the man appointed. Other members of the Va'ada agreed with him. Ottó Komoly sent a telegram to Istanbul requesting a Turkish visa for Joel and an urgent meeting with the Agency's Executive. Stern and Freudiger prepared a letter appointing Brand as the representative of "the whole of Hungarian Jewry" and requesting "all qualified Jewish people and institutions to accord him all the support in their power," signing it in the name of the Central Council of Hungarian Jews.

On April 29, 1944, the first transport of 1,800 Jews left Hungary for Auschwitz-Birkenau. The train carried only able-bodied men from the Kistarcsa prison camp. They, and the next transport of 2,000 men from the Topolya prison camp in southern Hungary, were to be part of the 100,000 Jewish laborers Regent Horthy had agreed to supply for urgent work detail in the Reich. The Hungarian parliament had approved this deal, and word was passed to the Jewish Council that these men were part of a workforce to replace Germans who were in the army.

There were daily warnings of the terrible consequences to gentiles of hiding Jews or Jewish wealth. The fascist press—the only newspapers published since the day after the German invasion—ran stories about friends of Jews who had concealed property and who were now to be punished according to the law. There were arrests and criminal charges, Jaross warned: "There is reason to suspect that many members of the Christian community have procured and concealed Jewish valuables, partially out of misguided humanitarian considerations."[5]

On May 5 Kasztner took the "Auschwitz Protocols" to the residence of Carl Lutz. The Swiss consul lived in a beautiful nineteenth-century manor house in old Buda, the former British legation in Hungary, and received Kasztner in one of the vast reception rooms, decorated with gold chandeliers, gold-framed mirrors, and romantic paintings celebrating ancient, heroic Hungarian battles. The whole building, but especially this room, was in terrible contrast to the horrors recounted by Vrba and Wetzler. Kasztner, though he felt parched after his long hike across the Chain Bridge and up the hill, refused the glass of chilled wine the embassy's butler offered. Lutz read the report while Kasztner stood at the window, his eyes gazing across the river at the peaceful, genteel view that belied all they already knew.

When Lutz had finished reading, he walked to the window and stood next to Kasztner, shaking with rage and grief. The two men got into the consul's car and went to see Moshe Krausz at his new office in the former American embassy. They were joined by Ottó Komoly, who had already read the report. Once again, they talked about the possibility of helping to arm some of the halutzim who were still busy with rescue work at border crossings and in ghettos. There was no chance of large-scale resistance—the men who could have created a tangible force against the Germans were all disarmed and in labor service. Thousands of Jews were in guarded ghettos, and there was practically no communication between Budapest and the provinces. All they could do, they decided, was use unreliable couriers to send messages to the Jewish councils in other cities, where some people, perhaps, could escape when they learned the truth. Lutz promised to step up his efforts to reach Horthy, and Kasztner said he would continue his negotiations with the ss. They still believed that the bribes to Wisliceny had stopped the deportations in Slovakia. And Lutz felt sure that once the news of Auschwitz reached the Allies, they would bomb the crematoria and destroy the rail lines leading to Poland.

Copies of the document had been distributed by the underground Jewish network to the Hungarian Roman Catholic bishops, the papal nuncio, the Lutherans, and Admiral Horthy's politician son, Miklós. Yet no news had spread to the outside world. There was nothing in the newspapers in Switzerland, nothing on the BBC, and no mention in the American news.

When Lutz asked the Swiss minister in Hungary whether he could take or send the report to Bern, the answer was no. It would be viewed as anti-German propaganda, and it was dangerous in these times for a neutral country to show such overt involvement in the Jewish issues of another country.

On May 9, the former inmates of the Kistarcsa prison camp

outside Budapest were murdered in Auschwitz.

At the May 13 meeting of the Hungarian government, the foreign minister read into the record a letter from Angelo Rotta, the papal nuncio, urging that it distinguish between Jews who had become practicing Christians and those who had not. The former, he insisted, should not be forced into ghettos. His request stemmed from a meeting he had attended with the Association of Christian Jews, whose membership had swelled over the past few months. But Pope Pius XII's representative met with the same response that the Jewish Council had received from the government: these measures were a necessary part of Hungary's efforts to sustain its relationship with its allies. The Jews were to be foreign workers in places where they were most needed; their treatment had been uniformly humane, and they were able to leave in orderly family groups.

Responding to the letters of protest, members of parliament firmly denied that Hungary was planning to deport its Jewish citizens. The minister of finance reassured Ernő Pető, a member of the Jewish Council, that no deportations were planned, and Ottó Komoly received the same promise at the Ministry of the Interior. Jean de Bavier, the Hungarian representative of the International Red Cross, tried and failed to bribe his way to an appointment with Regent Horthy.

In early May, the logistics of human transportation were reviewed during somewhat heated discussions at an SS conference in Vienna. Some of those in attendance argued that all rail lines should be reserved for troops and their provisions, but Captain Franz Novak, representing Eichmann, overruled their concerns and established the fact that the Reich considered the elimination of Jews to be its top priority, even as bad news continued to arrive from the frontline. The immediate priority was the transportation of Hungarian Jews to Poland.

The deportees were to include whole families, women and children, old people, the sick from the hospitals, the inhabitants of mental institutions, the lame, the blind, newborn babies with their mothers. De Bavier, who had seen the Auschwitz Protocols, reported to his boss that he was sure, from his own sources in government circles, that the trains were headed to a camp in Poland "where there are up-to-date installations for gassing people. The Jewish community here says it has credible evidence that their religious kin in Poland perished this way."[6]

On the day that Krumey completed Brand's travel arrangements for Istanbul, the mass deportation of Hungarian Jews began. On May 15 the trains from Hungary began to cross Slovakia and southern Poland. Within two weeks the areas in the north of Hungary would be empty of Jews. Before transportation, the Jews, irrespective of age and sex, were searched, including body orifices, in public. To Kasztner, Krumey still insisted that the deportees had all been able-bodied workers sent to a labor camp at Waldsee, Germany. When Kasztner asked why not one of them had sent home a letter or a postcard, Krumey assured him that there would be cards once the deportees had settled into their new lives. When Kasztner asked why these people had been selected, Krumey replied: "We took only professional workers." "Professional workers?" Kasztner remonstrated. "They were all bourgeois!"[7]

"Well," Krumey replied, "they'll learn a profession in the Reich."

Mel Marmelson from northern Transylvania called out through the slats of the wagon when he saw another boxcar on a nearby siding: "Who are you . . . where are you from?"

"We are Dutch," came the reply. "We are Jews. We are going to a labor camp."

There was a short burst of machine-gun fire, then silence.

In Transylvania, the Jews had been assembled in the brickyards, tile works, barricaded areas, and surrounding fields of smaller towns, without food and water. The roundups had been organized in the mayors' offices and were carried out by local gendarmerie and police units. Kasztner's family and friends were mostly in the brickyards at the northern periphery of Kolozsvár. In the covered but only partly walled sheds, a total of eighteen water faucets and four ditches for latrines served the eighteen thousand people incarcerated there. They had very little food.[8] Bogyó's father, József Fischer, had been in hospital when the order came for him to join the rest of the Jewish Council in the ghetto on May 15.

Most of the people had heard stories about the fate of Jews elsewhere, but they still did not believe that they, too, had been marked for annihilation. Those who had fought in the First World War carried their decorations with them, and many had briefcases containing their diplomas and degrees, their commendations from various officials. The women brought the birth certificates of their children. Fischer was already aware of Kasztner's dealings with the ss and his belief that three hundred people might be selected to go from Kolozsvár to Budapest by train, but the list had not arrived when he joined the group in the brickyards. When the list did arrive, it was delivered to one of the other members of the Kolozsvár Jewish Council.[9]

As the ghetto formed, the majority of the inhabitants' non-Jewish neighbors simply watched and went about their daily chores as though there was nothing unusual in such events in times of war. Some were afraid of being seen as sympathetic, while others helped themselves to property left unguarded. Those few who tried to deliver water or food to the camps were themselves beaten.

On May 15 in the city of Munkács, a large group of Jews, deprived of all they had owned, were marched to the trains. Along the road, they were watched by their former neighbors, none of whom intervened. Their march was accompanied by horrific screams from the synagogue, which had been transformed into an interrogation center where the formerly wealthy were tortured to reveal whatever might remain of their valuables.

Once the assembled groups arrived at the designated train station, they were ordered into freight cars that were padlocked from the outside. Some trains rolled through Budapest's Eastern Station during the night, partly because the army needed the rails during the day, and partly because the authorities worried about the noise of the condemned reaching sympathetic ears in the capital. Sometimes women begged for milk for their babies, while others asked for medication for diabetics and painkillers for those removed from operating rooms when the roundups began.

Mihály Salamon, one of the young men in the Information Office at Sip Street, remembered being told to drive a truck with loaves of bread to the Western Station and await further orders once there. It was early in the morning, but already too hot for that time of year. A train had stopped past the station and along the most distant set of tracks. It was surrounded by gendarmes, their guns aimed at the doors of the boxcars. Some men and women emerged from the darkness inside the cars and walked slowly toward the back of the train. Salamon was ordered to dump his load of bread at the siding and leave immediately. He thought there was something profoundly sad about those people filing toward the bread. He didn't realize, then, that they were some of the lucky ones. Most of the boxcars filled with Jews received no food and no water.

In a small town on the Hungarian plain, a train from the east stopped on a siding overnight while the main rail line transported a mass of wounded from the frontline to hospitals in Budapest. During the night, there was the sound of singing from one of the cattle cars. Slowly, voices carried the tune to the next car, then down the line, until the slow, mournful sound filled the summer air and reached the villagers where they slept. People began to emerge from their homes, a little dazed, stunned, then saddened and angry. They stood and listened while the song for the dead continued in waves through the dawn, barely interrupted by the yells of gendarmes and a few disheartened soldiers who had been commandeered for guard duty. When one of the gendarmes fired his gun into the nearest car, the villagers moved closer. They stood like that till the early morning when the train pulled out of the station.

As every train made occasional stops on its journey, each car was opened in turn and divulged its dead, its crazed, its traumatized. Those who tried to help were beaten with rifle butts, and some were forced to join the Jews in the freight cars. Others were shot.

The Jewish Council in Budapest sent yet another letter of protest to Prime Minister Döme Sztójay. Council members had been informed that Jews were being moved out of militarily sensitive areas, but they asked that these people, many too young or too old to be a threat to Hungary and its allies, be treated in a humane manner and settled within the borders of Hungary, not in another country. Many Jewish leaders had heard by now about Auschwitz, and, although they still could not believe that people were being systematically murdered there, they were afraid of what might happen if Jews were taken to Poland.

László Endre, who was responsible to Eichmann for ensuring that the deportations went smoothly, decided to respond to the council with a blatant lie: "The leaders of the Jewish Council must be called in and informed that deportations are taking place only in combat zones where there is a lot of spying and sabotage," he wrote. "These Jews have not assimilated . . . If the others behave themselves, the resettlements will be discontinued."[10]

In his notes from the middle of May, Kasztner praised the halutzim who carried food supplies to the ghettos and warned the Jews to do whatever they could to avoid entering the wagons.[11] But what could they do? They were isolated, hungry, thirsty, and demoralized, hopeless, no longer resembling the people they had been. Most still chose to believe they would be taken to a better place, there would be work for them, and they could stay together with their families.[12]

On May 16, his last evening in Budapest before he departed for Istanbul, Joel Brand met Kasztner in an old tavern-restaurant on the Buda side of the river, a long way from what they had begun to refer to as "Nazi Central." The tavern was one of those old outdoor places that reminded Joel of Berlin in the days of his youth. There were wooden benches and long wooden tables. Joel lit one of his strong, aromatic Turkish cigarettes. He was nervous, too loud, too enthusiastic. He leaned in across the table, searching for some sort of reassurance. He knew how important this mission was: he had to return with news of a deal. If only Eichmann had agreed to halt the deportations while Joel met the Jewish Agency's men.

Joel believed that the survival of Hungary's Jews depended on the success of this mission and that, even if the Germans' bargain was rejected, the Rescue Committee would gain time. The deportations might be stopped, and, if the delay was long enough, the Allies could, in the interval, win the war. He was afraid to take the Auschwitz Protocols with him, in case he was searched before he boarded the plane.

Rezső rehearsed him in the statements he would make, the order of his presentation, the background on the situation in Hungary, what they knew about the deportations—and about keeping it brief. He advised that the best way to deal with Moshe Shertok,[13] the political leader of the Jewish Agency, was to be direct. The man would know more than he let on. The Agency would have its own spies. He had to understand the relationship between the Yishuv leaders and the British. Despite their apparent lack of power, they could influence the British Parliament. The British press, when they learned what the Nazis were doing to the Jews, would force Parliament to act. Churchill was on the side of the Yishuv, he had opposed the White Paper on Palestine, he had been friendly with Chaim Weizmann, and he had frequently expressed his outrage over German atrocities. Rezső said he was certain that both Shertok and Weizmann would want to meet Joel, that they would recognize this mission as the final chance to save Jewish lives in Europe. As for the blood-for-goods deal, Kasztner believed that "the Allies would give neither trucks nor money since either one would help the enemy . . . and, on the Jewish side, there had been many attempts at rescue through ransom and Eichmann's subordinates had taken money . . . and sent their victims to their deaths." But what else could they do but pretend that the deal might be credible? They had no alternative rescue plans, and there was hope that this one could at least delay the deportations.[14]

At the end of the evening, Joel asked Rezső to look after his children. "And Hansi, of course, but I know you are going to do that, anyway," he said with a sad smile. He explained that all he had told Kasztner about the marriage . . . well, it might have been so once, but if he survived, if they survived the war, he would try to be a better husband. "The boys need me," he said.

CHAPTER 12

Mission to Istanbul

We must make some serious counterproposal so that the negotiations can continue. Tomorrow I'll cable Eichmann and tell him that all goes well . . .

Joel Brand, to the Jewish Agency in Istanbul[1]

It is impossible to prepare a list of 600 from 800,000.[2]

Ottó Komoly, "The Diary of Ottó Komoly"

Joel Brand and Bandi Grosz left Budapest for Vienna on May 17, 1944, in an ss car. They spent a night in the Austrian capital at the Metropole Hotel, which doubled as the Gestapo's headquarters, and arrived in Istanbul by German courier plane on May 19.

Immediately on his arrival, Brand was arrested by the Turks. He had the wrong kind of Turkish visa (it had been provided by the SD, in the name of Eugen Brand) and all the appearances of a German spy. To make matters worse, he was traveling with Bandi Grosz. The

Turks knew Grosz was an agent, but, being neutral, had allowed him in and out of the country on many previous occasions. In exchange for his freedom of movement, Grosz provided them with dribbles of information, warnings about the arrivals of new German and Hungarian agents, some troop movements in the Balkans, Jewish refugee ships, and American efforts to recruit and turn agents. He had been posing as a representative of the Danube Navigation Company, a cover for Grosz's smuggling and money-laundering businesses. Despite his unprepossessing appearance, he had attracted a local dancer and rented a fine apartment for the two of them.

While Brand waited for his Jewish contacts to arrive at the airport to claim him, Grosz left in a limousine with a short, well-dressed man. The Turks interrogated Brand, who would say only that he had important business with the Jewish Agency's representatives and they were expecting him. They didn't arrive. The Turks were on the point of putting Brand on another plane destined for Germany when Grosz returned. He had called Chaim Barlas of the Jewish Agency and, after bribing the appropriate Turkish officials, Brand was granted a temporary visa. Grosz had already booked a room for him at the Pera Hotel, which was, coincidentally, the headquarters of the Agency's Rescue Committee[3] and of various Zionist leaders, including Barlas. Grosz was the Agency's most frequently employed emissary/smuggler.

Despite the telegrams from Komoly and Kasztner outlining the nature of his mission, Brand got the impression that the Agency's men were surprised to see him. Perhaps, he thought, they did not believe that the ss would send a Jew out of Europe to meet other Jews in a neutral country. In fact, Barlas and his colleagues were inured to Nazi extortions. They had tried to extract Jewish children from Romania and Hungary; had sent money to Slovakia (about $200,000 by the end of September 1943 and a further $200,000 in 1944), earmarked for Weissmandel's Europa Plan (which sounded remarkably like Eichmann's blood-for-goods offer),[4] and had bribed German officials in Poland, Bulgaria, and France.

Brand, exhausted and furious at what he perceived to be a slight, insisted that Barlas and the other Agency men immediately arrange a meeting. He handed over his letters of authorization from Samuel Stern and Fülöp von Freudiger, the map of Auschwitz he had hidden, and Eichmann's list of required goods, and delivered a detailed verbal account of the deal Eichmann had offered. He told them what he knew about the extermination camps—they had heard of their existence at least two years before—and the situation of the Jews in Hungary. He confirmed what they already knew about the fate of Poland's Jews, paraphrasing what Vrba and Wetzler had reported in the Auschwitz Protocols. Throughout the long speech, his listeners kept interrupting in Hebrew, which he didn't understand, and in English, which he sometimes did. He yelled at them to stop talking among themselves and to speak a language he knew. They seemed genuinely unable to decide what to do with him, even though he kept repeating that he had to send a cable to Eichmann to advise him that the Jewish Agency Executive, or its Rescue Committee, or the Joint had met him and were very interested in the deal— that progress was being made.

Their initial reaction to the blood-for-goods proposal was one of genuine astonishment. The British, they were certain, would never go along with giving the Germans trucks. The Germans would surely realize that. Why, then, send Brand, and why with Grosz? When Brand demanded to see Chaim Weizmann or Moshe Shertok, the Agency members told him it was not easy for either of them to gain entry to Turkey from Palestine. Moreover, they explained, their own situation in Turkey was precarious.

Exhausted and angry, Brand asked how they could worry about their own situation in Turkey when hundreds of thousands of Jews were being murdered. Did they not understand that the delivery of trucks was not the point, that this mission was simply about starting negotiations that could, and would, drag out for months and that, while they were negotiating, lives would be saved? Eichmann, he argued, would not destroy the Jews if he thought a deal was imminent. Brand was certain that if either of the well-known Jewish leaders Weizmann or Shertok were seen in Istanbul in the next twenty-four hours, German agents would let Eichmann know that his offer was being considered at the highest levels.

Venia Pomerantz, one of the Agency's Rescue Committee emissaries, flew to Jerusalem with a typed summary of Eichmann's proposal hidden in a tube of shaving cream and reported on Brand's mission to David Ben-Gurion and Moshe Shertok, as well as to a hastily called emergency meeting of the Jewish Agency Executive. "We had no illusions about the German offer," Pomerantz recalled in his memoirs. "We knew that half of Hungary's Jews had been deported, but we had to try . . ."[5]

Barlas cabled Shertok and Ben-Gurion,[6] both later to become prime ministers of the new State of Israel, asking whether they could come and listen to Brand's incredible story. Shertok immediately applied for a Turkish visa. Ehud Avriel, who worked for the Agency's Rescue Committee, went to see Harold Gibson, the head of British Intelligence in Turkey, to inform him about Brand's mission and to gauge his reaction. Avriel recalled later that Gibson refused even to consider the possibility of pretending to negotiate to gain time. Perhaps he feared that the Russians would find out and suspect the British of double-crossing them. It was not something the British would be willing to risk.[7]

Two days later, Eichmann summoned Hansi Brand to the Majestic Hotel. She felt it was strange arriving in her former refuge now that it had become the stronghold of the enemy. She remembered lazy summer afternoons in the gardens, listening to the three-man band play the popular tunes of the day while she fed her children or played cards on the terrace in the cool shade of the acacia trees. Eichmann seemed cheerful, lounging in his chair, his gray officer's jacket flung over the back of another chair and a glass of wine on the table to the side. He was smoking a short Turkish cigarette, his head angled at her.

"Mrs. Brand," he said, "we have not heard from your husband."

"It's been only two days," Hansi replied, "a difficult time to gather all the right people who can make the kinds of decisions you need here, Herr Obersturmbannführer." She had walked the hundred yards or more from the cable-car station in her uncomfortable, white high-heeled shoes. She had wanted him to see her confident and composed. She stood very straight, her shoulders back, feet together.[8]

Eichmann took a long sip of his wine and glanced up at her. "You may cable your husband, Mrs. Brand, that if he doesn't come back at once and bring me news, he'll have no family to come back to. You understand, Mrs. Brand? He is on thin ice."

Hansi glanced at the photograph on Eichmann's desk. "You have children, too, Obersturmbannführer—"

"Don't you dare! Don't you dare!"[9] he shouted as he leaped to his feet and slammed his fist on the table.

Hansi fled the room and ran down the steps, where at first the guards stopped her, then let her go. They were used to Eichmann's rages. She moved her children from André Biss's apartment and took them to that of a gentile acquaintance who had offered to hide them in exchange for reasonable compensation.

During these first two days that Joel Brand was away, 23,363 Hungarians were deported. By May 19, the number had increased to 62,644.[10]

Kasztner begged Hermann Krumey to arrange for him to meet Eichmann. He knew that every day, every hour, mattered, that he had to convince Eichmann that Brand's silence was caused only by wartime communications problems. Kasztner wanted to introduce himself as the leader of the Va'ada, to set up a line of communication, to claim that he could produce whatever the Germans needed—anything to slow the pace of the deportations. In the end Hansi called Eichmann's adjutant and requested that he see "Dr. Kasztner, the executive director of the Rescue Committee." She accompanied him to the Majestic.

During that first meeting,[11] Eichmann suddenly leaned forward in his square-backed club chair and asked Kasztner, "Do you know who I am?" Not waiting for the answer, he continued: "I am the commissar of World Jewry. I decide how many Jews will live and how many will not. I am charged with cleaning the streets of Europe of Jews."

Kasztner stood transfixed in the doorway. He would always remember the fog of cigarette smoke, the dutiful adjutant, the shadows in the summer light lingering around Eichmann. "We knew we were facing the main stage manager of the Jewish destruction," he wrote later.

He noticed a copy of Theodor Herzl's *The Jewish State* on one corner of Eichmann's otherwise bare desk. "Fascinating book, don't you agree?" Eichmann inquired. "You Zionists want a territory where you can live in peace. That's what we National Socialists want—for you to have your own territory. Far away from ours. I wanted nothing less than firm ground under your feet!" he shouted. "Loved that book! Like you, I am, at heart, a romantic. It appealed to that side of my nature. Love the mountains, rivers, woods. Amazing that a Jew could write so well."

Eichmann indicated a couple of chairs for Hansi and Kasztner, more or less across the desk from himself but much farther back than his. Kasztner recalled similar configurations with his schoolmaster in Kolozsvár when he had done something wrong. Eichmann lit another cigarette.

"I speak fluent Hebrew," he said, his hand fluttering over the ashtray, "more than most of you do. Our Jews in Germany spoke only Yiddish, a bastardized German. They never learned their own language."

Eichmann was still proud of Hermann Göring's original Europa Plan, a fantastic notion of resettling Jews in the southeastern area of Poland where the local population had been eliminated. To make sure that the Jews would learn to fend for themselves, existing houses had been bulldozed, crops ploughed under, and wells poisoned. "They would learn to build, to plant, to drill for water," Eichmann told Kasztner. "Work. We found the perfect place in Nisko on the San River. You know, I even sent some Jews to look the place over. Big territory, I thought to myself, why not resettle the Poles and move the Jews here? Heydrich approved the plan! But then 'Polish Frank'[12] got into the act. That dumb bastard had just been appointed to head the General Government and, would you believe, he didn't want my Jews. He had his own!" Eichmann laughed, a loud, mirthless explosion of a laugh, his mouth open, his eyes squinting shut. Polish Frank had complained to Hitler that the new deportation policy would use the General Government as a "racial dustbin."[13]

But Eichmann had not given up, he told Kasztner, his cigarette waving frantically as he punctuated each point. He had thought of Madagascar. "Didn't Herzl himself consider Madagascar?" That is, if Palestine was not available? "I went to see your Palestine, once. Wanted to make sure there was room for the Jews from Germany. And from Austria—not Poland, not the Polish Jews. Vermin like the people they lived among." But once the Grand Mufti of Jerusalem arrived in Berlin, seeking refuge from the British,[14] promoting further immigration to Palestine became impossible. Surely the Jewish leaders here were aware of the British blockade of the area and of the United States' resistance to more Jewish immigrants? "The Bermuda Conference was so much shit!" he shouted. "The Reichsführer-ss himself had been ready to let you go, but there were no takers."[15]

"You and I," he told Kasztner expansively, "are idealists. We want the same things, and we just have somewhat different approaches."

Kasztner had been well aware of the Nazis' old Europa Plan: the confiscation of Jewish property in exchange for exit visas to Palestine. After an hour's uninterrupted lecture, Eichmann stopped and waited to see what Kasztner had to say.

First, he tried to convince Eichmann that he, Kasztner, represented that mythical World Jewry in which Hitler so fervently believed. "World Jewry," Kasztner said, would step in and save the Jews if given a chance. He begged for the deportations to stop while Brand negotiated with World Jewry's "leaders" in Istanbul. Kasztner claimed that he had talked with the American Joint Distribution Committee in Switzerland and had its instructions to make deals. The truth was that Saly Mayer had told Brand that his coffers were bare: he had received less than us$10,000 for 1940 and 1941, and nothing for the next year and a half while the Swiss banks pondered how to deal with American charitable donations. At one point, Mayer had suggested that eastern European Jews tended to panic too easily. He still did not believe the reports of systematic killing camps.

Kasztner asked about the terrible cruelties in the ghettos and the packed boxcars from Carpathian Ruthenia. "If there were more than ninety people in a wagon from the northeast," Eichmann said, "it's only because these are small people. Jews in that region have lots of children, and children don't need much room, as you know."

Kasztner asked if Eichmann would stop the deportations while Brand negotiated for the trucks and other goods that Eichmann wanted. "I will not stop the trains!" Eichmann shouted. "Do you all think I am stupid?" If he slowed the deportations, World Jewry would imagine they had won a reprieve. They wouldn't bother to negotiate.

Kasztner reminded him of his offer to Brand to send ten thousand Jews, 10 percent of the one million offered, to the border for emigration to prove that he would honor the blood-for-goods deal. Eichmann said he remembered the number as maybe a few hundred.

Kasztner pointed out that it would be impossible for Brand to prove that the ss would keep its promise in the deal if, at a minimum, half of the six hundred he had discussed with Krumey were not sent to Budapest from the eastern provinces now, before they were all deported.

"I have not seen your list," Eichmann replied.

And so the bargaining began. Eichmann offered lives he was unwilling to give; Kasztner offered goods he didn't have. It was a high-stakes poker game in which one player had nothing to offer but his own life, and the other had nothing to lose but face.

As Kasztner was leaving the meeting, he ran into an anxious Carl Lutz, who was still hopeful that at least a small portion of the seven thousand children and young people the Hungarian government and later Eichmann had agreed could leave the country would be allowed to go. Lutz told Kasztner and Hansi that he had finally received his ambassador's support for sending a copy of the Auschwitz Protocols to Switzerland, so long as the Nazis could not find a connection to the Swiss Consulate.

Hansi was silent most of the way down the hill. She and Rezső were the only Jews in the cable car, and she was sure the other passengers could tell they were Jews even without their distinguishing stars. Jews were no longer allowed to ride in these cars. Rezső admitted to her that he had been terrified of Eichmann. The man "ruled over life and death" in Hungary, and he had, in fact, made them no promises. He thought Eichmann had treated him dismissively, and, if that was so, how could he hope to appear as a negotiating partner? Although Eichmann kept up his chain-smoking, he had never offered Kasztner even one from his fancy cigarette case. Hansi laughed. "Next time, take your own cigarettes," she advised. Once home, she taught him how to chain-smoke heavily scented cigarettes, to match Eichmann's habit but primarily to show himself unafraid.[16] "In a game of chicken, Rezső," she cautioned, "you must not seem to be the one with the ruffled feathers."

Kasztner cabled the Istanbul Jewish Agency office that the deportations would continue. Each day was another day in the martyrdom of the Jews, and surely they would understand the urgency now. There was no reply.

Kasztner could not bear to make the selection for the list of six hundred people he had previously discussed with Krumey. He was unable even to contemplate the names that would not be on it. The thought that all they would save was a few hundred lives was unbearable. He asked the Rescue Committee's Ernő Szilágyi and Ottó Komoly to meet Fülöp von Freudiger and Samuel Stern to compile the list. They would try to be fair to all factions, keeping in mind the plight of the refugees and the hopes of those who had been lifelong Zionists, community leaders, and rabbis, Jews in the capital and in the provinces alike. The selection group had to act now, before the daily transports took them all.

The next meeting with Eichmann was on May 22. Before he even sat down that day, Kasztner removed his first cigarette from the elegant, gold-plated cigarette case Hansi had given him, tapped it lightly on the lid, and lit up. Again he reminded Eichmann about the million-lives-for-trucks deal that he had discussed with Joel Brand. If Eichmann did not act soon, he warned, World Jewry would not negotiate. What would be the point of negotiating with the world's Jews after all of the European Jews were gone?

Eichmann, in jackboots, his legs apart for additional balance, his hand casually resting on his pistol, shouted a string of obscenities.

"What do you take me for, Kasztner? One of your stupid Hungarians? Don't forget I know you for the *schweinhund* you are. I am not interested in your whining. If I weaken, you people will think you've won. I am not slowing down the deportations. Rather, I am going to speed them up. One hundred people to a wagon? Hell, those wagons can take more than a hundred!"

"Have you read *Der Stürmer*, Kasztner?" Eichmann continued.[17] "Thousands on thousands of our people believe that magazine. It gives you no chance at all, did you know? None." He was pacing again, making abrupt turns in the corners of the room, his cigarette wedged between his lips. "Me, I am willing to give you one last chance!"

Kasztner handed him a list of six hundred selected Jewish families—not individuals—and showed him the earlier cable from the Agency about the ship in Constanta. Eichmann declared, just as Krumey had done, that Constanta was out of the question. He could not permit emigration to Palestine. Didn't Kasztner know of the Führer's close relationship with the Grand Mufti of Jerusalem? The ss would never be a party to breaking the Führer's promises to an ally. The group would have to travel through Germany, France, and Spain, then on to Africa.

The formerly lovely grounds around the Majestic Hotel and the Little Majestic were in the process of being dug up to create bunkers for further expected Allied air attacks. Eichmann's men had requisitioned a group of boys, too young for the labor battalions, too old to be considered children, for the task. While Eichmann yelled and Kasztner listened inside the hotel, the boys, in their midteens, dug in the field between the two buildings. They were supervised by a man called Slavik, who wore overalls over his bare chest. He seemed to delight in beating the boys with his thin, leather truncheon whenever he thought they were slowing down.

As Kasztner was leaving the compound, Slavik grabbed a tall, thin, dark-haired kid and accused him of stealing cherries off the trees. Eichmann came out onto the veranda, ordered the boy into the toolshed at the end of the garden, and he and Slavik followed, as the youngster kept screaming that he had done nothing wrong.

Weeks later, Kasztner found out that Eichmann and Slavik had beaten the boy to death.[18]

At the Central Information Office on Sip Street, a cable had arrived from Joel Brand saying the discussions in Istanbul were going well. Delegates from the Joint, along with senior Jewish officials, were on their way to meet him.

Meanwhile, the ghettoization in the provinces north of the capital had begun, even as the trains kept coming from the east, four a day, seven days a week. A railway engineer from Munkács went to Sip Street with the news.[19] When he began to talk about the last day of the Munkács ghetto, he could not stop wiping his eyes, describing the way the men and women were rushed to the station and beaten with whips and rifle butts, the babies wrenched from their mothers' arms. As a final humiliation, people were ordered to undress and step away from their clothes. Many were infected with typhus and could barely stand. Policemen ransacked their clothes and tore up their identity papers while they stood naked, then pushed them into the wagons of the train.

Next it was time for the Jews of Zone IV, southeastern Hungary. They were driven into ghettos and their homes and belongings confiscated. In each ghetto, rooms or cellars designated as "the mint" became torture chambers where affluent Jews were tormented until they gave some information about their hidden valuables. They were beaten with rubber hoses, and women had electric wires inserted into their uteruses in front of their families. Between sessions, some people took the opportunity to commit suicide. Dieter Wisliceny, who served as a German adviser in two of the districts, claimed later that he was shocked by the savagery of the Hungarian gendarmes.

Although Samuel Stern had written several letters to State Secretary László Endre about the terrible situation in the ghettos, he had not received any answer. At long last he received a cursory reply. Endre had visited the ghettos, he said, and he found them rather like "sanatoria." Accommodation and food were better there than for soldiers at the front. When Stern arranged a brief audience at the

Majestic, Eichmann sneered that, in his opinion, "the open air would only be good for the Jews."[20] As for deportations, these tales were "malevolent distortions and alarmist propaganda," he said. The Russian armies were approaching the borders, and the Jews simply had to be removed from what could become "military operational territory."

Stern's heart had been giving him trouble, and he had lost weight, yet he dragged himself up to the fifth floor of the Sip Street building every day and withstood the tears and accusations of his former admirers.

For days there had been rumors in the city about the amazing deal Lieutenant Colonel Kurt Becher had made with Ferenc Chorin. Becher had been given legal rights to the Chorin-Weiss-Kornfeld-Mauthner assets, and the families had left the country for Spain or Portugal on May 18. Now the Hungarian minister of finance was raising questions in parliament and demanded an investigation.[21] Jewish assets were frozen and deemed to be the property of Hungary. The industrial complex in the Csepel District of Budapest, and the aircraft and munitions factory, had been among the big plums on the Hungarians' platter. To have them snatched by the ss was an insult.

Kasztner became convinced that he needed a private meeting with Kurt Becher. He wanted a new negotiating partner, one who might live up to his promises. Becher, after all, had allowed the Chorin group to leave for a neutral country, and he had been sent to Budapest in the first place by Himmler. Eichmann, in contrast, was not even acknowledging the original bribes the Va'ada had paid to Wisliceny, Hunsche, and Krumey. Wisliceny claimed that the full amount had been deposited with the appropriate Reich ministry and that he had withheld nothing for himself. He mentioned that additional payments would be necessary if Kasztner's six hundred "sample Jews" were to be sent out of the country, but he was unwilling or unable to suggest the amount. He did not know exactly how much the Chorins had paid, but he was happy to divulge that the totals—

even if you ignored the current value of the factories—were well beyond the sums deposited by Kasztner's group.

Eichmann, Wisliceny told Kasztner, would not spare a single Jew if such decisions were up to him alone. The Master was not interested in deals, and he "endeavored to wreck all negotiations." Becher had a very different approach to the Jewish question, and, unlike Eichmann, he had a direct line to Reichsführer Himmler.[22] Eichmann reported to Heinrich Müller and, if he needed additional backup, to Ernst Kaltenbrunner, but he rarely had occasion to see Himmler.

At first Jozsi Winninger agreed to make the contact with Becher, for a modest fee, but then he changed his mind. Now he recommended that Kasztner stay away from Becher. "Bad for your health," he advised. Eichmann would not like it. Himmler, Winninger said, had deliberately set up rivalries among his officers, to make sure that everyone did his best in the ensuing competition. And there was a natural rivalry between Eichmann and Becher, to the point where they actively disliked each other.

There are several accounts of the way Kasztner managed to arrange the meeting he wanted. Becher himself gave two versions during his testimonies at Nuremberg.[23] It is also probable that Becher, having known of the blood-for-goods proposition, tracked down the Va'ada himself. He had an unerring sense for finding good sources of money.

CHAPTER 13

A Million Jews for Sale

During two thousand years of persecution, it often happened that Jewish lives were bought for gold and valuables. This was neither the fault of the Jews nor of the money.

Rezső Kasztner, "A Nagy Embervásár"

J oel Brand had not been able to extend his visa, and he was again arrested by the Turkish police. He was amazed to find that none of the Jewish Agency's functionaries there was able to get him released. It was beginning to dawn on him that the Va'ada had greatly overestimated the Agency's influence. Briefly, Bandi Grosz joined him in the makeshift prison where the Turks had confined him, then Grosz bribed their way back to the hotel. There Grosz made a series of intense phone calls, had numerous visitors, and sent several cables while Brand waited for one of the Agency's people to arrive to help him prepare some sort of answering document that they could send to Eichmann. Unbeknownst to Brand, Grosz had already been to the offices of Western Electric Company, fronting for the OSS, and had reported in to "Dogwood."

Once again Grosz had bribed and cajoled Brand's way out of prison. Brand worried that Grosz would let the ss know he had been detained, assuming that Grosz's assignment was to keep an eye on him and report back to Eichmann. How could he pose as an important emissary for World Jewry if his contacts couldn't even keep him out of jail? His anxiety increased when Chaim Barlas told him the Agency's people were unhappy that Grosz had procured his freedom—illegally. "You have no right to check into a hotel when you are under arrest," one of them said. "The whole delegation could be in jeopardy. We could be expelled."

Brand was outraged. What did he care if they were all expelled? The worst that could befall them was a return to sunny Palestine. If he were expelled, he'd be killed. Worse, he was convinced that his mission was the last chance for European Jews. "If I am sent back for lack of a lousy visa, a million Jews will end up in Auschwitz!" he pleaded.[1] Eichmann had to be led to believe that he was meeting with the most important people in the Agency. If news of Grosz's engineering Brand's exit from jail got back to Budapest, it would not look right.

But Bandi Grosz, the German-Hungarian-American-Turkish quadruple agent, had an agenda that neither Eichmann nor Brand knew about: he had been chosen by Himmler to carry a message to the Allies. The fact that as agent "Trillium" he was used by the oss was, in Himmler's view, an asset.

Grosz's mission was to let the Allies know that, under certain circumstances, Himmler would be interested in suing for peace.[2]

Eichmann was becoming comfortable with Kasztner's visits. He even complained to Kasztner about Kurt Becher, saying that his promotions had come too easily. He, Eichmann, had had to struggle for each speck of recognition, while Becher had used "connections" to rise to the top. He had not been informed of Becher's mission in advance, and he considered all interference in dealing with "his" Jews as cutting across his turf. He referred to the Chorin deal as *schweinerei*, pig swill, and also as bad business because it annoyed local associates who had had every reason to think they would assume full control of the Weiss-Manfred Works and the broader Chorin interests. Besides, how was he to safeguard his personal friendships with Hungarian state secretaries László Endre and László Baky, given Becher's behind-the-scenes maneuvers, or justify letting rich Jews out of the country at German expense?

Kasztner grew even more anxious to meet the mysterious young cavalry officer.

Chaim Barlas assured Brand that he had alerted the American ambassador in Ankara, Laurence Steinhardt, to Brand's presence and that he would be able to meet the Americans. Barlas said he understood Brand's misgivings about talking with the British, though it could not be avoided: the British already knew of his mission. Brand was afraid that if the British rejected the German deal officially, it would mean the end of his quest. Barlas assured him that the Agency would continue to make every effort to extend his Turkish visa.

Meanwhile, they drafted a "memorandum of agreement" authorizing Brand to act on behalf of the Jewish Agency in negotiating a deal with the ss. Preconditions of the proposal set out that the deportations would cease and that emigration to Palestine and to neutral countries would be permitted. In exchange, the ss would be paid $400,000 for every one thousand persons allowed to leave for Palestine; $1 million would be paid for each transport of ten thousand persons allowed to leave for other countries.[3] The Agency would supply food, clothes, and medication for those held in concentration camps. The memorandum stated that delegates of the Jewish Agency were on their way to Istanbul and would be ready to meet "authorized representatives of the opposite side."[4] As for the trucks, there seemed to be a few problems that would have to be ironed out.

Brand cabled Kasztner that a formal agreement had been prepared. Proudly, he quoted some of the terms. Once Kasztner received the cable, he took a taxi up to the Majestic to show it personally to Eichmann, though he was sure that Eichmann, given that all communications were censored, would know about it already.

On that day, or the next, Kasztner saw Kurt Becher for the first time, lounging against the wall of Eichmann's office, his arms crossed, his face turned toward the windows. He did not look at Kasztner or give any hint of his interest in Brand's cable.

Otto Hunsche, Dieter Wisliceny, Hermann Krumey, and Franz Novak stood behind their leader. They knew Eichmann was drunk. These past few days he had been drinking more than usual, and he had been angrier than usual. His normally tidy uniform was creased, and the dark stubble under his chin attested to a hurried shave that morning. There had been a raucous party at László Endre's the night before, with a local band, a deep-voiced chanteuse from the Corso singing sad, romantic German ballads, everybody dancing, and, later, vomiting in the lush rosebushes that lined the path from what had once been another wealthy Jew's house. The singer had gotten into Eichmann's car just before 4 AM.

Kasztner begged Eichmann for patience. "Please give Brand a chance to deliver on your deal. You must stop the deportations— you see our friends are doing their utmost to meet your terms." Eichmann shouted that he would step up deportations rather than halt them. "I will show you and your swine you can't play games with me," he swore. He had waited too long already for such minimal promises. Now there was no mention of the merchandise he had asked for. He had already made it clear that the Reich did not need money. Where were the trucks?

Kasztner was now smoking as feverishly as Eichmann, and had become so used to the other man's ravings that he knew how to wait them out and present his case again. Over and over, he threatened that there would be no deal with World Jewry unless the deportations stopped.

Eichmann took a mimeographed letter from his pocket. It had been scrunched up, so he had to flatten it on the table, smoothing the edges with the palm of his hand. "This is what your people are spreading. This shit. This . . ." It was an appeal written by some members of the Jewish community, addressed to Hungarian Christians, reminding them of their thousand-year-long common bond with the Jews of Hungary and telling them of the terrible suffering of the provincial Jews in the ghettos, the lack of shelter and water in the brickyards and deserted mills, the horror of being driven into freight cars by men pointing bayonets, the suffering of the children. How, the appeal concluded, could the extermination of helpless old people, infants, and veterans, unarmed and defenseless people, be reconciled with the always chivalrous Hungarian nation?[5]

"More horror stories, Kasztner, more of the filth—and you know the penalty for that!" Eichmann's voice had risen so high that he was practically screaming. His arms braced, he leaned over his desk and spat his words into Kasztner's face. "The penalty is death! Hanging! And you want me to stop deporting this rabble? Germany has a war to win, and your filthy lot is trying to rouse these . . . savages . . . against us." Eichmann often referred to the Hungarians as savages. He strode up and down the room again, his heels slamming into the old parquet floor.

Kasztner took a long, deep breath and waited, measuring his own silence, waiting for the right pause in the Austrian's invective, the opening in the wall of words. When the moment came, Kasztner repeated quietly that if the deportations continued, there would be no lives to trade. He said, firmly: "Herr Obersturmbannführer, I must insist on the terms of our agreement." He had decided there was nothing left to lose. He was going to bargain for at least some lives. He asked for a hundred thousand Jews selected from across the country.

Hunsche, Krumey, Wisliceny, and Novak stared at Eichmann, waiting for the next explosion. He had jumped from his chair and stood leaning back on his widely planted feet, his back straight, his head wobbling from side to side. Then, with only the slightest change in his tone of voice, he sat down behind his desk and announced that he would let two hundred Jews from Kolozsvár evade deportation to the "work camp." After that, well, maybe that total of six hundred that had been talked about, half from Kolozsvár—"It's where your family is, right, Kasztner?"—if the Hungarians agreed to let them go. "I will *not*," and he slammed the table with his fist, "go against the Hungarians. You know we need their help here? They, and they alone, insisted on no special treatments."

Kasztner was quiet, waiting again for the storm to pass. He knew, as did they all, that six hundred Palestine certificates had been received before the German occupation. Each one could include a whole family. For this group, there would be no problem with entry into Palestine.

Then Krumey said, diffidently: "Obersturmbannführer, I think we can solve that problem. We tell [Hungarian Intelligence head Peter] Hain and [Hungarian gendarmerie colonel László] Ferenczy that we have uncovered a Jewish plot. Something far-reaching, affecting the Reich, and that we need to bring these people to Budapest for interrogation."

Wisliceny, who had had his back to Kasztner until then, said: "I believe, Adolf, that you'll have no trouble with the Hungarians. I've already told Ferenczy that we are tracking a dangerous Zionist conspiracy. I told him these conspirators have to be isolated from the rest of the Jews. They could cause a disturbance if they are left with the others."[6]

"They'll fall for that?" Eichmann asked, obviously amused by the ruse. He was usually amused by jokes at the expense of the Hungarians. He considered them *untermenschen*, somewhat above the Jews and the Poles, but still unworthy of their partnership with Germany.

"Kasztner will have the list," Krumey continued. "And the Hungarians will be pleased to oblige."

Eichmann nodded. An advance group, a gesture, to be matched by Istanbul, he said, what he agreed to do when Brand left. Six hundred was not a large enough number to attract attention here, yet the Jews—the Joint—would think it was a sign. Eichmann spoke of the Joint as of something almost mythical, a huge, powerful presence. "I told Brand to make sure he meets with Steinhardt. He is connected with the Joint. Like all Americans."

Kasztner asked if the selection of the people from Kolozsvár could be left to the Jewish Council there. They would know best which names to include. Eichmann began to shout. "You take the Hungarians for fools, Kasztner? How in hell can we convince them of a conspiracy if we can't even give them a list of the conspirators? No. The list will be done here and by you and your people."

At the end of the afternoon, Kasztner was given permission for just the six hundred Jews, and Hunsche added that the cost would be $800 a head.[7]

Eichmann had mused that if the Americans could charge new immigrants $1,000 a head to let them in, then he, too, would charge $1,000 a head to let them out. "It would be only fair, don't you think?" he asked. He turned to the other ss officers and gave one of his quick, mirthless laughs. "A fair offer?" The group could go via Spain or Portugal, but not from Constanta, where a ship was still waiting to take them to Palestine.

Kasztner gave his larger plan one more try: ten thousand people from the provinces, including Kolozsvár. "If it's going to be a conspiracy, it may as well be a big one," he said.[8]

"You can't bring them back, Kasztner, once they are gone," Krumey said, referring to those already deported. "No power on earth can bring them back. But we could see about that lot in Kolozsvár. If they are still available," he added, ominously.

"And maybe some additional conspirators in other provinces where the transports have not yet left," Wisliceny murmured.

"About two hundred from Kolozsvár, Kasztner, and that's my last word!" Eichmann pronounced. And, as an afterthought: "The head price will be determined later. You know they'll pay whatever you want, Kasztner; those Jews will find their hidden money as soon as they know it'll buy them their lives."

Kasztner was about to argue for the numbers agreed on earlier, but Krumey gestured to him to be silent. "We'll send this man to Kolozsvár with your list," he said, indicating a young ss sergeant near the doorway into the connecting rooms.

"Where will you keep them?" Eichmann asked. "They can't be allowed into the general population! Like letting poison back into the system. Vermin!" Krumey suggested they could be gathered in tents, in a field outside Kistarcsa.

Kasztner would not agree to any site near Kistarcsa. He said the courtyard of the Wechselmann Institute for the Deaf, Dumb and Blind on Columbus Street in Budapest would serve the purpose. It had been emptied by the Gestapo, and had a garden and spacious grounds for tents or barracks.[9] He had seen it on his way from Biss's apartment building and had thought of it as a possible hiding place for Jews.

"It's a Reich secret, Kasztner," Eichmann pronounced as Kasztner was leaving. "A word of this to anyone and the deal is dead. Dead!" he shouted. "Dead, you understand?" His laughter followed Kasztner down the corridor and the few steps to the guardroom.

The sergeant who had been ordered to go to Kolozsvár with the list stopped Kasztner as he was about to cross the footbridge onto the street. "About two hundred, Dr. Kasztner," he whispered, "can be more than two hundred. Perhaps a lot more than two hundred?" He had brought his sweaty young face close to Kasztner's, his head tilted to one side, emphasizing that he was, indeed, asking a question.

"If you think so, Scharführer," Kasztner said, carefully. "We would be most grateful." The code word was "grateful." The pimply young man whose uniform needed some tailoring would have understood.

*   *   *

Kasztner decided he would have the list delivered to József Fischer. He would know what to do. Meanwhile, every day, Kasztner took the cob railway to the top of Swabian Hill and walked on to the Majestic. He always returned on foot, giving himself a chance to think. If he could not slow Eichmann's plans for the deportations, he would have to work at expanding the list. The draft agreement from Istanbul had not yet arrived, there was no further word from Joel Brand, and Kasztner had not yet been able to meet with Becher, though William Billitz had promised to see what he could do. Now that Billitz worked for Becher, representing the new owners of the Csepel works, he had occasion to speak with him every day when the young ss officer was in the city.

In a desperate gamble, Kasztner showed Eichmann the German translation of the Auschwitz Protocols. "How long," he asked, "will it take for the Jewish Agency, for American Jewry, for the world, to find out about this?" And how would they respond to a deal—any idea of a deal—with a man who was sending tens of thousands of people to their deaths?

Eichmann leafed through the document casually, smiling his half smile of derision, as if he and Kasztner were sharing a joke at someone else's expense. Suddenly he stopped reading and threw the pages across his desk. "Herr Doktor, do you really believe this nonsense?"[10]

Kasztner said nothing.

"I had thought better of you, Kasztner. Surely you recognize this as another *greuelmärchen* [horror story]. I warned you people to stay clear of horror stories. This is the kind of bullshit that will get your slandering body in front of a military judge. It's treason to spread this kind of nonsense, Kasztner—the kind of treason that would see you and your stupid little bunch hanged!"

But at the end of the tirade he said he now had permission from Berlin for the sample group to leave Hungary. One train, he stipulated, straight from Budapest, across Germany, perhaps to Lisbon.

While the negotiations continued, the gendarmerie continued to gather up the Jews from the countryside. Very few tried to escape. Families stayed together, still imagining they were being resettled in another part of the country. Life would not be easy, but they would survive. Those who had understood that deportation to Germany was inevitable would explain that the Reich was desperately short of workers, that factories were idle, that farmers couldn't gather the wheat come harvest time. And when this madness was over, everyone would come home.

When a couple of young Zionists tried to tell a group of Orthodox Jews in southern Hungary about Auschwitz, they were chased out of town by the angry rabbi. God would never allow such a thing as Auschwitz.[11]

As Allied bombing raids continued, whole streets in Budapest became uninhabitable. The Budapest City Council made plans to move all Jews out of their apartments and into designated buildings so that non-Jews could occupy the space. The Jewish Council's Housing Department was charged with ensuring that Jews left their homes in working order.

Copies of the Auschwitz Protocols had begun to circulate. Stern thought that Horthy's son had given his copy to the Regent. Ottó Komoly had slipped a copy to the Hungarian foreign minister, who was raising questions in parliament about foreign reaction to a film the Germans had made about gendarmes shoving people into boxcars. A member of the council had given a copy of the document to a local priest, who then gave it to Justinian Cardinal Serédi, the head of the Roman Catholic Church in Hungary. Angelo Rotta, the papal nuncio, wrote to the government accusing it of being complicit in the murder of its Jewish subjects. "When old men of over seventy or even eighty are carried off, elderly women, children, the sick, one must ask: What kind of labor can these human beings perform? To the answer that this is an opportunity for Jews to take their families along, I ask: if this is so, such departures would be of one's free will." When the government responded with the formerly effective lies that the deportees were being sent to work in Germany, the old nuncio spoke of his "terrible fear" that innocent blood was being shed against the will of God and, therefore, "His blessing cannot remain on this country."

The message did finally reach Horthy, Stern reported to Komoly and Kasztner. Disregarding all the information he had received, the Regent had remained adamant that the Jews were sent to work camps and that they would not be harmed if they continued to cooperate. Surely, now, he would not ignore the pope's emissary in Hungary. Something, Komoly was sure, would be done.

As a last resort, Kasztner tried to contact Kurt Becher through Otto Klages. The Budapest SD chief had been party to Brand's meetings with Eichmann; Kasztner hoped Klages could be made to understand that tangible evidence of SS goodwill was needed to close the deal in Istanbul. A few hundred people gathered into the Columbus Street buildings would not be enough. Thousands were needed, but, as the days passed, fewer Jews remained in their home countries, and perhaps fewer still were alive in the camps.

Eventually, Becher made the first contact.[12] His adjutant went to the Information Office at Sip Street and requested that Kasztner present himself at the Chorin mansion on Andrássy Avenue. The four-story white stucco building was fronted by a large pillared portico, with wide marble steps leading to the carved oak doors. The front hall was decorated with brass wall lamps, paintings in gilded frames, a long Turkish carpet. The high-ceilinged living room had a long oak bookcase along the wall facing the windows.

Becher stood when Kasztner entered. A broad-shouldered, pale man with a square jaw and light-blue eyes, he seemed to Kasztner every inch the German archetype Hitler had selected to rule the world.

Kasztner tipped his head at the German: "Herr Obersturmbann-führer," he said. He had learned not to stretch out his hand when he met Germans. Even Becher's return nod was a novelty these days. He asked Kasztner to sit and motioned to the narrow, gold-edged Louis Quatorze chair in front of a small, antique side table and offered coffee from the monogrammed silver set in delicate Herendi china cups.

"Herr Obersturmbannführer," Kasztner repeated, still standing.

"For God's sake, Kasztner, will you sit down?" said Becher.

Kasztner sat rather carefully—the chair did not look as though it would support his weight. Becher smiled. "It's stronger than you think," he said. "Those spindly legs have supported bigger asses than yours in centuries past—and will again when this one is over. I expect you know who I am."

Kasztner said yes, he knew.

"Your train," Becher said before long. "There are a few people I will ask you to accommodate. Not many. Maybe fifty."

"My train?" Kasztner stammered. "We are still not sure how many will go . . . or whether it will ever go . . . All he said was that I could make a list of two hundred for Kolozsvár."

"It will go—and there will be about fifteen hundred Jews on board," Becher stated. "I want fifty, well, maybe a hundred seats. I will let you know."

"And Eichmann?" Kasztner asked.

"Don't worry about Eichmann," Becher said, with another easy smile. "Your train will be safe."

The draft memorandum that the Jewish Agency in Istanbul issued on May 27 asserted, without the slightest factual foundation, that the basic agreement was ready. Only a few legal and procedural issues had still to be ironed out. It stated that the Jews accepted Eichmann's offer and the ransom would be paid, if deportations ceased immediately.

Brand asked for additional money for bribes in Hungary and wondered, afterward, whether Menachem Bader, another Agency representative in Istanbul, had agreed too quickly to his request,[13] knowing that he had no chance of assuring success for this mission. Brand's expulsion order had been postponed for a few days, but so had his meeting with Laurence Steinhardt. The American ambassador in Turkey had alerted his State Department to the facts of the blood-for-goods deal and had been told that a special emissary would arrive in a few days to meet Brand.

On the same day, the Hungarian security police arrested Kasztner and Hansi Brand.[14] They were picked up at André Biss's apartment and bundled into police cars, their bodies bent over to hide their faces. They were driven across the river to an interrogation center, an unassuming, white stone building with small rooms and a deep basement where Peter Hain's Hungarian Intelligence men kept prisoners they found particularly interesting. The basement was so far underground that no sound would be heard outside, no matter how loudly the prisoners screamed. For five days, they were kept in their respective cells, each questioned separately. There were, of course, no official charges, but Kasztner guessed from the questions that Hain wanted to know why Joel Brand had gone to Istanbul, on whose orders, and the nature of Kasztner's dealings with the Germans.

The pretext was the discovery of a large number of fake Christian identity papers that a group of Slovak and Polish Jews had been carrying when they were captured at the Romanian border. Early on the first day, Hansi was confronted with the limp body of a printer the Va'ada had paid to produce the papers. The man was barely alive, his fingers crushed and his teeth missing. Two men held him by the shoulders, some distance from their own suits; he had been lying in his own vomit and excrement. Only with the lamp directed at his ravaged face did Hansi recognize him.

Quickly she took responsibility for his actions. She admitted to having paid the man to forge documents, but she denied all knowledge of her husband's whereabouts. She had no idea why the Germans had sent her husband abroad. She knew that if she revealed what Eichmann had referred to as "the state secret," she and her children would be killed. Hansi was badly beaten. The soles of her feet were so raw and swollen that she could neither walk nor stand.

Kasztner, ever the fast talker, suffered only a few minor bruises. In his later retelling of events, he characteristically boasted that he had been freed by a direct phone call from the German plenipotentiary, Edmund Veesenmayer, to Prime Minister Döme Sztójay. What he did not talk about was how he had doubled over in pain when he saw Hansi's bleeding feet and how he had held them in the back of the car that the Germans had demanded they get for the journey home. Nor that, still weeping over what Hansi had endured, he could not speak when Eichmann's man called, demanding a meeting that evening.

When Eichmann heard of her suffering, he paid her the highest compliment he knew: "Mrs. Brand has the courage of a true Aryan."

* * *

By the end of May 217,000 people had been deported from Hungary, a daily average of 12,056, or 3,145 per train. Body searches, in the name of the "preservation of national wealth," continued up to the moment the victims were packed into the rail wagons. Gendarmes in the city of Nagyvárad warned that they would shoot ten Jews for every one who had hidden money or jewelry. A woman who had gone into labor was thrown in with more than eighty people standing, packed tightly, in the sweltering heat. Near the Hungarian border, gendarmes provided a last chance for Jews to leave their belongings on Hungarian soil, offering buckets of water in return for jewelry. "The guards told us," one woman remembered, "we would not need anything where we were going, so why not leave it for the people in our homeland rather than let the Germans take it in Auschwitz."[15] Most of the boxcars were opened at the Slovak border, the corpses removed, and those who had gone mad were shot.

The trains rolled through the countryside toward Auschwitz. Sometimes a piece of paper thrown out of a train, bearing a name, a town, a district, betrayed where the people had come from. Some begged that relatives be told of their fate.

All this was kept out of the newspapers. Neither of the large-circulation dailies in Budapest reported on the deportations; nor did the Sonderkommando-censored Jewish newspaper. There were more dire warnings about "illegal propaganda activities"—the horrors in the countryside were forbidden from being reported to the foreign press still in Budapest.

Family and friends had started receiving postcards from Waldsee, where the deported claimed they were well and healthy, though working hard. But all the cards used almost exactly the same wording, and soon everyone realized that the text had been dictated. Most of the senders, Komoly said, would have been murdered before the cards were posted from the so-called labor camp.

When Kasztner implored Otto Hunsche to ease the suffering of the people on the trains, Hunsche warned him to stop spreading rumors again. However, he agreed to look into the matter.

On June 1, at a short meeting with Kasztner and Hansi Brand, Eichmann announced that if he did not hear from Joel within three days, "the deal he had offered would be off."

Joel Brand was interviewed in Istanbul by a couple of minor American functionaries who recommended that the negotiations with the Nazis be kept going.[16] They were concerned, however, that the undertaking for the trucks to be used only on the Eastern Front meant that the Germans were testing British/American interest in betraying the Soviets. The fact that Brand had been accompanied by Bandi Grosz cast further suspicion on the motives behind his journey.

Meanwhile, Grosz continued to have long, secret meetings, and Brand began to suspect he had a secondary agenda. Grosz urged Brand to travel with him to Aleppo, in British-controlled Syria. "We will get in direct touch with the Allies there," he told him. Grosz saw no point in further talks with the Jewish Agency's local people.[17] Moreover, he thought, the British were rightly suspicious that Jewish interests might not coincide with their own, and that the Jews would do anything, even betray an ally, to save their own people. While welcoming a Polish force, and the Free French forces, Czechs, and Romanians, the British had not been enthusiastic about creating a Jewish battalion, which, they reasoned, could be used in Palestine as well as in Europe.

While at the hotel, Grosz was visited alternately by his wife and his mistress. His wife, Brand discovered, had not found it difficult to obtain an exit visa for Turkey, nor did she have problems with the Turkish officials. What he found puzzling was how a man as ugly as Grosz could maintain both a wife and a mistress and how he paid for two lodgings. And while Brand waited, Grosz attended meetings and returned shuffling stacks of papers. He held long discussions with various Turkish businessmen, who all assured him that his interests were being safeguarded. He had already obtained a travel permit from the British, and told Brand that he had excellent relations with both the English and the American attachés, and that he had been advised to travel to Syria. Kasztner had warned Brand about the British, and Eichmann had told him to stay with Grosz. Brand was hoping that Moshe Shertok, the political leader of the Jewish Agency, would arrive soon from Palestine and decide what he should do.

Brand feared that, in spite of his best efforts, Jewish representatives in Istanbul remained unimpressed with the importance of his mission. Delegates of the various political factions were fighting over the best way to assist illegal immigrants, how far they could go to defy the "Mandatory Power" (the British presence in Palestine), and how to foment Jewish military resistance in Hungary. They didn't seem to be paying much attention to his pleas that illegal immigration could save only a few, whereas he was there in the interests of a million Jews, or to his caution that developing a strategy for military resistance in Hungary would take longer than whatever time they had left. "Five hundred Jews are sent into the gas chambers every hour!" he kept repeating. He was hysterical, crying in his hotel room. Teddy Kollek, a member of the Jewish Agency's Political

Department, recalled, "It was impossible to explain to Brand how helpless we were."[18] Brand did not understand the international context, Kollek said, no matter how hard everyone tried to tell him about the various preoccupations of the British and the Americans, their fear that the Soviets might withdraw from the war, and how low the Jews ranked on the Allies' own agendas. Venia Pomerantz wrote to Shertok that he feared Brand had become suicidal. "He did not understand that our very presence in Turkey was tenuous . . . that our ability to deliver was weak."[19]

The American emissary's visit was postponed, and then there seemed to be problems with Shertok's visa application.

Ten days after their arrival in Istanbul, Grosz decided to level with Brand and tell him what his own mission had been. The Nazis, he said, knew they had lost the war. Himmler's men wanted to start conversations with the Allies. Did Brand seriously think that Eichmann would let a million Jews go? "The whole Jewish business is just a blind."[20]

Brand did not believe him.

On June 1, Grosz left for Syria. That afternoon, Brand was informed that Shertok had not been able to obtain a visa from the Turks. Brand would have to travel to Syria, where Shertok would have no problems with a visa. Worse, Chaim Barlas told Brand that British delegates would be present at his meeting with Shertok.

Brand tried to reason with Barlas: if he did not return to Budapest with a concrete agreement now, his mission would be lost. Eichmann's machinery would continue its murderous rampage. All he needed was the draft agreement, and he was sure he could hold off further deportations.

By June 3, the number of Jews deported from Hungary reached 253,389.[21] The Jewish Council in Budapest rushed to whatever meetings they could arrange with members of parliament and their underlings. They were relieved to listen to the usual lies about Jews being Communist sympathizers and their removal being temporary. When news of deportations from Zone III reached the council, with a unanimous vote they decided not to tell the membership in Budapest. They feared that the news would create panic, and that panic could result in a massacre. They had to play for time and pray that the Allies would reach Hungary soon.

Minutes of Hungarian cabinet meetings for the months of the German occupation repeat the phrase "the Germans demand . . . the cabinet agrees," as if each German demand was viewed as an order. Prime Minister Sztójay would not allow discussion of arrests by the Gestapo, even when those arrested were members of parliament. Meanwhile, specialists in the government's Jewish Affairs Office had started to draft new explanations for coming "operations," such as the discovery of explosives in Jewish clubs or synagogues.[22] Edmund Veesenmayer, the Reich plenipotentiary, responded that he did not deem it necessary to invent new reasons for the actions against the Jews.

Joel Brand boarded a train to Syria with Ehud Avriel of the Jewish Agency, who, he discovered in conversation, had been a Viennese youth leader before landing in Palestine and joining the Mossad Le'Aliya Bet—the Department of "B" Immigration, or illegal immigration to Palestine, established in 1938.[22] Avriel had himself been in touch with Eichmann to arrange for ships during the years when Jews could still escape from Europe.[23] He was therefore not surprised to learn of Brand's ransom arrangement. He had negotiated such deals in the past, except that the price was lower then and the proposed outcome more credible.[24]

Two men stopped Brand at the Ankara station as he was walking out of the men's washroom. They told him they were Jewish Revisionists[25] and were convinced that Moshe Shertok and his party, the Mapai, would only betray him. They warned Brand that he would be arrested by the British once he reached Aleppo. They were zealots, Brand thought, crazed revolutionaries. He had met their chief, Vladimir Jabotinsky, in Istanbul. The man had been dismissive of all but his own efforts to save Jews. The British had to be forced to leave Palestine, he said. It was the only hope that Jews could be offered—

a safe haven. His visceral hatred of the British was supported by long explanations, as were his fears of the Mapai-controlled Jewish Agency's complicity with the British. Brand could no longer indulge in such suspicions: the British were, after all, fighting the Germans. However misguided their policies in Palestine, he reasoned, they were, at least, on the right side in this war.

CHAPTER 14

A Game of Roulette
for Human Lives

*If Eichmann could not be forced to back down here and now, then
the Va'ada had put its chips on the wrong number in this game for
human lives and was as much of a loser as so many others had
been in occupied Europe. The loser in this game could then be
called a traitor.*

Rezső Kasztner, *Der Kasztner-Bericht*

Rome fell to the Allies on June 5. The next day, Allied troops
landed on the beaches of Normandy. The final phase of the
Western Front had finally opened.

On June 5, not having heard from Kurt Becher, Rezső Kasztner
went to see Otto Hunsche at the ss offices at the Majestic. Again, he
lodged a complaint with as much formality as he could muster: hundreds of Jews were dying in the sealed boxcars, he stated, and thousands were being gassed shortly after they arrived in
Auschwitz-Birkenau. It would be impossible for the Germans to
make any kind of deal with the Allies if they knew what had been
going on in Hungary.

Hunsche said he had looked into the matter and, at most, sixty persons had died in each transport. That was not a large number, considering the circumstances. As for Auschwitz, the talk was all rumors. He knew of no such place.

On that same day, Florian Manoliou, a Romanian businessman, arrived in Budapest with two hundred Salvadoran *schutzpässe*, or immigration papers, and an urgent inquiry about what had happened to the Jews of Transylvania. He had been sent by George Mandel-Mantello, a Romanian refugee from Transylvania, whose parents had remained behind in Bistrita when he left the country before the borders closed.[1] Since then, Mandel-Mantello had acquired Salvadoran citizenship and a posting as consul in Switzerland. He now had access to citizenship papers and was eager to help his parents and their friends.

Manoliou's initial contact was Kasztner, and found him at Columbus Street, in a hastily assembled barrack outside the Wechselmann Institute. Kasztner had nothing but dire news. All the transports from Bistrita had gone across the Slovak border on their way to Auschwitz. He told Manoliou what Auschwitz meant for most people. Mindful of Eichmann's warnings, Kasztner did not mention the list.

Manoliou's return journey to Bistrita confirmed Kasztner's bone-jarring information. The Jewish community was no longer in the city; many of the members had been deported—no one knew where—and the rest were in ghettos, completely sealed off from any communication.

Back in Budapest, Manoliou called on Carl Lutz at the former American embassy to give him the schutzpässe. Though too late for his friend's parents, they could at least save others.

Lutz realized that he now had the opportunity he had been seeking: Manoliou could take the Auschwitz Protocols out of Hungary.[2] The horrific details would shock world leaders into immediate action. Auschwitz could be destroyed, the whole murder apparatus stopped. Lutz's idea was that Manoliou would act as courier for the Jewish Agency; they would disguise the document as a regular weekly communication. Lutz implored Moshe Krausz to write a note with the Vrba-Wetzler report. As the Jewish Agency's official representative in Hungary, Krausz was expected to send reports out of the country. The only risk he took was that this particular report would be carried by Manoliou. Lutz could not put his own signature to the covering letter; he would be recalled if the Germans found the Auschwitz Protocols.

Krausz, ever the stickler for formalities, resisted. He could not send anything to a Salvadoran Consulate, because he had not been authorized to deal with foreign governments. Krausz was not going to jeopardize his own job. When Lutz reminded him that he had personally benefited from Lutz himself breaking the rules and giving him and his family refuge, Krausz insisted that was a different matter. The consul had good reasons to house the Agency's representative.

In the end, Krausz agreed he would address Chaim Posner of the Jewish Agency's Palestine Office in Switzerland, absolving him of blame when Manoliou delivered the package to the Salvadoran Consul.

Within days, Mandel-Mantello sent copies to all the major newspapers in Switzerland, the United Kingdom, and the United States. Now, finally, the world learned about Auschwitz.

Unfortunately, news of the annihilation of European Jewry had to share center stage with other war news. The BBC broadcast some sections of Alfréd Wetzler and Rudolf Vrba's report, but the commentators construed much of it as propaganda, intended to vilify the enemy. Swiss and Swedish papers reported on the gas chambers amid day-to-day coverage of the war in Europe. The Jewish press in Palestine treated the extermination of Hungarian Jews with silence, whether because of British censorship or policies imposed by the Zionist leadership, Kasztner did not know. What he did know was that time was running out.

On June 9 Eichmann declared that, if he did not receive final word from Istanbul within three days, he would "let the mills work in Auschwitz."[3]

Joel Brand was arrested by the British even before he stepped off the train in Aleppo on June 6. He was escorted to their well-appointed barracks, where they assured him the food would be to his liking. For two days, he was questioned, unaware that the British had already reviewed Eichmann's proposition at a war cabinet meeting a week earlier. Moving a million Jews across Europe and into Spain would mean temporarily stopping the war. Such a prospect would be unpalatable to the British high command. The British high commissioner for Palestine, Sir Harold MacMichael, asked the obvious questions: Why would the Nazis propose a plan to save Jews? And why would they ask for trucks, knowing that trucks were war materials and that no goods could be shipped to the Germans in the middle of the war? However, the British had not yet discussed the matter with the Americans, and they needed them onside for any decision potentially affecting a million lives. No matter what the Nazi ploy, the American War Refugee Board was openly in favor of negotiations.[4]

Moshe Shertok arrived in Syria from Palestine with an entourage of four intelligence officers, including the head of the Mossad, by then a branch of the Haganah. He questioned Joel for ten hours in the presence of both his own men and four British agents. Brand became increasingly distraught. He stressed that time was being wasted, that the failure of his mission would mean the annihilation of Hungarian Jews, including his wife and children, who were being held by the ss as surety against his return. "Do you know, Mr. Shertok," he asked, "that while you and I have been locked in this room, at least twelve thousand of our people have been murdered?" He broke down and cried when Shertok told him the British might not let him return to Budapest.

Shertok, convinced that Brand was not a spy (though perhaps an unwitting pawn in a German plot) and that the slender thread of his strange deal might be the last chance to save what was left of Europe's Jews, recommended to the British that a neutral nation be used to enter into discussions with the ss. He urged that Brand be sent back to Hungary with some sort of promise that would never be met. Then he returned to Jerusalem to put the matter before the Executive Committee of the Jewish Agency. He said that, of all institutions, the Jewish Agency must keep the door open to trading goods for lives, no matter how offensive the prospect. "If there is even one chance in a million," he said, "we must take it."[5]

On June 7 Chaim Weizmann met Britain's foreign secretary, Anthony Eden, and asked him not to reject the German proposal out of hand. In return, he promised that the Agency would do nothing on its own without informing the British government.[6]

Contrary to Shertok's recommendation, Brand was taken to Cairo by the British and confined to a large furnished room in a prison for finer gentlemen. He was allowed out for lunches, given wine and Arab sweets, provided with tea and biscuits, but he was not allowed to leave the country. During the numerous interrogations that followed, he was asked hundreds of questions about the ss in Hungary, about the various former Abwehr and sd agents and the Hungarian intelligence network, about troop movements and fortifications, but nothing about the essence of his mission. The goods-for-blood deal had been referred to a higher authority. To his proposition that just the appearance of negotiations would keep the Jews alive, a British officer responded that His Majesty's government could not make promises it had no intention of keeping.

A British envoy told Brand that, even if the Germans were negotiating in good faith, "what in the world would we do with a million Jews?" They could not be allowed into Palestine in contravention of the agreement with the Arabs to limit immigration. There was no more room for refugees in Britain, which could barely feed its own people and its armed forces. America, while generally supportive, had not offered to lift its immigration bar. The British and the Americans had come up with the harebrained notion that they could, together, examine the possibility of accommodating these Jews on the Iberian Peninsula.[7] The Swedes, the Swiss, and the South Americans had produced their own acceptable numbers, but nowhere could you settle a million impoverished souls.

After several days of meetings in London, the Foreign Office concluded that Joel Brand's whole mission was a crude Nazi ploy. When Anthony Eden saw Shertok and Weizmann about the proposals, he told them there was no effective action the British could take. In

Washington, however, John Pehle, director of the War Refugee Board,[8] informed the secretary of the treasury, Henry Morgenthau Jr., that the Brand proposals were of less importance than the chance to save lives by talking, and that talking with the ss was what the War Refugee Board should do.

*   *   *

When it seemed clear in Budapest that Joel's mission had been a failure, only Hansi managed to remain calm. Rezső wept like a child. She cradled his head in her arms and kept repeating that they could not give up. He had to tell Adolf Eichmann again that Eichmann's own actions were making the trade impractical. They had to pretend that the Joint was still waiting for proof that the ss was serious; that the documents would not be delivered until World Jewry was satisfied.

One afternoon, in the bar of the Gellért Hotel, Dieter Wisliceny told Kasztner that Eichmann had been opposed to the deal all along. It hadn't been his idea. It was Himmler's. "Eichmann is frustrated that he can't carry out his mission as he planned. He has been slowed down, unnecessarily. His idea is to carry on with the deportations till not a single Jew is left in Hungary. Or didn't you know that?"

"But what about Brand's mission?"

"Oh, that," Wisliceny laughed. "Eichmann's one regret is that this one Jew has escaped him. He doesn't expect to see Brand again."[9]

Kasztner decided not to tell Hansi. He continued to send increasingly furious cables to the Jewish Agency in Istanbul and the Joint in Switzerland.

In Kolozsvár, eighteen thousand people were crammed into the tight space of the brickworks ghetto. Conditions had deteriorated with the summer heat, the lack of washing facilities, the overflowing latrines, and the sense of hopelessness. The Hungarian gendarmerie's Lieutenant Colonel László Ferenczy, dissatisfied with the thoroughness of body searches, had ordered the hiring of obstetricians and nurses to ensure that women could not hide jewelry or money. Gendarmes used pliers to wrench tight-fitting wedding rings from fingers.

József Fischer, still head of the Jewish Council in Kolozsvár, was gravely ill and barely aware of the terrible task he had been asked to perform: making changes to a preliminary list for the "Kasztner train," as it had started to be called. As Dieter Wisliceny and Hermann Krumey had insisted, the list would have to feature the names of those who could, conceivably, have been part of a Jewish conspiracy. Although children would be allowed, they could not form the majority of the names. Kasztner was given leave to talk on the phone with his father-in-law, but the list had to originate in Budapest and purportedly be taken to Kolozsvár by the ss.

The first couple of hundred names (no one is sure how many) were selected by Sigmund Leb, a member of Kolozsvár's Orthodox congregation, who had happened to be in Budapest when the Germans marched in; he had not been able to return home. The list was changed several times to include Zionist leaders, intellectuals, former parliamentarians, doctors, Polish refugees, orphans, widows, and some members of Rezső's and Bogyó's families. Because Fischer was ill, the young sergeant delegated by Krumey to accompany Kasztner to Kolozsvár delivered the list to the Jewish Council in that city. There it was changed by local Jewish leaders, by several Hungarian city officials who favored a few among those to be deported, and by ss men who had been bribed. It ended up with 388 names, including those of Kasztner's mother and older brother as well as several members of the Fischer family.

Fischer was still in the Jewish Hospital, a building near the ghetto that the authorities had permitted to operate until the last transport was ready to leave. In the tight space of the brickworks, with part walls on the only buildings and no privacy, the news of the list traveled swiftly. There were fierce arguments about whom to exclude and include and why. Some of those chosen refused to go, suspicious that occupants of a special train would be the first to be massacred. Some did not want to live in Palestine—they planned to return home once the war was over. Others still believed in the myth of a safe place in western Hungary where everyone would work. A few doctors had volunteered to be on the first trains, choosing to believe they would be needed where the trains went.[10]

Many who were not on the list clamored to be included, and those who survived Auschwitz remembered the ghastly scenes of begging and vituperations, of threats and humiliations. They would never forgive.

Fischer had no power to help anyone now. The ghetto granted no recognition to his past achievements. His local council tried to keep order, distributed food and clothing from the Aid and Rescue Committee, and attempted to delay the deportations. But by June 8, the only people left in the ghetto were those few who had been selected.

An ordinary cattle train carrying the 388 people left Kolozsvár on June 10.

They arrived at Columbus Street in Budapest starved, beaten, and ill, dressed in rags. The first priority was food and clothing, milk for the children, medicines for the sick. Because Jewish doctors had been denied their right to practice, there was no shortage of specialists. Over a four-day period, a group of Jewish builders had erected five wooden barracks and sanitation facilities in the large courtyard behind the Wechselmann Institute. A twenty-five-bed hospital had been set up in one of the barracks.[11]

There were bunk beds, simple tables, and makeshift shelving. Men and women were in separate buildings but shared the kitchen, and the food, prepared by the inmates, was tasty and plentiful. The institute's basement gymnasium had also been transformed into sleeping quarters.

The buildings were protected by five ss guards, ordered to behave with courtesy toward their charges. Kasztner observed that they followed these orders with the same exacting attention they would have accorded orders to machine-gun everybody and bury the corpses in lime.

The Wechselmann Institute was a massive, red brick building with dormer windows, an elaborate facade, decorative fencing, a high-ceilinged foyer with a brass bas-relief commemorating the architect and philanthropist Dr. Ignaz Wechselmann's efforts to help the deaf, the dumb, and the blind. It was in a quiet, tree-lined neighborhood. When Hansi Brand arrived with armloads of clothes and toys for the children, its halls were filled with noisy, anxious people trying to find a place for themselves. She and Kasztner designated a room in one of the barracks as an office, and Kasztner's secretary moved there from Sip Street.

Word had spread in Budapest about a train for Jews who could leave this hell and go to Palestine. At the Va'ada office in the Jewish Community Center on Sip Street, frantic people waited for hours, all day, even overnight, for a chance to see Rezső Kasztner, Ernő Szilágyi, or Ottó Komoly. Mothers with children, women whose husbands had gone for labor service and disappeared, all waited to explain why they had to be on the train to carry them toward Palestine. They begged as Kasztner had begged Eichmann; they promised money and jewelry, as he had promised bribes to the ss. Initially, "one hundred spots on the transport had to be offered to those people who could supply the most valuables and money," Kasztner recalled later. The trade-off to accommodate the German demands was the only way the Jewish planners could include those who had nothing left— the widows, the rabbis, community leaders, the young Poles and Slovaks who had been risking their lives at border crossings, and those who had worked for the Zionist cause without compensation. "Discussions with applicants for the 'spots for sale' were held under the leadership of Komoly," Kasztner said. "Unfortunately most Hungarian Jews had obeyed the law and turned their wealth over to the government months ago. That's why we had to raise the number of the 'paying' to 150. In the truest sense of the word, a battle was waged over those places."

One survivor remembers Kasztner asking her mother, wife of a former textile merchant from Kolozsvár, whether she could still lay her hands on a few valuables. A gentile friend then made the dangerous journey from Transylvania to Budapest, carrying a bag with jewelry and a set of silver cutlery. Had she been caught, she would have been imprisoned; had she confessed to transporting Jewish valuables, she would have been executed.

Bogyó, anxious about her father's health and suffering from the heat, the airlessness and loneliness, decided to join her family at the Wechselmann Institute. Since the German occupation, she had barely seen her husband. Even during the few hours when Jews were allowed out into the streets, she was too frightened to leave the Biss's apartment. Rezső rarely returned even at night. She knew he was with Hansi and that their relationship had become a love affair, but now was not the time to deal with it. She had wanted children, but Rezső insisted that no child of his should be born in a place ruled by the Nazis. Unbeknownst to him, she had endured a barely medicated abortion in an illegal Jewish clinic.[12] When the war was over and the world returned to sanity, Bogyó hoped to reclaim her husband and have children and a real home.

Hansi and Rezső worked together every day. They spent their evenings in the small apartment Hansi had rented with fake Christian papers. She visited her boys, but did not dare take them back there. If Joel didn't produce what Eichmann wanted, she was sure he would destroy them.

By now Kasztner was lighting one cigarette from the butt of another, slouching forward, blowing smoke at the Germans when he met with them, acting as though he had equal authority and could match Eichmann, "the Master," in power. He had taken to pacing, like Eichmann, with a furious stride, shouting, gesticulating in frustration. During the night Rezső and Hansi curled up together, to feel alive. His need for her had become the sustaining force of his life.

CHAPTER 15

Rolling the Dice

To anyone who was not there, most of these events will seem to be
incomprehensible, paradoxical, unbelievable. We lived in insane
times. Even to us, everything that happened remains impossible to
grasp. In those times, the human mind could not apply normal
rules of logic.

Rezső Kasztner, "A Nagy Embervásár"[1]

On June 16, both Rezső Kasztner and Hansi Brand were summoned to the Majestic Hotel. The guards were now so used to seeing Kasztner that they just waved them in without a search. Eichmann kept them waiting outside his office while members of his staff entered and left carrying files, cowed by Eichmann's shouting and swearing. The Master, one of his aides informed Kasztner, was in a bad mood again. It had been another late night. He had not had time to shave or bathe today because the party he attended the previous evening had still been going when he left at 6 AM.

When Hermann Krumey finally let them into the room, Kasztner was surprised to again see Kurt Becher with his back to Eichmann, gazing out the window. In the garden the waiters were serving breakfast. Eichmann, pasty-faced, with dark shadows under his eyes, screamed that he had had enough of the whole stupid exchange idea, that the Americans, the British, and the Jews had taken him for a fool, that Germany was not about to feed hundreds of thousands of *untermenschen* while they, on the other side of the Atlantic Ocean, were thinking things over.

"It is my duty to ask you," Kasztner asked, "what happens if Istanbul comes to an agreement? If you let the Hungarian Jews be gassed in Auschwitz, where will you get the merchandise to trade for the trucks?"[2]

"You're telling *greuelmärchen*, again, Kasztner. Auschwitz is like all the camps in the General Government." Another short burst of laughter. "Only the food is better. And don't worry about where we find extra Jews. We have children between twelve and fourteen. We have some Polish Jews. We have some in Theresienstadt [concentration camp]. And there are your sample Jews. Didn't I already agree to give you six hundred?"

"Don't you think, Lieutenant Colonel," Kasztner asked, "that it would be wise to keep a large number of Jews—say, 100,000—in the country in the event of a deal with the Jewish Agency?"

Kasztner was determined to steer the conversation, pull the one card from the deck that would make his opponent change his game. He reminded Eichmann that not so long ago Hitler himself had been willing to allow Jewish emigration to Palestine or to neutral countries, that the exchange deal would fit with the original National Socialist policies that had been altered rather abruptly to please an uncertain ally, the Arabs. In the past, they had not proved themselves to be reliable in any situation.

Kasztner's ploy worked. "I, personally, emigrated about a quarter of a million of them," Eichmann said, proudly. "A great deal for everybody, except the Mufti. And now he may be the best friend we have down there. Guest of the Führer."

Kasztner saw his chance. He offered the equivalent of five million Swiss francs as down payment against the eventual Istanbul deal in jewelry, foreign currency, and Hungarian pengős. He called this a gesture. Not the full amount the Germans could expect from the Jewish Agency, the War Refugee Board, and the Joint, no. Just a gesture. In exchange, he asked only for those 100,000 lives, calling that an advance, too. The money, Kasztner said, could be used to feed those already in ghettos but not yet in Auschwitz.

"I am not interested in money!" Eichmann shouted. "I sent that *dummkopf* to Turkey for trucks, Kasztner."

But Kasztner could see that he had Becher's attention. The cavalryman had turned when he mentioned five million Swiss francs and now appeared to be studying one of the newly installed paintings, an indifferent watercolor of little girls in dirndl dresses.

Kasztner said he and World Jewry would pay such a price—indeed, they were ready right now to do so. All they needed was a show of goodwill, a sign that Eichmann's promises were going to be kept. Not by him—*selbstverständlich*, naturally, they knew Eichmann would keep his promises—but there were others who could interfere with his orders.

"You look tired, Mr. Kasztner," Eichmann said, feigning sympathy. "Perhaps we should send you for a slow cure in Theresienstadt. Or would you prefer a fast cure in Auschwitz?"

Undaunted, Kasztner argued that the world knew about Auschwitz now. "If you drive the Hungarian Jews into gas chambers, what are you going to trade?" he repeated.

Then Hansi joined the conversation and took it in a different direction. "You were talking about the hundreds of thousands of Jews who still needed to be fed, Herr Obersturmbannführer. We could relieve you of the problem. While we wait."

"Well," Eichmann said, at last, "I may be able to put another thirty thousand on ice, while we wait for your husband."

They couldn't believe what they had just heard. Eichmann was ready to exempt another thirty thousand people from the deportations. Perhaps there had been a message from the British or the Americans. Perhaps there really was some higher authority in Germany, as Kasztner came to believe, someone above Eichmann who had decided the killings would end.

Once back at their Columbus Street office, Kasztner sent another cable to Switzerland, asking for money and for the agreement. Within an hour one of Eichmann's junior officers came running in. "Obersturmbannführer Eichmann wants to see you. Now." The sand-colored Mercedes was waiting outside the gates to carry Kasztner back up Swabian Hill. This time Eichmann was alone.

"What has Becher told you?" Eichmann asked as soon as he saw Kasztner.

"Nothing, Herr Obersturmbannführer," Kasztner replied. "Nothing."

"Has he got his fingers into our deal?" Eichmann demanded to know. He stopped with his face a few inches from Kasztner's. "The sample train is mine. Or it's nobody's and going nowhere."

"No," Kasztner lied. "He has not spoken to me about the train."

His glasses, he noticed when he was walking down Swabian Hill, had Eichmann's spit on them.

A few days later, Krumey went to see Kasztner. If the Rescue Committee assumed responsibility for food and clothing, medications, and all unforeseen incidentals, the Sonderkommando was ready to ship thirty thousand Jews to work in Austria. "They will be divided into groups and sent where they are most needed," Krumey said. "We'll keep them in families. The able-bodied will work."[3]

Krumey took some credit for the deal. He said he had reasoned with the Gestapo that killing all the Jews would be more expensive than keeping them alive. "And you'll remember this when the time comes, won't you, Kasztner?" he asked.[4] It was the first time Kasztner had heard one of Eichmann's men admit that their war would be lost. He did not acknowledge what Krumey said.

"Of course, we'll compensate for all the expenses," Kasztner said. He watched Krumey's clouded glasses—it was another warm, humid day. "A deposit of 100,000 pengős." He wanted to sound like a businessman, as if this were a piece of business. "But we want some from the provinces for this and for the transport to Spain or Portugal."

"You'll have to hurry, then, Kasztner. There aren't so many left in the provinces. And it won't be cheap," Krumey added. "But not the whole five million francs? And what does that matter to you people? It's only money." He chuckled. "Why not come to the casino tonight, Kasztner? If it's still standing, you'll be my guest."

On his way to the guarded gate at the Columbus Street camp, Krumey had encountered Hansi hurrying, as always, now with a bundle of children's clothes in her arms. One of her sons was holding on to her skirt, and the other trailed behind. Despite her misgivings, she had moved them to the Wechselmann Institute compound to reassure those who doubted Kasztner's deal with the ss.

Krumey stopped her, smiled, and stretched out his hand, "Frau Brand," he said, with impeccable politeness. All around them, she thought, people were watching, as if the scene had been ordered from a theatrical troupe. She transferred the bundle to her hip and shook the Nazi's hand. Later, she remembered: "I couldn't eat that day or the next. I scrubbed my right hand till the skin turned red. Oh yes, by then he knew he would be charged when the war ended. He was going to need us."[5]

Kasztner went to see Samuel Stern again. "In principle, we have an agreement," he said. "It's thirty thousand people, and I think we can make it fifteen thousand from the provinces and fifteen thousand from Budapest. All those who can work will work; the others won't have to."

"What did you promise them this time?" Stern asked, wearily. He had shrunk into an ailing old man, bent over the edge of his desk for support. Kasztner wondered how long it would be before Stern collapsed under the weight of all he had to endure.

"They never tell you exactly," Kasztner replied, "but they will accept 100,000 pengős on deposit. And perhaps only two million Swiss francs later. All on deposit against the Brand deal."[6]

"That's what they asked for?"

"No. Not exactly. It's the number I guessed. I had offered five million francs for 100,000 lives."

Stern sighed. "Why?"

Kasztner looked out the window at the bare, grimy bricks of the courtyard. The sun lit up a corner where someone had hung a small basket of blue flowers, now withered. Perhaps the woman who had tended them had been dragged away to the Sárvár prison, or Kistarcsa, or was already on her way to Auschwitz-Birkenau. "Because, Herr Hofrat, it was the best I could do. And we have to supply everything: medicines, baby food, blankets if—God forbid— winter comes and we are still waiting . . ."

Stern nodded.

Kasztner took his hat and bowed slightly, respectfully, as he left the old man's office. For the first time since they had met, they understood each other.

By June 16 the Jews of Zone III had all been transported to Auschwitz. The gendarmerie's Lieutenant Colonel László Ferenczy reported the number to state secretaries Baky and Endre as 51,829. By June 18, when the Russian ambassador to the United States visited the White House to protest any possible deal with the Germans, whatever the nature and origins of Joel Brand's mission, most of them had been murdered.

On June 23, when the ghettoization of Zone IV, southeastern Hungary, was complete, the Jewish Council was confronted by a delegation made up of labor servicemen and relatives of people in ghettos. A young physician gave an emotional speech accusing the council of not dealing with the emergency. "Don't you see, don't you want to understand, that our fathers, mothers, and brothers are crammed into freight trains by gendarmes' bayonets, eighty or more in a boxcar, and they are taken to their extermination? Can one tolerate this further, is it possible to be satisfied with petitions and servile requests . . . ? We must shout to the whole world that they are murdering us. We have to resist and stop this cowardly submission."[7]

Seemingly unshaken, Stern responded that the council was doing all it could under the circumstances. He and the other council members were in touch with all the government ministries and church officials. That very day, the cabinet was meeting to review complaints from the Jewish Council. Unfortunately, the Germans were in command. Resistance, he said, would accomplish immediate reprisals.

"It's not what people know or don't know," Hansi said to Rezső when she heard about Stern's response. "The question is what do they wish to know. It is easier to sleep at night if you do not believe in Auschwitz-Birkenau. It is easier for Samuel Stern to believe that Jews are somewhere in a work camp than to admit that they are being murdered by the thousands, and there is nothing, absolutely nothing we—any of us—can do about it."[8]

The young doctor, in protest and despair, committed suicide.

* * *

The Va'ada had been trying to send food to the prisoners in the Zone IV ghettos, but everything was confiscated by the guards or the self-declared Arrow Cross bands even before it reached the gates. The gendarmes had refined their methods of extracting the last vestiges of wealth, the last pieces of paper identifying each person as a person. The first two trains left Zone IV on June 25; some of the cars carried no water and most of them no food. The sorting of new arrivals at Auschwitz-Birkenau had sped up, and fewer people were selected for work. Despite continued whispered warnings by the Jewish kapos, mothers continued to cling to their children. No mothers with babies or toddlers, no children under the age of twelve survived the selection.

Krumey granted the Va'ada two days to compile its lists of the thirty thousand Jews "on ice." The Rescue Committee was still working on lists for Kasztner's train, which would travel through Austria to Germany, France, and Spain or Portugal, from where its passengers would travel on to Palestine. The Va'ada had to balance those who could afford to pay against those who had worked hard for others, the young who would be useful in a new country, Zionists who already had their Palestine permits, refugees, and Hasidic Jews who had been snatched from the ghettos by young religious halutzim. Once it was known that Baron Freudiger had a hand in the selections, there were desperate scenes in the courtyards of the Orthodox synagogue. Freudiger felt he had to fight for every place on the train and that the Va'ada resented even his modest allocation of sixty Orthodox Jews, though the committee relied on him to help raise the funds for the ss.[9] At the Emigration Department in the former American embassy, Moshe Krausz was busily writing out each permit himself.

Dozens of people now were working on the lists of families for the train. Kasztner, Ernő Szilágyi, Ottó Komoly, and André Biss—the latter had become more involved in rescue work after Joel Brand left—decided that except for a few people, perhaps a hundred, who were known for helping other Jews in the area, they would leave the lists to the local councils. Szilágyi wrote them letters asking that they select large families with many young children, especially families of labor service men and prominent Jews, both religious and secular.[10] More than one hundred of the "prominents" were given dispensations by the ss to go to Columbus Street, where they would join the group to be sent to Palestine.

At the Columbus Street camp, there was relative calm. Each day more people arrived, and they were admitted once their names were ticked on the list at the gate by a German in uniform. Visitors were allowed, and salami, liver pâté, or even the occasional plucked chicken were passed in through the gates. The guards seemed indifferent to the comings and goings—their task appeared to be to protect those within from outside danger, rather than to forbid contact with those outside. The Va'ada set up a workshop with sewing machines, obtained wool and cotton fabric for clothes, organized a kitchen and a medical center, and provided Hebrew language courses and agricultural lessons as preparation for new lives in Palestine. If the Germans noticed that the numbers in the camp had swelled beyond the previously agreed limits, they did not protest.

On June 20, Kasztner and Szilágyi paid the advance for the passengers on the Kasztner train: three huge suitcases full of various currencies, jewelry, precious stones, share certificates of foreign companies, gold bars, Napoleon coins, silver, and other assorted valuables.[11] Stern, Freudiger, and Szilágyi had sold 150 seats on the train to wealthy Jews at a price much higher than Eichmann's suggested $1,000 per person. In each instance, they had to judge how much they thought the person had hidden. Some paid as much as $5,000, others $1,500. From the beginning, the plan had been for the wealthy Jews to pay for those who were selected on the basis of other pressing reasons. Wisliceny had extended the numbers traveling to twelve hundred by including family members of the original six hundred. The Va'ada was debating whether toddlers should carry a price and at what stage children should be charged at the going rate.

To this day, the exact value of the bribe to the Germans is impossible to determine. Each person involved with the payment remembered the valuation differently, especially as the currencies of the day fluctuated wildly, the price of gold was erratic, jewelry is always difficult to evaluate objectively, and the Va'ada had every reason to estimate the payment high while the ss wished to keep it low.

Becher's select group, which he had decided would be fifty wealthy Jews who had compensated him for various privileges since he arrived in Budapest, paid about $25,000 directly to Becher for his "protection" and nothing to the Va'ada.[12] Becher, much against Eichmann's wishes, had somehow inserted himself into the final stages of the negotiations. Hansi knew that Becher had gained the upper hand, though she had no idea how, and that Eichmann's threats about canceling the train from Columbus Street were now only a game. Somebody else above both of the lieutenant colonels stationed in Budapest was pulling the strings.

On June 20, a junior adjutant named Argermayer had appeared at the gates of the Szeged ghetto in Zone IV, with a letter to the local Jewish Council from Szilágyi in Budapest, asking them to select three thousand Jews for special labor service in Austria, to choose families with children, especially the families of those in labor service.[13] By the time they got into the designated boxcars, the Szeged group "on ice" was almost six thousand people, according to the German records.[14]

Argermayer then drove to other ghettos in Zone IV and in Zone V in southwestern Hungary, where the ghettoization had begun on June 30, and repeated the process.[15] In each center, he also delivered the Va'ada's separate list of those to be sent to the Columbus Street camp at Wisliceny's special instructions. At the end of June Wisliceny reported to Eichmann that 20,700[16] Jews had been selected for transport to Strasshof, Austria, and requested further orders. Kasztner was busy collecting the deposit of $100 a head for those to be held "on ice" in Austria, a surprisingly low amount given how much it had cost to set aside the passengers of the Kasztner train. Kasztner was unaware that ss Brigadier General Karl Blaschke, the Nazi mayor of Vienna, had requested relief workers from the chief of the Reich Security Main Office, Ernst Kalten-brunner, and since Kaltenbrunner was above Eichmann in both rank and influence, Eichmann had little choice but to comply.

The 40,500 people from zones IV and V who were not included in the Strasshof selections were transported to Auschwitz-Birkenau[17] in fourteen transports of 3,000 people each—somewhat over the maximum the gas chambers could handle in any one day.

Time was running out for Budapest's once vibrant Jewish community. The Va'ada had known since the end of May that Zone VI, the last ghettoization and deportation zone after the gendarmes had emptied western Hungary of its Jews, was to be their city.

On June 17 the Budapest City Council ordered all Jews into 2,680 designated "Yellow-Star Houses," apartment buildings marked at the outside entrance with a canary-yellow, six-pointed star, one foot in diameter, against a black background, for maximum visibility. Those whose apartment buildings had not been designated for Jews had to leave their homes within three days. If they had not complied by June 24, they were to be arrested and deported immediately. The Jewish Council was charged with finding accommodation for Jews in designated houses. In the Star Houses, a Jewish family of four was entitled to only one room. Few could fit their furniture into one room, so the city was overwhelmed by desperate people searching for storage space, trucks, wagons, or handcarts, even wheelbarrows, to transport their belongings.

A Christian family could appeal the designation of its home as a Star House and, while waiting for a decision, affix a large, white cross to its doorway to make sure it was recognized as non-Jewish. Some gentile petitioners openly laid claims to Jewish homes, stores, or warehouses. The Hungarian government, following the German model, held auctions for furniture and perishable goods left behind by the former owners.[18]

On June 25 a new regulation issued by the Ministry of the Interior restricted Jews to their "living quarters" except for the hours between 2 PM and 5 PM, when they were allowed to shop for food. Another new ordinance forbade Jews to entertain guests in their homes or to go to city parks. Henceforth they could travel only in the last car of streetcars and were to use a separate area in the air-raid shelters, if such an area was provided. If no separate section could be made for them, they were not to use a shelter. The superintendent of each Star building was ordered to make a list (in triplicate) of all the Jews in each apartment and on every floor. One copy of the list was to be posted at the main entrance, a second copy submitted to the city, and the third kept by the superintendent, responsible for ensuring that only those on the list lived in the building.

On that same day, the primate of the Church of England, William Temple, denounced the deportations, and Francis Cardinal Spellman in the United States called on Roman Catholics to rise up against the evil of racial persecution. Both messages were carried by the BBC and widely heard in Budapest, despite the prohibition against listening to enemy broadcasts.

Swiss newspapers kept reporting on the fate of Hungarian Jewry, and the BBC attacked the Nazi regime and its Hungarian fellow travelers. The American press threatened that Hungarian society, as a whole, and Regent Miklós Horthy, personally, would be judged guilty of complicity. King Gustav V of Sweden sent an urgent appeal to Horthy, citing traditional Hungarian chivalry and warning that if he did not step in, Hungary would become a "pariah among other nations." Max Huber, the president of the International Red Cross, wrote to Horthy: "We implore the Royal Hungarian government to avoid anything that might provide even the slightest cause for such monstrous rumors . . . as the deportation and murder of its Jewish subjects."[19] Huber offered to send a mission to Hungary with food and clothing for the deportees. The Red Cross had not been helpful to Europe's Jews until now, reasoning that the organization's function was to help prisoners of war; Jews were prisoners in their own countries, or in countries allied with their own, and therefore they were outside Red Cross jurisdiction.

The American secretary of state, Cordell Hull, issued repeated warnings that all who participated in the murder of civilians would be dealt with as criminals after the war. Meanwhile, the Allies were pushing inland from Normandy, and the Russians were undefeated in the east. But the deportations continued.

In Istanbul, Chaim Barlas had kept apostolic nuncio Monsignor Angelo Roncalli (later to become Pope John XXIII) fully apprised of the persecution of the Jews under Nazi rule. The nuncio had informed the Vatican as early as 1943 that millions of Jews were being murdered, and, in May the following year, the Vatican received a copy of the Auschwitz Protocols. The Vatican's special emissary, Monsignor Mario, had even met one of the two young men who had written the document. Rudolf Vrba was now hiding in a monastery near Bratislava. Gizi Fleischmann was certain that the monsignor had been convinced of the truthfulness of the document; when last seen, she said in a letter to Kasztner, Mario was heading to Budapest to meet the Regent. Of course, they all knew that Horthy had already read the text but had decided it was a piece of ill-conceived propaganda.[20] Now he would hear about Auschwitz from the pope's own emissary. On June 25 Pope Pius XII, who had remained silent on the subject—he said he preferred to use quiet diplomacy—telegraphed a personal message to Horthy entreating him to intervene. Monsignor Angelo Rotta, the papal nuncio and most senior international representative in Budapest, finally succeeded in gaining a private audience with the admiral.

Horthy convened a meeting of the Crown Council of Ministers on June 26 and directed the government of Prime Minister Döme Sztójay to stop the deportations. That day State Secretary László Endre and the gendarmerie's László Ferenczy met Dieter Wisliceny, Brigadier-General Hans Geschke, and other members of Eichmann's Sonderkommando to pin down the last details of the plan to deport Budapest's Jews. The date for the start of the Aktion was fixed for July 5, with the last Jew scheduled to leave Budapest eight days later. Eichmann was furious when he heard of Horthy's Crown Council announcement.[21] He ordered Kasztner to the Majestic, only to tell him that he would not give up on his master plan to "extract all Budapest's Jews." When Kasztner protested in the interests of the Istanbul deal, Eichmann said he still had enough "ethnically valuable Jews" left in western Hungary to complete the transaction should it ever materialize. "And I no longer believe it will," he stated flatly.[22] He gave orders to complete the deportations in western Hungary, and Sztójay, according to Kasztner, simply lacked the courage to intervene.

Justinian Cardinal Serédi, head of the Roman Catholic Church in Hungary, finally appealed to his flock, if only on behalf of converted Jews. He insisted that the latter should be treated differently from those of the "Israelite faith." The reaction from Jews was immediate. Kasztner saw long lines of Jews in front of both the Franciscan Church and the smaller Rókus Church. According to rumors, the cardinal had also threatened to have a pastoral letter read in all Catholic churches the following Sunday condemning the government's actions against Jews. Where, Kasztner wondered, had the kindly prince of the Catholic Church been when the deportations started? And where was he when the definition of "Jew" had been decided in the Hungarian parliament along purely racial lines?

The proposed June 29 letter to Catholics throughout the country was withdrawn at the last moment after intervention by the minister of justice and religious affairs.[23] One of Samuel Stern's contacts reported, however, that the bishop of Eger ignored the official cancellation and read the letter to his congregation in northern Hungary. To Stern's surprise, Cardinal Serédi's letter asked for the repeal of all deportation orders against Jews, not only the converted. The cardinal admitted that his behind-the-scenes negotiations with the government had not been effective and that he had to appeal to his "Catholic brethren." The letter was not all good news: Cardinal Serédi went on at some length about Jewry's purported earlier "subversive influence on the Hungarian economic, social and moral life," but he deemed deportation too great a penance.

Kasztner's view was that the cardinal showed a certain amount of chutzpah in talking to his brethren about Christian virtues and morality, but at least that was preferable to encouraging them to loot the property of the recently departed. He sent Saly Mayer in Switzerland a request that a list of war criminals should be published as widely as possible and announced on the BBC, along with a news story stating that the Allies would insist these individuals stand trial after the war. A lot of people in Budapest were listening to the forbidden voice of the BBC, and some of them were members of the government.

On June 27 the gendarme commandant of the Debrecen ghetto in eastern Hungary sent his proudly penned report to Lieutenant Colonel Ferenczy that his men had extracted the last wealth from the area's Jews: "7.5 kilos of gold, 45.67 kilos of silver, a fine selection of women's dresses and men's suits, plus 70,000 pengős." It had taken only five days of beatings and torture with electrical wires to accomplish this hoard.

By the end of June, more than 400,000 Hungarian Jews had been deported to Auschwitz, and most of them were dead.

CHAPTER 16

Blessings from Heaven

[A]nd, by the way, [one of the parachutists] said they wanted us to help them find British and American parachutists, pilots who had bailed out of their planes. And how do you imagine we do that? I asked. We put an ad in the paper and suggest they contact us? We put our address in the advertisement? In June 1944, in Budapest! How could these boys come here and think such a thing?

Hansi Brand[1]

A week before the end of the month of June, the week that Eichmann's "Jews on ice" were being gathered for the work camps in Austria and mere days before the Kasztner train was to leave on its journey to Palestine via Portugal or Spain, the Yishuv parachutists whom Moshe Schweiger had talked about in March arrived in the capital. The original plan had been for an expeditionary force, as Schweiger had expected, but after months of negotiations Lord Moyne, the British minister for Middle Eastern affairs, had proposed only three Hungarian-speaking Jews,[2] part of a tiny group of thirty-two parachutists who had been selected for service in Slovakia, Bulgaria, Austria, and Hungary. Moyne remarked that the parachutists were all "active and resourceful Jews," and, therefore, removing them was a good idea, as "the chances of many of them returning to give trouble in Palestine seem slight."[3]

Their mission would include opening escape routes for downed British airmen, sending back military information, and helping to foment a Jewish uprising.[4] They had received some training by British Special Operations in Egypt and Italy, more in Yugoslavia with Josip Tito's partisans, and recently had received their specific instructions from the British command. Had they arrived a year earlier, their mission might have had the smallest chance of success. Now the plan was utterly ludicrous.

Kasztner remembered Schweiger's anticipation of some military assistance, but that seemed a lifetime ago, on the eve of the German occupation, before the arrival of the Sonderkommando, before 400,000 Jews had been deported. Now Schweiger was in a concentration camp,[5] possibly dead, and neither Kasztner nor Hansi Brand had given the matter any thought until, suddenly, Hans Geschke, the Gestapo chief, stood in the doorway of the Va'ada's temporary office, smoking one of his thin cigars, and asked whether they had been in touch with the Tito partisans. The Germans obviously suspected the Aid and Rescue Committee leaders of something, but Kasztner and Hansi had no idea what. When they shook their heads in sincere innocence, Geschke left.

The next day, equipped with fake Swedish and real British military papers, two of the parachutists arrived at the Va'ada office. Emil Nussbecher and Ferenc Goldstein had crossed the Yugoslav border and taken a train from Szeged to Budapest. Born in Transylvania, they had no problems with the language. When most of the other passengers on the train had been asked to show identity papers, they were not. Having no experience with the reigning terror in Hungary, neither had thought this treatment strange. Once in Budapest, they had gone in search of Moshe Schweiger. When they found his apartment occupied by a man who had no knowledge of a previous lodger by that name, they went to the temporary office of the Va'ada in the narrow street behind the Gresham Café and asked to speak with

Rezső Kasztner. British Intelligence had suggested Kasztner as an alternative to Schweiger. Nussbecher had been one of the young halutzim in the Zionist camp that Kasztner had helped to organize some years before in Kolozsvár. A little younger than Kasztner, inspired by the same idealistic Zionism, he had emigrated to Palestine as a teenager. Both of Goldstein's parents had been active Zionists and had often attended meetings with Kasztner at the home of József Fischer, but they had remained in their own homes until recently, when they were included in the Kolozsvár group at the Columbus Street camp.

Hansi was sure they had been allowed to come this far because the Hungarians or the Germans, or both, had wanted to know where they were headed. She had no doubt that they had been shadowed to these offices. "Do you think that they will ever trust us again if they find them here? It's a trap. Or a test. Peter Hain needs a reason to have us arrested. Or Eichmann suddenly suspects we are working with the Yugoslavs. As does Geschke."

Kasztner was at a loss. Certainly the two young men's presence would have been known to the ss. Everything he and his colleagues had worked so hard to achieve could now be lost.

"You must be mad to have come here," he chided, in his first words to Nussbecher,[6] who told Kasztner that they were working for the Yishuv, assigned to British Special Operations. He showed his identity card with considerable pride. It featured a fine photograph of him over the signature of a senior officer. He and Goldstein hoped that Hanna Szenes, the third member of their team, had already arrived and that Kasztner knew where she was. They explained the importance of their mission.

"In other words," Kasztner said, "you have come here to die. And just before you get on with that effortless task, you are going to make sure we all join you in the hereafter."

Hansi was appalled at the stupidity of the Yishuv and the simple-mindedness of the British—unless, of course, the British had planned the whole excursion to embarrass the Jewish Agency. When Nussbecher pulled out of his pocket a sock with fifty Napoleon gold coins in it, Hansi started to laugh hysterically. As she recalled later,

"This is what he was going to use to save Hungary's remaining Jews."[7]

Kasztner's immediate fear was that both the Columbus Street camp and the Strasshof labor camp in Austria were in jeopardy. If the ss caught the parachutists here, they could cancel the train to Spain or Portugal and murder all of the Strasshof Jews "on ice."

Although certain the two young men would be caught and questioned, Kasztner risked telling them about the group that was about to leave for Palestine. Ferenc Goldstein's own parents were in the "privileged" camp, and they devised a plan to write him with his parents, hoping he would be just another passenger on the train. Kasztner gave Ferenc a contact name and sent him on his way. Much to his relief, the young man managed to bluff his way into the Columbus Street camp. He was only nineteen years old—too young, they thought, to survive in this duplicitous environment where you could trust no one, not even the members of the Jewish community. Samuel Stern had warned them that some of the people at the Sip Street Community Center were German spies, or Jews working for the ss in exchange for whatever favors they would be granted.

Kasztner cautioned Nussbecher to be careful what he said and whom he spoke to in the building, but he encouraged him to try his luck with the refugees' aid workers at Sip Street. The refugee office there might be able to help him find accommodation. It was not safe for him to stay in the Va'ada office. Obviously, Hans Geschke had been expecting him there.

Not surprisingly, Hansi Brand and Kasztner were picked up by the Hungarian security police and bundled into the usual waiting car as soon as they ventured outside. Peter Hain's security officers demanded an explanation for the presence of the two young men: Where had they come from, were they involved in smuggling Jews, were they spies, what prior knowledge did the Va'ada have of their arrival in Budapest, and from whom? What did their contacts in Palestine say about these people? Were they here for the British or only for the Jews? Did they know what their mission was? They seemed to have lost track of Ferenc Goldstein after he left the Va'ada office. Where had he gone? Most important, was there a connection between these two men and the ss? "We are going to find out one way or another, Kasztner," they told Rezső. "Why not make it easier on yourself and Mrs. Brand?" The officer in charge winked at Kasztner when he mentioned Hansi. "This line of questioning can be particularly hard on women," he added. They mentioned that Hanna Szenes was already in custody. She was certainly going to tell them everything they needed to know, so why not corroborate whatever her story was while they had a chance?

The officers suggested that Kasztner and Hansi think the matter over and then released them. The searchers would be back at the same time the next day. An hour later, Nussbecher arrived at Hansi's apartment. He had found the Sip Street Community Center in disarray. No one had wanted to talk to him. He had failed to make contact with the halutzim underground. And he had been warned that he would be arrested if he did not wear a yellow star when he was outdoors.

There was no question now of Nussbecher's being able to hide. They talked about a variety of escape options, but none seemed feasible with both the German and the Hungarian security police on his trail. In the end, they hatched a fantastic plan. Hansi would go to the ss and tell them that both Goldstein and Nussbecher had been sent by the Jewish Agency to ascertain whether Joel Brand's mission was real and fully supported by the Germans. They had come to ensure that the Agency's funds were not wasted, that the Sonderkommando would live up to its end of the bargain. The young men's task, Hansi would claim, was to confirm that the fate of the Hungarian Jews was not yet sealed, that there were still a million lives ready to be traded for trucks and coffee. Hansi thought the ss wouldn't fall for it, but no one came up with a better idea.

When Nussbecher left, he hugged them both and wept.

The next day, they learned from Geschke that Nussbecher was in custody. Geschke mentioned, casually, that they would execute Nussbecher if the other man was not found within the next twenty-four hours. "Your train," he told Hansi, "could still be redirected, you know. It's easier for us to send another lot to Auschwitz than to reroute one through the Reich. Your friends are bombing the lines, barely a station left in all of Germany. It's hard to find soldiers to keep Jews safe these days . . ."

Kasztner sought out Goldstein at the Columbus Street camp and told him that Nussbecher would be killed unless Goldstein turned himself in. They coached him in the details of Joel Brand's mission and the story they had cooked up with Nussbecher, and left him to decide what he wanted to do: he could try to hide at the camp for a few more days, and he might be able to slip onto the train with his parents, or he might be caught. In any event, Nussbecher would be dead.

Goldstein turned himself in, but his story was not believed. He was taken to the Mauthausen concentration camp in Austria, where he was murdered with most of the other inmates. Emil Nussbecher, who later changed his name to Yoel Palgi, escaped from the ss transport to Auschwitz and survived to return to Jerusalem, a terribly damaged aspiring hero.

The third parachutist, twenty-three-year-old Hanna Szenes, a poet, a dreamer, an idealist, told her captors nothing in spite of being tortured and was executed on November 7, 1944.

The ss must have decided that Kasztner and Hansi Brand had not been directly involved with the parachutists, because they continued to deal with them over the next several months of the war.

CHAPTER 17

Strasshof: The Jews on Ice

We were confronted with the most serious dilemma, the dilemma with which we had been faced throughout our work: Should we leave the selection to blind fate or should we try to influence it? We tried . . .

Rezső Kasztner[1]

Eichmann reneged on the "Jews on ice" agreement even before the Va'ada provided all the lists. There were to be fifteen thousand people from the provinces and fifteen thousand from Budapest, but the second group was never selected. The fact that the final numbers came close to twenty thousand was due to bureaucratic bungling rather than to any effort to make up the shortfall. In some ghettos it was too late for a selection—the boxcars were packed, the people counted. The gendarmes in charge were not about to start afresh with new lists and new numbers. The local Jewish councils still alive in the western ghettos had tried to make the lists for Strasshof voluntary, but few people realized that they had a better chance of survival in one train versus another. By then their one, overwhelming desire was to get away from the horrors of the ghetto as fast as they could.

The boxcars were unbearably hot and airless. Some of them had liquid lime covering the floor; the fumes were toxic. And there was a ghastly human error: shift workers at the Hungarian border had routinely switched the tracks toward Auschwitz-Birkenau, as they had been doing every day since the beginning of May. They did not notice that two trainloads were supposed to have been redirected to Strasshof. By the time the other trains arrived at Strasshof between July 3 and 5, many people were comatose from lack of water and suffering from unbearable pain in their legs and open sores in their throats and mouths. Since a chief criterion for selection had been families with young children, the trains were full of shrieking infants and inconsolable toddlers. Ukrainian volunteer workers with long, rubber whips tried to drive the new arrivals into the already full barracks. Most could not be accommodated and spent the first few nights and days in the fields and the adjacent cemetery. The dead and the dying lay side by side with the living. Traumatized babies clung to their exhausted mothers, children snuggled up to corpses. Two women gave birth while lying on gravestones.

On arrival, the Vienna commercial and administrative office, headed by Hermann Krumey, registered only 6,889 men and 9,812 women—it did not register small children under ten years of age.[2]

The Hungarian families stayed together in the barracks and fields, each group selecting its most robust members to line up for water and soup rations. Beyond a barbed-wire enclosure, they could see hundreds of Soviet prisoners of war milling about.[3]

Much to Lieutenant General Ernst Kaltenbrunner's surprise and Major General Karl Blaschke's consternation, fewer than half of these new arrivals could work. Blaschke had expected to receive able-bodied men to toil in the factories and on farms, and to clear rubble from the bombed streets in towns and the capital. All able-bodied Austrian males were serving in the armed forces. Now Kaltenbrunner had to explain to his friend the mayor that the young children and the very old were to be kept safe despite their inability to work. They were a special group of "exchange Jews."[4]

Paul Varnai was only six years old when he arrived at the Strasshof distribution camp.[5] His father and older brother had been drafted into labor battalions, but the rest of his extended family stayed together in a lice-infested barrack with wooden bunks and bits of damp straw bedding. No one could sleep. The heat and the lice were maddening. His two baby cousins cried themselves hoarse.

The family was taken to a farm in Annahof on the Czech border. The Polish overseer allowed the youngest children to pick apples and potatoes in the fields on Sundays. The grandparents cooked and mended clothes while the others worked on the farm. Paul's grandmother made jam and apple cider. On Sunday afternoons they were allowed to bathe in the River Thaya. His memories of anxiety and constant hunger are idyllic compared with the wretchedness of the Bergen-Belsen camp that was to follow Annahof.

Hermann Krumey had been ordered to set up the new office in Vienna and charged with the fate of the Hungarian "exchange" Jews. The Nazis arranged to rent them out of the Strasshof sorting camp and collected their wages from family farms, construction companies, wood-processing plants, paper mills, city maintenance and cleaning operations, manufacturing industries, and small businesses. The Jews sent to Vienna fared worse than those, like Paul Varnai's family, who worked on farms. Allied bombardments had destroyed entire streets; dead bodies had to be carted to the cemeteries, roads had to be cleared and rebuilt. The Jews were barred from entering bomb shelters, and many were wounded, and some killed, by bombs and falling debris. They were forbidden to speak with gentiles even when they were standing near them or working with them at bombed sites.

Children over ten were regarded as adults and worked the same long shifts. István Hargittai wrote that he was in one of the special labor units in Vienna comprised of children between ten and fifteen years old.[6] "We were taken into buildings immediately after a bombing. We had to reach places that adults couldn't have reached. We brought out cadavers, the wounded, and all valuables. If we found limbs or other body parts, we had to bring them out as well." The German guards encouraged small children to climb up brickworks and along smoldering beams by unleashing bursts of machine-gun fire. When István tried to replace his own torn, newspaper-stuffed shoes with new shoes off a corpse, the guards threatened to shoot him. They wanted everything for themselves. The prisoners lived in bombed-out buildings with little or no roof, in stables, or in woodsheds, storage facilities, or factories.

The Vienna Jews were moved from place to place, depending on where labor was most needed. No trucks were available to take the prisoners to their work sites, so they walked or traveled by streetcars, which led to local residents seeing their pitifully thin, grimy clothes and their hungry children. It was impossible for the guards to prevent chunks of bread, apples, or bits of cookies from being slipped into Jewish hands. To the surprise of the German authorities, many local Austrians who came into direct contact with the deportees were not without humanity.

At family farms, some local villagers volunteered to send letters home to relatives in Hungary and provided their own addresses for return mail. Despite their own strained circumstances, a few farmers gave clothing to their Jewish workers. Many ignored the prohibition against giving the Jews anything other than the prescribed near-starvation diet. When villagers saw emaciated elderly people being marched to the farms in the half dark of early dawn, they felt angry at the system that caused such things to happen. A boy named George, only seven years old when he was deported with his family to a farm near Wiener-Neustadt, would slip through half-open doors and beg for food as the group marched to the fields. He was rarely disappointed and never betrayed. To underline the warnings, the ss arrested and interned a number of local Christians, some of whose lives ended in concentration camps alongside the Jews they had tried to help.[7]

Reports from civilian employers to Nazi headquarters in Vienna about the behavior of the forced laborers were, overall, very positive. Only a few of the managers found it necessary to insert derogatory phrases about Jews so that they would be viewed as trustworthy Reich citizens and continue to receive Jewish workers.

CHAPTER 18

The Memories of Peter Munk and Erwin Schaeffer

*I became a proud Jew, which I hadn't been before. When they said
"dirty Jew," I was proud.*
                Peter Munk, talking about his experiences at school[1]

I think I should have killed him myself . . .
                Erwin Schaeffer, speaking of Rezső Kasztner[2]

Peter Munk almost missed Kasztner's train. Seven months
before, in November 1943, he had turned sixteen. His
extended family were all still safe in their homes. He had
heard rumors that some Jews, elsewhere, were being mistreated—
but that was in Poland, in Czechoslovakia, in the Russian countryside. In Lipótváros, a district of Budapest where the rich Jews lived,
there had been few hints of change. The Munks had a five-story
house there. Until the Germans marched in, they thought they
would be safe from persecution.

"I had a large group of friends. We went to one another's homes.

We played card games. I never heard of the deportations," Peter said. His grandfather Gabriel Munk had made his fortune in the chocolate-importing business, invested in apartment buildings in Budapest and in land that he sold for residential development. By 1944 he was retired. Peter remembers special occasions when his grandfather would offer the children bonbons wrapped in shiny red and gold paper. When they undid the wrapping, they found gold pieces. "He was awesomely formal," Peter remembered. "Never let down his guard. All through my childhood, I would click my heels when I went to see him, and I would kiss his hand. He demanded that kind of respect—no, I don't mean he demanded, I mean his mere presence inspired the respect, awe. His word was the law. For all of us."

For a while after his parents' divorce ten years earlier, Peter had lived with his mother, Katharina, and his maternal grandmother. His best friend then, and probably today, was Erwin Schaeffer, a tall, burly boy of his own age with a sense of mischief Peter had not yet acquired. On their way to and from school, it was Erwin who protected the smaller Peter from bullies. Once his father, Louis Munk, remarried, Peter was taken back—kicking and screaming—to live in the big, white house in Lipótváros with the rest of the Munks.

In the years that followed, Peter was sent to a strict Calvinist boarding school in Miskolc for sons of high-placed Magyar officers and bureaucrats. "It will toughen him up," his father said, "and teach him to respect the comforts of home." Louis was right at least on the first count. One of the teachers used to call Peter "Jew Munk." He was set upon by groups of boys and beaten for being a Jew. He learned how to fight, and he also learned tactics: when to fight and when to wait for the right opportunity to attack. Both of these lessons would serve him well, later, in the boardrooms of the world.

After Louis's second marriage also failed, he took his son home to meet his third and, he was sure, his final wife, Olga Brunner. She was a widow, equipped with reasonable finances and a son of her own. Peter, ten years older than his new stepbrother, John, could come and go as he pleased.

When the German army marched into Budapest on March 19, 1944, Peter, almost seventeen, was on the Danube embankment with his brand-new camera, a birthday gift from his grandfather. Fascinated, he watched the long columns of jeeps in military camouflage, the gray tanks, the motorbikes with sidecars, the disciplined march of the smartly uniformed foot soldiers. He snapped photographs and waved to the men who smiled and waved to him.

"I wasn't frightened. All I thought about was my new camera and that I should try various angles to see how it worked. I was concerned there wasn't enough light."

Days later, when the new law was issued ordering all Jews to wear the canary-yellow Star of David on their outer clothing, Peter and a couple of his friends briefly ventured into the Star of David—making business. There were strict rules about the size, the color, the dimensions. In Lipótváros, at first, few people bothered to wear them. There was no one to report infractions: the shopkeepers were Jews, as were the families in other houses and in the apartment buildings. Only when Peter went to visit his mother did he have to be careful. He always kept the star badge in his pocket, in case he was stopped.

By early June, Grandfather Gabriel and Louis had realized that life was getting extremely dangerous for Jews in Budapest. When they heard word of Kasztner's train, they immediately bought fourteen places on it and delivered a large suitcase full of money and gold to Rezső Kasztner's office; the payment represented most of what remained of the family's Hungarian fortune. Peter doesn't know how they had managed to keep this much after the regulations regarding the surrender of all Jewish assets, but he had seen his father open a hidden safe and empty all its contents into the suitcase. There was a ticket for every member of the family except for his mother. Katharina had, after all, left Louis of her own free will, and Gabriel felt no obligation to pay Katharina's way out of the country.

For the first time in his life, Peter opposed his grandfather. He wanted to stay in Budapest. Gabriel Munk refused, aware that the days of Budapest's Jews were numbered. "You are the last male heir of the Munks," he told Peter. "Your responsibility is to obey. Mine is to make sure you are safe."

Three weeks earlier Katharina had received the official notice to report to the detention center at the former Jewish Rabbinical Seminary on Rökk Szilárd Street. In the end, his mother cast the deciding vote for Peter's life: she insisted that he should leave with his father's people, persuading him that she would be all right, that her detention would be temporary. Still, Peter was not convinced. "My father assured me that if we left enough money for food and bribes, my mother would be fine . . . But I think he knew she would be deported," he still believes.

On June 28, the day before the Munks were to go to Columbus Street, Peter accompanied his mother to the Rökk Szilárd Street building. He carried her elegant leather suitcase, a memento of easier times, and they talked all the way there about future plans once the war was over and they could be together again. She wore her cream-colored summer suit and her Italian shoes and carried a small purse. They said goodbye at the gate.

The next morning was humid, with a haze over Pest and the Danube rolling heavily in the summer heat. Yet Peter wore his warm, English-tweed jacket, wanting to take something for the journey that would suit him well in the capitals of other countries. He did not feel awkward riding on top of the horse-drawn cart that took the Munk family to the Wechselmann Institute on Columbus Street. Now that they were on their way, he was excited, looking forward to the adventure. "I was sixteen years old, I was tough, I thought I was rich. I was supremely confident. Riding through the streets of Budapest, looking down from the top seat on that cart, I felt like a conqueror."

They could see several long, wooden barracks in the courtyard of the red brick mansion. Everyone was quiet. Not even the usually chatty Munk sisters talked. When they climbed down from the cart in front of the gate, they dusted off their clothes and stood waiting.

There was Gabriel Munk in his formal, dark traveling suit; Louis in something lighter, less functional—he had always been a flashy dresser; Louis's third wife, the lovely Olga, holding hands with her son, John; the aunts, with their husbands and children. The family had left behind their dogs, entrusted to the care of one of Gabriel's former business associates. They hauled down their luggage and waited in line.

Two uniformed ss men read out the would-be passengers' names in guttural German. As each person stepped forward from the crowd, the guards ticked off the name, checked the travel documents, and allowed the individual to enter the camp. The family reassembled on the other side of the gate.

Before leaving the Columbus Street compound to board the train on June 30, Peter phoned the commandant of the Csepel detention center, to which his mother had been transferred. Strangely, he was allowed to talk to her one last time, and the commandant reassured him that she would be fine. She sounded cheerful, unconcerned, and said that the commandant had been most polite, the food was good, and her maid had come from home with freshly washed and ironed clothes.

A few days later, Katharina Munk boarded a transport train of boxcars bound for Auschwitz.

Erwin Schaeffer's family didn't make it onto the Kasztner train. They had paid for their seats, of that Erwin is sure. It was June 18, 1944, a Sunday. His parents had already moved to the Star House next door to their old home, but that day they returned to the cellar.

He remembers listening to two men[4] tell his father that the rumors they had heard about the death camps could well be true. There was a train leaving in the next few days for Palestine via Spain or Portugal, they said, and a few seats were still available. But only a few.

He remembers his father going into the wine cellar with a shovel and digging under the wooden shelves of fine wines while Erwin waited and watched. His father had been a wealthy man, a wine and spirits importer, and the house servants took care of everyday things. Digging up the cellar floor was the most physical thing Erwin had ever seen his father undertake.

His father dragged out a small, metal box and extracted from it handfuls of gold sovereigns and a velvet bag of jewels. With all those pieces packed into his pockets, he returned to his old study, where the same two men were waiting. They had enjoyed glasses of Schaeffer's most expensive brandy and smoked and chatted with Erwin's mother while his father dug in the cellar. When they took the bag of gold and jewels, the men asked if Erwin's father could buy a couple of extra tickets for orphans who had no money of their own. Erwin is certain his father obliged. He had always been a generous man.

Erwin was sixteen, a tall, good-looking lad with light-brown hair, blue eyes, the build of a football player. He and his sister did not want to go on the train, and he was finally able to convince his father that they would be safe with gentile friends in Budapest. Their older brother, who had returned there from Paris, had an apartment and perfect gentile identity papers, though he was in hiding from the Gestapo. They could live with him and the whole family would be reunited when the war was over in a few months.

On that hot day of June 29 as people started gathering for the train's departure, the clothes Erwin's parents wore included warm sweaters and socks and their winter coats. There wasn't much room for suitcases in the wheelbarrow, and they wanted to make sure they had adequate attire for the long journey.

When Erwin accompanied his parents to the Columbus Street camp's gate, they found a swarming mass of people jostling to get in. The crowd formed into three or four lines, all angling toward the narrow gate where a uniformed German stood. Erwin wore a belted leather overcoat and stayed well apart from his parents. He hoped he would be mistaken for a youth member of the Hungarian Arrow Cross, and he circled the crowd until their names were called.

Some sixty years later, Erwin Schaeffer, on another hot summer day in Budapest, walked to the back of the Great Synagogue in Dohány Street, past the rescued gravestones and the memorials. There, in the shadow of the new reconstruction, is a silver tree. About ten feet tall, its branches reach out and up, its leaves are all shiny metal pieces. The whole tree shimmers in the afternoon light. Each leaf bears the name of a person who was murdered in the Holocaust. One leaf, a small one nailed to the trunk of the tree, holds his father's name.

His hand touching the leaf, Erwin stood quietly, gently rocking backward and forward, murmuring a prayer for his father—and perhaps also for himself.

"My parents were thrown off the Kasztner train," he said, softly.

"Kasztner, I think, had oversold the train. In the end he had more people than tickets. So when the train was about to pull out of the station, he sent a couple of German goons down the length of the train to remove some passengers. When my father showed his ticket, the goon didn't even look at it. He tore it up. They accused my father of traveling with false papers, claiming he hadn't bought the tickets in the first place. Then they frog-marched my parents to the doors and threw them down on the siding."

For six months thereafter, the Schaeffers hid in their older son's apartment on the Pest side of the river. Erwin, the most Aryan-looking, shopped for food and essentials. He is certain that Rezső Kasztner sent a messenger to his father to apologize for the dreadful misunderstanding in all the confusion at Columbus Street and to explain that another train would be leaving shortly. That was the last time they had word from Kasztner.

Then, on January 13, 1945, with the Soviet army bombarding the city, the Germans retreating across to Buda and the war almost over, Erwin's father ventured out for fresh air. He thought they would check on his daughter Klara, on the Buda side of the river. Erwin was walking with his father along Városház Street. It was almost five o'clock, near curfew. A drunk in an Arrow Cross uniform recognized Erwin's father and shouted: "It's the Jew Schaeffer! I know him. I used to work for this pig, guarding his wine! How do you like me now, Mr. Schaeffer? How do you like the new rules?"

Several of his fellow thugs grabbed Erwin's father by the arms and handcuffed him. One of them hit him in the chest. The other went after Erwin.

Until that day, Erwin had thought he was brave, but now he denied he was with his father. "Never seen this man before. Don't know him." He heard his father's voice over the loud voices of the Arrow Cross men: no, he had never seen the young man before. Never.

A passing German army officer stopped to watch the commotion. "Let's settle this now," he ordered. "You," he pointed at Erwin, "unbutton your pants." They were a few steps from City Hall, near the Palace of Justice. No one stopped to stare when Erwin unbuttoned his pants by the side of the building. The German didn't wait to see his circumcised penis. He yelled: "See, the boy is a gentile!" And he grabbed Erwin by the shoulder to propel him toward Váci Street. "Run, dammit." And Erwin did.

They took his father to 14 Városház Street, the last stronghold of the Arrow Cross in Budapest. Two days later, with a group of about thirty naked, beaten, terrified men and women, he was marched to the edge of the Danube and shot.

Erwin Schaeffer and Peter Munk have remained friends for more than sixty years. They do not talk about Rezső Kasztner or the train.

From left to right: Moshe Schweiger, Bogyó Kasztner, Rezső Kasztner, and Joel Brand. *Courtesy of Yitzhak Katsiri*

From left to right: Rezső Kasztner's brother Ernő, Rezső, and their parents, Helen and Yitzhak Kasztner, in Kolozsvár (Cluj). *Courtesy of Yitzhak Katsiri*

From left to right: Ernő (seated); Ernő's wife, Ella; Gyula's wife, Martha; Ernő's son, Yitzhak, on the table; Rezső's brother Gyula; Rezső; and Helen Kasztner holding Gyula's daughter, Gila. This photo was taken during a 1938 visit by Gyula's family from Palestine to Kolozsvár. *Courtesy of Yitzhak Katsir*

Regent Miklós Horthy arriving at Komárom, November 6, 1938. *Copyright © Magyar Távirati Iroda*

Members of the Budapest Relief and Rescue Committee, 1944. *From left to right*: Peretz Révész, Hansi Brand, Rezső Kasztner, Ottó Komoly, and Zvi Goldfarb. *Copyright © Beth Hatefutsoth, Photo Archive, courtesy of the Zehavi Family, Jerusalem*

ss Lieutenant-Colonel Karl Adolf Eichmann in civilian clothes. *Copyright © USHMM, courtesy of Yad Vashem Photo Archives*

Clockwise from top left

Mug shot of Edmund Veesenmayer, former Reich plenipotentiary in Hungary. *Copyright © USHMM, courtesy of Robert Kempner*

SS Colonel Kurt Andreas Becher. *Courtesy of Szabolcs Szita. From Szabolcs Szita,* Aki Egy Embert Megment, a Világot Menti Meg, *Budapest: Corvina, 2005*

Joel Brand in 1944. *Courtesy of Szabolcs Szita. From Szabolcs Szita,* Aki Egy Embert Megment, a Világot Menti Meg, *Budapest: Corvina, 2005*

Hansi Brand in 1944. *Courtesy of Szabolcs Szita. From Szabolcs Szita,* Aki Egy Embert Megment, a Világot Menti Meg, *Budapest: Corvina, 2005*

ews on the first Kasztner rescue train upon their arrival in Switzerland, ugust 1944. *Copyright © USHMM, courtesy of Yad Vashem Photo Archives*

wish women escorted along Wesselényi Street, on their way to collection mps at the start of the death marches toward Vienna, October 17, 1944. *opyright © Bundesarchiv, Bild 101I-680-8285A-04, Photo: Faupel*

Peter Munk and Erwin Schaeffer, boyhood friends in Budapest. *Courtesy of Peter Munk*

Kasztner's train passengers on the way from Bergen-Belsen toward Switzerland. *Courtesy of Memorial Museum of Hungarian Speaking Jewry, Safed, Israel*

rowds of people clamoring for safe passes or passports in front of the Glass
louse, October 1944. *Courtesy of Memorial Museum of Hungarian Speaking
wry, Safed, Israel*

wiss Consul Carl Lutz amid the ruins of his residence. *Courtesy of György
ámos, The Glass House, Budapest*

Bogyó and Rezső Kasztner with baby Zsuzsi, December 1945. *Courtesy of Yitzhak Katsir. From Zsuzsi Kasztner's private collection*

Zsuzsi Kasztner and her father in Tel Aviv, shortly before he was murdered. *Courtesy of Yitzhak Katsir. From Zsuzsi Kasztner's private collection*

PART THREE

The Highway of Death

*I am not so naïve as to believe that this slim volume will change
the course of history or shake the conscience of the world.
Books no longer have the power they once did.
Those who kept silent yesterday will remain silent tomorrow.*

Elie Wiesel, *Night*

CHAPTER 19

The Journey

*He who saves a single life, it is as though he has saved the entire
world.*

Sanhedrin, Chapter 4, Talmud

On Friday, June 30, 1944, Rezső Kasztner's "token" group, its
num-bers swelled to around 1,500,[1] left the Columbus
Street camp on foot in heavy rain and walked in rows, five
abreast, toward the Rákos Street railway station.[2] The passengers had
come from all parts of Hungary, from villages and cities, and from
all social standings. There were forty rabbis, including Joel Teitel-
baum, the fabled Szatmár *rebbe*, the chief rabbi of the ultrareligious
Hasidim; well-known Zionists; eastern European Jews in traditional
garb; several secular scholars; a world-famous psychologist; two
opera singers; a number of journalists, farmers, and landowners;
peasants and former officers in the Hungarian army; ladies of leisure,
and old women who had worked in the wheat and potato fields.
Baron Fülöp von Freudiger, whose family and congregation had
contributed the major share of the original deposit, had been

allotted only sixty places for his Orthodox congregation, not including his relatives.[3] There were Slovak and Polish refugees, Communists and Conservatives, Neologs and Orthodox young halutzim who had trained for *aliya* (the return to the land of Eretz Israel, or Palestine) and were singing in newly learned Hebrew, and seventeen Polish and about forty Hungarian orphans.[4] Some of the industrialists and bankers on board had paid handsomely for their seats but were now no different from the other passengers.

Joel Brand's mother, sister, and niece Margit were on the train; so were Kasztner's brother Ernő and their mother, Helen, and Bogyó, her father, József Fischer, and other members of Bogyó's family. Samuel Stern's daughters, Ottó Komoly's daughter Lea, and Ernő Szilágyi, the man who had been most responsible to the Va'ada for the list, were also there.

Peter Munk thought all these people had been selected to represent the myriad lives of the Jews—a kind of Noah's Ark.

Each person had been allowed to take two changes of clothing, six sets of underwear, and sufficient food for ten days' journey. The train was nothing but boxcars, and the suitcases and food were packed into wagons attached to the end of the train. During the hours they waited in a railroad yard for departure from Budapest, about sixty additional people boarded from Bocskay Street, where a small area around the synagogue had been assigned for the last of the Kasztner transport. A young woman who had escaped from Poland with her two-year-old nephew threw the boy through the open doors of one of the boxcars. She had heard of the train from one of the Polish halutzim and had been waiting for it to pass. Margit Fendrich, Joel's niece, remembers persuading one of the Hungarian families to take responsibility for the child.[5] That night the train moved slowly to the outskirts of the city, where it stopped on a siding to take on more coal. During the dark hours, some of the labor service men from a nearby train stealthily scrambled aboard.

Most of the passengers settled on the floor of the boxcars, surrounded by a few of their bags. Some made nests for themselves with clothing; others just leaned against one another. A few had brought pillows and blankets. Babies cried, children had to be kept quiet and entertained.

Unlike those of the trains going to Auschwitz, the boxcar doors were not padlocked, so, as they waited, the passengers could let in the night air. Some men sat on the ledges, their legs dangling over the sides of the wagons, smoking, looking at the stars and for the last time at the antiaircraft lights over Budapest. Peter Munk remembers lying on the roof of a wagon, looking at the sky and seeing the sudden flashes of light where the bombs landed. Later, he, too, sat on a ledge, smoking one of his grandfather's gold-tipped cigarettes and talking with a beautiful, blond-haired girl.

The train finally left Budapest a half hour after midnight on Saturday, July 1.[6]

Munk isn't sure how many passengers left Budapest in the end; he has read several versions of the story, and they all give different numbers. He has no recollection of anyone being taken off the train or anyone scrambling onto it, unidentified, but the excitement surrounding their departure was so great that he concedes it could have happened. The guards seemed not to have counted the more than two hundred babies and toddlers. In any event, there were more people than Kasztner had paid for. The ss demanded to be paid in full for every one in the final count of 1,684—and, as it happened, they were paid twice for the people to whom Kurt Becher had sold his tickets.

Once on their way, many gave in to their exhaustion and slept in snatches; some talked loudly, edgily, all night and through the next day; others seemed dazed, caught in their own private horrors. The train stopped for several hours while a nearby town was lit up by heavy bombardments and planes rumbled overhead so close that those on the ground could make out the silhouettes of British pilots in the blinding antiaircraft lights. Some of the halutzim were quickly shut up when they started singing about Jerusalem. "Damned fools, they're going to draw enemy fire," someone muttered in the dark.

"Who is the enemy?" another gruff voice inquired. "And who is the fool?"

They spent the nights of Sunday and Monday in a field, surrounded by a few gendarmes and a couple of German guards. They dug latrines at the point farthest from the train and erected a plank fence around them. Fortunately, the rain had subsided. There was a clear sky, with myriad stars and a million mosquitoes. One of the poets recited a long poem of farewell to the night sky or some other abstraction, but no one paid much attention.

On the fourth day, a baby was born in one of the wagons, with two doctors (one of them a renowned obstetrician) in attendance. It was the last day for Hungarian signs and Hungarian newspapers. The German guards supplied extras if they were offered Swiss francs—they didn't want Hungarian pengős anymore. Most people cried when they said goodbye to Hungary. Even the Zionists kept quiet, out of respect for those who still felt that the country was their home. The passengers saw their last Hungarian soldier, and then they rolled into Austria.

Jewish labor brigade workers brought them food on a railway siding on the way to Vienna. When they were informed that there would be hot showers in Auspitz,[7] many protested that they were fine without them. They had heard rumors of the kinds of showers that awaited Jews in German camps, and the word "Auspitz" sounded a lot like "Auschwitz." In hindsight, Peter Munk wonders how so many of the passengers knew about Auschwitz. He had not heard of it.

In the end, it was Linz where the showers waited. Each person had to stand naked in front of a German doctor before being sent to wash. Some of the women were ordered to have their hair cut off and their bodies shaved to prevent the spread of lice, or so they were told. Bogyó remembered standing before the German with her head held high, her shoulders back, and thinking, "I am a proud Jewish woman." Peter Munk's aunt, Eva Speter, looked straight into the doctor's eyes, ignoring the grinning guards who watched the whole process. She would not be humiliated.

Munk remembers the excitement he felt when the train stopped at Vienna, one of the grand European cities where he had always longed to be. "My grandfather was inside reading for most of the journey. I was getting a suntan, watching the scenery go by, still excited about the adventure. I could scamper onto the roof, stand there with the wind in my face . . . taller than all the bombed-out

buildings." He shared his cigarette with a young German guard, sitting by the open doors at the side of the wagon, basking in the
morning sunshine. The guard was not much older than Peter, and
he, too, had always wanted to see Vienna, but not now. The escorts
had strict orders not to let the passengers off the train here. Vienna
had become proudly *Judenfrei* some time before.

On July 8 they stopped and changed trains for one with fewer
boxcars. They camped that evening in a field outside Hannover. The
sky was alive with hundreds of Allied bombers, and the earth shook
and vibrated as they dropped their lethal loads on the city. József
Fischer gathered the group of former leaders together on the railway
siding late that night and told them that the train had been refused
permission to cross France, so they could no longer go to Portugal or
Spain. The Allied forces were gaining ground: U.S. units had liberated Cherbourg, while British and Canadian units were at the
outskirts of Caen. He had received a telegram, via the local ss, from
Rezső Kasztner. The Sonderkommando had assured him that they
were all safe. No one should panic. There would be a short delay
while the ss found another way to the west, but the deal was going
to be honored.

In the small circle of those who surrounded Fischer that night, he
may have been the only one who believed his son-in-law. There had
been too many rumors about Kasztner falling for the Nazis' lies.
Moshe Krausz had told those who sought his opinion that "the
convoy was headed for destruction."[8] He had warned the Joint and
the Jewish Agency that Kasztner and Ottó Komoly had become
tools in Eichmann's hands and that the ss, having extracted the Jews'
remaining valuables, would send the special train's passengers to
their deaths. Krausz's influence had been so great that several of
those originally on the lists had changed their minds and stayed
behind in Budapest.

"We did not know where the train was going," Olga Munk
remembers, and they had "no idea if we would be alive at the end of
the journey. But we were absolutely certain we would not live to see
the end of the war if we stayed in Budapest."

The train arrived at Bergen-Belsen, about forty-five miles

northeast of Hannover, Germany, on Sunday, July 9. They received an armed reception from Hungarian guards in German uniforms, some holding onto tightly leashed dogs. The passengers stood in lines of ten to be counted, and to be counted again. There were 972 women and 712 men, including 252 children; the oldest was eighty-two, the youngest but a few days old.[9] The counting took three hours, during which they stood in heavy rain. It was dark by the time it was over, and the guards were not willing to start looking for the luggage then. "When we arrived in Bergen-Belsen we thought it was an extermination camp," says Olga Munk. "We were given a single blanket each, a wooden bowl, a spoon, and herded into long barracks with double wooden bunks." Her little boy, John—he was only six at the time—wanted her to sew on a second yellow star. He thought they were beautiful. The next morning there was milk and rice pudding for the babies and toddlers; for the rest, thin turnip soup.

This part of the camp became known as the *Ungarnlager*, "the Hungarian camp," a separate part of Bergen-Belsen for the Hungarian "exchange Jews." In 1944 parts of Bergen-Belsen still retained the camp's original 1942 purpose of holding only those the German government considered useful—persons with influence, foreign Jews, those who could serve in case of prisoner exchanges or be traded for goods.[10] The so-called privileged area was divided by high barbed-wire fences and landmines into separate units, one for each nationality. There were separate cages for Greeks, Romanians, Spanish, Dutch, North Africans, Yugoslavs, Albanians, and two hundred French women. In addition, there was a separate area for Jewish working prisoners, who were treated considerably worse than the rest of the inmates.[11] ss guards with machine guns at the ready manned the watchtowers to ensure that there was no mixing of nationalities. "There can be no logical, sane explanation for this camp," Béla Zsolt remembered. "It was as if some crazed people had given vent to a maniacal, pointless collecting passion. And even now that there are few Jews left to categorize, the insane collecting and sorting goes on unabated."[12]

In the Ungarnlager, the daily diet was black gruel, a thin cattle-turnip stew, a tiny piece of dark bread that tasted like sawdust, and sometimes a bit of cheese, sausage, jam, and even margarine. Children got milk and oatmeal.[13] The little ones were exempted from the daily roll calls. The denizens of the Ungarnlager did not work. As they settled in, the men elected a camp executive—József Fischer was president—to help run daily activities. The halutz youth organized themselves into subgroups for studies in Hebrew and outdoor gymnastics training. The women ran exercise classes. The Orthodox started a yeshiva for the children.[14] There were lectures by professors of philosophy and psychology, history and political science, and also religious education, including Orthodox Jewish. Some evenings there were concerts—Hanna Brand, Joel's sister, sang Handel on the second evening after their arrival.[15] One of the great bass singers from the National Opera House joined her the following night. The Polish children told stories about their *shtetl* childhoods, and everyone cried when they remembered the dead. They held readings of poetry by Ady, Jozsef, Heine, and Petőfi; they listened to dissertations about the work of Kant, Thomas Mann, and Dickens. Some of the theater people created a musical revue with hilarious takeoffs of others in the camp, re-enacting various verbal jousts among the inmates.

Inevitably, as the days marched on and their future remained uncertain, there were more arguments; small differences grew into monsters from living at such close quarters. The halutzim managed to acquire alcohol and sometimes got drunk in their barracks. There were numerous accusations of hoarding food or stealing precious items, of not keeping clean or of spreading lice in the barracks; there were jealous rages, heated religious arguments, and fistfights. One evening Bogyó Kasztner slapped the face of a young man who had dared to address her disrespectfully; another night a woman committed suicide over a tiff with her recently acquired lover. Sometimes there were letters from Budapest and parcels from the Red Cross. Ernő Szilágyi was the only Va'ada member to have made the journey. He said he wanted to be there to reassure the young halutzim. The Poles and the Slovaks would not have come if they hadn't seen him lining up for the train. He was their insurance against going to Auschwitz. In the camp, he gave lectures on Herbert Spencer, astronomy, Chinese culture, Plato, and ancient cultures. Professor Lipót Szondi, a world-famous psychologist, offered evening lessons on the applications of modern psychiatry and new developments in the field since Freud. He even provided the occasional private consultation.

In another, separate camp adjacent to the Ungarnlager was a large contingent of Dutch exchange Jews who had been there for a couple of years. They had their own hospital and storage rooms. "We were kept apart by barbed-wire fences. Sometimes we could hear them singing Dutch songs," Margit remembers. "It was as if a madman with too much barbed wire had decided to create a series of cages for groups of mice. We could run all day in and out of the barracks in our own enclosure but were not allowed to have any contact with the mice on the other side of the cage." There was also a *häftlinger* camp, where emaciated men with shaved heads, dressed in striped pajamas, could barely walk to their barracks after twelve hours of hard physical labor. They stared over the barbed-wire fence at the exchange Jews with wonder and hatred.

Every morning and afternoon there were the dreaded roll calls. Sometimes it took two or even three hours for all the people to be counted—then recounted if the numbers did not match the previous tally. An old man and a ten-month-old baby in his mother's arms died while waiting in the heat.

But Peter Munk had fallen in love with a dark-haired beauty from Budapest. Her name was Kitty, and she was the only member of her family on the train. Her father had asked that the Munks look after her, and Peter had volunteered for the service. He spent most of his time in Bergen-Belsen trying to be alone with her, stealing his grandfather's expensive cigarettes to bribe the guards to allow them an hour or two in the guardhouse or the storerooms.

On August 1, Hermann Krumey visited the Ungarnlager. He told Fischer that the group would be able to leave soon, though definitely not for Spain or Portugal, but perhaps Switzerland. "When you are free, don't tell horror stories about us," he warned the men surrounding him as they persisted with their questions.

Two of the passengers on the Kasztner transport, lawyers from Kolozsvár, found out that their daughters were on the other side of the barbed wire and tried to give them food. They were allowed to join their children, and they died, later, with them.

CHAPTER 20

The End of the Great Plan

You will understand the mental condition in which I am writing this letter. The dream of the big plan is finished . . .
                    Rezső Kasztner, in a letter to Nathan Schwalb[1]

Don't believe anything the Germans say! They will promise much and keep little. If you can, give them money, valuables, maybe you will be able to get something in return. And give them coffee, they go crazy for coffee.
                    Leiser Landau, a Polish refugee, speaking to Fülöp von
                                                              Freudiger[2]

On June 28 Rezső Kasztner cabled Menachem Bader,[3] the Zionist from Galicia who was now working for the Jewish Agency in Istanbul, to inform him that the ss was willing to meet with a bona fide representative of the Yishuv, the Jews in Palestine. His ss contacts had suggested that Bader or another credible person should travel to Budapest for discussions. He could no longer pretend that Joel Brand was continuing the negotiations. Bader cabled David Ben-Gurion to ask whether he thought this could be a viable plan. Hermann Krumey, whom Kasztner described as "a fair man," guaranteed Bader's safe return to Istanbul. Two days later in London, Moshe Shertok and Chaim Weizmann, leaders of the Jewish Agency in Palestine, met George Hull of the British Foreign Office. They demanded that Brand be allowed to return to Eichmann with the assurance that the German offer was being discussed in the British war cabinet and that the British were coordinating their efforts with the American government.[4] Hull agreed to take the matter to his superiors.

Meanwhile, Brand was being held in a comfortable prison in Cairo. His cell was a large, well-appointed room with a view. His bowl of fresh fruit was replenished every day.[5] He discovered that Sam Springmann, his Va'ada colleague from Budapest, was also a prisoner there. Having left Budapest when the Germans marched into the city in March, and even though he had a valid emigration certificate for Palestine, Springmann had chosen to remain in Istanbul to help the Yishuv representatives, but they turned out not to want his assistance. And when the Turks had expelled him to Syria, where he was promptly arrested by the British, the Agency's people failed to assist him. As Brand saw it, both of them had been betrayed by the Jewish Agency. Strangely, Brand continued to believe that the Agency could take command of matters regarding the fate of the Jews and that it had a special relationship with both the British and the Americans, but, for reasons unknown to him, it stubbornly failed to meet his expectations. In his deepening depression, he was intensely aware of his own failure and placed the blame on the Agency's men.

The interrogations of Brand continued despite the existence of extensive manila files containing all the information he had already given to the British. As he recalled later, his questioners were now asking him to guess what the Germans' real motives had been in sending him and Grosz on this crazy errand. He told them that, in his view, the Nazis—not Hitler—were looking for a way to share the blame for the murder of the Jews. "They would be able to say: 'We wanted to be rid of the Jews, to expel them, but the others wouldn't accept them, so we had to exterminate them.' "[6] The British were seeking other reasons. They kept asking how Brand and his group could ever imagine that the Allies would give or grant permission for someone else to give the Germans ten thousand trucks, and whether he ever thought that such a bargain would work.

He was told numerous times that the matter of extracting even a hundred thousand, never mind a million, Jews from Germany was complicated, involved agreements by several countries, and could not be accomplished at the same time as fighting the war. Military action would have to cease while the refugee Jews crossed borders, accommodation would have to be found for them, countries would have to agree to accept them, and, while everyone focused on this humanitarian action, the Germans could gain some military advantages. Brand continued to repeat that winning the war would be of little interest to the Jews if they had all been annihilated before victory was declared.

Brand found the War Refugee Board's delegate, Ira Hirschmann, more sympathetic than his British captors. Hirschmann, a key executive with Bloomingdale's department store in New York, had been chosen by President Roosevelt as the board's man in Turkey. He met Brand on June 22 and, in his report, recommended that the United States not close the door on the blood-for-goods proposal, no matter what the British decided. He considered it likely that Eichmann's deal was just a cover for a larger, more important proposal—that of beginning peace negotiations with the ss.[7] When Hirschmann asked Brand whether he thought his not returning to Hungary would risk losing the chance for a deal with the ss, Brand replied that Eichmann had indicated he could take his time if he saw a chance of success.[8] During a later meeting, the British minister for the Middle East, Lord Moyne, told Hirschmann that Brand would be taken to London.[9]

In London the British foreign secretary, Anthony Eden, after his meeting with Weizmann and Shertok, recommended that Brand be returned to Budapest with an immediate counteroffer for 6,500 children with safe-conduct passes to Palestine. It was a ridiculously small number, but even that proposal seemed unacceptable to the British government. The very idea of negotiating with the enemy, of ransom payments, of wheeling and dealing about lives was abhorrent to the other cabinet ministers, no matter how fervently the Jewish Agency pleaded as the rumors about Auschwitz became established facts.

Around the time that the Kasztner transport arrived in Bergen-Belsen, Eden reported Brand's view that the German plot behind the mission was to blame the Allies for "extreme measures against the Jews." Privately, several British functionaries expressed the opinion that the Zionists (Joel Brand being one of them) were in cahoots with the Germans and that the expulsion of a million Jews to Palestine would destabilize the Middle East. A strong British force would be required to restore peace there—and that distraction would, in turn, ease the German army's current situation in Europe. On July 11, Prime Minister Winston Churchill sent Eden a memorandum expressing both his horror at the German actions against the Jews and his decision that there "be no negotiations of any kind on this subject."[10]

The American response to the Jewish Agency's pleadings was to consult the Soviet Union over any action they should take.[11]

Brand went on a hunger strike. To restore his appetite, his friendly British guard gave him a letter from the Mossad's Ehud Avriel informing Brand that Shertok was meeting with the appropriate levels of government in London and that their "basic demands have been as good as met." Avriel said they had also heard from Kasztner that deportations in Hungary were to cease and that Hansi Brand and Joel's children were doing well.[12]

A couple of days before the Kasztner train left Budapest, Adolf Eichmann had been replaced in the "business" process by Kurt Becher. It was "Himmler's decision," Becher said, and, obviously, another "Reich secret." Eichmann had been told to focus his attention, instead, on the deportations. "They left me the dirty work," he complained to Kasztner, who pretended sympathy. Kasztner was

relieved to be dealing with the calmer, more personable Becher, who
was willing to accept all currencies, even declining pengős, as long as
the amounts were stated in Swiss francs or American dollars and
converted at prevailing black-market rates. Naturally, he preferred
foreign currencies, jewelry, gold, diamonds, foreign share certificates,
and paintings, but he accepted even soon-to-be-worthless Hungarian
stocks and bonds. There was still the matter of the total amounts to be
paid for the 1,684 passengers now parked in Bergen-Belsen. Eichmann
had originally asked for $200 a head. Becher had suggested $2,000, but
he had been prepared to settle for $1,000 each as Heinrich Himmler
had specified. "Businessman to businessman," as Hansi Brand had
prompted, they had agreed that the Jews-for-sale account would be
kept open and replenished as each side delivered on its promises.

The trick was to agree on the exchange rates to be used. The U.S.
dollar was not officially rated at the bank. It could be worth 4.25
pengős at a bank, but between 30 and 40 pengős on the black market.
"Our position was," Kasztner said later, "that we have already paid
more than the full tariff of 1,684,000 dollars."[13] Becher insisted that
the original deal had included the trucks, and if trucks were not going
to be available, the Va'ada had to substitute other goods of equal value.
Freudiger, after all, had offered Wisliceny textiles and medicines worth
10 million francs if he would intervene with Eichmann to stop the
deportations immediately. Freudiger claimed he had sources in Spain
and Switzerland, though Kasztner doubted they were real. The Orthodox leader had become more and more desperate, and Kasztner
thought him capable of inventing foreign associates in a bid to gain
valuable time. Kasztner had been able to get 16.5 tons of coffee[14] from
Istanbul, but Becher discounted 25 percent of the shipment for cleaning the merchandise. At Samuel Stern's suggestion, he offered Becher
$20,000 to close the account for the Bergen-Belsen group. If Eich-
mann stepped in to stop the group's departure, Becher would intercede with Himmler.

The two men were now sufficiently friendly that Becher would
casually invite Kasztner to dine with him at the Weiss mansion, and
sometimes they went to the casino for late-night drinks and a short
game of roulette. Kasztner was grateful that the pit boss knew

Becher well enough to make sure the ss officer always won. The train was still in Bergen-Belsen and, as Eichmann had threatened, it could easily be transferred to Auschwitz. The Strasshof families, "the Jews on ice," were in even greater danger. Though he was repeatedly reassured by Becher and Krumey that they had been kept together and alive, Kasztner knew how tenuous such promises could be.

Hansi encouraged Rezső to act as Becher's social equal.[15] They both spoke faultless high German. Although Kasztner had read more broadly, Becher had a better understanding of military strategy, including historically brilliant strategists such as Napoleon. Hansi suggested that Rezső present the lieutenant colonel with tickets to the opera, give him volumes of classic German poetry, and listen spellbound to his revelations about the tactics of Roman warfare.

On July 7, when the long-awaited draft agreement finally arrived from the Jewish Agency in Istanbul, Becher could be assured of substantial top-ups in Western currencies, and the issue of trucks could be raised again. Becher suggested that he or Fritz Laufer, the former Abwehr agent, would go to Lisbon if the Jewish Agency could not send someone to Budapest to sign the formal agreements. Kasztner cabled another urgent request for funds.

The sudden presence of large numbers of cock-feathered, fully armed gendarmes in the capital, Stern told Kasztner, was a prelude to the attempt by the two Hungarian state secretaries, László Baky and László Endre, to take over the government from the Nazi administration. The Sip Street building was filled with panicked men and women who feared that the Hungarian gendarmes, who had so effectively and mercilessly driven the Jews out of the provinces, would now do the same in Budapest. Many still had a few hidden valuables that they drew out of their pockets and flashed before Stern, begging to be included in the next train to Palestine.

In the Zionists' Information Office, the noise was so loud, the cries of the women so shrill that Kasztner avoided going there. When he did, the people who recognized him tugged at his sleeves or grabbed his arms as he passed. Stern tried valiantly to calm everyone. He still believed in Regent Miklós Horthy's ability to intervene, and he knew that a few members of the Crown Council were now ready to back

Horthy when he took a stand against the Nazi invaders. In no event, Stern reasoned, would the Regent allow Baky and Endre to take over the government. Stern had been able to get a long-awaited audience with Mihály Arnothy-Jungerth, the deputy foreign minister, who said he had been opposed to the deportations from the beginning. "Not because he was sympathetic to us," Stern hastened to add, "but because he thought these measures were extreme and could do irreparable harm to Hungary's foreign relations."[16]

Kasztner arranged a meeting with Ottó Komoly and the Swiss consul, Carl Lutz, at the former American embassy to discuss how each of them had fared in the previous few days. On his way there, he was twice asked to identify himself. Some of the main streets were so bomb cratered that he had to take a detour and found streetcar tracks had buckled, and firefighters and volunteers were removing a burning streetcar to make way for repairs. The embassy building, its stairwells, corridors, and bathrooms, were filled with the destitute who had lost their homes during the bombardments and had not been able to find relatives to allow them into their crowded apartments. Many of them had lived there for weeks.

Lutz admitted that his efforts to rescue more of the people who held entry permits for Palestine had not been successful. He talked about his several meetings with German plenipotentiary Edmund Veesenmayer, with Admiral Horthy, and with Prime Minister Döme Sztójay. Lutz's main concern now was that the government should respect his visas. Veesenmayer was bent on the total destruction of Hungary's Jews and stressed that the time for emigration was over. The Grand Mufti of Jerusalem, condemned to death in absentia by the British, had dined with Hitler in Berlin and had assured the Führer of Arab assistance in the Middle East, but only if he could be sure of no further Jewish immigration.

Friedrich Born, on behalf of the International Red Cross, had formally appointed Komoly to be in charge of its Section A, international affairs, allowing him to gather refugees in the Swiss Consulate and other "safe houses" should the need arise. The Red Cross had delivered a strongly worded letter to Horthy, urging him to obtain transit visas for would-be emigrants to Palestine.[17]

Kasztner reported on the "German line." He told them about his meetings with Becher and his conviction that the ss lieutenant-colonel was more interested in cash rewards than in deportations. He was driven by greed rather than ideology, and, in the end, he might turn into a reluctant ally of the Jews. Lutz offered Kasztner a Swiss protective passport, in case his meetings with the Germans came to a dead end, but he declined. In this game of roulette, if he bet on the wrong number he would be dead before he could reach for a new identity.

Komoly said that he and Moshe Krausz had also been pursuing the "Hungarian line."[18] They had not given up on Horthy's ability to step in. The old man might be ineffectual, but he seemed to have made up his mind this time now that the pope had pleaded with him to intervene, and the added encouragement of Endre's and Baky's plans to oust him.

Kasztner begged Lutz to use his influence with Krausz to speed the production of Palestine entry certificates. If Horthy made a decisive move, regardless of what Veesenmayer had decided, maybe forty or fifty thousand people could reach safety. The seven thousand certificates would, as Lutz had assured Kasztner, be stretched to seven thousand families, and some families would be enlarged with additional children. A couple could have seven, even eight children, and parents as well as aunts and uncles. He offered his help, along with Hansi's, to make sure that all the papers were in order, if only Krausz could be persuaded not to follow the rules so mulishly.

On his way to Krausz's office, Kasztner was stopped by several Slovak halutzim involved in the rescue of Jewish families. Lutz had given them Swiss papers and fake jobs as emigration officials. Krausz, they complained, would not allow them to help. He had thrown Rafi Benshalom out of his office and insisted that he would tell Lutz not to provide protection for people who kept disrupting his work.

In the basement, behind the door of the Emigration Department, Krausz sat over piles of paper, his floor littered with boxes filled with more documents, each representing a person begging to be allowed into Palestine. Krausz was still typing each letter himself on his old typewriter, its worn ribbon constantly getting tangled with the keys.[19]

When Kasztner offered Krausz his personal assistance with the forms, Krausz merely glanced up from his letters and laughed. "You go back to your Germans," he sneered. "You're not needed here." He had already contacted Chaim Barlas in the Jewish Agency office in Istanbul, he said, asking for Turkish ships to transport the new emigrants from Constanta.

On the morning of July 8, one day after the last of the Jews from western and southwestern Hungary had been transported, Admiral Horthy demanded an immediate stop to the deportation of the Jews. He accused Baky and Endre of misinforming the government about the handling of the "Jewish problem." Horthy already knew that Baky planned to have him arrested and that he had ordered László Ferenczy's gendarmerie to the capital to make sure that the coup was successful. Horthy countered with an order for the Hungarian army's Esztergom Armored Regiment to stand by in case it was needed.[20] If it came to a conflict, Horthy would not lose. The gendarmes might be battle hardened against unarmed civilians, but they were not trained military men.

When the gendarmes buckled under and left the capital, Stern informed the Jewish Council that the Regent had, finally, stepped in to stop the Germans. Within an hour, the Sip Street building was almost deserted. It was a warm, sunny day, and Stern told Kasztner he was going home to enjoy an afternoon sleep.

By July 1, 1944, according to Wisliceny, 475,000 Hungarian Jews had been deported to Auschwitz-Birkenau.[21] Eichmann was disappointed at the total; he had set his sights on a minimum of half a million people by that date. Ferenczy gave the number as 434,351 human beings, who left for the Birkenau ramp in 147 trains.[22] Three-quarters of them were murdered within an hour of their arrival.

CHAPTER 21

Still Trading in Lives

*I had no confidence in Horthy or those around him. They were
all lacking in courage . . . We had only one chance to gain time
and that was to negotiate with the ss, to have recourse to ruse
and to make, if necessary, a few deliveries.*

André *Biss, A Million Jews to Save*

In Istanbul, Menachem Bader was invited for coffee with a man
who called himself Stiller and said he was attached to the
German Consulate. Stiller claimed he was authorized by the
appropriate parties on the German side to offer Bader safe conduct
and a plane ride to Vienna so that he could continue the discussions
begun by Joel Brand.

The invitation was reviewed for two days by the Jewish Agency
Executive. They concluded that Bader should not be allowed to make
the journey, because, as a British subject, he was forbidden to travel in
areas controlled by the enemy.[1]

The question for David Ben-Gurion and Moshe Shertok was how
to continue negotiations without the knowledge of the British,

whose spy system was better than the Yishuv's and who seemed unwilling to make something of the Brand proposition. Ben-Gurion would have preferred British cooperation, but he was not going to give up on any deal that might save Jewish lives, even if the British tried to veto it. He sent two cables to Franklin Roosevelt pleading with him "not to allow this unique and possibly last chance of saving the remains of European Jewry to be lost."[2]

In Palestine, Shertok reported to the Jewish Agency Executive on the whole "heartrending, discouraging affair" and his determination to "try every possible avenue" to persuade the British government to allow him to proceed.

In Cairo, a dispirited Brand was allowed to meet Lord Moyne in a private club, where the British minister reportedly asked him: "But Mr. Brand, what can I do with this million Jews? Where can I put them?"[3]

Eichmann ignored Regent Horthy's command that deportations cease and continued to instruct the eager Hungarian Nazis to round up Jews from the areas close to Budapest. Hitler, he reasoned, had never agreed to accede to anything but the "correct course" of action. To make his point, Eichmann had the remaining inmates of the Kistarcsa and Sárvár camps put on trains and consigned to Auschwitz. He told Kasztner that, no matter what arrangement Kasztner had come to with Becher, unless the required goods began to appear at the borders Eichmann would add the passengers on Kasztner's train—still waiting at Bergen-Belsen—to the next transport and "have the whole lot of them gassed without a selection."

"An interesting idea, Herr Obersturmbannführer," Kasztner replied, "but it would end any chance we had of negotiating for goods the Reich might need in exchange for Jews it does not want."[4]

On July 10, following Admiral Horthy's orders, the Hungarian police intercepted one of Eichmann's trains and returned it to Kistarcsa. When Eichmann discovered that the Regent had countermanded his orders, he flew into a rage. He rampaged around his rooms at the Majestic, shouting at his staff and threatening to clean up the whole damned place. He ordered Wisliceny to go to Kistarcsa and get those *übriges mistvolk*, those superfluous shit people, back into the wagons.

Otto Hunsche went to Sip Street with a small, armed ss contingent and demanded that the members of the Jewish Council accompany him to an urgent meeting with Eichmann at the Majestic. Stern tried to reach the Regent, but the ss would not allow him time even for a phone call. The matter was, Hunsche insisted, of the utmost urgency.

When the council members reached the Majestic, they were offered chairs and coffee while they waited for the commandant. When one of them tried to use the phone, he was told all the lines were down. Meanwhile, Wisliceny's men packed the Kistarcsa camp inmates—most of them bankers, industrialists, accountants, and lawyers who had been arrested soon after the German occupation— into trucks and transported them to the Eastern Railway Station.

By the time the council was allowed to return to Sip Street late that evening, the train had crossed the border into Austria. Wisliceny laughingly asked Kasztner: "Do you think Eichmann would let that old fool Horthy slap him in the face like that?"

Horthy tried to convince Veesenmayer that his orders regarding the Jews were not in contravention of the Regent's agreement with Hitler and that he was merely re-examining his undertakings in respect to workers that Hungary now needed at home. Meanwhile, Andor Jaross, the Hungarian minister of the interior, reassured Eichmann that he would devise a way to circumvent the Regent's orders.[5]

On July 12, Kasztner wrote another desperate letter to Joseph Schwartz of the American Joint Distribution Committee, explaining his sense of isolation, the whirlwind of events, the speed of deportations, the hopelessness, the horror of helplessly watching the tragedy unfold in the streets of Hungary. Had Joel Brand returned, had the Jewish Agency or the Allies listened to the call for help from Budapest, more people could have been saved. He was convinced that the Germans were negotiating in relatively good faith, that they had been ready to sell what they called "valueless human material" in exchange for goods of value to them.

His letter passed the German censors unchanged: ". . . hundreds of thousands went to Auschwitz in such a way that they were not conscious until the last moment what it was all about and what was happening. We who did know tried to act against it, but after three-and-a-half months of bitter fighting, I must state that it was more like watching the unfolding of a tragedy and its unstoppable progress, without being able to do anything to prevent it . . . The speed of the collapse was so wild that help and actions of rescue could not keep up with it; even thoughts were too slow. I cannot give you a picture of the annihilation or of its impact; I could only feel it. The thing that happened here between May 15 and July 9 is like the burial of the last scion of an aristocratic family as they lower him into the grave and turn the face of his ancestors' shield to the wall."

Three days later, four plainclothes Hungarian policemen confronted Kasztner as he left the Columbus Street building. When he refused to go with them voluntarily, they handcuffed him and shoved him into the backseat of their car. One man sat on either side of him, blindfolded him, pushed his head down between his knees, and drove him in silence over rough roads at tremendous speeds for what seemed to Kasztner about an hour. He was so stiff when they stopped at their destination that he had to be half carried into a building and down some stairs. They removed the blindfold in a cellar that smelled musty, unused, and damp, where he was interrogated while standing facing the wall. They wanted to know the exact details of the deal the Va'ada had with the ss. How had he persuaded the ss to let a trainload of Jews out of the country and not consign them to Auschwitz? What was the idea for the "exceptional" camps, and how had they paid for all these concessions? Where had the valuables come from? Despite the ceaseless interrogation, after five days and sleepless nights Kasztner had told them nothing of value. He admitted that some money had changed hands, but he swore that he was not sure of its source.[6]

On the sixth day, gendarmerie captain Leo Lullay appeared. He had been Ferenczy's representative at the Vienna conference at which the train schedules were organized, and he was now Ferenczy's second-in-command for the deportations, a man with a reputation for uncompromising brutality toward and complete lack of sympathy for the unfortunate people in the boxcars traveling to Auschwitz. He was in full dress uniform, as though he intended to visit not a bedraggled prisoner in a guarded cellar but some dignitary. Lullay put his hand on Kasztner's shoulder and said, "Don't be afraid, our country needs you."[7] And he smiled.

Kasztner was blindfolded once more and taken for another long ride in the back of a car. When his captors allowed him out, they removed the blindfold and led him into the guardroom he would share overnight with the duty sergeant. They slept on narrow bunks and with the door locked, with a washbowl and bucket to share. At dawn, Lullay took over the interrogation. He seemed convinced that Kasztner was a member of the American spy service. Because he was unsure which answer was more likely to get him released, Kasztner was reluctant to admit or to deny the allegation. Lullay went to great pains to explain his role in the deportations, insisting that he had not known until quite recently what Auschwitz was used for. He told Kasztner that the Germans had filmed the gendarmes pushing Jews into boxcars and that these films were being shown in foreign capitals to prove that the Hungarians, not the Germans, had been responsible for what had happened to the Jews. Lullay said he was a living witness to the facts: the deportations had been ordered and carried out by the Germans. The gendarmes, with one or two exceptions who would be punished when the war was over, were innocent.

Kasztner guessed that Lullay had detained him only to secure an alibi for himself. He would, he said, be more than willing to testify to all he had learned during this grueling week. He was astonished by Lullay's stupidity, his cheerful assumption that he could continue his career after the Allies invaded Hungary, and his acknowledgment that he believed Germany's war would be lost. Lullay declared that he was a patriot, as if that explained his anti-Semitism, and he seemed quite touched by his own words. Kasztner told him that he was leaving for one of the neutral countries in a few days and that he could then tell the Allies the truth about the deportations. Lullay seemed satisfied for the moment and said he would let Kasztner go if his chief agreed.

As they traveled back to Budapest through the devastated countryside, they stopped to pick up Lullay's chief, László Ferenczy. The lieutenant colonel, even in civilian clothes, had the bearing of a military man: He stood at least six feet three inches tall, with broad shoulders, and short, graying hair, a clean-shaven, ruddy face, and a cheerful disposition that belied his notorious brutality. This was the man who had insisted on savagely torturing men and women in the ghettos, recommending to his troops that torturing children would often lead parents to reveal where they had hidden their valuables.

Ferenczy folded himself into the backseat next to Kasztner and smiled. He would, he said, be willing now to prevent further harm to the Jews. His forces could resist German orders and, if necessary, use arms in their defense. He asked that Kasztner arrange for him to meet members of the Jewish Council—in particular, Hofrat Samuel Stern.

Kasztner should, Ferenczy said, deny that they had arrested him. If asked by the ss, he would have to fabricate something. It had to be understood that the gendarmerie would have no option but to have him killed if he betrayed their confidence. "The smallest indiscretion," he said, "will cost you your life." With that, Kasztner was deposited in front of André Biss's apartment building.

Kasztner concluded that Ferenczy had refrained from torturing him only because of his presumed close connections with the ss. He later learned that both Becher and Eichmann had known who had taken him and why, and that they were concerned the Hungarians would glean some information about the nature of their deals.

Hansi Brand, unlike the ss, had not known where Rezső was. Rumors suggested that he had been arrested for spying and might have been executed. She had gone to the Majestic to seek an appointment with Eichmann. He claimed no knowledge of Kasztner's whereabouts and threatened her with immediate reprisals if he discovered that Kasztner had left the country. "Those children are still here, Mrs. Brand, aren't they?" he inquired, referring to Hansi's youngsters. She demanded that Eichmann make every effort to find Kasztner; otherwise, she threatened, the negotiations with the Jewish Agency could come to an end. She tried not to panic, but with every day of Rezső's absence she became more fearful that he had been killed by Peter Hain's people, or even by Eichmann himself in reprisal for Joel's continued absence.

Biss went to see Otto Klages, the Budapest SD chief, and told him that the Va'ada was still ready to negotiate on the basis set out by Kasztner, that the deal could still be made. He asked Klages to intervene directly with Reichsführer Himmler to have the Bergen-Belsen group released. Biss described Klages as a gentleman, even-tempered, considerate, faultlessly polite. Even on this occasion, it seemed, he had managed to let Biss down gently.[8] If neither Eichmann nor Becher was willing to intervene with the Reichsführer, Klages said, he wouldn't either.

"How much did you tell them?" Eichmann demanded when Kasztner presented himself, once more, on Swabian Hill. "Only so much that they would let me go, Herr Obersturmbannführer," Kasztner replied. "And nothing they did not already know."[9]

The Hungarian government sent a formal announcement to all its representatives at home and abroad: "The dispatch of Jews abroad for the purpose of labor is temporarily suspended." It went on to declare that it had authorized the emigration of all Jews with valid certificates (close to eight thousand at the time)[10] to Palestine through the mediation of the International Red Cross[11] that four hundred to five hundred more who had acquired Swedish citizenship would also be allowed to leave the country, and that an agreement had been offered to the War Refugee Board allowing children under the age of ten to leave for Palestine. Horthy's representative in Turkey met Chaim Barlas to inform him of the Regent's announcement and to urge him to make suitable travel arrangements for all those wishing to leave.

The Jewish Agency immediately appealed to all countries to accept a substantial influx of refugees, mostly children, and petitioned the British government to ease the restrictions of the White Paper that capped Jewish immigration to Palestine at twelve thousand people a year. Several countries agreed to take a limited number of the refugees, but both Britain and the United States hesitated. They worried about a flood of refugees at such a critical time in the war. Britain did not want to cause further Arab disturbances in the Middle East and resented Horthy's interference in its governing of Palestine. Edmund Veesenmayer conveyed his agreement to Horthy's plan, provided that deportations of the rest of the Jews could resume immediately.

In the early evening of July 20, Lieutenant Colonel Ferenczy, wearing a gray, formal suit, went to Samuel Stern's home for an audience. Rezső Kasztner and four members of the Jewish Council also attended this strangest of meetings. Hansi, though she had been invited by Rezső, refused to attend. She did not wish to breathe the same air as "that brute." For the first fifteen minutes, while introductions were made, they all stood close to the door—to make a hasty getaway if needed, Kasztner thought. Ferenczy towered over the other men. "He had a strongly chiseled, attractive face, a thick, muscular neck," one of the participants recalled. "I hoped the hangman's rope would look good on it."[12]

Ferenczy wanted to confirm his willingness to change sides. His orders had been, as they knew, to clear the city of its Jewish population. Coming directly from Eichmann, they were no different now except that the date had been moved. Ferenczy informed his audience that the Germans were ready to complete the "cleansing" of Hungary and would take over the government if that was what they had to do to achieve their goal. What he had come to offer was a new idea for saving Jews: he would pretend to follow the ss's orders and start concentrating the Jews into a couple of camps outside Budapest, but they would, in fact, be safe there from the ss. The gendarmes would guard the camps, which would be model modern facilities— not the kind the Jews had experienced in the ghettos.

Ferenczy feigned surprise when the others told him about the gas chambers. He remonstrated that he had helped to ship Jews to labor camps in Poland.

"Including the children," Komoly said into the silence that followed Ferenczy's statement.

"I asked if I would be permitted to visit Auschwitz," Ferenczy asserted. "I wanted to see for myself that all your people were reasonably well treated and fully employed."

"In Auschwitz . . . ," Komoly said, choking on the word.

"They wouldn't give me the travel pass," Ferenczy continued. "I would be allowed to visit only after the last of the trains left, they said, and that would be the last transport from Budapest."

All Ferenczy asked for, in return for his change of heart, was that the group arrange a meeting for him with Regent Horthy. He could not, he explained, ask for it himself without arousing suspicions. In fact, given his station in the defense of the nation, he could not request such a meeting on his own. He had to go through "proper channels"—and that, as everyone knew, would lead to his immediate arrest.

Stern agreed.[13]

"In these times," Stern explained later to Kasztner, "we can't be choosy about where we find help." Ferenczy was certainly no worse than the Sonderkommando members whom Kasztner had been visiting daily.

At the next meeting, Ferenczy was joined by Leo Lullay, who seemed as eager to help their newfound Jewish friends as he had been, only a few days earlier, to have them murdered. To prove his own reliability, Ferenczy provided Stern with a list the Germans had approved for emigration to Sweden. The original list had been expanded by the newly arrived Swedish attaché in Budapest. Ferenczy claimed he had managed to get approval for all the 2,600 Jews named. He tried, again, to persuade the council to move Budapest's Jews into the protected camps he had proposed. He claimed he had found suitable accommodation outside the city.

Stern did not even consider this plan. Jews concentrated in a camp would be too easy to put into boxcars. Rather than argue with Ferenczy, however, he insisted that the proposed sites be pre-approved by the International Red Cross. As good as his word, Stern did arrange for Ferenczy to meet Horthy at his private quarters in Buda

Castle. Having sensed that the German presence in Hungary might be coming to an end, Ferenczy was now desperate to present himself as an ardent nationalist whose chief interest coincided with the Regent's—whatever that might have been. He informed Horthy of Gestapo activities and Wehrmacht manpower in Hungary, presented his plans for the first-class camps for Budapest's Jews, and pledged his support to Horthy should the Regent demand the withdrawal of German troops.[14]

Horthy made the mistake of trusting Ferenczy with his own plans. First, he would frustrate Eichmann's efforts to deport the Jews of the capital, and then he would remove Baky and Endre from all positions of power. He suspected that they would try to gain German assistance for their coup.

To speed the production of emigration papers, Carl Lutz rented a building on Vadász Street close to the former American embassy for the Emigration Department: a glass house, a showpiece of Bauhaus architecture. It belonged to a Jewish wholesale glass merchant named Arthur Weisz, who was already out of business and was living in the loft with his family. He was thrilled to hear of the rental offer and even happier to accept the Swiss consul's protection certificates.

Krausz moved most reluctantly with his ancient Remington from the basement of the Swiss legation to the second floor of the Glass House, where he established a new domain behind locked doors. Despite his hesitation, however, he sent a triumphant cable to the Jewish Agency headquarters in Palestine, declaring that his own work through Lutz and the "Hungarian line" had succeeded in a large-scale rescue. The eight thousand individual permits would be translated into eight thousand family permits, stretching the numbers to at least three times what had originally been offered.

The glass building now bore the insignia of the Swiss Consulate, with a large Swiss flag and, for all to see, the words "Department of Emigration" engraved in black against a white metal board. As such, it was neutral ground and its employees, young halutzim appointed by Lutz, would all be under the protection of the Swiss government.

As employees, they would not be obliged to wear the yellow star.

Thousands of would-be immigrants lined up in front of the house seeking entry forms and refuge while they waited for their departure date. People whom the halutzim managed to extract from the provincial ghettos also ended up here. They made makeshift sleeping quarters in corners of the building, and a group of Orthodox Jews from the east started a kosher kitchen in the basement.

Meanwhile the British, after pondering the matter both in Parliament and in secret meetings, decided to turn down the blood-for-goods proposition. The *New York Herald Tribune* carried the story on July 19, claiming that the real purpose of Joel Brand's mission had been to split the Allies over the matter of trucks to be used against the Soviets. The July 20 issue of the *Times* in London reported Brand's mission to Istanbul under the heading "A Monstrous Offer—German Blackmail—Bartering Jews for Munitions." The Germans were blackmailing the Allies with threats of murdering all the Jews of Hungary, it said. "It has long been clear that, faced with the certainty of defeat, the German authorities would intensify all their efforts to blackmail, deceive, and split the allies. In their latest effort, made known in London yesterday, they have reached a new level of self-deception. They have put forward, or sponsored, an offer to exchange the remaining Hungarian Jews for munitions of war—which, they said, would not be used on the Western front." The newspaper called the deal "loathsome." The BBC talked of "humanitarian blackmail."

The blood-for-goods deal was over—or so it seemed. Fortunately for most participants, Hitler's immediate circle paid no attention to the news from London. That very day, a group of senior army officers attempted to assassinate the Fuhrer, hoping for an immediate peace with the Allies. At 12:42 in the afternoon, at Hitler's eastern headquarters near Rastenburg, a bomb was left under the heavy oak table of a conference room that had recently been vacated by several high-ranking German officers. It exploded while Hitler was still in the room, but, apart from a small wound on his arm and some damage to his hearing, he left unscathed. For five days no one knew about this incident: Hitler and Propaganda Minister Josef Goebbels decided the news must not slip out uncontrolled. Even Becher, who was fond of mentioning his close relationship with Himmler, did not find out until a week later, when the first trial of the conspirators was scheduled for hearing before the misleadingly named People's Court.

Nathan Schwalb, the European emissary of the Hechalutz, certainly would not have known about the assassination attempt when, on behalf of the Joint, he sent a long cable to Kasztner offering continued negotiations at a meeting in Switzerland. The Joint had appointed Saly Mayer to conduct further negotiations and was ready to begin immediately. Nor did Kasztner know, when he rushed to see Becher at Andrássy Avenue. The guards posted at either side of the doorway simply waved him in.

Becher was lounging on one of Ferenc Chorin's blue-and-pink, silk-covered couches. He offered Kasztner a glass of wine and then introduced him to his German mistress in Budapest, Countess Hermine von Platen. Tall and lithe, perhaps a dancer, she invited Kasztner to dine with them—"I shall call you Rudolf," she purred. It was a quiet evening of Viennese platters and piano music at the Gellért Hotel. Afterward, they went to the casino, where Becher won modestly and spent his winnings on champagne. At the end of the evening, Kasztner handed Becher the $20,000 he had recently received from the Joint and explained that the organization in Switzerland was prepared to convene a meeting with Becher to discuss the details of how further payments would be made.[15]

That week, Horthy's government requested forty thousand Jewish exit visas from the Germans. The Allies continued their wrangling over lives. The British still worried about the possibility of large numbers of eastern European Jews arriving in Haifa, while they were stuck with their White Paper limiting immigration to Palestine. Spain offered to take three thousand children. Switzerland declared it would "receive" seven thousand to eight thousand holders of Palestine entry certificates, provided it was assured that the emigrants would use Switzerland only as a transit point.[16] Sweden would take anyone who was guaranteed by a Swedish citizen.

The newly arrived third secretary at the Swedish Embassy, Raoul

Wallenberg, who was prepared to do whatever was necessary to save lives, began to hand out hundreds of Swedish protection papers.[17] A converted Lutheran, he was the great-great-grandson of one of the first Jews who had settled in Sweden. His family controlled the Eskilda Bank, a financial institution that continued to deal with both the Allies and the Axis.[18] His own convictions had been bolstered by information from the Joint, the War Refugee Board, the World Jewish Congress, and the United States intelligence service, the OSS. At first the Swedish Embassy's list included only those with proven connections to Sweden, but the process was slow and, after a few days, Wallenberg arranged that holders of Swedish papers could move into a number of protected houses—all marked with the Swedish colors—on the Pest side of the Danube.

As an afterthought, Horthy asked Veesenmayer for written assurance that the already deported Hungarian Jews were not being put to death. Both men were still pretending that the Hungarian Jews were going to work in aircraft factories in the Reich. In dress uniform, his chest bristling with medals unearned by a man who had never seen battle, Veesenmayer visited Horthy with a personal message from Hitler: "The Führer expects to see the measures against the Budapest Jews carried out by the Hungarian government without further delays . . . At the end of the war, Germany and its allies, not America, will stand victorious in Europe." He then informed Horthy that the exit visas were conditional on rounding up the Jews of the capital.

Caught in the middle, between fear of the Allies and terror of the Germans, Horthy vacillated. "If this ever ends," Rezső told Hansi, "Horthy should be given the Légion d'Honneur for extraordinary bravery in the face of the enemy and, immediately afterward, taken out and shot for cowardice."

The bomb-damaged streets of Budapest boiled with rumors. The Germans were going to take over the city and round up the Jews; Horthy had been taken prisoner; he had made a separate peace deal with the Allies, and the British were coming up through Yugoslavia to occupy Hungary. The leader of the Orthodox community of Budapest, Fülöp von Freudiger, went to see Dieter Wisliceny. Their relationship had remained cordial since those first few days of the occupation when Freudiger had been able to obtain the release of his brother in exchange for the two rubies in a chocolate box. Freudiger continued to supply Wisliceny with desirable baubles—a string of pearls, a diamond brooch, a gold watch—and the occasional wad of foreign cash for such small favors as extensions of immunity certificates and travel passes for friends and family, as well as the rescue of individuals from ghettos. It was Freudiger who had arranged to extract the venerated rabbi of Szatmár from certain death.[19]

Now Freudiger was asking for more favors and found the rotund ss captain jovially receptive. Of late, he had been left out of negotiations, and he was missing the excitement of the chase and the joys of receiving gifts. Freudiger presented him with a cash bonus and several more pieces of antique jewelry. As they were saying goodbye, Wisliceny said, "You should go away now." Freudiger took it as a warning, and, on August 9, he escaped from Budapest with his family and forty friends and managed to reach Romania. Moshe Krausz had known of the plans in advance and had succeeded in changing the composition of the group to include some people who were more at risk than others. They were all traveling on Romanian passports that Freudiger had obtained while in temporary hiding with the Romanian Embassy staff. He left a note for Kasztner explaining his actions and why he had chosen this particular time to escape.

Samuel Stern knew that Freudiger had made his own deal with Wisliceny and that Eichmann's people would now be looking for him, Stern, but he had nowhere to hide. He was, nominally, responsible for the Jewish Council, and Freudiger had been a member of his governing group. Stern told Kasztner that if he did not survive the next few weeks, Rezső himself should write the story of how he had, despite the odds, done his best.

Eichmann did indeed have Stern and two other members of the council arrested. Someone was going to suffer for Freudiger's escape. The three men were kept standing in ankle-deep water in the Gestapo's Buda jail. They were all given an hour-long lecture, but only Ernő Pető, the youngest of the group, was beaten.

Eichmann then ordered Kasztner up to his office in the Majestic

Hotel. Becher was there, lounging in one of the chairs, his feet on a filigree-covered table. The room was thick with cigarette smoke.

"You knew about this pig swill, of course," Eichmann accused Kasztner in greeting.

"Only afterward, Herr Obersturmbannführer."

"If I catch him, I'm going to have him beaten to death. I'm going to watch when he dies. Why hasn't Stern killed himself yet? You've got to tell him it's time. Once I get angry, he won't escape! Does he know that?" Eichmann shrieked. "A dog. Smart little terrier. Dog. Does he have any money left?"

Becher shrugged. "There are some rich Jews still," he said. "Why don't you go after them, Adolf?"

"It's Horthy!" Eichmann shouted. "*Ich habe die Schnauze voll* [I've had it up to here]!"[20] That "dimwitted little seaman" would have to learn the hard way, Eichmann raged at Kasztner. "No one can threaten me into letting go of the prime objective." In direct defiance of the Führer's orders, he shouted, the Soviet army had been allowed to seize the Majdanek concentration camp without a shot being fired and with the gas chambers and furnaces intact. No one was following orders any longer. And, Kasztner noted, Eichmann no longer pretended that the gas chambers did not exist.

The government demanded that the Jewish Council immediately provide two thousand laborers for rubble clearing. They would be paid a nominal amount but fed two meals a day. Thousands of the unemployed lined up at Sip Street to apply for the jobs. Former lawyers, engineers, bankers, architects, and doctors were eager to show that they were, despite their age, physically fit. They needed the wages to buy food for their families.

The international community continued to debate how to accommodate the Regent's attempt to win exit visas for Hungarian Jews. As the weeks passed, it showed no sense of urgency and still offered no refuge for forty thousand people. The United States had already filled its Hungarian quota. The camp it had established in upstate New York for around one thousand stateless persons was full.[21] Smaller nations were afraid to offer temporary homes if the United States, Australia, and Canada were not going to take the refugees off their hands once the war was over. Australia refused on the grounds of "unpromising shipping," Ireland agreed to take five hundred children, and Canada did not respond at all. Various South American countries were examining their options.

But the Germans did not provide exit visas even for those who had obtained legal entry papers to other countries. The children's transport to Spain and the Swedish transport of 640 people were stalled. Despite all the paperwork on the collective Swiss passport that Lutz had authorized, no one had been allowed to leave Hungary.[22] Kasztner cabled Saly Mayer in Switzerland that he was convinced no exit visas would be granted without ransom payments.[23] A whole month had passed since Horthy had offered the last chance of "a large rescue," as Krausz had described it.

On August 17, Horthy demanded the resignations of the most overtly pro-Nazi members of the government, including Andor Jaross, the minister of the interior, and sent Prime Minister Döme Sztójay on extended sick leave. Then he waited to see what the German reaction would be, and, when there was none, he appointed Géza Lakatos, a former general in the Hungarian army, as prime minister.[24] During his first week in office, Lakatos dismissed both of the state secretaries, László Baky and László Endre. He tried to pacify the Germans by announcing an immediate increase in production for the war effort.

The official announcement regarding Jewish refugees was finally made by the British and the Americans on August 18, when the *New York Times* reported that the Allies assumed responsibility for providing shelter for the refugees, even though they did not, "in any way, condone the action of the Hungarian government in forcing emigration as an alternative to persecution and death."[25]

The same day, Eichmann ordered a show of strength in Budapest with an hour-long ss parade of goose-stepping, fully armed troops, armored cars, jeeps, and tanks.

Kasztner's repeated requests that Joel Brand return home to report directly to Eichmann went unanswered. He sent daily pleas to the Jewish Agency in Istanbul and to Saly Mayer at the Joint in Switzerland, asking that a date be set for the meeting with Becher. Mayer finally agreed to this encounter, despite his own misgivings and his instructions from Schwalb that he could not offer the Germans anything concrete. He knew that the Joint was expressly forbidden to offer money or goods to enemies of the United States.

On his next visit to Becher, Kasztner demanded that the Bergen-Belsen group be released now, as a token of German goodwill in preparation for the first meeting with Mayer. They had already been paid for, and, if this small concession could be made, he was sure the meeting would bring additional financial rewards. It was, he said, what the Jewish Agency and the Joint would expect. Becher told Kasztner he was "an uppity dog"[26] and suggested he could relax about the mutual undertakings now that he was dealing with Himmler's representative.

"We must clear the air before we meet with any foreign representatives, Herr Obersturmbannführer," Kasztner said. "You need to understand that promises have been broken, that Wisliceny did not deliver his end of the bargain when we paid to avoid the deportations. He said the ss was not interested in deportations, yet that was exactly what followed. Now, at least 300,000 of our people are dead."

"How do you know that?" Becher demanded. "Does Istanbul know?"

"I expect everyone knows, in Istanbul and London, even in New York," Kasztner replied. "This is not the kind of information you can hope to keep hidden."

Becher said it was not information, only rumors, but he immediately asked Eichmann to release half of the original 1,684 passengers on Kasztner's train. Eichmann agreed to only 500,[27] but then, in his instructions to Hermann Krumey, reduced the number still further to 300. Krumey traveled to the "privileged" Ungarnlager, planning to pick the 300 quickly and alphabetically. He had no stomach for the scenes that greeted him on August 16. The previous day there had been a suicide and a funeral in the camp, and, that same evening, everyone had been restricted to the barracks as a large group of newly arrived women were marched past the barred windows to some distant section of the camp. The women were barefoot, their striped cotton dresses hung off their thin shoulders, and they walked with their eyes fixed on the ground and their faces expressionless, hurried along by gun-wielding guards.

The Ungarnlager's inmates became hysterical and grief-stricken when they discovered that Krumey's orders did not include all of them. When Fischer stood on a wooden crate to read out the names of those selected, some screamed and shouted accusations of influence peddling and bribery. Too many had been chosen from Samuel Stern's list, they claimed, and not enough of the halutzim or the Orthodox. Olga Munk was listed, but not her son, John. When she tried to take his hand, at first the guards prevented her, but Krumey relented and added another eighteen to the list for a total 318, risking Eichmann's displeasure but, he hoped, gaining some praise from Kasztner and the others when the war was over.

Krumey had brought letters to the camp from Kasztner, telling the transport's leaders that this smaller group (though he was expecting it to be five hundred) was an advance on the whole deal and that they would all be leaving for Switzerland in a few more days. The letters helped to calm those who stayed behind, especially given the fact that Rezső's and Bogyó's families were still with them.

In a long, coded note, Kasztner reassured Fischer that discussions in Budapest had gone well. He mentioned his own imprisonment and its strange outcome, but it took some days for the imprisoned leaders to interpret what he had said in code.

The entire Munk family was on that first train. Peter remembers stopping at a bombed-out railway station near Frankfurt and watching the burning fires destroy the city. He lay on the roof of the boxcar and delighted in feeling the earth shake as repeated bombing flights attacked Germany. The train reached the Swiss border on August 21, the same time that an ss car arrived on the Austrian side of the Saint Margarethen Bridge, carrying Becher and Kasztner to their first meeting with Saly Mayer.

CHAPTER 22

The Bridge at Saint Margarethen

I should like to add that my efforts to protect Jewish and politically persecuted persons were the reason why I pretended that I wished to carry out these business deals.

Kurt Becher, testifying for the trial of Adolf Eichmann

A company of men passed . . .
I ran to see, are you amongst the men?
You wore prisoner's stripes and a prisoner cap,
Easy to recognize, you looked like your old self.
I, with boundless joy,
Arms raised called out to you
Father, Apukam, look at me, here I am.
You looked at me puzzled,
Questions rose in your eyes,
I did not know why, I did not see myself.
A crazy woman waving,
Hairless and in rags . . .

Baba Schwartz, speaking to her murdered father on the
sixtieth anniversary of the liberation of Auschwitz

W hen Kurt Becher and Rezső Kasztner arrived at Bregenz, Austria, Hermann Krumey, who was waiting for them at the hotel, told Kasztner about Eichmann's orders to reduce his first group to leave Bergen-Belsen to just 300 people, now expanded by Krumey to 318. Kasztner knew, then, that his own family would not have been chosen; Eichmann would keep them as long as he could as a bargaining tool.

The three men traveled to the Swiss border near the Austrian town of Höchst with an armed ss driver and Becher's aide, Max Grüson. They had planned to cross into Switzerland over the Saint Margarethen Bridge, which spans the Rhine Canal between Austria and Switzerland. It was a warm, rainy day in August. Becher wore a bulky black raincoat and dark civilian clothes and stood waiting at the Austrian end. Saly Mayer, a short, balding man in his early sixties, approached the middle of the bridge and waited there for the German party to come closer. Under his raincoat, he was wearing dark-blue pants and a sport jacket with a tidy white handkerchief poking out of its upper left pocket, as though he was expecting a casual invitation to cocktails rather than an ss officer with a life-saving proposition. Mayer, as it turned out, had not obtained Swiss visas for the Germans, so Becher and Krumey moved to the midway point with Kasztner but could not cross to the other side.

Mayer had been a very successful businessman, a lace manufacturer with political ambitions, and he was also the former head of the Association of Swiss Jews. He had retired early from the association amid accusations that he had too easily accepted Swiss restrictions against Jewish refugees.[1] In June 1940 he was appointed as the local representative of the Joint, and he had then been chosen to negotiate with the ss because, as a Swiss citizen, he was not tied to rules governing the actions of Americans. He was set in his ways and conservative in his outlook.

Becher, in contrast, was on the cusp of an outstanding business career—at the moment, it was in trading goods for lives. He had received the entire amount for the Bergen-Belsen transport, yet he still had the majority of its members in the Reich. He had been praised by his chief, Heinrich Himmler, and he was sure he could deliver additional war materials to earn even further promotions. He knew that Himmler had great hopes for this meeting, and that his task included finding a way to make direct contact with the Americans.

Both men were clever and confident negotiators, but on this occasion, neither had much to offer: Mayer had no trucks, and Becher did not have a million Jews left to trade. Nevertheless, both were determined to appear as though they had been dealt a winning hand. They stood halfway across the bridge, each on his side of the border. Mayer refused to enter the Reich, stating explicitly, "My feet would not touch such soil." Nor could he allow the Germans to enter Switzerland, saying, "I am a Swiss citizen and we are a neutral country."

Kasztner was appalled. It had been months since Joel Brand had, presumably, explained what was at stake. Kasztner had sent at least a hundred cables and several coded letters, yet the Joint and the Jewish Agency seemed unable to grasp the seriousness of the situation, the deadly consequences of being rude to a man who held lives in his hands.

Becher introduced himself as Himmler's personal representative. He then made it clear that the survival of the Hungarian Jews depended on how great a sacrifice World Jewry was willing to make.

Mayer replied that he was not empowered to negotiate on behalf of World Jewry, but he was willing to listen, "as a private Swiss citizen," to any proposition that could save lives. He would take these proposals to the American Joint Distribution Committee, provided the Germans stopped deportations and blew up the gas chambers immediately.

"I shall report this to the Reichsführer-ss," Becher replied, with icy politeness. "However, we have already shown our goodwill by letting 318 Jews out of Bergen-Belsen. What do you have to offer in return?"

Mayer mentioned humanitarian considerations. Becher was not interested. It seemed to Kasztner that Mayer was unaware that all he had to do was to pretend he had been contemplating, reviewing, and discussing the German deal with his colleagues in the United States or Palestine or Great Britain or anywhere that sounded halfway impressive. He should have been trying to convince Becher that the British press, with its "Monstrous Offer" headlines, did not speak for the Americans and that Brand was in high-level talks with somebody.

Kasztner could barely control his impatience. He kept interrupting to remind Mayer that the meeting had been instigated by the Joint and that the American War Refugee Board was in favor of supplying the goods requested. He would have settled for mentions of coffee or sugar, or even a truckload of cigarettes, unaware that Mayer's instructions were to negotiate but to promise nothing.[2]

Mayer asked if the Germans would consider currency instead of merchandise. He explained that it would be difficult for him to send "war materials" across the Swiss border in times of war.

"No," Becher replied. They had made their terms clear to Joel Brand and Kasztner, and he saw no reason to waver.

Kasztner was deeply disappointed in Mayer's inability to offer anything the Germans wanted. He felt let down by the Jewish Agency and the Joint, convinced that they had sent the wrong man to negotiate, that they had failed to understand how high the stakes were. When he was given permission to speak with Mayer alone, he said that Eichmann's ss faction was impatient to continue the extermination of the Jews even if Germany was losing the war. Their only hope now lay in some kind of bargain with Himmler's "faction," who "do not oppose the release of Jews if they can obtain goods of value to the Reich."[3]

Mayer was equally impatient with the insistent Kasztner. His own instructions were clear: he was not to promise anything to the Germans. Yet he was here, on his own, on a wet day, in the middle of a bridge, in no-man's-land, shaking hands with the devil, playing for time. He had withheld any indication that he represented no government, not even an organization like the Joint. The Joint, in fact, was expressly forbidden to deal with the enemy. He did not reveal that he had seen the orders signed by the U.S. secretary of state confirming that the United States "cannot enter into or authorize ransom transactions," and that "Saly Mayer should participate only as a Swiss citizen and not (repeat: not) as a representative of any

American organization." Mayer knew that the Germans would not agree to meet a Swiss citizen who lacked the authorization of either the U.S. government or the Joint, so he continued to play the part of a real representative. However, all he had to offer were words.

When it appeared that the meeting was coming to an end without results, Mayer suggested they set a time for a week later, after each of them had consulted his superiors.

Once they had crossed the Swiss border, the 318 passengers from the Kasztner train were offered hot showers, chocolates, warm milk for the children, and a dinner of rice pudding. They traveled by bus to Basel, where they were examined by doctors and given a grand meal of potatoes and chicken in the Mustermesse. Everyone spent the night in agony, vomiting—they were no longer used to food fit for humans.[4] Two days later they were moved to the picturesque Caux-sur-Montreux overlooking Lake Geneva. The Orthodox were given rooms in the Regina Hotel,[5] and the rest of the group were housed in the Bellevue and Caux Palace. They were able to read their first newspapers in a long time and hear the first broadcasts about the true state of the war. Some began to make plans for a quick return to their Hungarian homes, some filled out application forms for their departure for Palestine, and others tried to reach friends and relations in other countries, hoping for entry visas now that the war seemed to be near its end. In József Fischer's absence, they elected Kasztner's old law-school friend Dezsö Hermann as leader.

Becher and Kasztner returned to Budapest, angry and afraid. Kasztner was terrified that his wife and the remaining Bergen-Belsen hostages would be transferred to Auschwitz. Becher was furious with Kasztner. He had, obviously, not briefed his associates about the seriousness of a senior ss officer traveling to negotiate with a bunch of Jews who had not even bothered to provide a suitable reception. He was afraid for his position as Himmler's man of choice for the negotiations and even worried about his own life. The meeting with

Mayer had been his idea. The ss Reichsführer would be enraged about this failure, particularly now that the enemy was advancing steadily on the Reich from both west and east—the Americans were about to enter Paris, and the Soviet army had already arrived in Romania. The Ploesti oil fields that had fueled the German armies in the east would be under enemy control. The Bulgarians had announced their desire to withdraw from the war, and the Finns, never an enthusiastic ally of Germany against the Soviet Union, were becoming surly.

On August 23 the Wehrmacht lost the battle for Romania at the cost of 380,000 soldiers. King Michael immediately had the violently anti-Semitic and pro-Nazi Ion Antonescu arrested and replaced his government with one that did not support the Germans. In response, the Luftwaffe bombed the Royal Palace in Bucharest. Romania eagerly joined the war against its former allies, just as it had done at the end of the First World War. Now, as before, its immediate priority was to invade Transylvania and try to wrest it away from the Hungarians. Romania signed an armistice with the Soviets and, thereby, sealed Hungary's fate. Hungary was now the frontline.

Two days later, General Charles de Gaulle, chief of the Free French armies, walked down the Champs Élysées to the sound of church bells ringing and wild cheering from the crowds. The French Resistance had risen against the German occupation and, in close coordination with both the Americans and General Philippe Leclerc's French armored division, it took back the City of Light from the German occupying forces.

Somewhere on the road toward Vienna, Becher decided not to tell Himmler the truth. His August 25 wire to his chief reported that the release of the 318 Jews from Bergen-Belsen had convinced the Americans of the seriousness of the Germans' willingness to negotiate, and he recommended that they should accept alternative products such as raw materials (chromium, nickel, aluminum) in place of the trucks they had originally demanded. He emphasized that if the deportations from Hungary continued, the Jewish leaders would break off discussions, and he humbly requested Himmler's permission to continue with his mission to wrest material rewards for the Reich.

On August 29, Regent Horthy sent word to Edmund Veesen-mayer that he had decided there would be no more deportations, at least for now. At 3 AM, a cable arrived from Berlin for Becher. Himmler approved the suspension of deportations and authorized Becher to continue his negotiations. It seemed that the ss Reichs-führer was more interested in keeping Hungary onside than in pur-suing his original plan of "cleansing" the country. Besides, by the end of August 1944 the German armies had lost half a million men and most of their tanks in the west. Himmler had been thinking about finding an acceptable way out of the war.[6]

Once back in his office in Budapest, Kasztner was astonished to learn from Dieter Wisliceny that Eichmann and his unit had been ordered out of Hungary. "You have won," the Nazi officer told him. "The Sonderkommando is leaving."[7]

For a while, Eichmann remained hopeful that the orders were temporary. He sent Wisliceny back to Berlin to see if Himmler would change his mind, and, if not, whether his orders might be overruled by Hitler. But Himmler wouldn't even see Wisliceny, and the Führer was preoccupied with war business. Eichmann, furious at Becher's soft technique and Himmler's vacillations, retired to sulk at his estate near Linz in Austria. To compensate him for the disap-pointment, Himmler later awarded him an Iron Cross–Second Class.

Kasztner, unlike members of the Jewish Council, had no faith in Horthy's protestations that he had been duped into allowing depor-tations in the first place and even less faith in Himmler's change of heart. Increasingly, he began to rely on Becher's fear of his superiors while they were still in power and the lieutenant-colonel's anxiety about retribution once they were gone. Kasztner cabled Mayer that the second meeting had to be arranged immediately and that Mayer had to come with something concrete to offer Becher, perhaps gaso-line or engine parts—something the Germans needed but would never get because the war would be over before the Joint had to deliver on its promises. The telephone lines to Switzerland were broken, so Becher arranged for Kasztner to travel to Bratislava to make a call to Mayer to finalize the arrangements.

During the phone conversation, Kasztner told Mayer bluntly that his failure to arrange some plan as a basis for negotiation might be construed later as his participating in the murder of Hungarian Jewry. "It's easy for Mayer to express his loathing for the Nazis," he wrote in his diary. "They [the Joint] are on the outside, we are on the inside. They moralize, we fear death. They are sympathetic but believe themselves to be powerless. We want to live and therefore believe that rescue is possible."[8] He told Hansi that "the next meeting at the Swiss border cannot be another fiasco."

While he was in Bratislava, Kasztner visited Gizi Fleischmann, who asked him not to forget the Slovak Jews if he made a deal with the Joint. Their situation had not changed since Wisliceny stopped the deportations,[9] but she was afraid that the Germans would begin the roundups again with a vengeance once the Soviet armies neared their borders. She confided that her own experiences had convinced her that Mayer was the wrong man for these desperate negotiations. Their lives were hanging by the slender hook of hope for more cash to keep Wisliceny on their side.

Saly Mayer agreed to a meeting on September 3, but Becher refused to attend. He told Kasztner that he was not prepared to be humiliated by "that Jew" again and instead sent his aide Max Grüson, Hermann Krumey, William Billitz, the man who was now running the Weiss-Manfred conglomerate, and, of course, Kasztner. Mayer was accompanied by his lawyer, another dapper Swiss named Marcus Wyler-Schmidt.

Once again, the meeting was midway along the Saint Margarethen Bridge. This time, Mayer had a few more cards to play. He had been granted $2 million of bargaining money by the U.S. War Refugee Board, but it could not be used for ransom payments. He upped this to $5 million (the additional $3 million was entirely fictitious) and offered to deposit the amount in designated Swiss accounts. He said he would do his best to persuade the Swiss to allow the Germans to buy whatever they needed.[10] As a further delaying technique, he told the delegation to return with a list of their likely requirements. His condition was that all the Jews under Nazi rule be kept alive. Having heard from Rabbi Dov Weissmandel, he was particularly concerned about the Slovak Jews.

Grüson said the ss always delivered on its promises. Deportations in Hungary had already ceased, and the first group of "Kasztner's Jews" had been handed across the Swiss border. World Jewry had not yet reciprocated. Joel Brand, who had been sent on an important mission, had vanished. Grüson pointed out that Mayer was only a middleman, a Swiss citizen who could not make deals on the spot. He was wasting their time. He demanded that, at the next meeting, Mayer bring along someone who had full authority to negotiate, so that the Germans would leave with a signed agreement.[11]

Mayer, it seemed to Kasztner, had nodded his assent.

The next night, back in Budapest, Hansi brought out a small bottle of old French brandy she had saved from before the war. Both of the dreaded state secretaries, László Baky and László Endre, had been discredited; Mayer was now talking about $5 million, and the deportations had ended. It was a hazy, hot, late-summer evening, with clouds of mosquitoes buzzing through the open window. They did not dare light a candle during the blackout, as they waited for the next bombardment to begin and the sirens to start. Huddled over a meal of cold eggs and ersatz bacon, they drank to the victory of the Allies and their own success. They were, finally, beginning to make a difference.

CHAPTER 23

The End of Summer

If I pass through this difficult period, I believe I will be able to say
that my life was not in vain . . .

Gizi Fleischmann, in a letter to her daughter
in Palestine, summer 1944

In the late summer of 1944 a bloody insurrection erupted in Slovakia against the government of Josef Tiso, aka Father Tiso, a Catholic priest and one of the most feared, hysterically anti-Semitic leaders of the Nazi era. Since early June, there had been sporadic partisan attacks in the area around Banská Bystrica. Partisan forces had been strengthened by the addition of some Slovak army deserters and by French and Soviet escapees from concentration camps. A few parachutists from Britain and two Soviet airborne brigades also took part in the uprising, as did some Jewish partisans, including Rudolf Vrba, who finally got his chance to hear a German scream in pain. In his autobiography, Vrba wrote of the extraordinary joy he experienced when he realized that Germans could be hurt, that they were not as invincible as they had seemed in Auschwitz.

Tiso requested Hitler's help to hold on to power. On August 29, ss Lieutenant General Gottlob Berger arrived with an elite ss force to quell the rebellion, and Adolf Eichmann dispatched Captain Alois Brunner for immediate reprisals against the Jews.

Brunner was one of Eichmann's most reliable acolytes. He had joined the National Socialist Party when he was only nineteen years old. His dream had been to become a member of the elite ss corps, but he was too short, too thin, and too ugly to be immediately accepted. He worked as Eichmann's secretary at the Central Office for Jewish Emigration, in Austria after the Anschluss and managed to have 47,000 Austrian Jews sent to the death camps. He then teamed up with Dieter Wisliceny in Salonica, where 44,000 Jews were packed into boxcars destined for Auschwitz. Wisliceny thought Brunner was too eager to prove himself because of his "black kinky hair and hooked nose."[1] Brunner commanded the roundup of Jews in France and their transport to Auschwitz. His hatred for Jews was legendary—Eichmann had chosen him carefully. He looked on his mission in Slovakia as an opportunity for further career advancement, as his chance to destroy those Jews whose lives had been spared against payments to Wisliceny. The deportations of all participants in the uprising in Slovakia and of all Jews were publicly announced. Of the 19,000 people who were driven to the Sered transit camp, about half were Jews.

Kasztner first heard of the Slovak uprising at Hermann Krumey's headquarters in Vienna. He had been working with Krumey's staff to allow the Red Cross to distribute shoes and clothing to the Strasshof deportees, who had been robbed of the last of their meager possessions by the Ukrainian guards on arrival at the transit camp. By now, all of them had worn out their summer clothes. Some had made wooden soles and tied them to their feet with rags; others wore rags with newspaper lining. Those prisoners used for fieldwork in the countryside had received pieces of clothing from villagers, but the Vienna groups had nothing to protect them from the cold. Kasztner had also brought in corn and potatoes from Győr in Hungary, but Krumey insisted that the Austrians were as deprived of food as the prisoners and had confiscated the entire truckload.

As soon as Krumey told him the news from Bratislava, Kasztner cabled Saly Mayer in Switzerland, begging him to ask for another meeting. His previous cable had inquired whether Mayer was still alive, for only Mayer's demise, Kasztner thought, could explain the void into which he had been sending his desperate pleas. Next he called on Kurt Becher at the Grand Hotel in Vienna. He found the English somewhat surly. Not enough was being accomplished at the meetings with Mayer, the German complained, and he did not want to be blamed for the lack of progress. Mayer's request for a list of goods was just another delaying tactic, he felt. Kasztner told him that the Sonderkommando had rounded up seven or eight thousand Jews already in Slovakia. Becher would not even discuss the Slovaks, nor ask Himmler to intercede on their behalf. He did not want to be perceived by his superiors as an advocate for Jews. However, he did grant Kasztner another travel permit for Bratislava.[2] He would be accompanied by Max Grüson to make sure he made no contact with suspicious elements.

Becher did not tell Kasztner that he was concerned about Himmler's own position in the Reich. Although Himmler had enthusiastically organized the arrest and interrogation of the leaders implicated in a July 20 plot to kill Hitler, there had been rumors that he might have had contact with former colonel Claus Stauffenberg, the presumed mastermind behind the attempted assassination. The Reichsführer had shown himself particularly diligent in rooting out the perpetrators and all their friends and relations. There had been a wave of arrests, gruesome torture filmed for the edification of the masses, and public executions, some of which were carried out with meat hooks and piano wire. Fortunately, news of Joel Brand's failure had been drowned out by the news of the retributions. No, Becher cautioned, it was not the time to mention Jews to Himmler.

Kasztner reached Bratislava on September 15. No sooner had he arrived at the Carlton Hotel than Brunner's Gestapo agents arrested him.

"Are you a Jew?" a young ss officer demanded.

"I am not considered a Jew," Kasztner replied.

"Are you circumcised?"

"Yes, but I am still not considered a Jew."

"By our laws, you are a Jew!" the officer shouted as they dragged the protesting Kasztner across the lobby and down the steps to a waiting car.[3]

When Becher heard about the arrest, he called Brunner. Soon after, Kasztner was released.

Kasztner went to see Gizi Fleischmann and Rabbi Weissmandel, who were still in their offices at Edel Alley. Their Working Group had been bombarding Mayer with cables, asking for immediate financial assistance. They were sure the government-supported Hlinka Guard militia would not oppose the ss. Kasztner offered to ask Becher to set up an "economic branch" in Bratislava where he could negotiate to exchange lives for more cash or merchandise. "On the spot we drew up a list of deliverable merchandise" for presentation to Becher, Kasztner remembered, and he returned to Vienna the next day to beg Becher to consider the Slovak proposition. Becher declined because he still had no word from Mayer.

On September 16 Ottó Komoly met Miklós Horthy Jr. in Buda Castle to discuss the removal of the anti-Jewish laws. The Lakatos government had announced its intention to return Jews to productive life, though not to their previously held positions. The young Horthy had spoken openly about stepping out of the war, about joining the Americans. His father had ordered the arrest of several Arrow Cross leaders. Horthy Jr. asked Komoly whether the Jews in labor battalions would be willing to join with the Hungarian army to fight against the Germans, should defending Hungary be necessary. Komoly was certain the Jews would welcome the opportunity to meet the Germans on a battlefield. They did not discuss how his father was going to regain control of the army from the largely Swabian senior staff. When Komoly mentioned his concern that the Germans would not give up Hungary, Miklós Jr. smiled. The Germans needed friends to the east of their Reich, he said.

When Komoly told Kasztner and Hansi Brand about the meeting, he described Horthy Jr. as an uninformed, hot-headed chip off the old block, a traditional anti-Semite, but with some decency—and that, he believed, was about all that was needed from men of

influence in these times. A willingness to look at the facts might have
been helpful, but one should not expect too much. Young Horthy
had seemed genuinely horrified that extermination camps existed,
Komoly reported, and had not tried to argue, as his father had done,
that Auschwitz was merely another tough labor camp.

"They don't have a chance" was Becher's view of Horthy's late
resistance to the Germans. "We will hold the territory, no matter
what the loss of life," he told Kasztner. "Budapest is the cornerstone
of the Margarethen line [named for Margarethen (or Margit) Island
in the Danube between Buda and Pest]. We will defend it to the best
of our ability and to the last man. Germany will not accept your tin-
pot Regent's desire to make a separate peace." The fact that Finland
had just, on September 19, signed a separate peace treaty with the
Russians was going to make Horthy's disobedience more irritating to
Hitler now than it might have been earlier.

On September 24, Kasztner returned, empty-handed, to
Bratislava. At his request, Grüson went to see Brunner to tell him,
without due authorization from Becher, that important negotiations
were taking place between the Reich and certain members of the
Slovak Working Group and that they involved the delivery of war
materials.[4] He demanded that therefore Fleischmann's group be
allowed to continue its work. Brunner refused. He took his orders
only from Eichmann, he insisted. Grüson was arrested a few days
later.[5]

Kasztner offered Becher a deal that included 30,000 Slovakian
kronen and 110,000 yards of ready-to-wear canvas in exchange for
fifty people. This small group would be taken directly to Switzerland, and the rest of the Jews who were awaiting their fate in the
Sered camp would go to Theresienstadt. No Slovak Jews would be
sent to Auschwitz. Mayer, Kasztner assured Becher, would compensate generously, and the War Refugee Board would supply food and
clothing through the Red Cross. But this time Kasztner failed.

"You've done the best you could, Rudolf," Becher tried to console
him. "If we lose the war, there will be statues commemorating your
efforts, streets named after you in Tel Aviv and Budapest." Mayer's
September 26 cable to Kasztner, asking for a meeting—his first after

a three-week silence—was, they agreed, a good sign, but Becher predicted it was too late to save the Slovak Jews. They had been taken into custody for "military reasons."[6] A large number of them had been picked up in areas formerly controlled by the partisans, he said, and Eichmann had succeeded in "poisoning the atmosphere in Berlin." Becher showed Kasztner a copy of Brunner's telegram to Eichmann, sent after Kasztner had offered goods for the Slovak Jews. It read: "The claims of the Jew from the Joint, Kasztner, are a lie. And delivery of goods from the Jews would disturb German-Slovak relations. The Jewess, Fleischmann, has been caught by the Slovak police as she was composing horror stories to send abroad. I have taken the necessary steps."[7]

Kasztner feared that Mayer's cable, indicating that the Joint (or whoever was behind Mayer) was no longer stalling, would not impress Eichmann. In it, Mayer reiterated his agreement to put money in a Swiss bank account for the Nazis' use. So Kasztner returned once again to the passengers on his train and urged Becher at least to allow the rest of the Bergen-Belsen group into Switzerland. The "other side" would expect nothing less. Kasztner always presented his own views as though he were merely conveying the demands of this other side. Frequently, he acted aggrieved by the intransigence of the Joint or the Jewish Agency, an unwilling middleman who was doing his best.

"Surely this group can be considered as paid for long ago," he urged.

Becher replied that, because the deemed exchange rate for the dollar had changed considerably since the group had left and given that all the financial details were based on the old conversion rates, money was owed now. He showed Kasztner Himmler's personally signed telegram: "The other side must be crazy. The fee for a Jew from Europe to enter America is $1,000, the emigration fee for a Jew to leave Europe is also $1,000. Himmler." The original deposit, as estimated by Becher's new man, First Lieutenant Karl Grabau, was worth only $400,000 to $500,000, not enough to pay for even half of the remaining Jews in Bergen-Belsen.[8]

Kasztner protested that the rates at the time of departure from

Budapest would, surely, apply. Becher demurred. The payment was only a deposit against the Brand deal, and the first group had been allowed to leave Bergen-Belsen without a single truck in return. There was continued silence from Switzerland on the important issue of trucks and on meeting with a suitable negotiating partner, someone other than Mayer.

On September 28 Kasztner traveled to Switzerland for another meeting with Mayer. Becher, when he learned that Mayer would once again have no one of higher authority to accompany him, decided not to attend himself and not to attempt the release of the remaining "Kasztner Jews" from Bergen-Belsen. Instead, he sent Herbert Kettlitz, another of his ss aides.[9] And Becher proved to be right. The third meeting was as inconclusive as the previous two had been. There was still no money in any bank, nor had any goods been bought. Mayer's lawyer, Marcus Wyler-Schmidt, did most of the talking. He promised to advance the $2 million after the Germans stopped all the deportations. He specified their awareness of the imminent danger facing Slovak Jews, and demanded improved conditions for both Jews and slave laborers in concentration camps. Mayer told Kasztner in Yiddish that he had nothing more to offer and that his total budget was frozen by U.S. government orders.[10]

Kasztner was relieved that Kettlitz did not understand Yiddish and that Becher had not come to another pointless meeting. As he recalled later, even Kettlitz had been reduced to entreating Mayer for some written agreement, something "my chief could use. Otherwise," he warned, "it will be impossible for him to intervene further with the Reichsführer-ss on behalf of the Jews."

Mayer's response was delivered with his usual stiffness: "A Swiss gives only those promises he knows he can keep," he said.[11]

Kasztner was enraged by Mayer's seeming intransigence. Mayer had full knowledge of the impending fate of the Slovak Jews, and he knew how many Hungarian Jews had been deported to Auschwitz-Birkenau. Yet there he was, "an old, venerable, neurotic retiree, vain, overbearing, ignoring how many lives are involved and congratulating himself on his personal sacrifice of negotiating with the Nazis." Mayer's notion of "playing for time" was no longer effective—a few more days and there would be no more time left.[12]

Becher, following Himmler's orders, now insisted that there would be no further meetings or discussions unless Mayer produced a representative of the Allies, preferably an American.

The Allies had liberated France. In Italy, Canadian and American forces were fighting their way north toward Rome. The Soviet army was at the gates of Warsaw; they had been there since the beginning of the Poles' uprising against the Germans on August 1, but Stalin had determined that he wanted Poland weakened. He did not wish to see any more attempts at independence. So the Soviet army sat and sunbathed on the far side while the Germans fought back, destroying whole city blocks in Warsaw and massacring some forty thousand unarmed civilians on the western bank of the Vistula River.[13]

Krumey called Kasztner in Budapest. With winter approaching, he could now give the International Red Cross permission to deliver the shoes and some warmer clothes for the Strasshof exchange Jews. He implied that further payments would be needed for transmitting the clothes—in other words, the usual ss bribe—but did not mention the sum. He complained that some local Austrians were handing their own clothes to the Jews, a situation he said had to be stopped if only for the benefit of the would-be humanitarians. They were endangering their own lives. Kasztner ordered five thousand pairs of shoes from a Slovak supplier and requested the money to pay for them from the Jewish Agency's Rescue Committee.

The Columbus Street camp continued to attract the displaced and the desperate. Some people hoped for another train, and, in the meantime, the camp seemed calmer than the rest of Budapest. There was still a hospital, a baths barrack, and even an ambulance service. Many of the new arrivals had been rescued from the provincial ghettos in exchange for steep bribes to the ss.[14] Ottó Komoly was a frequent visitor, delivering letters and packages and collecting mail for relatives in Budapest. He believed the camp would be handed over to the Hungarian authorities now that Eichmann's contingent had departed from the city. Unlike Kasztner, Komoly had faith in the Hungarians' ability to sustain their regained independence.

Kasztner moved his secretary from the pension where she had been living to the Columbus Street camp, with fake papers. He spent the nights dictating letters and cables to the Joint and the Jewish Agency. His reports on the situation in Budapest were starting to show the strain of his daily efforts, his lack of sleep, and his frustration over Joel Brand's failure to return. Unlike Samuel Stern and the Central Jewish Council, Kasztner was unconvinced that these days were any more than a brief lull in the terror.

The illusion that the Germans would pack up and go home had taken hold of the capital. The cafés and restaurants were full, and no one left even when the sirens sounded. It was a sunny, cool fall after the over-hot summer months. The kiosks along the Danube Corso played less Mozart and more Chopin. The Jews of Budapest gathered in their overcrowded Star House apartments to celebrate the two days of the New Year and the day of Yom Kippur.

The Soviet army, now joined by units of Romanians and encountering light resistance, rolled into Transylvania in northeastern Hungary with 59 divisions and 825 tanks, outnumbering German and Hungarian troops by more than two to one.

Joel Brand was, finally, released by the British on October 5. He had been given the choice of returning to Budapest, where he would probably have been killed for coming back empty-handed, or going to Palestine. He chose Palestine. He saw Teddy Kollek, a fellow Hungarian[15] he had met in Istanbul, and David Ben-Gurion, and, as he poured out his story to them, he blamed both of them for the failure of his mission. He was not comforted when Ben-Gurion tried to reassure him that the negotiations were ongoing. And he exploded when he learned that Saly Mayer was representing the Joint in meetings with the ss and that Brand's role had been assumed by Rezső Kasztner.

Brand continued to write reports, bombarding the governments of Great Britain and the United States with demands for action in Hungary. He called himself the "emissary for the dead" and believed he was speaking on behalf of Hungary's murdered Jews. He spent hours waiting outside the offices of various Jewish leaders in Tel Aviv and Jerusalem, hoping to tell them how they had let down half a million Jews by not listening to his pleas in Istanbul. Everyone, he found, was too busy with his own unimportant tasks to pay attention to mass murder in Hungary. "Well-trained secretaries," he recalled, "would tell me facilely that their bosses had gone out and that no one knew exactly when they would return."[16]

Brand was still unaware of how little influence the leaders of the Jewish Agency and the various American Jewish organizations had on the policies of the Allies. Furious with the British for arresting him in Syria and with the Agency for not making an effort to meet Eichmann's demands, he joined the bitterest enemies of the Jewish Agency and the British occupation forces, the Stern Gang, a Jewish terrorist group named for its founder, Avraham Stern, who had been killed by the British in 1942. The Stern Gang did not accept the policy of the Haganah, the Jewish underground army under the command of the Jewish Agency, to cease fighting the British while the Allies fought the Germans; nor did it accept the British mandate, the White Paper limiting immigration, or any of the British policies governing the Jewish presence in Palestine. Its methods of showing disagreement included blowing up British installations and attacking British soldiers. In November 1944 the Stern Gang murdered Lord Moyne, the British minister for Middle Eastern affairs who had played an active role in Brand's blood-for-goods mission.

In mid-October, Captain Alois Brunner began to empty the Sered camp of its almost twenty thousand Slovak Jews, even as the Slovak insurrection was defeated by four German ss divisions. Some of those who were sent to Theresienstadt survived the war. A few survived at the Sachsenhausen camp in Germany, Stutthof in Poland, and Bergen-Belsen. The rest, including all the children, were murdered in Auschwitz. Brunner had always taken great pleasure in the murder of children.[17]

Rabbi Weissmandel, the man who had first tried to buy Jewish lives from Wisliceny, escaped from the train. He hid in the cellar of a villa on the outskirts of Bratislava with seventeen other Jews. His wife and children were murdered in Auschwitz-Birkenau.

Gizi Fleischmann, the woman Wisliceny had commended for her extraordinary courage, was given a last chance to live: Brunner asked her to reveal the whereabouts of Jews in hiding.[18] When she refused, she was chained to the floor of a boxcar. For the twenty hours it took the train to reach its final destination, she could move neither her arms nor her legs. Brunner had her transport marked "Return Undesirable." On arrival at the Birkenau rail ramp, she was taken directly to the gas chambers.

CHAPTER 24

The Dying Days of Budapest

Voluminous books will be written to show in full light all that occurred in the course of those ten months . . . That epoch without one quiet day, a day without one quiet minute, was like a limitless expanse of water, a flood sweeping away everything . . . Those who outlived it were the true favorites of Providence.

The man who was forced to head the doomed asks himself: Have I blundered on this or that occasion? Have I omitted things that ought to have been done? And seeing our enormous losses and our minute remnants—those few still alive—is it a wonder that he looks into the deepest recesses of his soul to examine his conscience? . . . He who, in those times in that situation, could have contrived to accomplish something more and better, let him cast the first stone.

Samuel Stern, "A Race Against Time"[1]

The Soviet army broke through German and Hungarian defenses west of Transylvania and pushed onto the Great Hungarian Plain and then into Bulgaria. In Sofia it was joined by the defecting Bulgarian army; together, they routed the Germans from Belgrade at a loss of fifteen thousand Wehrmacht soldiers killed and nine thousand taken prisoner. Marshal Josip Tito's partisans paraded down the streets of the Yugoslav capital, cheered by the remnant population. By mid-October 1944 the Second and Third Ukrainian Fronts were ready to execute Stalin's order to "take Budapest quickly."[2]

Heavy Allied bombardments of Budapest had destroyed the Museum of Fine Arts, the Museum of the Capital, and most of the Millennial Monument. The sound of sirens had become so common that some people rarely came up from their cellars. The running joke in the city was that the Americans, being young, still needed their beauty sleep, so they dropped bombs during the day. The British bombed during the night. At sunset, you could never be sure which one it would be. On both sides of the Danube, along the boulevards where the chestnut trees stood in silent witness to the insanity of man, whole apartment buildings had been leveled. The Csepel factories had been destroyed. The government, through the Jewish Council, called up all able-bodied Jewish men and women for local labor, removing corpses from the rubble and putting out fires. The bodies were laid out in school auditoriums and gymnasiums, where they could be identified by relatives.

Arrow Cross newspapers accused the Jews of signaling bombers from rooftops, directing bombs to specific targets. "You can imagine this little Jewish guy," Rezső told Hansi. "He is sitting on top of his apartment building and he is signaling like mad at the next building, where his mother-in-law lives. And, what do you know, the British pilot can spot him in the dark with the antiaircraft strobe lights in his eyes and he says, thank you little Jewish fellow, and bombs the next building . . . They are all mad. Every one of them. It's as if they had all caught some disease of the mind."

Another newspaper headline reported that American pilots had dropped thousands of booby-trapped dolls that exploded as children played with them. There were posters of mutilated children holding decapitated dolls. Through brilliant investigative work, a young Arrow Cross boy discovered that the dolls were all manufactured in Budapest by Jews. The question of how these devilishly clever Jews managed to get the dolls with explosives to the American pilots was never asked and never had to be answered.

Raoul Wallenberg had opened the door of the Swedish Embassy and directed his staff to hand out Swedish protection papers to all Jewish applicants. The certificates claimed that the holders were Swedish citizens awaiting exit visas. A lively underground market for protection papers developed—Swiss, Swedish, and Spanish. Some people had all three, as well as certificates of baptism, army discharge papers, and old *levente* identity papers (the Levente were a Hungarian paramilitary youth movement), proving that they had taken some junior military training in a Christian environment. As Kasztner said, "You could never have too many identity papers." Most young halutzim carried levente cards, army discharge papers, or army sick-leave papers. A person stopped on the street by a policeman and asked to identify himself had to be careful which pocket he reached into before he announced who he was.

The number of Jews with official Swedish protection papers would exceed 4,500 by the end of October. At least another 3,000 fake Swedish certificates were handed out by the Rescue Committee and its halutz workers. They all waited for permits to leave the country and be allowed into Palestine. With each passing day, Moshe Krausz's dream of personally saving a large number of Jews evaporated.

Miklós Horthy Jr. told Ottó Komoly that he was concerned about the vast number of Jews ready to leave the country. Hungarians, he said, needed the competition from the Jews—it egged them on to accomplish more. He opined that when the situation normalized, the government would petition some of those eager to leave for Palestine to stay behind to assist the nation's economy. Komoly, always polite and thoughtful, had found it difficult not to laugh.[3]

The Swiss Red Cross had received over three million Swiss francs from the Joint to pay for food for the people in the protected Star

Houses that bore the Swedish colors and in the Columbus Street camp. Unlike the houses, the camp had not been marked with the Star of David, though everyone knew it was providing a refuge to Jews. Now Komoly and Kasztner asked Friedrich Born to allow the emblem of the International Red Cross, a large red cross against a white background, to be placed to the right of the main entrance. The Red Cross, Kasztner thought, was even more reliable than protection passes.

Throughout the period when Géza Lakatos was prime minister, rumors spread that Horthy was getting ready to exit the war, that all he needed was "an honorable way out," and that he had sent emissaries to the Allies through Istanbul and Lisbon. He wanted to sue for peace—but not if peace included Stalin. The British and the Americans were not interested. President Roosevelt had announced that nothing less than "unconditional surrender" would do. Contrary to Horthy's assumption, the Allies had no interest in marching up from the Balkans and taking advantage of his desire to welcome them.[4] Later, historians would explain that a deal with the Soviet Union had already been made, that Europe was to be divided into "spheres of influence," with Hungary falling into the Soviet sphere. Resistance to the Germans did not save the Poles from Soviet domination at war's end, and Hungary's increasingly reluctant alliance with the Germans did not help Horthy's case.

In final desperation, having lost all faith in the British and the Americans, Horthy sent Lieutenant General Gábor Faragho, his former military attaché in Moscow, across the front lines to present Hungary's case to the Russians. On October 11 Faragho returned with a draft armistice agreement requiring Hungary to give up, once again, its historic territories, those that had been reacquired after the shameful Treaty of Trianon—in other words, everything Horthy had fought for during his career as head of state. In this dilemma, the Regent did what he had always done when faced with a tough decision: nothing. His hesitation gave the Germans the time they needed to prepare a coup.

Ferenc Szálasi, the leader of the Arrow Cross Party, was seen coming and going from the residence of the German plenipotentiary,

Edmund Veesenmayer, as were several ultra-right-wing politicians, including the former minister of the interior, Andor Jaross. Horthy's efforts to have all the Arrow Cross leaders jailed had met with effective resistance from the Germans, and many of them were now grateful guests at Veesenmayer's opulent residence. Himmler called in the chief of antipartisan units from Warsaw to take command of the local ss.

In full view, right outside the Hungaria Hotel, three ss men pushed a uniformed Hungarian general into the backseat of a car. His two senior officers were abducted from their hotel rooms.

Meanwhile, Miklós Horthy Jr. invited Samuel Stern to another secret meeting in Buda Castle. Stern received so many instructions to take precautionary measures that he got lost as he followed a map through the underground tunnels and surfaced in the wrong court-yard, only to be directed back the way he had come and into another set of tunnels. Young Horthy wanted to know whether the Jewish Council had been able to reach the labor service brigades to ascertain that the 150,000 men there were ready to fight alongside the Hungarian army. It was the same question he had asked Komoly a few days earlier. Surprised that someone like Horthy Jr. would understand the fear and suspicion Jews now felt toward Hungarians, Stern was certain that not one of them would refuse to fight for what had once been his country—as long as the enemy was the Germans and not the Soviets.

On Sunday morning, October 15, Hansi Brand told Ottó Komoly that she had heard rumors that the Regent's son had been abducted. German planes had dropped leaflets over the city urging a rebellion against the government. Gestapo cars had been seen in various parts of the city, and politicians and high-ranking soldiers had been arrested. It was a gray, moist, cloudy, windless autumn morning, as though the whole city was holding its breath. On street corners, in shop windows through loudspeakers, in apartments that still had radio sets, Hungarian Radio announced that the Regent would make a general proclamation at 1 PM.

A few minutes before the appointed hour, regular broadcasts ceased. When Horthy finally spoke, his voice was soft and shaky. In a long, detailed statement, he announced his decision to sign a separate peace treaty with the Allies and withdraw Hungary from the war. He spoke of the lost territories, the injustices of the Treaty of Trianon, and declared that "Hungary was dragged into war against the Allies through German pressure resulting from our geographic location. In this war we had no aims of conquest: we did not wish to take away so much as a square metre of territory from anyone else," only to regain what Hungary had lost. "Today it is obvious to any sober-minded person that the German Reich has lost the war," he said. The Reich had broken its obligations to its Hungarian partner when it invaded the country in March and arrested many Hungarian citizens. Germany had shown that it would lead Hungary to total destruction. He blamed the Gestapo for dealing with the "Jewish problem" in an inhumane way and claimed that his nation had been forced to persecute the Jews. He announced that he was ready to protect the honor of Hungary now that its former ally was assisting his enemies in an attempted coup.

At the end of his proclamation, Horthy called on Hungarian soldiers to remain loyal and to obey only his instructions.

Regent Horthy's desire for Hungary to exit the war was heard throughout the country several times that day, but on that day only. It had turned into a glorious fall afternoon: the sun was shining, and the trees along the boulevards displayed their startling red, yellow, and deep-purple colors as if the horrors of the past few weeks had not happened, as if the houses lining the avenues had not been turned into rubble by the bombardments. People came out of their cellars, put on their good clothes, and walked, holding hands and greeting each other just as they had done in peacetime. Many Jews who had been in hiding paraded their newfound freedom; some tore the yellow stars off their breasts and ordered shots of pálinka in bars where they used to go, or dared to use a public telephone and take rides on the streetcars where the tracks had not yet been bombed.

But the general euphoria did not last.

Horthy's proposed surrender may have been a surprise to some, but certainly not to the Germans. They had watched his preparations since the end of August, listening to every conversation in the castle.

They were aware of his plan to bring two Hungarian regiments into the city, knew of the arming of the Jewish battalions, had seen the draft capitulation agreement, and were ready with their own surprise for the Regent.

Horthy Jr. had indeed been captured, by two Gestapo agents posing as Yugoslav emissaries from Tito's partisan army. The capture had been laughably easy, though not without casualties: One of young Horthy's friends and the SD chief, Lieutenant Colonel Klages,[5] had been wounded in the battle between the Horthys' guards and the Germans. Pistol-whipped and rolled up in a carpet, the Regent's son was traveling toward Germany. His capture had been the chief reason for Regent Horthy's shaken voice on the radio. At seventy-seven, having lost one son already in a plane crash over Kassa, at the outbreak of the war, Horthy was devastated by the abduction of the other. The Germans now raised the stakes and threatened that his son would be executed unless the admiral withdrew his surrender plans. Without further remonstrance, the Regent handed over power to the Arrow Cross.

In the late afternoon, the radio went silent; when it resumed a short time later, it played German marching songs. Along Olasz Avenue, one halutz on his way to the Slovak border saw a long column of German armored trucks and tanks rumble into Buda, their turrets swiveling, their trapdoors shut, ready with their machine guns. The Arrow Cross took over the national radio station. The Regent's orders to the army were replaced by new ones from the chief of the Hungarian general staff, ordering soldiers in the Hungarian armed forces to fight against the Soviet invaders. The gendarmerie was urged to continue its fight against bolshevism. Horthy, under duress and in fear for his son's life, signed a document nullifying his earlier statements and confirming the orders from the chief of the general staff. He handed over the leadership of the Hungarian government to the Germans' handpicked successor, Szálasi. While not their first choice—his complicated ideology gave precedence to a renewed "Hungarist," or racially Magyar, state, rather than an abject German servant—he and they agreed on the need to win the war and the desire to be rid of all the Jews.

The radio played the Hungarian anthem, followed by the German anthem. As head of state, Szálasi awarded himself a new title: "protector of the Hungarian people." He announced that Admiral Horthy had been flown to Germany and was in protective custody. The "traitors" who had attempted a takeover of the government had been arrested and would pay dearly for their black deeds. Hungary would stand firm with its great friend and ally, Germany. The Jews and Communists who had engineered the "putsch" would be taught a lesson. Friedrich Born of the International Red Cross described the arrival of Szálasi and his gang as "the revolution of nonsense."

The ss arrested some high-ranking officers thought to be loyal to Regent Horthy, all democratically inclined representatives in the former parliament and members of the Regent's personal guard. Leaflets began to appear accusing the Regent of being a "hireling of the Jews and a traitor."[6] Horthy and his family were taken to Bavaria, where, guarded by a hundred ss soldiers and nine Gestapo officers in Schloss Waldbichl,[7] they awaited the end of the war. Horthy Jr., after several weeks of merciless interrogation, was taken to Mauthausen concentration camp in Austria.

The next day, the streets were filled with jubilant Arrow Cross youths strutting in their jackbooted, green-shirted uniforms and waving Nazi flags. Kasztner thought they appeared to have emerged from Goya's drawings for *The Disasters of War*. He noted in his diary: "Execution scenes in the twilight, murder in the fog, in the night and by full daylight. Gunshots along the banks of the Danube and hundreds of Jewish corpses floating in the beautiful river." The gangs invaded several Star Houses and marched their inhabitants to the river, where they shot them.

Szálasi announced that the government would no longer honor safe passes, visas, or protection certificates from neutral countries. Jewish inhabitants of houses marked with the Star of David were not to leave their homes. The order applied to members of the Jewish Council, to all aid workers, and to the Va'ada. Kasztner's and Komoly's immediate concern were the children's homes under Red Cross protection. They had to make sure these houses were safe from the Arrow Cross marauders.

Born did not succeed in gaining an immediate audience with Szálasi, but he did get a message delivered to Veesenmayer reminding him of what the Red Cross was expected to do for Germans in Allied prisoner-of-war camps, not to mention the threatened ethnic Germans in Transylvania. How could its staff members, he argued, continue to do such good work if their own lives and the lives of those they were protecting were threatened?

Carl Lutz gained admittance to Szálasi and suggested that the Swiss would not be able to recognize the new government unless it, in turn, recognized Swiss protection papers. He had been particularly concerned about the Arrow Cross harassing members of his staff—he didn't mention that most members of his staff were Jews. He said he insisted on continuing to do his work for his country and for the other countries he represented. That would include keeping his Emigration Office open.

Szálasi, though he portrayed himself as a populist figure, had always thirsted for the honors that come with being "the leader." He had chosen his own title in homage to Hitler, and certainly wanted recognition for his government, which had so far been branded by all nations as a German puppet regime. He treated Lutz with deference and bored him with a long lecture on his plans for resettling the Jews—but only after the war. In the meantime, they would do useful work in Hungary.

Szálasi complained about the lineups and noise surrounding the former American embassy and its extension, the Glass House, occupied by Lutz and his various Jewish departments, calling them a blot on the face of the city. Still, he conceded that Lutz's protection papers would be recognized as long as the Swiss were planning to recognize his government.

Born's plea to Veesenmayer met with some success. Section A, run by Ottó Komoly, could reopen. The International Red Cross's plaque would be respected on the doors of the children's homes. Those taking care of the children were provided with papers by both the Red Cross and the Swiss Consulate. Kasztner estimated that about six thousand children were in the homes, some from Poland and Slovakia, a few from Yugoslavia, but most Hungarians whose parents had been deported or imprisoned.

István Weiszlovits, whose parents had been deported from Eper-jes, Slovakia, had first heard of the homes that offered some protection to Jewish children the day after Szálasi assumed power. He had been hiding with relatives, but, once the Arrow Cross began patrolling the streets, that no longer seemed safe. He went to the Glass House on Vadász Street and found hundreds of people outside and hundreds more lining up inside the gates, but when he said he was from Slovakia, he was hustled off to a small house on Budakeszi Road that enjoyed the protection of both the Red Cross and the Swedish Embassy. He was twelve years old.[8]

Peretz Révész, who had delivered many of the Slovak children to the homes, was now assigned to guard a home with over a hundred small children. Most of them had been so traumatized by their experiences that they were silent. It was strange, he recalled, to be in a building filled with children, some only three or four years old, where there was no laughter and no sound of play.[9]

Adolf Eichmann returned to Budapest on October 17. He moved back into his offices at the Majestic Hotel and ordered Rezső Kaszt-ner to go to see him that first afternoon. Once again, Kasztner took the cogwheel railway—incredibly, it had not yet been destroyed by bombs—to its last station, at the top of Swabian Hill. It was a cold, foggy day, with a slow drizzle in the air. Hundreds of birds were chattering in the trees; amazing, he thought, that they would still be there. Hansi Brand accompanied him to the small, concrete bridge that connected the street to the Majestic, but she waited outside.

"I am back, as you see," Eichmann announced, glowing with confidence, wearing his full uniform, revolver on the desk in front of him.[10] "My arm is long enough to reach you and your useless dung people. They will all be deported now, you hear me, Kasztner?" he shouted. "You hear me? Not one of them will be spared. This time, there are no trains, no lorries—they will march all the way. I don't want to hear any of your damned excuses. I don't care how old they are or how sick they are. It's all lies, Kasztner, I've heard it all before. We need workers for the defense of Vienna." Eichmann was convinced there were more than 200,000 Jews in what he called Jew City, all pretending to be gentiles, and he would root them out. "I am a bloodhound, Kasztner, don't you forget that!"

Kasztner said not a word during the tirade.

"Now, if you can supply us with the trucks, we'll use trucks to move them. Or doesn't that suit you?"

Still silence.

"You think I can't do it?" Eichmann shrieked. "You think my teeth have been pulled by Himmler? Your pretty boy Becher, you think he had it all arranged? Your dumb plans, you think they were going to work?"

Kasztner asked Eichmann's permission to leave. He would contact the people in Switzerland, he said. He would talk to them about those trucks Eichmann had wanted. He left the room slowly, every step accompanied by Eichmann's barking laughter.

Dieter Wisliceny was in the stairwell. "Didn't think we'd be back so soon, did you, Kasztner?" he said, with a grin. Then he told Kasztner that Eichmann's Hungarian mistress had left him while he was in Linz. "The obersturmbannführer is in a foul mood—I wouldn't even try to argue with him. Perhaps after the next fifty thousand have gone, then you may have a chance at bargaining again."

"Fifty thousand?"

"Yes, fifty thousand Jews to work protecting the Reich."

Kasztner walked down the steps, measuring the distance, wanting to be sure he neither said anything to indicate he was a human being nor cried. He walked by Brigadier-General Hans Geschke—"the Butcher of Lidice"[11]—in the outer hall, made sure his stride was wide and confident, casually waved at the familiar guards in the small cubicle by the front door, and strolled down toward the railway car, where he knew Hansi would be waiting.

He didn't cry until they were back in the apartment.

The Hungarian government announced its urgent requirements for Jewish males between the ages of sixteen and sixty to dig antitank

trenches at the banks of the Tisza River and at the eastern periphery
of Budapest. Roundups began immediately. Arrow Cross gangs
invaded Star-marked buildings, broke into the apartments, and
ordered all the men, irrespective of age and health, into the central
courtyards. While in the apartments, they took anything they
fancied—money, jewelry, military decorations, preserves, clothes,
pieces of furniture. They force-marched the men—many were over
eighty years old, some were disabled, others were boys of barely
twelve or younger—to the racecourse or to Teleki Square. Those
who lagged behind were beaten or shot.

Lieutenant-Colonel László Ferenczy was, once again, the faithful
follower of orders, as he had been throughout the first months of the
occupation. His cock-feathered gendarmes served alongside the
young, undisciplined Arrow Cross ruffians. The pretext was to
search for able bodies who had not yet "volunteered" for service, but
in reality the boys were searching for valuables.

Inadvertently, Ferenczy did one good deed for the Jews of
Budapest. When an Arrow Cross band arrived at the Sip Street
building two days after the takeover by Ferenc Szálasi, Miksa
Domonkos, a Jewish Council member, was able to call Ferenczy's
office in front of the surprised Arrow Cross men. He asked for
Ferenczy by name, reported that the building was being threatened by
thugs, listened attentively for the response, hung up the phone, and
told the young marauders that Colonel Ferenczy was sending a
gendarmerie force to throw them out. What Ferenczy had said, in fact,
was that the Jews were about to get what they deserved, but nobody
except Domonkos heard that. The Arrow Cross left empty-handed.

Domonkos continued to benefit from his brief acquaintance with
the gendarmerie colonel during Ferenczy's efforts to ingratiate himself with the Jewish Council. Though not a member of the Council,
he led its technical office. He invoked Ferenczy's name whenever he
was stopped for questioning, and also issued certificates of safe
conduct over Ferenczy's name. He wore his own First World War
captain's uniform and claimed to issue Ferenczy's orders, ensuring
that food and medical deliveries were made to the Star Houses.
Pretending to represent the Ministry of Defense, he eventually

appointed himself police chief of the ghetto, where all but a few of the initiated thought he was an officious, overdressed but basically decent Christian.

On October 20, Szálasi reluctantly agreed to "lend" fifty thousand Jewish workers to the Reich. He hesitated initially because his traditional stance had been to find a made-in-Hungary solution to "the Jewish problem." He saw himself as a patriot, a descendent of Hungarian tribesmen, a Magyar with egalitarian convictions, all of which, he thought, explained his tolerance for the Arrow Cross rabble. They needed some guidance, some education, but they were the new generation that would rule his ideal country. He did not want to lend Jewish workers to the Germans, simply because he wanted them to work at home. Pressure from Veesenmayer, however, overcame his reluctance. Szálasi had been appointed at the Germans' pleasure, and the Jews were a small sacrifice to make.

Ostensibly the job was to build fortifications southwest of Vienna, the so-called Southwest Wall, which would stop the Soviets in the "unlikely event" that they broke through the defenses in Hungary. That, at least, had been the order from Ernst Kaltenbrunner; Eichmann, as usual, had his own agenda. The march toward Ostmark, the Reich's name for its province formerly known as Austria, was a fine excuse for the resumption of Jewish extermination as he had begun it in April. Fifty thousand Jewish men and women were to report to sports arenas and Budapest's Ferihegy airport for "recruitment" and mobilization. They were given no food, no water, no medication. Now and then a Hungarian policeman helped someone escape along the way to the collection points, but, once inside, there was little hope of returning home.

Carl Lutz and Raoul Wallenberg petitioned government departments, claiming they had countries ready to accept Jewish refugees by the thousands. Hansi Brand and her team of counterfeiters printed and distributed fake passes and Aryan papers, most of which were produced at such speed that they no longer even hoped to resemble the real things. Kasztner organized shipments of food and water to those awaiting orders to march to Ostmark. Peretz Révész and his group of young Zionists were digging bunkers and shelters for children in bombed-out homes. They delivered letters of protection and fake immigration papers.

The Glass House was now a refuge for more than two thousand people. The halutzim took over the area to the right of the main entrance, Moshe Krausz still worked feverishly in his closed office (now on the third floor), and the Orthodox had their own area in the basement. Desperate newcomers were trying to claw their way into the building. Andor Schwartz remembers arriving shortly before eight o'clock one evening. The street, they told him, was "a death trap" at night; the secretary who registered the new entrants gave him an identity paper with a gigantic red stamp on it signifying that he was under the protection of the Swiss Consulate. He knew that this paper would exempt him from the forced march toward Vienna.[12] The makeshift kitchen in the courtyard of the Glass House produced big cauldrons of soup every day, and young Jewish couriers brought bread from bakeries ordered open by the government.

Giorgio Perlasca, an Italian-born former volunteer in the Spanish Civil War on the Franco side, used his war-hero status to claim Spanish citizenship and the keys to the Spanish legation once the real chargé d'affaires had fled home. Shocked by what he saw in the streets of Budapest, Perlasca extended to all Jews the protection that neutral Spain had offered to Sephardic Jews. He had his driver take him through the streets of the city in the evenings, when Arrow Cross gangs were most prevalent, stopping whenever he saw Jews in danger, and claiming them for Spain. In six weeks, he handed out about two thousand Spanish protection papers.[13]

Arrow Cross boys—most of them under eighteen—paraded through the streets, shot or arrested anyone wearing a yellow star, broke into Red Cross safe houses while wielding machine guns, entered the protected children's homes and murdered every child there. In one building they shot the babies in their cribs on the first floor, then the toddlers on the second, before they were stopped by a couple of armed policemen on the third floor. Some survivors of Jewish labor brigades were rounded up, marched to the Danube, shot, and pushed into the river. Seven-year-old Charles Fenyvesi, who had been hiding in one of the children's homes, witnessed murders from the Margit Bridge. "People lined up by the river were shot in the nape of the neck so they fell into the water headfirst," he recalled. When they ran short of ammunition, the Arrow Cross lads tied several people together with wire and rope, shot one, and pushed them all into the river to drown.

There were men hanging from trees in most of the city's parks. The murderers usually affixed cardboard signs to the corpses, proclaiming their alleged deeds. The signs ranged from the simple "Traitor" to the more cautionary "Long live Szálasi" or "Warning to Jews."

Joe Lebovic remembers fondly the counterfeit levente papers that saved his life. He was employed as a Christian child trainee cleaning floors in one of the workshops. His brother was in an orphanage, and his mother was a volunteer nurse in a hospital. He had no idea where his father was, though he seemed to materialize at prearranged times inside a closed store on Rákóczy Avenue. One day, when he didn't appear, Joe searched the length of the street, gazing intently at the corpses hanging from lampposts. He was relieved not to recognize any one of them.[14]

On October 24, a desperate, near-hysterical Kasztner, after a long, seemingly inexplicable silence, received a cable from Saly Mayer proposing to resume the negotiations. Kurt Becher refused even to see Kasztner until he had concrete financial results to show and a meeting had been arranged with an official representative of the United States. Fortunately for Kasztner and the second group from his train, Mayer had become sufficiently friendly with Roswell D. McClelland, whom he described in his cable as "Roosevelt's emissary" in Zurich, to be able to persuade him, against his government's policy, to go to a meeting with the ss.[15] McClelland was a representative of the War Refugee Board, a U.S. government agency, and therefore someone who could be viewed by the ss as an American official.

By an October 26 order of the Ministry of Defense, seventy companies of labor service men were to be handed over to the Reich. They, too, were to be employed in building the wall to protect

Vienna, but their progress west turned into another death march supervised by brutal Arrow Cross irregulars.

The Szálasi government issued a new decree in Budapest, yet another of the more than one hundred anti-Jewish laws that had been passed by parliament since March 1944. It read: "The Hungarian State herewith assumes possession of all Jewish property and assets, which it considers to form an integral part of the cumulative wealth of the nation."

Finally, one of the political parties, the formerly fascist Hungarian Socialists, turned against the government and offered clandestine assistance to the persecuted Jews. One of their members contacted the Jewish Council and offered Arrow Cross papers, uniforms, and arm-bands to young Jews who were involved in rescue operations. It was a slender lifeline, but the halutzim grabbed it with no questions asked.[16] One of the halutzim, Rafi Benshalom, wrote about members of his group who, dressed in Arrow Cross uniforms, rescued other members from prisons under the pretext of transferring them to higher authorities.[17]

Kasztner and William Billitz left in an ss car for Switzerland on October 27. Becher flew to Berlin for further authorization to sign a contract with the Americans and to accept goods of reasonable value to the Reich. But the October 29 meeting was yet another waste of time. Mayer talked of $2 million on deposit and of "moral obligations," but he admitted he had been unable to procure the trucks. Becher was to join them on November 5, and for that day Mayer promised to produce his American emissary.

The marches toward the border began in early November. "There were grandmothers and small children among us," Aviva Fleisch-mann remembered. "We walked the whole days . . . many fell; those who could not move were shot and left to die . . . we got no food, we stopped in the dark and slept where we could."[18] They were marched about 120 miles, not allowed to rest more than an hour at a time, and had no food and no shelter. They were guarded all the way by a brutal force of young Arrow Cross men. When they arrived, even the survivors were almost dead.

Magda Létai escaped after three days of marching along the road to Vienna.[19] She saw hundreds of corpses in the ditches, people falling, beaten by Arrow Cross boys, shot, and left for dead, even though a few were still moving. She was captured by a group of gendarmes and by Christmas 1944 she was in Ravensbrück concentration camp.

The long, tortured march of Jewish laborers from the Bor copper mines in Yugoslavia began on September 17 and ended in the deaths of most of the former prisoners a few weeks later. Before they reached the borders of Hungary, over three hundred of them were murdered by their German guards. In Crevenka, the guards decided to kill a thousand men and bury them in large pits that had been dug for the raw materials for making bricks. The remnant arrived at the Austrian border, where they met the other death-march victims from Budapest. Miklós Radnóti, one of the great young poets of the war years, had been at the Bor mines and survived until he reached Győr, near the Austrian border. There he was murdered along with a group of other young Jewish men. When the mass grave near Győr was opened years later, he was found, his pockets filled with poems scribbled on dirty bits of paper. A Catholic convert, Radnóti had kept his faith until his last hour.

CHAPTER 25

In the Shadow of the
Third Reich's Final Days

*Roosevelt's representative and Himmler's agent sat opposite each
other, the two representatives of the two nations who played a
decisive battle of life and death.*

Rezső Kasztner, *Der Kasztner-Bericht*

The meeting between Kurt Becher and Roswell McClelland
took place on November 5, a Sunday afternoon, in a small
conference room in the Savoy, an upscale Zurich hotel.
McClelland was composed and at ease; Becher, in rumpled civilian
clothes, tired after his long trip from Berlin and irritable after the previous day's preliminary discussion with Saly Mayer in Saint Gallen,
Switzerland,[1] was visibly nervous. Both men were in their midthirties. On the sidelines sat Mayer and Kasztner, witnesses rather than
participants. McClelland was a Quaker, head of the War Refugee
Board, a highly educated man whose erudition impressed even the
usually dismissive Kasztner.

Becher opened with a statement that Himmler was ready to allow
the emigration of the group still held in Bergen-Belsen once certain

conditions were met. McClelland, well aware of the European tragedy as it had unfolded in every country the Germans had occupied, replied that the average man had no sympathy for a regime that raised murder to a form of government policy.

Becher countered that the death of hundreds of thousands of innocent German women and children, victims of Allied bombardments intended specifically to kill civilians, was tantamount to murder. He mentioned the systematic destruction of entire cities.

McClelland stated that the end of the war was in sight, that Germany was going to be defeated, and that Becher's role in saving lives at this critical moment would count in his favor in the war criminals' trials at the close of hostilities. When Becher insisted on returning to the essence of the original agreement, that he could guarantee nothing without concrete results from these negotiations, Mayer said they were present to make a deal.

McClelland—without due authorization from his superiors—offered Becher 20 million Swiss francs in return for the immediate cessation of deportations, the safety of the remaining inmates of all concentration camps, and respect for the lives of all civilians "without regard for their race or religion." Mayer showed Becher a telegram from the American secretary of state, Cordell Hull, that confirmed $5 million was to be transferred to Mayer's special account for rescue efforts. The ss could use the funds to shop for whatever it needed, except, of course, war materials. Becher, in turn, and without due authorization from Himmler, agreed that men and women under sixteen and over forty would be spared.

At Kasztner's urging—he thought McClelland's demands too general and impossible to supervise—Becher agreed to make an effort to release the Bergen-Belsen group. But he said he could not allow the Slovak Jews to emigrate, because he had orders from Himmler that they were to be eliminated "for military reasons."

The meeting ended at 1 AM the next day. Becher was satisfied with his performance on behalf of the Reich, so he went shopping in the morning for a gift for the countess, something smaller for his wife, and a special Swiss medication for Himmler's ailing kidneys.

Kasztner was up all night writing a report on the meeting. He was not pleased with the day's events. The agreements were all fine in principle, but they failed to make concrete demands of the Germans. McClelland's requirement that the Germans "respect the lives of all civilians" was nice, but it ignored the urgent needs of Hungary's remaining Jews. Kasztner had asked of Mayer that demands from the Joint include at least a guarantee for the security of those still alive; that the deportations of Jews stop immediately; that those who had foreign passports or protection papers be allowed to leave; that the Red Cross be permitted to enter the concentration camps, and that the Bergen-Belsen group depart at once for Switzerland.[2]

When Mayer accompanied the delegation to the Swiss border for their return to Budapest via Vienna, Kasztner produced the text he had been working on all night. It contained the conditions he thought essential in exchange for the 20 million francs.

Becher said he would consider those demands, except for the one about deportations. He was not about to leave behind Jews who could attack German soldiers once the Russians were close to Budapest. Then he turned to his ss aide, Herbert Kettlitz, and ordered him to remain behind to begin locating material goods to purchase with the 20 million francs. "When will you deliver the suitcase?" Becher asked Mayer.

"The suitcase?" Mayer asked.

"The one with the money," Becher replied.

"What do you think?" Mayer shouted. "That we are throwing our millions at you now?"

Everyone froze. Finally, Becher broke the silence. "Herr Mayer, it seems, has lost his nerve," he said.[3] He had obviously decided to treat Mayer's outburst as an ill-conceived joke.

On the long drive back from the Swiss border to Vienna, Becher soon fell into a talkative, confiding mood. He complained to Kasztner about interference from the Gestapo in ss affairs, about being under observation himself because of his relationship with Kasztner, about his suspicions that Eichmann would continue to evade Himmler's orders. He made a serious, though to Kasztner completely ridiculous, effort to explain Himmler's sincere convictions regarding Jews, his idealism, and his honorable intentions. "He is, basically, a good-hearted man," he told Rezső. "You should see him with his daughter, Püppi. He is devoted."

Himmler, it seemed to Becher, would have preferred another way to rid Europe of the dominant Jewish presence. "Did you know that Himmler has never insulted the Jews in a single one of his speeches?" he asked Kasztner. And he would have preferred not to be at war with the British and the Americans. Himmler was a brilliant man, one who could see into the future. In the end, the British and the Americans would come to their senses and realize that the common enemy was Soviet Communism.

Hitler, he continued, had characterized the Slavs as *untermenschen*, subhumans, like the Jews. He planned to use them all as illiterate slave labor and to annihilate those who were not capable of useful work. Becher said he was sure that Hitler's medications caused his fits of uncontrollable rage. Since the attempt on his life, the Führer had lost his sense of balance, not only physically but also psychologically. But Becher still admired him and knew how difficult his task must be: it required superhuman strength for him to continue to command the nation.

From Vienna they continued their journey with Lieutenant General Hans Jüttner, the head of the ss Führungshauptamt and technically Becher's boss. While the shiny Mercedes was avoiding the craters from recent American and British bomb attacks, the strafing by low-flying aircraft, and the trucks carrying the wounded to hospitals in Berlin and Nuremberg and Vienna, the relentless "death marches" of Budapest's Jews toward Austria had begun.

Jüttner saw the battered columns of women, children, and old men staggering along the Budapest–Vienna road, dead bodies lying in the ditches, and claimed later to have been horrified. No preparations for rest or food along the 140-mile route had been made. Those who became ill were shot or left behind along the highway without medical help. The International Red Cross reported ragged, starved, exhausted people force-marched by truncheon-wielding gendarmes and Arrow Cross irregulars. Most of those who saw them were afraid to interfere. A few brave souls found the courage to take people out of the marching columns, claiming they were needed for urgent work elsewhere. Five men prepared a rough film to show to the papal nuncio and to send on to Red Cross headquarters in Bern.

As they drove toward Budapest, Jüttner asked Becher directly: At whose orders were these civilians marched to their deaths? Who had the authority to order such an atrocity in full view of the population?

"It's Eichmann's regiment," Becher told him. "They are marching at Eichmann's orders."[4] Initially, 27,000 civilians had been rounded up for the exodus, supplemented with 17,000 labor service men, but the numbers grew as the horrific state of those who arrived hardly met Ernst Kaltenbrunner's order for able-bodied workers.

Once Jüttner arrived in the capital, he sent an urgent request to Eichmann for a meeting to discuss the matter. In response, Eichmann sent one of his junior officers, a lad no more than twenty years old, who treated Jüttner's outrage with a smirk and suggested that, if Jüttner was willing to sacrifice military transports for Jews, perhaps they could discuss the matter further. Otherwise, the Sonderkommando had its orders for laborers to build fortifications against a possible attack along the Ostmark (Austrian) border. Becher promised Kasztner that he would also contact Himmler, and, in the meantime, he would have his adjutant deliver a hundred ss passes for the use of Jewish aid workers.[5]

Eichmann commanded Kasztner to attend his office again. He screamed, swore at his adjutants, and seethed about both the clerics and the interfering foreign governments. He raged that there were still too many Jews hiding in Budapest, that "others" were attempting to thwart his plans for the new Europe. But he was determined to show them all. They had told him it was impossible to "lift out" the Jews of Hungary, but he had almost accomplished the impossible. And he had done it in record time. It was the victory of National Socialism over the *untermenschen*. Now there were a mere 200,000 to 300,000 left. Rewarded with his lieutenant colonel's stripes after he exterminated Poland's Jews, he now expected to be made a full colonel after his Hungarian campaign.

Himmler, he complained, had taken false counsel. He had been trapped into negotiations with "the Jew." As for Hungary, the country was run by rabble, the government did not know how to govern, and the Arrow Cross was nothing but a bunch of kids with guns. In a real war, most of them would not know how to hit a moving target. If the Russians came close, the Arrow Cross would be even less useful than the Hungarian army.

Kasztner interrupted the invective with a plea for the Columbus Street camp. These were Jews he had brought in from the provinces with Eichmann's "help," but now the ss guards were no longer there to keep away the thieving and marauding "rabble."[6]

Eichmann replied that he would arrange to have all the inmates of the camp taken to the Bergen-Belsen Ungarnlager, the section of the camp set aside for Kasztner's "exchange Jews," once the first twenty-five trucks arrived. Then he turned his back on Kasztner, barked orders at his staff, buckled on his belt, and departed the meeting with long, swinging steps.

Kasztner raced back to the still intact Va'ada offices and called everyone together to organize help for the survivors among the marchers he had swept by in the car. The news from the "Hungarian line" was terrible. Ottó Komoly and Samuel Stern learned that the men they had been meeting to organize effective armed resistance to the Arrow Cross had been betrayed, and many of the Hungarian leaders, including Endre Bajcsy-Zsilinszky, were charged with treason.[7]

Becher went to see Raoul Wallenberg at the Swedish Embassy and offered to provide his protection and exit visas for four hundred Jews with Swedish passports in exchange for only 400,000 Swiss francs.[8] But as Wallenberg's Hungarian activities were financed by the Joint, he could not enter into ransom negotiations any more than Mayer could. Becher suggested similar deals to the Portuguese and Spanish embassies, but there was not enough time for the transactions. The Russians were starting to encircle the city.

Jüttner cabled a furious report to Himmler about the forced marches. Both Jüttner and Becher claimed credit when the marches were stopped by the ss Reichsführer. Becher's cable to Himmler regarding the meeting with Roswell McClelland, Kasztner thought, would have been the decisive factor in Himmler's decision. That was certainly how Becher presented the decision. "Now I hope," he said, "that your Mr. McClelland will appreciate Himmler's willingness to meet him halfway: 20 million francs is a laughable sum in light of what I have just accomplished."[9] But at the end of the war even Rudolf Höss, the former commandant of Auschwitz-Birkenau, claimed credit for stopping the death march. He said he had complained to Himmler about the poor condition of the new arrivals; he had been put in charge of the trench-digging in Vienna and had asked for able-bodied men. Yehuda Bauer, one of the foremost historians of this terrible era, suggests that the Swiss negotiations were the deciding factor.

Mayer continued to assure Becher, through telephone calls and telegrams to Kasztner, that the money was now ready for use for whatever materials the Reich required, in exchange for lives spared. Unbeknownst to Kasztner, this message, too, was a bluff. The U.S. State Department had cabled to expressly forbid any ransom deal. It was time, it said, for more "gestures" from the Germans.

The remaining captives in the Bergen-Belsen camp had heard little news about their fate either from home or from Hermann Krumey. Many of them had succumbed to illness, and they were suffering from hunger and the infernal lice, from cold and damp amid the persistent rains, and, most of all, from mind-numbing boredom. Every day, they watched the hundreds of Allied bombers flash overhead on their way to their German targets. They had seen new groups arrive in other "privileged" camp enclosures, as well as in the *häftlinger* camp, where walking skeletons worked night and day.

At last, on November 18, the Ungarnlager welcomed its first visitor since the first group had left—Bergen-Belsen's commandant, Adolf Haas, a handsome young man in an immaculate uniform. He informed József Fischer that a train would be leaving for Switzerland in a few days. Polite and deferential, he asked to see Mrs. Kasztner, personally. When he was told that she was too ill to come—Bogyó had been suffering from pneumonia—he asked Fischer to tell his daughter that "Dr. Kasztner sends his good wishes and I send mine for her speedy recovery. In a few days she will see her husband again."

"And the rest of us?" Fischer asked.

"All of you," the commandant lied, and he respectfully nodded his head at Fischer before leaving.

November 18 was also the day that Becher received word from Kettlitz in Saint Gallen in Switzerland. Kettlitz still had not seen any of the Joint's promised Swiss francs, so he concluded that Mayer and McClelland had been bluffing when they met Becher earlier in the month.

Becher was outraged. He told Kasztner he would have to report the facts to Himmler. He was not going to take further responsibility for the Joint's inaction. Kasztner immediately cabled Saly Mayer, but, without waiting for Mayer's reply, he informed Becher that the "payments had been held up due to unforeseen technical difficulties" in Switzerland. But, he added with a flourish, "I guarantee that the money will be there."

Eichmann ordered Kasztner to appear for another audience at the Majestic Hotel. "I need 65,000 to 70,000 Jews," he announced. "Immediately—20,000 for the Ostmark wall; the rest for factories in the Reich." He said that all the women and children could stay in their Budapest homes, and he would respect the protection papers—even the fake ones—if Kasztner would make the Jewish Council understand that it had to produce the required number of workers.

"You are actually asking that I locate the Jews who you claim have been hiding and force them to appear for your convenience?" Kasztner asked, incredulous. Eichmann assured him that he, personally, would root out everyone with or without cooperation, so why not cooperate to mutual advantage? Kasztner politely declined. He was hoping he could reach Becher and persuade him to intervene again.

Eichmann started up the marches anew. About thirty thousand Jews, mostly women and children, began the journey toward Austria.[10] This time, though, there were a great many more helpers along the highway—Hungarian gentiles, priests, and even some former members of parliament who dared now to show themselves once more. It was obvious to everyone that Germany was losing the war. The new Romanian government announced its intention to deport Germans from Romania to Siberia, unless the Germans returned the Transylvanian Jews.[11] Kasztner noticed how shocked Becher appeared when he registered the news that others were willing to use ss methods to free themselves of unwanted people. They both knew that few Transylvanian Jews would be left in Auschwitz and that extracting even those few would be impractical. "Perhaps," he suggested to Becher, "we could engineer a fair exchange? Our live Jews for their live Germans?"

On November 28 the Hungarian police, following orders from the Ministry of the Interior, began to herd Jews from the Star Houses into the Seventh District, which would now be designated Budapest's ghetto. The Jewish Council had been given a few hours' notice about the boundaries of the ghetto, where all Jews who lacked international papers or protection certificates were to be located. The ghetto contained 290 buildings, but only 240 could be used to house the 45,000 people—by the end of December, they numbered about 85,000—who had been ordered to live there. Given the number of apartments and rooms in the area, this meant an average of six persons in each room.[12] Those with papers from the different embassies were put in their own "protected houses," duly identified by both the Star of David and the emblem of the particular country granting its protection.

Kasztner had been waiting for Becher in the foyer of the Chorin house. If Becher was as much a realist as he appeared to be, he would, surely, have started planning for his future after the end of the Reich. Kasztner wondered whether Becher had been fooled by Mayer's tactics or McClelland's inspired speeches. Perhaps they had all been playing for time. The vast sums of money they had been discussing were a mirage, and perhaps smaller amounts would do, if only to grant Becher some grounds to continue his pretense to Himmler that the negotiations were going well.

Becher, however, arrived in high spirits, with startling news. "I have convinced the Reichsführer-ss to stop the Final Solution," he announced. "Himmler has authorized the destruction of the gas chambers and the crematoria in all the camps—not only in Auschwitz, in all of them."[13] He poured Kasztner a glass of champagne. "It's French," he boasted. "The real thing, not the phony stuff you Hungarians make."

At first Kasztner did not believe what he had just heard. If they were blowing up the death machinery, they had to be destroying evidence, and the Allies were closer than he had realized. Or had the meeting with McClelland led to some sort of exit for the Germans? "Has there been another meeting with McClelland?" he asked.

"And what exactly would be the point of that?" Becher asked. "Another explanation? Another wait?"

When Kasztner told him that the delays in Switzerland were caused by misunderstandings, that the deal was still substantially in place, Becher just smiled. "What's wrong with you, Rudolf," he said, "is that you cannot enjoy the moment. Tonight we are going to the Hungaria [Hotel]. There is a chanteuse I want you to hear and, tell you what, why don't we fetch Hansi on the way over? God knows, she looks like she needs a bit of fun in her life . . ."

Kasztner started talking about the ghetto, the Arrow Cross, and the random shootings, but Becher waved him aside. "There is a time for everything, Kasztner. Tonight is one for celebrations."

At the Hungaria the crystal chandelier was still in place, in defiance of the bombings. The waiters were still in tails, their starched shirtfronts gleaming in the candlelight. Becher's companion, a Hungarian baroness, enchanted by the atmosphere, clung to his arm as if in a trance. She was about nineteen years old, a bit unsteady in her studded high heels. The chanteuse, her lips brushing the microphone as if it were a lover, sang "Lili Marlene"—"Vor der Kaserne, vor den grossen Tor . . ." An ss officer near the entrance was crying.

On Sunday, December 3, the Ungarnlager group at Bergen-Belsen was ready for departure for Switzerland by train, as promised by Haas. Everyone had packed and lined up for the last head count. Hermann Krumey arrived to personally oversee the transfer of the remaining Red Cross packages to the Germans and to ensure that Eichmann's final orders for the "Kasztner transport" were obeyed: Joel Brand's family was not to be included. His eighty-year-old mother knelt in the mud before Krumey and begged that at least her granddaughter, Margit, be allowed to leave. "We are very sorry," said Krumey, and he turned his back on the weeping woman.[14]

Margit, ill with scarlet fever, remembers the misery of the days after the others left. The family was put into the neighboring Dutch enclosure, where she was allowed to remain in the hospital until her fever subsided. It was there that she met a young girl of about her own age, tall and pale, with short, dark stubble where her hair had been cut off. The other members of her family, the girl told Margit, were all dead. She, too, was ill with the fever. Her name was Anne Frank.

That same day, a large force of Arrow Cross thugs attacked the Columbus Street camp, murdered many of the people inside, and dragged some survivors to the ghetto. The commander of the camp and his entire family were among the victims. About four thousand others were herded into boxcars and transported to Bergen-Belsen, where they met some of the Strasshof exchange Jews.

Later, Ferenc Szálasi's secretary explained the attack to the Red Cross, whose flag and emblem at the gate had been ignored. "There were some shots fired from inside the camp," he claimed. André Biss, in Kasztner's absence—once again, Kasztner was on his way to the Swiss border—tried to reach Becher, but his appropriated house on Andrássy Avenue was locked up. Not even a guard had been left at the doors to say where he had gone. So Biss went to the Majestic and demanded to see Eichmann. He threatened Otto Hunsche with sending a message to Himmler that all negotiations should cease because the Sonderkommando was ignoring Himmler's orders.[15] After keeping him waiting for an hour, Hunsche confirmed that peace had been restored at Columbus Street and said there would be no further disturbances.

On December 5, Kasztner and Saly Mayer met again in Saint Gallen, with Erich Krell standing in for Becher. Kasztner carried an anguished letter from the Budapest Jewish Council, asking the Joint and the Jewish Agency to recognize that they were all about to die. Urgent help was needed to deter the killers.

As before, Mayer had neither money nor goods. He complained

to Kasztner that, while nobody had said no, neither had anyone said yes, and without that, the promised 20 million Swiss francs was unavailable. He was able to show only that a deposit of 207,600 Swiss francs had been made by the War Refugee Board into the account of a Lucerne manufacturer that could sell sixteen tractors to Germany. (As it happened, no tractors were delivered, and the Board defined the amount transferred as "show money.")

While he was in Switzerland, Kasztner received a cable from Biss. The situation of the Budapest Jews in the ghetto had become intolerable, Biss warned. There was an immediate need for further funds. Telegram in hand, Kasztner returned to Mayer's room and exacted further promises, though Mayer was still unable to give Kasztner any money to bribe the Germans. Although Kasztner never believed his claim that he didn't have any real cash, Mayer was telling the truth. The best he could hope for was to reach an agreement with the Swiss Red Cross to increase its supply of food for Budapest. When Kasztner accused him of complicity in the murder of Jews, Mayer said he would resign his position. These had, he made clear, been terrible months for him, and he did not want abuse from Kasztner.

Kasztner refrained from further criticism, but it took him the rest of the day to persuade Mayer to stay on the job. His resignation now would have signed the death warrants of all the Jews that Kasztner had worked to save. Having softened Mayer's stance, Kasztner went to cajole the Germans. He persuaded Krell to send a cable to Becher telling him that the Joint would take it as a sign of good faith if the Bergen-Belsen group was allowed to cross the border.

On December 7, at seven o'clock in the evening, the second Kasztner group, including Bogyó, arrived at Bregenz in Ostmark, near the Swiss border in an ordinary passenger train. Rezső was waiting for them along with Becher's adjutants, Kettlitz and Krell. The two Germans argued over whether to allow the passengers through to the Swiss side. Kettlitz kept insisting that, because Krell had not been able to collect the Swiss goods, further orders from Becher were required. Krell argued that their task was to deliver the 1,368 *stück*, or "pieces," not to ask unnecessary questions. His orders, however, included a final accounting; as the exchange rate stood, Becher was still owed $65,000. "According to my calculations," Kasztner insisted, "I am owed another four hundred people." They did not settle the argument, but each man agreed to discuss the matter with his superiors.

Krumey, who had been following the train in a German staff car, strolled down the platform, stopped to converse with the other ss officers, and finally approached Kasztner, who had been smoking near the compartment where he had seen Bogyó at the window. He told Kasztner that the dice were cast in his favor. The group could cross the Rhine into neutral territory. The guards said their suddenly polite goodbyes on the German side and asked to be remembered when the war was over. Bogyó and Rezső embraced and held each other, briefly, on the platform. He had worried she would be kept back as a hostage.

The Kasztner group was taken to the military barracks in Saint Gallen. There they found nurses and doctors to take care of the sick, medicines and warm clothes, and delicacies such as chocolates, fresh fruit, and pastries, gifts for the children, and fine underwear for the women. For the first time in months they had real news, both in newspapers and on the radio, so they could learn what had happened in Budapest and in Kolozsvár.

"Their departure," Kasztner recalled, "ended my five-months' nightmare."[16]

On December 8, five million of the long-awaited 20 million Swiss francs was finally deposited. Krell was able to cable Becher from Bregenz that the procurement of goods was in process, that the remaining 15 million "was being worked on," that Dr. Billitz was needed for further discussions, and that Kasztner should be allowed to go to Switzerland for a few days.

Becher agreed to a short trip for Kasztner because the Joint's European representative, Joseph Schwartz, was expected in Switzerland, but a follow-up telegram on December 11 demanded immediate information about the 15 million. "The situation in Budapest," Becher said, "has become precarious."[17]

Kasztner finally crossed the Swiss border on December 20. The next day, he was reunited with his family. Bogyó had been ill in Bergen-Belsen; she had become extremely thin, her once luxurious hair had been cut short, and her face showed the signs of stress, fear, and hunger. Rezső had trained himself to display no emotion, his face almost a mask of faked composure; his constant smoking had stained his teeth and his hands yellow, and he seemed a stranger even to himself. One night in Budapest he had promised Hansi that, if they survived this slaughter, they would remain together—he would leave Bogyó. Now, seeing his lovely, fragile wife again, he was no longer sure about that vow.[18]

There had been talk in the Bergen-Belsen camp about Rezső and Hansi, but Bogyó, when she was at last alone with her husband, gave no indication that she had heard anything at all.

On December 10 the Budapest ghetto was surrounded by a sixteen-foot wooden fence. By then, some 63,000 people had been crammed into 293 houses and 4,500 apartments, at least fourteen people to each room. There was little food, supplies of water were sporadic, and toilet facilities were few. Corpses lined the streets and piled up in central Klauzál Square. Ottó Komoly, still the nominal head of the Red Cross's Section A, now also took charge of delivering food to the ghetto, but delivery vans were frequently robbed on the way. "Inadvertently," he told Miksa Domonkos, "we are feeding the Arrow Cross mobs with subsistence suppers, courtesy of the Joint."[19]

Becher returned briefly from Berlin to supervise the packing of paintings, furniture, antique mirrors, and jewelry in the Chorin villas. He worked with Hans Geschke's group of ss men loading fifty-five freight cars with valuables that they and their fellow officers had collected while stationed in Hungary.[20] It was a small portion of the more than 600,000 tons of goods and valuables that the Germans looted from their ally when they finally abandoned all hope of turning back the Russians from invading Hungary. About a quarter of this total had come from the Jews. The Germans had also collected 2.5 billion reichsmarks from the Hungarian government for the removal of the Jews from the provinces.[21] Between October 20, 1944, and early May of the next year, they emptied the National Bank of all its deposits and sent to Germany 1,227 steam engines, 3,839 passenger wagons, 43,741 boxcars, 63,900 trucks, 605,000 beef cattle—and that was just the beginning. In his report to Szálasi, parliamentarian Endre Rajk complained in particular that he had difficulty preventing "ss Colonel Becher's countless excesses."[22] Some weeks earlier, the Hungarian government had already begun to assemble the contents of what became known as "the Gold Train." That train, containing the confiscated assets of Hungary's Jewry— precious stones, gold and silver objects, jewelry, valuable furs, rare carpets, and art, packed in sixty-one large cases—crossed the border into Ostmark just before the end of the war in Europe.[23]

Becher's mistress had returned to Budapest a few weeks earlier. The countess was sad to see the last of the city. The Allied bombings were difficult to endure, but they were bombing Germany, too, and in Budapest she had enjoyed some of the comforts of prewar Berlin.

While Kasztner waited in Switzerland for Nathan Schwalb's arrival, he was visited by two brothers, Elias and Yitzhak Sternbuch, who were part of the Orthodox relief work there. They had managed to funnel some cash to the beleaguered Bratislava Working Group and were pursuing a new contact, a man who had once been friendly with Himmler and could be persuaded to go to Berlin—even in these times—to negotiate the release of a group of Orthodox Jews. Voicing their visceral hatred of Mayer, who they thought was incompetent and unwilling to take any chances, they assured Kasztner that their new contact, former Swiss president Jean-Marie Musy,[24] had no misgivings about dealing with the Nazis. Kasztner, despite his own misgivings about Mayer, was reluctant to abandon his own line to the Joint. As he explained to the Sternbuchs and, later, wrote in his report, he decided that the Joint was a more reliable ally than even the most influential of Swiss leaders. He would stay the course.

Unfortunately, Kasztner's meeting with Schwalb did not produce any quick solution to his immediate problem of getting those 15 million Swiss francs to the Germans. The best he could do was to extract a letter from Mayer promising that the millions would be ready to transfer to the ss during his next meeting with Becher himself. Budapest was now surrounded by Soviet troops. Kasztner, determined to be of help, crossed the border again to Bregenz. He wanted to be in Budapest with his friends in the Va'ada. He explained to Bogyó that he could not sit in Switzerland knowing what those he had left behind had to endure.

On January 1, 1945, Kasztner traveled to Vienna, determined that his *tauschjuden*, or "exchange Jews," as Eichmann had billed them, should survive the war. He had been concerned that the ss would murder them all when the Soviet army reached Austria. He had a German passport, issued by the German Embassy in Budapest, which made no mention of his birthplace or of his being a Jew. Becher said this document would make it easy for Kasztner to move around, and it would save Becher the bother of extricating "Rudolf" again from tricky situations. Kasztner's German was fluent, faultless, literate, and witty, and he could easily pass for an Aryan. Becher was so confident of Kasztner's ability that he arranged with the assistant chief of the Vienna Gestapo that Kasztner be given a room at the Grand Hotel.[25]

At the ss Arbeitzentrals headquarters in Castellangasse, all the records of the Strasshof Jews were carefully filed by name and number,[26] a card for each arrival at the Strasshof transit camp. Every person, even the babies, had been examined by a doctor and judged suitable or unsuitable for work. Since then, the individual cards had been updated regularly with any piece of new information. This office also kept the books for amounts paid by the users of Jewish slave labor, all food or medication distributed, and the transfers from one work area to another. With each passing week, the health of the exchange Jews had deteriorated. There were more transfers to Bergen-Belsen and other concentration camps.

Krumey had allowed a small hospital to be set up at 16 Malzgasse, where Kasztner met Emil Tuchmann, the most senior of the ten Jewish doctors who were now working there. Naturally, they could not call the place a hospital, or refer to Tuchmann and the others as doctors, because all Jewish doctors had lost their medical degrees.[27] Nevertheless, they attended to the immediate medical needs of the

Jews in and around Vienna. Tuchmann told Kasztner that the doctors regularly lied to the ss about the seriousness of their patients' illnesses. They knew that those crippled in work-related accidents or seriously ill were often transferred to death camps. No matter how serious the illness, they claimed that patients would recover quickly and be able to return to work. They pretended that broken limbs were minor sprains, that dysentery was a temporary stomach ailment, that tuberculosis was a cold. They gave advice to diabetics about how to stay alive without medication. Anyone openly diagnosed with diabetes, even small children, was immediately sent to an extermination camp.

Rezső Seress, the Budapest composer of the hit song "Gloomy Sunday," occupied one of the hospital's beds. He had been on the forced march from the capital, and, when he tried to escape, he was wounded. The Gestapo officer who found him had delivered him to the hospital to recuperate; the officer had fond memories of the maudlin song.

On Himmler's orders, the last of the crematoria at Auschwitz-Birkenau were blown up in early January. A few days later, the German guards killed 700 prisoners at random and began the westward march of 65,000 others, lined up in rows of five abreast. In one of the harshest winters in Europe, in below-freezing temperatures and blinding, drifting snow, wearing only their thin prison clothes, they began their long journey from Poland to other camps in the Reich. Anyone who stopped was shot, and only half of them reached their destination camps. About 20,000 ended up in the overcrowded, typhoid-infected Bergen-Belsen camp.[28]

When members of the First Ukrainian Front of the Red Army arrived at Auschwitz, they found only about 8,000 prisoners. Most of them had been deemed too ill for the march, and there had not been enough time to kill them all. According to Gábor Kádár and Zoltán Vági's book *Self-Financing Genocide,* throughout the existence of the death camp "nearly 690 Norwegian, 7,500 Italian, 10,000 Yugoslav, 23,000 German and Austrian, 25,000 Belgian, 27,000 Slovak, 46,000 Czech, 55,000 Greek, 60,000 Dutch, 69,000 French, and

300,000 Polish Jews were deported to the Auschwitz complex. The largest contingent, 430,000 people,[29] came from Hungary. Of the 1.1 million Jews deported to Auschwitz, 1 million died."[30] Other accounts claim that out of a total of 1.3 million people deported to Auschwitz between 1940 and 1945, 1.1 million had been murdered by all the various means available to their captors.[31] Initially, Rudolf Höss, the camp commandant, himself had estimated the number of dead ("executed and exterminated") at around 3 million, including those who had died of "starvation and disease,"[32] but he lowered his estimate to 1,135,000 at his trial in Warsaw.

General Georgi Zhukov's armies launched a massive Soviet offensive against Berlin on January 12, 1945 and British and American bombers had already reduced Germany's major cities to rubble. The war in Europe was obviously coming to an end, but Hitler and his generals made a last, desperate move to enlist everybody into the defense of the tottering Reich. They also continued with their plan for the destruction of the Jews.

Having come to a tenuous understanding with Becher, Kasztner now tried to make a similar deal with Krumey. It was his last hope for the Strass-hof Jews. He promised Krumey that, when the war was over, he would put in a good word for him. "When the time comes," he told him, "you will be glad you helped me now. We always remember our friends." Krumey, who had been moved to Vienna by Eichmann as punishment for his relative friendliness to the Jews,[33] was at first reluctant, but Kasztner finally persuaded him to give the Red Cross permission to distribute ten thousand sets of underclothes, twelve thousand pairs of shoes, and five thousand lots of warm clothes to the prisoners. He also obtained Krumey's agreement to bring in more medical supplies, dental equipment, and even painkillers. Kasztner was particularly anxious that the Strasshof Jews should still be classified as *schutzhäftlinge*, protected prisoners or exchange Jews, even though no exchange goods had arrived from the Joint. He complained that his Jews were not allowed to use the underground shelters during Allied bombings. "It is not too late to prove your humanity," he advised Krumey, as General Zhukov's armies crossed the Oder River less than sixty miles from Berlin.

Kasztner traveled to Bratislava to purchase canvas, tobacco, woolens, and cooking oil for Becher, in exchange for sixty Bratislava "prominent Jews" who had been in hiding since the deportations resumed. He visited Rabbi Weissmandel in the cellar of a boarded-up villa on the outskirts of Bratislava. Weissmandel was hoping to be part of the last group to escape to the west before the Soviet army arrived and, indeed, he was driven to Switzerland on April 1, four days before the Russians took the city.

While in Bratislava, Kasztner bought forty pounds of tobacco for Krumey, along with clothing for the eighty-five babies who had been born in captivity in Vienna. The Red Cross had shipped two thousand pairs of shoes for this Strasshof group, not nearly enough, but even that number was difficult to sift through the thieving fingers of Krumey's officers. Most of the medical supplies had already been confiscated by the ss, and it took several more weeks for the warm clothing to arrive from the Red Cross. In addition to all the suffering these various wants caused, Vienna was now undergoing daily Allied bombardments. Already much of central Vienna had become a warren of ruins.

Kasztner tried to reach Budapest from Bratislava, but all roads and railway lines were blocked by the fighting. On his return to Vienna, he called on Dieter Wisliceny at his cozy apartment on one of the lower floors of an old building that had, so far, withstood the bombing. He was fascinated by Wisliceny's library. Considering that the ss captain had been an active participant in the implementation of the Final Solution, it was extraordinary that he had collected works by Stefan and Arnold Zweig, Emil Ludwig, and other Jewish writers. Like his former colleague Eichmann in Budapest, Wisliceny had become, in his own eyes, a savior of Jews. He talked fondly of Gizi Fleischmann and nostalgically of the evenings he had spent in Budapest's nightclubs with Kasztner. He claimed he had sent the sick and exhausted Jews from the border of Hungary to Vienna for treatment at the Jewish hospital, so it was fortunate that he had been in charge of receiving them at the end of their long march from Budapest.[34]

Kasztner considered this change of heart a very good sign: if Wisliceny continued to picture himself in the role of savior, he could perhaps be relied on to prevent more murders at the Austrian border. Wisliceny blamed Eichmann for everything that had happened to the Hungarian Jews, and, now that Himmler had decided to spare the remaining Jews, Wisliceny complained that Eichmann would ignore the order. Eichmann had given instructions to the camp commandants to "severely punish" Jews if they did not fully cooperate when the camps were evacuated, but, he complained, some commanders did not fully understand his message and left behind live Jews for the Russians to find. The last time they had met in Berlin, Wisliceny reported, Eichmann had said, "I will laugh when I jump into the grave because of the feeling that I have killed five million Jews." As Wisliceny saw it, only he had been blameless in this whole tragic story.[35] He confided in Kasztner that when he first learned of the gas chambers, he told Eichmann, "God grant that our enemies will never use these methods against us."[36] And in November he had ordered one day of rest for those who arrived on foot from Budapest. Once Eichmann found out, he threatened to have him court-martialed.

When Himmler visited Vienna, Becher tried to arrange a meeting between Kasztner and the ss Reichsführer. "He is deeply concerned about the fate of the Jews," Becher explained to the astonished Kasztner. "In these situations, there is always a chance that some hothead will decide to act on his own or refer to earlier orders." Becher and Kasztner were sitting in the Metropole Hotel bar, surrounded by senior German officers of various stripes. The air-raid sirens had been shrieking their regular warnings, but the piano player was still at the keys, singing with a deep, husky voice something soft about home, and the bar stayed open.

Becher showed Kasztner the new orders from Himmler: "Under no circumstances must they be harmed."[37] Those words meant that Kasztner's *tauschjuden* would not be dragged away to concentration camps. Better still, the camps would stop killing the surviving Jews. Himmler, perhaps, had discovered that his murder apparatus had disposed of a great source of labor for the Reich.[38]

"What will the ss commandants do with this order?" Kasztner asked. "Will they follow it?"

Becher thought they would have no option but to obey, although, he complained, Ernst Kaltenbrunner had been undermining his every action. He had gone directly to Hitler for authorization over Himmler's orders. The Führer, understandably after the attempt on his life, was suspicious of everybody.

Himmler, he confided, had told Becher that he would sign a treaty with the Allies if they did the sensible thing and united against the Soviet Union. The Führer had predicted that the coalition of the Allies would disintegrate, for the West had nothing in common with the Communists. Perhaps Kaltenbrunner knew that Himmler had dealt with the organization of Orthodox Jews and their emissary, former Swiss president Musy. Unlike Saly Mayer, Musy had not found it difficult to turn over the necessary funds to Himmler to save 1,200 Theresienstadt Jews. Now Kaltenbrunner was saying that while Becher shuffled back and forth between Budapest and Switzerland in the company of a Jew, Musy had successfully paid for his 1,200 Jews and trucked them out of Germany. "I have lost credibility, Rudolf," Becher complained. "As to your Ostmark Jews, under the circumstances, this was the best I could do."

It was not the first time that Becher had shared his concerns with Kasztner, but it was the first time he openly discussed his fear of Kaltenbrunner and mentioned the rift between Hitler and Himmler. Hitler had not agreed to the release of Kasztner's Jews to Switzerland, and he had been furious—after he recovered from the assassination attempt—about Joel Brand's failed mission. There were times, it seemed, when the ss Reichsführer had taken matters into his own hands.

"With Brand's mission?" Kasztner asked.

"No. With Grosz's mission. Or haven't you put the puzzle pieces together yet, Rudolf?" He had assumed that Kasztner, being so smart, would have known long ago that the Brand mission was just a front for another mission, the one that Bandi Grosz was to accomplish.

"Why would he have chosen Grosz?" Kasztner asked. Becher had now confirmed what he had learned from Palestine's Yishuv emissaries in Istanbul: Grosz was carrying a message from Himmler. "Why Grosz?" he repeated.

Becher shook his head in disbelief. "Rudolf, I have always admired your brains! Think about it. With someone like Grosz, the whole thing was deniable. It needed denying when Hitler heard about it on the BBC. Do you think the Reichsführer-SS was going to take any chances?"

Kasztner left the bar with a sense of unreality, not because of what he had heard about the Brand mission—he had suspected something from the beginning—but because a decorated SS officer had trusted him with information that could mean his own execution. He felt strangely elated, proud of his unique station.

When he went again to see Dr. Emil Tuchmann at the "Jewish hospital," the building was guarded by Hitler Youth, some as young as twelve or fourteen but swearing they would kill every Jew inside if the Russians approached Vienna. The youngsters had been armed and empowered to act on behalf of the Reich. They would not, they swore, let the Jews fall into enemy hands alive. Smiling, Kasztner reassured Tuchmann that they would all be safe now. After all, he believed he had Himmler's word for it.

Kasztner learned the next day that some of his "Jews on ice" were no longer in the Ungarnlager of Bergen-Belsen but had been transferred to the *häftlingslager* by the new camp commandant, SS Captain Josef Kramer, "the Beast of Belsen." Kramer had immediately canceled all the so-called camp privileges for "exchange Jews." Kasztner knew what they would be facing: starvation, brutality, stacks of corpses, the stench of burning bodies. He sought out Becher to tell him that the Germans had reneged on an agreement, and tried to get the Red Cross access to the camp, so that food and clothing would be available for the inmates.

Six-year-old Paul Varnai was transported with his family in a cattle car to Bergen-Belsen. He remembers the unbearable hunger, the thirst, the cold, the dirt, and the dreadful sickness that killed hundreds around him, along with the endless early morning roll calls in the snow, the prisoners' frozen black toes, and everyone's breath in the air. When the numbers did not add up as the guards expected, the roll call started again—and again, until the guards were satisfied.

In early April they were herded into boxcars once more. "The train was attacked by American planes. The guards took cover in the fields and woods nearby while the prisoners stayed padlocked in the wagons. The planes dropped bombs and strafed the flimsy roofs. The noise was horrific. The exploding shells, the screams of the wounded. Blood splattered all over the walls. So many died . . ." He barely recalls arriving in Theresienstadt. It was his seventh birthday.[39]

CHAPTER 26

Budapest in the Throes of Liberation

"Were you looking forward to the arrival of the Russians?"

"Yes, as if they had been our own family. Rafi, for example, ran to meet them like a madman and embraced the first Russian in tears. The Russian said: Here, Jew, give me your leather coat."
From István Benedek and György Vámos, *Tépd Le a Sárga Csillagot*

My neighbor—not long ago a keen Nazi supporter—invited a Russian officer to dinner. During the main course, my neighbor asked the Russian what the Bolsheviks thought of the Jews. The officer shrugged. "Send them to work, with everybody," he said.

I realized, then, that the remnant of Hungary's Jewry, those poor, suffering souls in the capital, would not see a restitution of their losses— the fact that they are no longer singled out would have to suffice.
Sándor Márai, *Ami a Naplómból Kimaradt*

By November 1944, the German and Hungarian forces were severely outnumbered by the Soviets, seven divisions facing twelve. There was little communication between these increasingly desperate allies, mainly because they did not trust each other. The Germans were convinced that their brothers-in-arms would, given the chance, cheerfully defect to the enemy;[1] the Hungarians not only resented their German commanders but realized that their own units were generally ill-equipped, disorganized, and untrained. They knew that it was pointless to try to defend Budapest, the symbol of Hungarian national pride.

Szálasi therefore asked Veesenmayer whether Budapest could be declared a "free city," sparing it the destruction of street-to-street battles. But the Reich plenipotentiary told him that Germany did not care whether Budapest and all its people were destroyed, so long as the Russians stayed pinned down in the east. Veesenmayer took his direction from the Führer, and he was still convinced that Hitler would launch a decisive counteroffensive and that, given time, the British and the Americans would come to their senses and realize that Soviet Russia was the real enemy. They would make peace with Germany in the west and focus, instead, on the common enemy of Bolshevik Russia in the east.

Even if Himmler was wrong about the Allies' interest in offering acceptable terms, Veesenmayer was determined to save Vienna. It was not a personal mission—Veesenmayer had only contempt for the Viennese—but he had to follow Hitler's orders to preserve the capital city of his native land. To do that, it was crucial to keep the Soviet army totally occupied with Hungary. On November 23 Hitler himself had issued a directive to his chief of staff in Hungary: the Wehrmacht was to hold its position to the last man. Every house in Budapest was to be defended, regardless of civilian casualties. For as long as he was Reich plenipotentiary, Veesenmayer would do just that.

On December 1 Hitler appointed Lieutenant General Karl Pfeffer-Wildenbruch of the Waffen-ss to lead the defense of Budapest. Otto Winkelmann, the ss commander in chief of both the German and the Hungarian forces in Budapest, had resigned his post, convinced that the city could not be successfully defended. By this time, the oil fields in western Hungary were the only source of fuel for the German forces. The once proud panzer divisions were frequently idle because there was not enough gasoline, and the armaments industry had slowed to a near standstill for lack of fuel and workers. In Hitler's mind, Hungary had to become the main theater of war in the east.

As he was preparing to leave the city, Eichmann ordered the execution of all members of the Jewish Council. In the general confusion, the order was not carried out, but Samuel Stern and his fellow councillors recognized that they were now marked men.

For most Hungarians, welcoming the Soviet army was a terrible prospect. Historically, the Russians had been among their most bitter and feared enemies. It was the last-minute intervention by the Russians that had crushed the Hungarian War of Independence of 1848–49. Now, however, a dishonorable surrender to their historic foe was preferable to the destruction of their city.

The Soviet troops who pushed into Hungary with overwhelming force had surprisingly low morale. They had been fighting for months; their food rations were poor; and the Tatars, Lithuanians, and Ukrainians among them had been pressed into service against their will. To keep some semblance of order, many of their commanders ordered the laggards in their units to be executed in front of their comrades for cowardice or sentenced to years of hard labor in Siberia. Others tried to cheer up their men by distributing vast quantities of low-grade vodka and encouraging them to gather up to ten pounds of gifts each week from the local population. They were allowed to send war booty to their families. This combination of drinking and looting drove many men to commit horrific acts. Some women were raped so often that they died; others had their backs broken. Some girls as young as ten were raped by whole platoons while their mothers waited their turn.

On December 24 the first Soviet units reached the outskirts of Buda. A woman cooking Christmas dinner saw Russian soldiers with submachine guns hurrying past her kitchen window. At the Number 81 streetcar terminus, a few Russian soldiers distributed loaves of black army bread. While Verdi's *Aida* played at the baroque Opera House to a packed audience determined to ignore the fall of their city, Soviet bombs rained down on Pest, and antiaircraft guns and air-raid sirens bellowed in protest. Among the ruins, families prepared for the traditional Christmas celebrations.

Ági Lantos had prepared for the festivities by making sure her parents were safe in their Buda hiding place with their Christian documents and sufficient food for a couple of weeks.[2] She had long since taken off the yellow star, acquired Christian papers, and lived with a family who gave her a back room in exchange for her services as a dressmaker. She was sewing a festive outfit for one of the children when the sirens started. They rarely stopped again until the city was taken.

Young István Weiszlovits saw his first Soviet soldier on Christmas Eve, and Christmas is still his favorite holiday. He was the only one among 150 children and 30 adults in the home who could speak Russian, and became an interpreter for both the Russians and the Hungarians. Major Maslov, the local commander, took István with him when he and his senior staff were hosted by Cardinal Serédi in Esztergom's Catholic basilica to a fantastic meal of salami, ham, fresh vegetables, white bread, and cheeses.[3]

Hansi Brand, although she was a frequent visitor at the Red Cross children's homes, had not taken her own two children to one of them. Her instinct told her that no one would be able to control the Arrow Cross gangs. Even when the government had wanted to cooperate with the Swedes and the Swiss, it had little influence on the mobs that ran the streets. Only six years old at that time, Dani Brand remembers hiding in the basement of a Christian woman's apartment building, having to pretend he and his brother were gentiles. He knew that if they were betrayed, they might die. Their mother had bought a single cot for them to share, but as the basement was always crowded, not everyone had a bed.

One evening an older man demanded their cot and Hansi's blanket. "Why should the Jews always get the comfort?" he asked.

"Then a bomb fell right through the ceiling one night and landed on what used to be our cot," Dani remembers. "Both the man and his wife died."[4]

By Christmas Day, Budapest was encircled by Soviet heavy armor. Remnants of the German army were trapped and still not allowed to withdraw. Bodies were hanging from lampposts, lying in gutters, drifting down the Danube. Corpses were left where they fell. Throughout the ceaseless bombardments, as buildings collapsed around them, the Arrow Cross continued their frantic rampage, murdering Jews in the streets. When they tried to remove the remaining children from the Red Cross orphanages to the ghetto, they were stopped by Friedrich Born. Throughout the city, posters warned that the punishment for helping Jews was summary execution. To ensure that the message was heard, the Arrow Cross killed a few sample Christians—nuns on Swabian Hill, building superintendents who had not reported Jews in hiding, and the managing director of the Bauxit Company together with his pregnant wife and two small children.[5]

The former American embassy building and the Glass House on Vadász Street were filled with Jews. Every space was occupied, with people sleeping on the stairs, in the closets, in the bathrooms. A unit of German soldiers had taken over the upper floors of the Glass House to shoot at the Soviet planes, and the responding fire shattered the massive glass walls and thick window panels. Bombs broke through the roof of the embassy. Still, no one left the buildings.

A group of Arrow Cross boys, led by an older, leather-jacketed Nazi enthusiast, blew up the gates of the Glass House with a shower of hand grenades. Waving their machine guns at the cowering people inside, they shouted for everyone to leave the building. Mihály Salamon remembered how scared he was when a hysterical boy of about fourteen pointed his gun at the small children in the upstairs "display" room; Salamon feared that the shaking weapon would go off accidentally. By the time Arthur Weisz, the former owner of the Glass House, arrived in the courtyard, dozens of Swiss consul Carl Lutz's protected charges had been shot, and the Arrow Cross boys were eagerly rummaging through abandoned belongings in search of valuables. Weisz stepped up to the gang's leader and tried to explain that the house was under the protection of the Swiss government. When that failed to impress, he demanded that he be allowed to make a phone call to the city's commander in chief. The refugees were then allowed to return to what was left of the once spectacular building, but Weisz paid for his intervention with his life.[6]

Samuel Stern had taken refuge with a former Nazi extremist and Hungarian journalist, who continued to file stories for an Arrow Cross newspaper to preserve his image. He assumed, rightly, that Stern would one day be his alibi. André Biss and his wife checked into the Hotel Pannonia, where the Hungarian government was guarding the now enemy Romanian diplomats who had not been able to leave the city, thinking it would be a safer refuge than his bombed-out apartment.

On December 28 two police officers went to Ottó Komoly's Mérleg Street office and politely asked that he go with them to a meeting to discuss the future of the ghetto. He escaped through the back entrance and checked into the Ritz Hotel under another name, but he was recognized by someone in the foyer, reported, and taken to the Arrow Cross headquarters on Városház Street. The drains in the building were clogged with blood. The few prisoners still alive after the beatings stood in two feet of fetid, bloody water, waiting for someone to kill them. And it was probably there that Ottó Komoly, too, was murdered.

More than 800,000 civilians lived underground in dank cellars, occasionally venturing out to search for food or for loved ones. Whenever a warehouse or a truck was shelled, people emerged from their bunkers to look for cans or boxes of food that were meant for the army. Farmers could no longer take their wagons into the city, so there was nothing left to eat. Dying horses wandering through the streets were hacked to pieces by men and women using scissors and kitchen knives. It was only because some 30,000 horses had been brought to the city and abandoned without food or shelter that the citizens of Budapest had any food at all, though a bakery near Rákóczy Avenue continued to bake bread with its rapidly diminishing supplies and sawdust-mixed flour. The army itself began to run out of food by January. Entire city blocks collapsed under the constant bombardment, trapping the inhabitants under the rubble.

Some 60,000 German and Hungarian soldiers fought against 180,000 Soviet and Romanian troops in house-to-house combat, and the streets were covered in broken glass and bits of brick. Dead bodies were no longer collected, and scavenging civilians competed to take the shoes, coats, and sweaters off the corpses.

No one without a special permit had been allowed into the ghetto since December 10. The gates were locked and guarded, and food deliveries had all but halted. Dead bodies were piled up in the former garden of the synagogue. Most had been stripped of their clothes. Frozen in the sudden December cold, they lay exposed to the dazed indifference of the living. It was a miracle that Miksa Domonkos still managed to commandeer a few meager supplies, but there was never enough. Wearing his army captain's uniform, he acted with enough authority to redirect a couple of trucks with flour through the guarded gates. He continued to fake Ferenczy's name on transfer certificates to rescue Jews from the Arrow Cross.

The patients, doctors, and nurses of the two remaining Jewish hospitals, both under the protection of the Red Cross, were massacred by the Arrow Cross. Only the hospital under the protection of ss officer Ara Jerezien remained safe. More than four hundred Jews, including Eva Zahler and her mother and grandfather, survived the war because of him. All that Jerezien demanded in exchange was a certificate, signed by all forty doctors, testifying to his good deed in saving their lives. This they did gladly.[7]

In their efforts to commandeer vehicles, Arrow Cross gangs frequently shot Hungarian officers and randomly selected civilians who they imagined might be hiding something valuable or whose appearance they simply disliked. They loathed all class distinctions, which they claimed had denied them their rightful share of wealth. The stench of burning buildings, refuse, and decomposing bodies was overwhelming. Congested with rubble and parts of bridges that had fallen, the Danube swelled and began to flood the northern parts of the city.

On New Year's Eve, units of the Soviet army overran Hungarian army positions around Pest. House-to-house fighting now extended into the working quarters of the city, and Soviet soldiers penetrated the culverts of the inner district. Often the two sides were separated by only one street or one house. Aircraft squadrons continued to drop bombs, and fighter planes strafed streets that were deemed to be in enemy hands, though sometimes they were shooting at their own men. On January 5, following direct orders from the government, police and Arrow Cross irregulars began emptying out the "international houses," those under the protection of various neutral governments. When the news reached Raoul Wallenberg, he offered a bribe of food and medications to leave his charges where they were.

The main military hospital received a direct hit on January 14. Dying soldiers were left in destroyed buildings. The wounded piled up in makeshift hospitals, without medicine or nurses, lying in the cold cellars of the burned-out Parliament Building and the Museum of Military History. A retreating German army unit blew up the Horthy (later Petőfi) Bridge. An Arrow Cross group advanced into the ghetto and murdered several people they encountered before being routed by Domonkos and a couple of policemen. In the streets, the advancing Soviet soldiers used captured civilians to shield them from enemy fire. In short order, the German military also adopted this tactic, but the strategy was ineffectual for both armies.

Hansi Brand and her two children survived the siege, underground. When a Soviet soldier entered their cellar, Dani told his mother to hide behind him in the corner. The Russians ordered the women to come and help "peel potatoes." The other women went, but Hansi stayed hidden in the corner by her two little boys.[8] She wondered how Dani knew what to do but later realized bitterly that "he had seen so much already, his childhood was lost."

The German military command in Budapest asked for reinforcements. Hitler had no one to spare. Ignoring advice from his generals, he had thrown eight divisions into a last, desperate attack on the advancing British, American, and Canadian forces in the Saar region. In his deteriorating mind, success in retaking the strategically important Ardennes borderlands to the northwest would prove that Germany was still worthy of its Führer. The attack, as predicted by the generals, was a disaster, with a loss of 120,000 men, 600 tanks, 1,600 planes, and 6,000 trucks.[9] When Hitler finally decided to send a panzer division to Hungary, it was too late.

There was one final, unsuccessful attempt on January 15 to blow up the Budapest ghetto. Major General Gerhard Schmidthuber, the last of a series of German commanders of Budapest, claimed later that he forbade the destruction of the ghetto and ensured that his order was followed by posting Wehrmacht soldiers outside the wooden walls.[10] Kasztner, in contrast, said that the destruction had been prevented by General Winkelmann, acting on direct orders from Kurt Becher.[11] Kasztner was actually in Vienna during the siege of Budapest, but he wrote: "When I gave him [Becher] Krell's receipt for the 20 million francs from the Joint, Becher called ss General Winkelmann, who forbade the Arrow Cross government's action. The Germans told Kovarcz, the Arrow Cross minister, that emptying the ghetto could seriously endanger Germany's interests."[12] At Nuremberg, Becher, too, suddenly recalled that he had given such orders—though by then there were many who claimed credit for heroism in the dying days of the Reich.[13]

On January 18 the ghetto was liberated by the Soviet army.

Hansi remembered that it had been snowing the night before and, when she finally looked outside, the smell of fresh snow seemed stronger than the stench of corpses and smoke. And she recalled the few moments of quiet after Pest fell.

In front of the Glass House, the young halutzim ran out to hug and kiss the first Soviet soldiers they saw. Their enthusiasm was so great that some of the Russians grabbed their guns to free themselves.[14]

Along the Danube, the hotels, the restaurants, and the entire Corso were on fire. Retreating Germans blew up all the bridges between Buda and Pest. Remnants of the German and Hungarian armies crossed over the badly damaged Chain Bridge into the ruins of the old Castle District just before the bridge was destroyed. There were thousands of casualties. The narrow streets and burning buildings made it difficult to reach the bridgehead, and the bridge itself was continually bombarded.

Buda came under heavy attacks both from the air and by advancing Soviet troops from the west. Still, the German command deemed that the hills were defendable. Both sides suffered enormous losses. Of the 30,000 German soldiers who eventually tried to break out of Budapest, against the Führer's orders, only 624 reached the German lines.[15]

Pest was taken by the Soviets between January 17 and 18, and Buda on February 13. The siege of Budapest had lasted one hundred days. The combined Soviet and Romanian losses in Budapest totaled more than 70,000 men; the Hungarian army lost 16,500; the German army, 30,000.[16] More than 40,000 civilians had been killed, including some 7,000 Jews. About 40,000 Hungarian soldiers were taken prisoner by the Soviets. To round out the numbers, they took 50,000 civilians as well. Everyone in uniform, even firefighters and postmen, was taken prisoner, as were men lining up for bread or going in search of water. Around one-third of the soldiers and civilians were returned to Hungary after a few years of forced labor in the Soviet Union.

Of the 50,000 Jews "lent" to the Reich to build fortifications around Vienna, only about 20,000 were still alive in April 1945. Fewer than one-tenth of the men in the Jewish labor brigades survived the war.

On February 13, crouched over the radio in the remnants of an old apartment building, Hansi Brand and Peretz Révész screamed with delight when they heard the news of Dresden's demise: 529 Lancaster aircraft had dropped thousands of high-explosive blockbuster and incendiary cluster bombs on one of Germany's proudest and oldest cities, consuming it in a firestorm. The city, and almost everyone in it, was dead. The Death Bureau later reported that 120,000 to 150,000 people had died there.[17]

When Rezső Kasztner heard of the bombing, he said that if there was a God, which he doubted, he had perhaps been thinking about the burning of all of Dresden's Jews in 1349 on massive pyres in the Old City Square. That, too, had happened on a February 13.[18] On the day Dresden was destroyed, Kasztner was again at the Saint Margarethen Bridge with Saly Mayer, Kurt Becher, Mayer's lawyer, and

Becher's adjutant, Erich Krell. Saly Mayer showed Becher a letter confirming that 20 million Swiss francs had at last been deposited in a Swiss bank account for him and Roswell McClelland to use at their discretion.[19] At Mayer's insistence, the Joint had transferred an additional $5 million to his account as "show money." Becher immediately demanded that the money be transferred into an account in his name only, but Mayer refused. The Swiss would never agree, he said.[20]

Becher asked to see McClelland again, then accepted Mayer's request that the Red Cross be allowed to deliver food and medications to the concentration camps. What caused the most difficulties was Mayer's demand for an estimate of the number of Jews still alive in German hands.

After Budapest was lost, Hitler's Sixth ss Panzer Division still tried to hold out west of Lake Balaton against the combined Ukrainian and Russian assault. At the same time that the main Soviet offensive under General Zhukov was only fifty miles from Berlin, the remaining few of the July 20 conspirators were executed by an ss firing squad. They were fortunate that there simply wasn't enough time for Hitler's entourage to stage another exhibition of degrading deaths.

When the Soviet army arrived in Vienna, more than eight thousand Strasshof Jews remained scattered throughout the city. They were cold, hungry, and terrified, but they were alive.

CHAPTER 27

Nazi Gold

The conversation between Himmler, Eichmann and me took place in Himmler's command carriage in the Black Forest, near Freiburg. Himmler talked to Eichmann in a manner I would call both kindly and angry . . . He shouted at him something like, "If until now you have exterminated Jews, from now on, if I order you, as I do now, you must be a fosterer of Jews."

Kurt Becher, testifying at Nuremberg

Rezső Kasztner had still hoped to return to Budapest in March, but, with the war raging across western Hungary, he had no choice but to remain in Vienna.

On April 5, as the Wehrmacht's last battles for Vienna began, Kurt Becher, who had been promoted to full colonel in January, told Kasztner that Himmler had appointed him to be the officer in charge of several concentration camps.[1] He asked Kasztner to travel with him to Bergen-Belsen and perhaps later also to the Neuengamme, Dachau, Flossenbürg, Theresienstadt, and Mauthausen camps to deliver Himmler's authorization to stop the slaughter.[2] When the ss driver called for Kasztner the next morning at his hotel, Becher showed him the orders. Given that the ss Reichsführer had previously been totally committed to the extermination of Jews, this document was truly extraordinary. "By this order, which becomes immediately effective," it read, "I forbid any extermination of Jews and order that, on the contrary, care should be given to weak and sick persons. I hold you personally responsible even if this order should not be strictly adhered to by subordinate officers."[3]

Becher had already delivered copies of the order to both Ernst Kalten-brunner and the chief of the ss Economic and Administrative Main Office, Oswald Pohl.[4] Now, he said, his task was to make certain that Himmler's commands were obeyed. These orders would supersede whatever previous orders had been given to the camp commandants, including Himmler's own decrees. Becher revealed that Kaltenbrunner had become vociferous in his attacks on Himmler's softening position toward the concentration camp inmates and had threatened to go directly to Hitler again. This time, however, Becher was not overly concerned. The Führer had dug himself into a bunker somewhere near the Reichstag in Berlin and was no longer in touch with the outside world. He seemed not to care what happened to the German people; one of his recent orders, for instance, had been to destroy all the country's military and industrial complexes. All communications installations were also to be blown up. The Führer, Becher told Kasztner, rather than hand Germany over to the enemy, would turn it into a wasteland. He had been raving about betrayals and reprisals.

By then, of course, it was already too late for six million Jews. The sight of Bergen-Belsen and its survivors was so horrific that Kasztner would never be able to speak of it again. In the mud and excrement, dead bodies were piled up next to the living. In the barracks, people slept ten or twelve to each narrow wooden shelf. Mere skeletons of men and women were staggering about or crawling, most of them dreadfully wounded, disfigured, maimed, afflicted with diseases, infested with lice, neither talking nor hearing. The last arrivals were lying outside in the mud—all young women, all dead.[5]

Yet the storehouse contained mountains of Red Cross food parcels, medication, and clothing; none of it had been distributed to the inmates. Years later, when an Israeli interviewer asked Becher why he had not commanded that food and clothing be distributed immediately, he stared into space and asked that the question be repeated. It was, but he still did not have an answer.

Becher negotiated with the commandant, ss Captain Josef Kramer, in his office for two days while Kasztner waited. On the second day, a filthy old woman in rags, her head shaved, her hands arthritic claws, shambled up to him where he stood, erect in his clean suit and tie. In a hoarse voice, she begged for bread for her daughter.

When he did not respond, she asked: "Don't you know me, Rezső?"[6]

Just at this moment, Becher came out of Kramer's office, and the two of them resumed their guarded walk through the camp. Suddenly Kasztner realized that the "old" woman was Joel Brand's sister Hanna. To his everlasting horror and shame, he did not return to try to find her.

All attempts at camp administration had already collapsed. The ss units guarding prisoners from outside the barbed-wire fences paid no attention to what was going on inside; their job was to prevent escapes. Becher had to persuade Kramer and the commanders of the nearby Wehrmacht units not to massacre the surviving inmates. His argument, according to later testimonies, was that the typhoid epidemic in the camp would spread to the soldiers.

Becher reported to Himmler that typhoid was killing the inmates faster even than starvation and the lack of water. The camp was overcrowded. Too many prisoners from other camps, including Auschwitz, had been brought to Bergen-Belsen on senseless, long marches when Poland was abandoned to the Russians.

Himmler issued another order—also shown at the Nuremberg war-crimes trials before the International Military Tribunal[7]—that the ss should fight the epidemic "with everything at your disposal . . . Do not spare doctors and medication. The prisoners are under special protection." It was an order few saw and no one obeyed. Waffen-ss units around the camp (their members included an ethnic German detachment from Hungary) were given the opportunity to shoot any *häftlings* they wished "just for the fun of it."[8]

Kasztner later credited Becher with saving the last sixty thousand of Bergen-Belsen's prisoners. The photographs and film footage taken there by the Americans still, even after all the carnage of war, had the power to shock the world. The liberators found seventeen thousand unburied corpses, and thousands of the skeletal survivors died within days of the surrender of the camp. The soldiers ordered a contingent of local villagers to dig trenches and help bulldoze the corpses into the mass graves. The British commander said there were no words, no pictures, that could adequately describe the horror they saw.

Joel Brand's mother, two sisters, and niece, Margit, were ordered into a train on April 9 just before the camp was taken by the British. The train was directed to Theresienstadt, but it never arrived at its destination. It was shunted in and out of bombed-out stations, its doors sealed tight and with no food or water for the people inside. It stopped when planes strafed the engine, but the guards allowed the prisoners out only once in the six- or seven-day journey.[9] The Russians finally opened the doors of "the lost train" near Frankfurt an der Oder. The villagers of Troeditz, accustomed as they were to horrific sights, had never seen anything like the few, emaciated survivors who stumbled from that train. Brand's mother had died during the journey, but his other relatives survived.

Becher was not as successful at Neuengamme, where the commandant ignored his demand that the camp be handed over to the Swedish Red Cross.

At Becher's behest, Hermann Krumey, Otto Hunsche, Dieter Wisliceny,[10] and Kasztner traveled to Theresienstadt to deliver Himmler's orders to surrender the camp. On the way, Krumey, unaware of the revulsion his words would elicit, boasted to Kasztner that he had been able to save 115,000 reichsmarks from the payments he received for work done by the Strasshof Jews.[11] He was proud of his modest contribution to the German war effort, unaware that these savings meant he had not purchased the food and medication intended for the Strasshof Jews, as had been agreed with Kasztner.

Vienna was taken by the Soviets on April 13. On April 20, Hitler's fifty-sixth birthday, all his faithful chiefs went to visit him once more: Hermann Göring, Josef Goebbels, Joachim von Ribbentrop, Martin Bormann, and, of course, Heinrich Himmler. However, at least three of the men had made concerted efforts to be picked as Hitler's successor and to lead Germany in negotiations with the British and Americans. They all disliked one another intensely.

Kurt Becher had not been invited to the celebration. Instead, he drove to the Mauthausen concentration camp, near Linz, with Himmler's orders.

ss Colonel Franz Ziereis, the commandant of Mauthausen, had received orders from Kaltenbrunner to kill at least a thousand people a day. Time permitting, he planned to send a few thousand down the Danube in barges to the Wels subcamp. He was determined not to hand a single live prisoner over to the Russians. As a finale to his reign of terror, Ziereis intended to collect the remaining inmates in the underground Bergkristall tunnels where they had worked and blow the whole place up.[12] When Ziereis questioned his authority, Becher phoned Kaltenbrunner in Ziereis's presence to inform him of Himmler's wishes, hoping Kaltenbrunner did not know that his appointment to supervise selected concentration camps did not include Mauthausen, and that the appointment had, in any event, been subsequently rescinded.[13] The two senior ss officers got into a heated argument. The Reich Security Office chief was unconvinced but did not dare to countermand the order. In the end, Becher had to agree to go to Kaltenbrunner's Salzburg headquarters to review the nature of his appointment and Himmler's orders.[14] Meanwhile, Ziereis reluctantly postponed the killings and evacuation. He also agreed to do a personal favor for Becher—to free Moshe Schweiger.

One of Kasztner's earliest Va'ada associates, Schweiger had been deported to Mauthausen a few days after the German occupation of

Hungary in March 1944. He would later recall that when he was summoned to the camp commandant's quarters in April 1945, he was convinced it would be his last hour. He had been very ill and hoped the end would be quick. A tall, handsome man in Ziereis's outer office introduced himself with extraordinary politeness, called him "Dr. Schweiger," and offered him a glass of wine and a sandwich of thinly sliced beef on white bread—the first meat and real bread Schweiger had seen since his incarceration. Schweiger declined the wine because he was afraid he would not survive the first sip. He could barely walk and had lost over thirty pounds as well as all his hair and fingernails. Becher ordered the camp's Jewish tailor to measure Schweiger for a suit of civilian clothes.[15]

"You are my gift to Dr. Kasztner," Becher told him. He explained that Schweiger would be transferred to an area of the camp where prisoners were fed and given medical treatment. He did not think that Schweiger should travel in his present condition. He said he would be back in a few days and hoped Schweiger would be well enough to accompany him. Becher then drove to Salzburg for the meeting with Kaltenbrunner. On the road to Flossenbürg, he was spotted by American troops and, according to his own account, was lightly wounded in the ensuing skirmish. He was awarded the Black Wounded Badge for his bravery.[16] Despite the wound, he stoically carried on toward Salzburg.

There are two completely different versions of what took place at the Reich Security office that day, Kaltenbrunner's and Becher's. The security chief claimed that the only concentration camp they discussed was Dachau. The Americans were close to Munich and could reach Dachau within a couple of days. The camp commandant, ss Captain Eduard Weiter, had received written orders from Himmler, dated April 4, instructing him that "no prisoner must fall into the hands of the enemy." Despite that instruction, Becher claimed in his account that he had managed to bluff his way to an agreement whereby both Dachau and Mauthausen would be handed over to the Allies and no more prisoners would be killed.[17]

Becher returned to Mauthausen on the morning of April 27, the day that Weiter began to evacuate Dachau. When the prisoners there resisted, the commandant phoned Himmler, who ordered that he execute them all immediately. Only the arrival of American forces prevented Weiter's successful compliance with these orders.

Meanwhile, in Mauthausen, Schweiger had responded well to the food and medication. The camp tailor had fitted him for a pair of trousers and a jacket, cut from a dead prisoner's suit. When Becher was ready to depart, an ss chauffeur sprang out of the car to open the back door for Schweiger. Becher chatted amiably with him all the way to a hunting lodge near the town of Bad Ischl.

According to Schweiger, Becher spent much of their three-hour journey explaining how Himmler had been misunderstood by so many people. The Reichsführer's orders had saved many thousands of lives, yet few seemed to appreciate how much he had risked over the past several months. Schweiger, who had never anticipated such a discussion with an ss officer about the man who had ordered the extermination of all Jews, just hoped he would never have to make Himmler's acquaintance.

After two days of food and music—the ss officer favored Mozart—Becher presented Schweiger with six suitcases that he said contained the gold and other valuables Kasztner had given to him in Budapest. Becher claimed the valuables were worth around three million Swiss francs. He maintained that he had always planned to return them once the war was over—and the war was, clearly, at an end. He asked Schweiger to hand the cases over to the Jewish Agency, and also to sign a document attesting to Becher's innocence. The paper stated that Becher had been instrumental in saving Jewish lives in Budapest, and that he had guaranteed the peaceful surrender of Bergen-Belsen, Neuengamme, Mauthausen, and Theresienstadt. Schweiger could not have known about all these good deeds from his own personal experience, but was happy to sign.

On April 29 in Berlin, Adolf Hitler and Eva Braun were formally married in Hitler's bunker. The bride wore a simple, cream-colored gown; the groom was dressed in a formal suit. They both attested to having no known health problems and to their being "of complete

Aryan descent." After the wedding breakfast, Hitler dictated his last will and testament, a long, rambling document that laid the blame for the millions of dead on everyone except himself and exhorted all Germans to continue murdering Jews. He expressed his hopes for the future. "Centuries will go by, but from the ruins of our towns and monuments the hatred of those ultimately responsible will always grow anew. They are the people whom we have to thank for all this: international Jewry and its helpers." After ordering poison for his favorite dog, Blondi (his two other dogs were shot), he made his farewells to his remaining staff and retired with his bride to his private apartments. Hitler shot himself at 3:30 PM on April 30. Eva took poison to join her groom.

The Thousand Year Reich survived him by only one week.

American troops reached the Mauthausen camp on May 3, a sunny spring day, and they found a mass grave with more than ten thousand people. Ziereis was shot while trying to escape. In his deathbed testimony, he admitted that Kaltenbrunner had reinstated the order to kill one thousand prisoners a day. Ziereis had not had time to blow up the tunnels. His testimony was entered in evidence against Kaltenbrunner at the Nuremberg Trials.

All told, Becher claimed credit for the survival of around eighty thousand prisoners at the concentration camps he had been ordered to supervise.

At midnight on May 8–9, 1945, Germany surrendered. The Second World War in Europe was over.

*   *   *

Schweiger tried, unsuccessfully, to reach the Jewish Agency in Istanbul and the Joint in Switzerland. He knew it was too risky to keep the valuables under his bed in Bad Ischl. Anyone found with Nazi loot risked execution, and he was afraid to leave the boxes unguarded; they could easily have been stolen. He made a careful inventory of the contents, then delivered them to the 215th Detachment of the American Counter Intelligence Corps in Bad Ischl on May 30. They were booked in as "Becher Treasure I" and were later united with "Becher Treasure II"—two more suitcases (containing 18.7 pounds of gold and 4.4 pounds of platinum) that were found in Weissenbach Castle.[18] Becher explained that he had been keeping it all for return to the Jewish Agency. The Americans arrested Becher on May 24. He told them he had been scheduled to meet Roswell McClelland and Saly Mayer regarding more transports for the Jews he was saving—as though it had all been a mutually agreed process and the war not already lost. If they doubted his word, he said, they should go to Switzerland and ask Mayer of the American Joint Distribution Committee. For additional proof of his goodwill and honesty, he showed them the letter Schweiger had signed.

The Becher Treasure was packed into twenty-nine bags. The first fifteen were deposited in the National Bank of Austria, the rest in the Bank für Oberösterreich in Salzburg.[19]

SS Reichsführer Heinrich Himmler had been dismissed from the government of what was left of the Reich on April 29 for his efforts to negotiate Germany's capitulation. Hitler had found out that Himmler had met twice with Count Folke Bernadotte and had asked the Swedish diplomat to act as a middleman with the Allies. In exchange, Himmler had agreed to allow all Scandinavian women and children still alive in the camps to be sent to Sweden and, later, he agreed that all the women from the Ravensbrück camp could join the exodus.[20] Somehow, despite his isolation, Hitler had learned the news from a Reuters dispatch. Becher's hero to the last, Himmler shaved off his mustache, stuck a black patch over one eye, and tried to escape in a Wehrmacht uniform. On May 23 he was captured by the British and committed suicide by biting down on a hidden cyanide capsule.

For many weeks after the end of hostilities, some Soviet soldiers raped and even killed Jewish women they encountered as these former concentration camp prisoners made their way back to their homes along the broken roads of Europe. In one account of a survivor, a mother and daughter, straggling home from Ravensbrück, were raped ten times before reaching Budapest. In another, a group of women had their clothes stolen and were left standing naked on the side of the road. Grandmothers in their eighties were raped while trying to gather firewood. In Hungary, homes were looted, churches vandalized, domestic animals butchered. Whatever could be carried off (and had been left behind by the Germans) was taken—furniture, carpets, curtains, clothing, even pianos. Soldiers ordered people to undress in the street if they wanted their coats. They consumed all the alcohol they found, even rubbing alcohol and bottles of perfume. What they could not consume or take, they burned.

As if to signal the next era of murky persecutions and fake charges, the Soviet secret service arrested Raoul Wallenberg[21] and took him to the Soviet Union, where, many years later, he died in prison. The officers were probably aware that Wallenberg had had discussions with the U.S. intelligence service before he went to Hungary and, despite the appearance of friendly relations between the two countries, the Soviet government did not trust the Americans. Perhaps, as Yehuda Bauer suggests, to the Soviets "the moral imperatives of a wealthy banker to endanger his life in order to save some Jews must have seemed incomprehensible and suspicious."[22]

Both the Swedish and the Swiss embassies were looted, some of their staff were killed, and others vanished into the Soviet Union. Carl Lutz, the man who had given his protection to thousands in the former American embassy and the Glass House, was sent out of the country in a third-class compartment of a train to Bucharest. He and his wife, Gertrud, shared the compartment with Angelo Rotta from the Vatican and Friedrich Born of the Swiss Red Cross. Miksa Domonkos was not so lucky. The courageous commander of the ghetto, having fooled the Germans, failed to convince the Hungarian State Police (AVO) that he was neither a German stooge nor an Arrow Cross recruit. He was tortured to death in 1953.[23]

Samuel Stern died in 1946, a year after the end of the war. He left behind three large notebooks about his own activities and the work of the Jewish Council from March 1944 to January 1945. Maria Schmidt, a historian and political activist, prepared them for publication in 2004. The museum she helped to found, the House of Terror, detailing both the German and the Communist regimes in Hungary, occupies the building on Andrássy Avenue that was once the headquarters for the Arrow Cross and, later, the state security officers of the Communist Party.

PART FOUR

Death with Honor

The problem with the Jews in the Exile is that they prefer the life of a beaten dog to death with honor . . . We must at the very least see to it that we leave a Masada legend behind us.

Yitzhak Grünbaum, at the Jewish Agency Executive[1]

CHAPTER 28

In Search of a Life

The cause we represented in Budapest was first and foremost rescue; in other words, the saving of human life. That goal was for us, in the first place, a series of commitments that we endeavored to fulfill. What should be written about our efforts is the fact that in the liberated areas of the west alone, more than 200,000 Jews remained alive, and another ten thousand were freed by the Russians.

Rezső Kasztner, in a letter to friends, August 1945[1]

Rezső Kasztner joined his family in Switzerland on April 19, 1945. His wife, Bogyó, had been extremely anxious about him in the previous few months. She listened to the news about the destruction of Budapest and Vienna and was sure he had been shot, perhaps maimed. Phone lines were no longer functioning in Europe, and his few letters arrived long after the war was over. She spent most of her time in the tiny pension room, waiting for news. Tommy Margittai, only fourteen at the time, spent many afternoons with her, talking and smoking cigarettes—since Bergen-Belsen, she had become a nervous smoker—while he gazed at her adoringly. He thought he was deeply in love with her. "Such a beautiful woman, graceful, elegant, with a low, sexy voice . . ."[2]

Bogyó had known that Rezső was traveling with Kurt Becher during those weeks, though she never understood how he accepted the company of an ss officer who could have had him killed without the slightest consequence. Earlier, in December 1944, after she and the second group of passengers on "Kasztner's train" crossed the border, she had tried to persuade him not to leave the safety of Switzerland when he had the chance to stay. But Kasztner had argued that he was needed in Budapest, that the Strasshof "exchange Jews" might not live if he did not return, that he needed to coax Hermann Krumey into collaborating with the Red Cross to provide food and clothing for these people—and, in any case, that Becher, the key person to fulfilling their few remaining hopes, would not deal with anyone else. He believed he had won the ss man's confidence, and, because they were now on first-name terms, that Becher liked him as a friend. Bogyó shuddered at the idea of such a friendship.

Now that the war was almost over, however, she thought they might be able to return to their old lives in Transylvania, which was again under Romanian rule. They would have children and a home of their own, and she hoped they would be able to forget the past. But Kasztner would not even think about returning to their old lives. The only place where he had any desire to live was Palestine, but not yet. He was consumed by memories of the past—a changed man, she thought. His vaunted optimism seemed to be missing.

He was honored at a banquet given in Basel by some of the passengers from the train. There were long speeches about the group's experiences, and professions of eternal gratitude, but Kasztner seemed preoccupied; he barely listened to the gushing words. He sat almost motionless, smiling, picking at his food. At the end, he rose to thank them all and, in a perfunctory kind of way, expressed his hope they would remain forever friends.

With very few exceptions, however, the passengers of the Kasztner train forgot about him once they scattered and began their new lives; they could not wait to wipe the dust and the humiliations of the

Holocaust from their feet. "A natural reaction," Ernő Szilágyi wrote. "We were all victims and deeply ashamed of the fact. We walked about the clean, well-tended streets with no sense of belonging. Even Kasztner, the *stadlan* [the middleman who negotiates the terms for survival], was at a loss how to live."[3] Here, in tidy, organized Switzerland, there was no call for his talents. Peter Munk's aunt, Eva Speter, said that Kasztner "was a born adventurer." Switzerland was much too quiet for him.[4]

On May 8, when the Third Reich surrendered, Kasztner sent a telegram to the Jewish Agency's headquarters in Tel Aviv: "Mission accomplished." Still the showman, he listed his most important life-saving accomplishments.

Kasztner and Bogyó moved into a pension in Geneva, but after the first days of freedom and the confidence of being safe, Kasztner grew restless. The welcome he had anticipated was short-lived. The honors he had expected from the Joint, the War Refugee Board, and the Jewish Agency never arrived. He had not been invited to Palestine to relate his experiences, and no new appointments had been offered. There had been no newspaper interviews, no formal acknowledgments. Instead, he lived on a subsistence income. His days in Budapest and Vienna began to haunt him. Some of his acquaintances wrote that they found his talk about his relationships with individual Nazis repulsive. He seemed to be boasting of his status in the Germans' midst, of the nightclubs in Vienna during the bombardments, his special treatment at the Metropole and the Grand hotels there, the use of Becher's car and driver, the courtesies he had been afforded by men like Becher and Dieter Wisliceny.

Kasztner was moody, brooding, impatient. He and Bogyó argued about everything but mainly about the time he had spent in Budapest with Hansi Brand. Kasztner didn't bother to deny the accusation that he had had a romantic relationship with Hansi. The more disgruntled he became, the more he thought about Hansi— her generosity, her support for their work, and her tireless efforts to save other lives. The arguments merely added fuel to his desire to be with her. A couple who occupied the floor below the Kasztners complained to the landlord about the loud arguments overhead, the door banging as Rezső walked out on his furious wife.

Amid the general confusion of Europe's displaced millions, a few hundred of the Kasztner train refugees—Szilágyi was one of them—returned to Hungary. They missed their familiar neighborhoods, and they yearned to be "home," speaking the language they knew. They wanted their houses or apartments, their furniture, and their books back again. They imagined, wrongly, that the postwar government would find ways to compensate them for their losses.

In July, seven hundred people with Palestine certificates, including Bogyó's parents, left for Haifa on a ship via Bari, Italy.

When Carl Lutz arrived home in Switzerland from Istanbul, he did not expect a hero's welcome, but he thought his government would want to learn of his life-saving work in Budapest. Not only did his government fail to recognize his rescue work in Hungary, but it also ordered a judicial investigation into his activities there. Why had he engaged in saving Hungarian nationals when his consular duties included no such endeavors? Worse, he had failed to obtain due authorization from Bern for all the Swiss identity papers he had handed out—more than fifty thousand Swiss schutzpässe—and illegal operators in Hungary had manufactured at least another fifty thousand. Now thousands of undesirables could claim Swiss citizenship.[5]

Several people who had given their valuables to the Budapest Aid and Rescue Committee—for safekeeping, they claimed—began to seek their return. Kasztner spent much of his time going over the accounts of the committee, wanting to prove to both the Jewish Agency and those looking for their property that he had not, personally, kept anything. He had used it all for bribes, for buying lives. He wrote long, anguished, often angry letters hectoring the complainers: What value did they put on their lives? he asked. Eventually, he stopped going to public functions held by the Jewish community. He avoided people who wanted to talk to him about their own past and those who were determined to find out how the passengers on Kasztner's train had been chosen.

He learned that there were rumors about him, and a whispering campaign had begun accusing him of collaborating with the Germans. One story had him handing Emil Nussbecher, who now called himself Yoel Palgi, and Ferenc Goldstein over to the ss, in exchange for favors. Palgi and Goldstein were the two parachutists who had gone to his office in Budapest the day before the train was due to depart. Palgi's book, first published in 1946 with a title that translated as *Behold a Great Wind Came*, had immediately become a best-seller in Palestine.[6] Although he praised Kasztner there for his leadership of the Rescue Committee, he suggested that he had not done all he could have to save the parachutists' mission. Yet, when confronted by one of Kasztner's friends, Palgi declared that Kasztner had been both brilliant and fearless in his handling of the negotiations in Hungary—that without him, thousands more would have perished.

Palgi, as he later testified, believed then that Goldstein was still alive and that he owed his life to Kasztner. He did not realize that he was the sole survivor of the ill-conceived foray into Hungary. Goldstein's parents, who had been on the train, claimed they had been reassured by Kasztner that their son was in good hands. They insisted, now, that Kasztner should explain to them what he believed had happened after their son gave himself up to the Nazis. Kasztner did not want to see them. "They don't understand," he told Bogyó, "that I could not save everybody."[7] His failures, it seemed, were as painful for him to bear as they were for those who had lost members of their families.[8]

Moshe Krausz, Kasztner discovered, had filed a complaint against him with the Jewish Agency Executive and with the Zionist Congress, accusing him of pointlessly hobnobbing with the Nazis while he, Krausz, had found a way to save thousands through hard work with the representatives of the neutral nations. He claimed credit for all those who survived in the "protected houses." He blamed Kasztner for the failure to gain exit visas for the Jews with immigration certificates for Palestine. He deemed Kasztner's apparent friendship with Becher suspect and described Kasztner as a megalomaniac with only his own personal glory in mind.

Furious, Kasztner wrote to the Jewish Agency's representative in Geneva, asking for an open hearing at which his accusers would state their case and he would be given an opportunity to respond. He became obsessed with the need to clear his name. He filed a complaint against Krausz. He said he had known of Krausz's efforts to discredit the Va'ada and his own dealings with the Sonderkommando. Krausz had made no secret of his personal dislike for him. Kasztner's accusations were bolstered by Rafi Benshalom, one of the former halutz leaders in Budapest (and soon to become Israel's first ambassador to Czechoslovakia), who accused Krausz of mishandling his office and holding up the rescue efforts.

The Agency's Executive held investigative hearings into both complaints and concluded there was no reason to proceed with either of them. But rumors continued to circulate. Kasztner's appointment to a mission in Budapest on behalf of the Agency was vetoed because of suspicions about his relationships with the ss. He heard from a journalist colleague in the city that a petition had been filed with the government, asking for an investigation of his activities during the German occupation.[9] A Mizrachi official from Hungary had filed a complaint against him with the World Jewish Congress, accusing him of keeping part of the money collected to buy lives. In vain, Kasztner insisted that he and his colleagues, some of whom had been murdered by the Nazis or the Arrow Cross, deserved a full hearing. But there would not be a public inquiry. The Agency was satisfied with its investigation and saw no reason for anything more. There were too many other pressing matters to deal with. Millions of the displaced—the disenfranchised, as well as concentration camp survivors, fleeing Nazis, and disarmed soldiers—were roaming Europe, trying to find missing relatives, confiscated homes, new identities, or ways of escape.

Meanwhile, in Palestine, there were armed battles between various political factions of the Jews and between the Yishuv and the British occupying forces. The Revisionists, under Menachem Begin, continued their harassment of the British.[10] David Ben-Gurion and the

Jewish Agency were at first vehemently opposed to Begin's terrorist tactics, but by October 1945 they, too, committed themselves to forcing the British to return to their islands. Without consulting Chaim Weizmann, Ben-Gurion ordered the Haganah to begin a campaign to drive the British out. However, violent disagreements between the two groups over their approach to the problem remained, as did their mutual distrust and hostility.

When Kasztner saw in the local press that Saly Mayer had been praised for the rescue of thousands of Hungarian Jews and for his selfless efforts on their behalf in Nazi Germany, he was incensed. It seemed to him that Mayer was assuming credit for his own, Kasztner's, work with the ss. Moreover, Mayer was praised for his courage in entering Nazi Germany to pursue the negotiations, yet it was well known that Mayer had never set foot there. He had done whatever he did in the secure knowledge of a comfortable bed in neutral Switzerland. Kasztner fired off long, angry memoranda to various officials, including Mayer himself: "All of us who have experienced the prisons of the Gestapo, the police, and the Arrow Cross, in the name of our dead colleagues . . . we raise our voice in protest . . . against the bizarre way in which we have been dispossessed of our work, our sacrifice, and our achievements."[11] Saly Mayer did not respond.

Most nights, Kasztner found it impossible to fall asleep. He wandered the streets alone or sat staring out of the darkened window, writing long letters on an old typewriter and working on his reports. He talked with Eliahu Dobkin and Chaim Barlas of the Jewish Agency's Executive about making plans to reclaim the funds and valuables that had been given to Becher and to Eichmann's deputies in Hungary, as well as the much larger theft of Hungarian Jewish belongings that had been sent by truck and train to Germany in late October 1944. No one was sure what the value of the latter might be, but estimates ran as high as $350 million. Dobkin and Barlas were concerned that these valuables could be viewed as war booty by the Americans or, once returned to Hungary, grabbed by the state.

The Jewish Agency, representing the six million murdered Jews of Europe, had been attempting to gain status at the planned trials of war criminals in Nuremberg, Germany. It failed. Kasztner, however, succeeded. He volunteered to help the Allied prosecutors of war crimes in their quest to determine the guilt or innocence of the various Nazi officers and officials he had come to know. At the Jewish Agency's expense, he flew to London in early September 1945 and submitted two sworn affidavits before the American Committee for the Investigation of War Crimes, a series of hearings that preceded the trials of the war criminals. His first statement dealt with the destruction of Jews in Hungary, mentioning also Slovakia, Poland, and Austria.[12] He detailed the role played by the Sonderkommando and, in particular, its murderous chief, Adolf Eichmann. He mentioned Krumey's tireless execution of Eichmann's plans in Hungary. His second affidavit outlined the roles of Becher and Wisliceny in Hungary, as well as the role he and the Va'ada played in preserving human lives. In these statements, Kasztner left no doubt that those who had cooperated with him in the final months before Germany's inevitable defeat did so purely to save their own skins.[13]

When Moshe Schweiger arrived in Switzerland in mid-October 1945, he thought his friend was pale, dispirited, listless; his vaunted sense of self-confidence had vanished. Traces of the former Kasztner surfaced only when the two of them worked on their detailed report about the Becher Treasure and Kasztner's own report about the work of the Jewish Rescue Committee. Kasztner had estimated the total amounts paid to Becher before December 7, 1944, at $2.1 million, or close to nine million Swiss francs, including the additional amounts Becher received from his small group of favored "clients"— not the three million francs Becher had mentioned when he presented the suitcases to Schweiger. The originally approved number of train passengers was 1,300, or $1.3 million at $1,000 a head. The final number on arrival at Bergen-Belsen was 1,684. Becher had demanded and received the additional payments. Passengers on the train estimated the true value of the two Becher Treasures to be 8.7 million Swiss francs.[14] Kasztner and Schweiger were not yet aware of the existence of the second Becher Treasure, but Kasztner was already determined to seek a meeting with Becher.

Their report to the Jewish Agency recommended that it immediately claim the Becher Treasure from the Americans. There was a danger, Kasztner feared, that the Americans would view any valuables as war booty.[15]

When Joel Brand arrived from Palestine, Kasztner met him at the Geneva railway station. After a moment's hesitation, they embraced—two old friends with a shared past. So much to talk about, Joel thought, so much to explain. He had traveled to Switzerland with his two sons to be reunited with his wife. He had picked up the boys in Bratislava from Peretz Révész, who was still helping to move small groups of Jewish children to safety. Joel had known about Hansi's affair with Kasztner, but he hoped that their relationship would be over. Hansi had been in Switzerland since early May, but already Joel suspected, rightly, that she had been with Kasztner again. All three of them were nervous about one another, careful of what they said. When they did get together, there were long silences, whole areas of experience each of them kept private.

It was not until Joel saw Bogyó again that he knew Hansi would not leave him for Kasztner. Bogyó was obviously and joyously pregnant, and she had regained her confidence. She had told Rezső to stop seeing Hansi if he wanted to have their baby. He had agreed.[16] Hansi told Rezső that whatever had been between them, it was over. In her heart, it ended when Joel's niece, Margit, told her what had happened in Bergen-Belsen. She could not forgive him for leaving Joel's mother to die.[17] As she told the story years later to a friend, Eva Carmeli, once she knew that Bogyó was pregnant, she broke off the relationship with Rezső. It no longer made sense to her.[18]

When Joel went to Hansi's small, rented apartment, he was determined not to talk about her affair, but in the end he did. He accused her of having become Rezső's mistress. She reminded him that their marriage had been a sham, an arrangement, and that they—especially Joel—had never expected to keep their vows. She was in no mood to deny her affair or even to apologize. She accused him of cowardice, claiming he should have returned to Budapest, no matter the risks and no matter what the Jewish Agency wanted. His continued absence had destroyed the one sure bargaining chip she and Rezső had held with Eichmann. Rezső, she told him, had saved all their lives.

She and Joel fought tirelessly, sometimes all night, about what had happened in Istanbul, about how she and Rezső had struggled for each one of those Joel had left behind, and why Joel had not returned to Hungary. He had known his wife and children were in danger of Eichmann's wrath. As for his heroic role in drawing the world's attention to what was happening in Hungary, Hansi said, he had failed even in that.

Zsuzsi Kasztner was born in Switzerland on December 26, 1945. There is a photograph of the proud parents grinning at the camera, the tiny bundle held between them. They seem hopeful, happy as parents usually are when they welcome a newborn.

Bogyó agreed to go to Palestine. Her parents had settled in Tel Aviv. She was sure her father's ill health would improve with her presence, and baby Zsuzsi would benefit from having adoring grandparents around her. But Rezső was still not ready to go to what would soon become the State of Israel.

Kasztner presented *The Report of the Jewish Rescue Committee of Budapest, 1942–1945*[19] to the Twenty-Second Zionist Congress in Basel in December 1946. It was the first postwar Zionist congress—the saddest and loneliest of conferences, because so many of Europe's Zionist leaders had been murdered. David Ben-Gurion compared it to sitting shivah, observing a seven-day mourning period, for all your best friends at once, all the brilliant, argumentative men, those familiar faces all gone up in the smoke of the Nazi annihilation machines.

Although Kasztner, unlike Moshe Krausz, was not given official status at the congress—he attended as a journalist representing a Budapest newspaper—his report caused a considerable stir among the delegates.[20] Hansi was also there, though she stayed in the lobby of the conference center. She went to the restaurant at mealtimes, hoping to see a few people she had known in Budapest. But she could neither understand what was being said by the delegates nor speak to them. "I didn't know Hebrew or their kind of Yiddish," she said. "And no one was interested in hearing from me." A stringer for one of the Palestine Jewish newspapers approached to talk to her but discovered they did not have a language in common. "After all the work we had done, it was strange," she said. "No one was interested."[21]

While she found her own situation ironic, she felt sorry for Rezső. They had risked their lives every day, and she was surprised by the lack of recognition for them both. She told Rezső it was only a matter of time. The horrors were too recent. As for the rumors, there would always be those who felt wronged. She and Rezső had known from the beginning that not everyone would make it. Even the grand, heroic gesture of the Warsaw ghetto uprising had saved few lives.

No one knows for sure how Kasztner came to change his attitude toward Kurt Becher. Only a few facts are certain: he and members of the Jewish Agency Executive were anxious to talk to Becher about the bribes he had accepted and about the confiscated wealth of Hungarian Jews; they were eager to locate Adolf Eichmann, who had disappeared only days before his offices in Berlin were destroyed by the Russians, and they believed that Dieter Wisliceny and Hans Jüttner, and perhaps Hermann Krumey, could shed light on these matters. Even before Kasztner appeared at the investigations before the war-crimes trials in Nuremberg, there was a marked alteration in his view of Becher.[22] In January 1946 he and Schweiger issued a statement in Geneva about Becher's courageous humanitarian activities.[23] They asserted that the "Becher Deposit" belonged to the Jews of Hungary and outlined how it had ended up with the American army. Their statement was delivered to the United States Embassy in Switzerland, but when the Americans checked with Saly Mayer about Kasztner's credibility they noted that Mayer—still the Joint's representative in Switzerland—had nothing positive to say.[24]

When Becher, who had been jailed by the Americans, sought Kasztner's help to prove he was innocent of war crimes, Kasztner volunteered to be an expert witness on Hungarian matters at the Nuremberg Trials, which had begun on November 20, 1945. He also offered to speak in the same capacity at any of the Subsequent Nuremberg Trials.[25] Once the trials began, a statement by Becher was read into the record and used against his fellow ss officer General Kaltenbrunner.

I, Kurt Becher, former Standartenführer, born 12 September 1909, at Hamburg, declare under oath:

Between the middle of September and the middle of October 1944, I caused the Reichsführer-ss Himmler to issue the following order, which I received in two originals, one each for ss Obergruppenführer Kaltenbrunner and [Obergruppenführer Oswald] Pohl, and a copy for myself: "By this order, which becomes immediately effective, I forbid any extermination of Jews and order that, on the contrary, care should be given to weak and sick persons. I hold you [Kaltenbrunner and Pohl] personally responsible even if this order should not be strictly adhered to by subordinate officers."

I took Pohl's copy to him in his office in Berlin and left a copy for Kaltenbrunner at his office in Berlin. Therefore, in my opinion Kaltenbrunner and Pohl bear the responsibility after this date of any further killings of Jewish prisoners.

When visiting Mauthausen concentration camp on 27 April 1945 at 0900 hours, I was told in the strictest secrecy by the commandant, ss Standartenführer Ziereis, that "Kaltenbrunner gave me the order that at least a thousand persons would still have to die at Mauthausen each day."

The facts mentioned above are true . . .

In his own testimony of April 12, 1947, Kaltenbrunner confirmed some of Becher's statements, at least as far as the timing of Becher's meetings with Himmler. He said that Himmler had been forced to issue an order in September or October 1944 to stop the murder apparatus. He was not very helpful, however, about Himmler's appointment of Becher to oversee the handover of concentration camps to the Allies. He recalled no such order.

When Kasztner received an invitation to testify, it was courtesy of Joel Brand's niece Margit, who had survived the horrors of Bergen-Belsen and found a job with the war-crimes tribunal.

After the Russians found the passengers of "the lost train" from Bergen-Belsen in Troeditz, Margit Fendrich, who spoke English, had claimed she was an American. The Russian army driver took her, along with her mother and aunt, to the American pow camp. The staff there sent her on to Reims in an American ambulance. She recovered in an American hospital filled with other English-speaking refugees. An extraordinarily beautiful, well-spoken young woman with large, wide-set brown eyes, long eyelashes, and a soft, pink complexion, she got a job first with the U.S. military and then applied for a position with the International Military Tribunal that was to conduct the trials at Nuremberg. "They were looking for people who could handle languages," she said. Fluent in German, English, Hungarian, and French, she was hired as office help and as an interpreter. She remembered that Kasztner was eager to participate. He called her as soon as he discovered where she was and, because he had dealt, personally, with several of those charged, insisted that his testimony would be vital—"being Rezső, what he had to say was always vital," she chuckled.[26]

Had she forgiven him for that walk through Bergen-Belsen when he had failed to recognize her mother and done nothing to repair the damage? Perhaps.

"We all did so many things in those days, just to survive," Hansi recalled. "Rezső was braver than most, but he was always afraid of Becher. He should have helped Joel's family, and he should not have testified at Nuremberg." Joel's mother had died about ten days after that visit to the camp. Years later in Israel, when an interviewer asked Hansi how that scene would have played had it been Joel with Becher and Kasztner's mother asking for a piece of bread, she replied, "How can anyone know what he or she would do in such a situation?" But her answer rings hollow. Clearly, Hansi had expected more of Rezső.

In January 1947, when the U.S. State Department released the "Becher Deposits" to the Jewish Agency, the contents of the twenty-nine bags were a painful disappointment. Once an inventory of all the items had been made, the total value was put at only $65,000.

The inventory of items handed to the Agency's representative, however, matched the one made when Schweiger handed over the suitcases to the U.S. military. In July 1947 most of the items were sold by the Jewish Agency, and the proceeds were split with the Joint.[27] The difference between this paltry sum and the bribes that he had paid to Becher was so great that Kasztner remained convinced there were further amounts to be found.

Kasztner received letters from Krumey's wife, asking for help. Her husband was in jail, awaiting trial, and she was living in strained circumstances. In February 1947 Kasztner wrote to Krumey, addressing him as Doctor Krumey (Krumey had been a pharmacist before the war) and asking how he could assist. He wanted Krumey to know that he had not forgotten how helpful Krumey had been during the last months of the war. He offered to testify at Krumey's trial, just as he had promised he would when the lives of the Strasshof prisoners were at stake.

Kasztner was not present at the interrogation of Dieter Wisliceny before the International Military Tribunal on January 3, 1946. However, he filed an intervention on the former Nazi captain's behalf after Wisliceny was transferred to Slovakia to stand trial for his role in the murder of the Slovak Jews. Kasztner made an appeal for his return to American custody, no doubt believing that Eichmann's former colleague could shed light on "the Master's" whereabouts. He was, after all, the last person to have seen Eichmann in February 1945, when Eichmann told him that he would gladly jump into the grave happy because he had killed six million Jews. "That gives me great satisfaction and gratification," Eichmann had said before he disappeared.[28]

In August 1947 Kasztner stated in the presence of Major Warren Farr of the United States Army, assistant trial counsel at Nuremberg, that he had survived only because "ss Standartenführer Kurt Becher extended his protection to me, albeit to prepare an alibi for himself. After the autumn of 1944 he definitely tried to demonstrate that he condemned the deportations and the extermination of Jews and he was tireless in his efforts to supply me with proof of his having saved Jews." Kasztner filed a sworn declaration before a Denazification

Court, testifying that Becher was one of the few good Germans: "There can be no doubt that Becher belongs to the very few ss leaders having the courage to oppose the program of annihilation of the Jews and trying to rescue human lives . . . In my opinion when this case is judged by Allied or German authorities, Kurt Becher deserves the fullest possible consideration." He signed this statement, rather grandly, "not only in my name but also on behalf of the Jewish Agency and the World Jewish Congress," and added, for good measure, that he was the "former chairman of the Zionist Organization in Hungary, 1943–45, representative of the Joint Distribution Committee in Budapest."[29]

Walter Rapp, assistant to the chief U.S. prosecutor at Nuremberg, remembered how Kasztner had approached members of his team in his "official capacity" representing some world Jewish organization: "I can state that Becher, until the arrival of Kasztner," he said, "was merely one of many suspects and it seemed probable that if put on trial, he would be convicted. He has Kasztner to thank for his freedom."

Kasztner was granted special status to question Becher directly in the presence of the U.S. prosecutor, and he gave Becher every opportunity to clear himself. During one of these interviews, he asked Becher about his role in the survival of the 85,000 Jews trapped in the Budapest ghetto. At first Becher appeared not to recall his part in this act of mercy, but, after repeated prompts by Kasztner, he modestly claimed the proffered credit.[30]

Through several interviews with U.S. personnel and in statements for the court proceedings, Becher claimed to have joined the ss only because of his keen interest in horseback riding. He rose quickly in the ranks (unlike Eichmann, who never got his heart's desire), reaching colonel in January 1945, just before Hungary was liberated by the Russians. The only medal he seemed to be proud of was the one he received for a firefight with American soldiers after his life-saving visit to Mauthausen. He took credit for freeing the Weiss-Chorin-Kornfeld families, for letting the Kasztner train leave the Reich, and for other assorted good deeds. As special Reich commissioner for concentration camps during the last few weeks of the war, he claimed to have been able to prevent the murder of the last prisoners at several locations.

Becher testified to having been an enemy of Eichmann and all that Eichmann stood for. He claimed responsibility for stopping the foot marches from Budapest to the Austrian border by intervening directly with Himmler. He produced the document that Schweiger had signed at Bad Ischl.

Margit, who took shorthand notes during this testimony, remembered Becher looking up during one of his statements and staring directly at her. He appeared not to be embarrassed by their changed positions; rather, he seemed mildly amused. When he was released from the internment camp in December 1947, Becher stayed on in Nuremberg to testify at further proceedings against some of his former colleagues. One afternoon, he went to Margit's first-floor office in the courthouse and inquired whether she could obtain six pairs of nylon stockings for him.

CHAPTER 29

The Jews of the Exile

He was the most brilliant journalist I have ever met. He could dictate a perfect column in sentences, paragraphs, without ever having to look it over or change a single word. Three months after I had started working for him at Új Kelet, he was still in the habit of crossing out the beginning and end of each of my pieces, without bothering to read what I had written. He just knew that a young reporter would not get to the story right away and would want to find some unnecessary conclusions at the end. He was quick-witted, sarcastic, smarter than anyone else and happy to show off in front of the less well endowed. I remember the day he grinned at me and said: "Now that you are a seasoned reporter, you're fully qualified to go to the kiosk outside and bring me back a package of cigarettes."

Tomy Lapid, Kasztner's former colleague at *Új Kelet*
and former member of the Knesset[1]

The Kasztners moved to Palestine in late 1947. They arrived at the end of the War of Independence, during the last days of the British in Palestine, the beginnings of the State of Israel, and the start of a war between Israel and the surrounding Arab states. The destruction of the King David Hotel in the middle of 1946 by Menachem Begin's Revisionist army (known as the Irgun), the murderous fights between the Jews and the Arabs, the continued attacks on the roads and railways, the pitched battles against the British, and the horrific, symbolic hanging of two British soldiers had successfully convinced the British government that it did not wish to continue its mandated occupation of Palestine. The initial plan, a three-part division of the area, had been rejected by both Jews and Arabs. The British turned the problem over to the United Nations,[2] where, on November 29, 1947, the General Assembly endorsed the partitioning of Palestine into two states: one Jewish, one Arab. The Jews accepted this; the Palestinian Arabs did not, and the partition plan was never implemented.

Palestine was too preoccupied with its own problems to notice the Kasztners' arrival. Little fanfare greeted them—a couple of newspaper articles and a small party given by one of the survivors from the train. Yoel Palgi wrote a warm, welcoming article in one of the local newspapers, presenting Kasztner as a hero, a man who had risked his life so that others might live. Kasztner was relieved to see that Palgi was not harboring ill feelings toward him. Even so, he had expected a more effusive reception. There were people here he had helped to save, people who would remember his role in Budapest and Vienna, people who would know that he had accomplished much on behalf of the Jewish Agency. He had kept in touch with several members of the Executive, including Moshe Sharett (formerly Shertok) and Chaim Barlas. His actions had been recognized, at least verbally, by David Ben-Gurion. Yet none of the Yishuv's leaders was there to greet him.

Only their families seemed delighted to see them. Kasztner's oldest brother, Ernő, and his mother were living near Haifa with the middle son, Gyula, who, as a small-arms instructor in the Haganah, was preparing young men for the next round of heavy fighting. The

Fischers lived in Tel Aviv, and that was where Rezső and Bogyó settled. They moved into a one-room basement apartment on Adam HaCohen Street. Kasztner found a job at *Új Kelet*, the reborn, small-circulation, Hungarian-language newspaper he had previously worked for in Kolozsvár. The publisher, Ernő Márton, had been his boss before Rezső left for Budapest in the spring of 1941. Kasztner was also commissioned to create programs for Hungarian-language radio. His columns were tough, analytical statements, much as they had been in his early days as a journalist. On radio, he was an engaging, witty interviewer. He applied himself to the study of Hebrew. He began to use his Hebrew name, Israel, and dropped the *z* from "Kasztner," as he had informally done already when dealing with the ss.

In April 1948, when Kasztner returned to Nuremberg, it was at the behest of the new Mapai-led government, headed by Ben-Gurion. They believed there was still a chance that more of the Budapest Jews' wealth would be traced and that Eichmann would be brought to justice. Kasztner testified about the fate of the Slovak Jews and his own attempts to buy their lives. He added some color to Becher's account of his efforts to save Kasztner and the others. This time he also credited Hermann Krumey with sparing the Strasshof Jews in the last three weeks of the war and in the rescue of twenty-nine Jews from Bratislava. In a statement he made at the office of the chief war-crimes counsel in Nuremberg, he gave Krumey credit for "full understanding and sympathy," as well as the rescue of thirty thousand Jews in the Theresienstadt camp who would otherwise have been murdered before the Soviet army liberated the area.[3]

While he was in Nuremberg, Kasztner visited Becher again. Afterward, he reported to the Jewish Agency's minister of finance in Israel, Eliezer Kaplan, that Becher told him of additional Jewish assets he had given to Lieutenant General Hans Jüttner in Hungary. In his report Kasztner labeled these goods "the new Becher assets" and recommended that Kaplan should make every effort to recover them.

Bogyó kept very much to herself. Even in company, she was quiet. Most people ascribed her sadness to her father's illness, her caring for a young child at the same time as for a dying father. József Fischer, once a leading citizen of Kolozsvár, was now destitute, as was his family. Nevertheless, as Zsuzsi remembers, despite her worries Bogyó remained an elegant, stately presence. Any store she entered was quick to serve her. Strangers opened doors for her and offered their arm when she crossed the street.

Kasztner had not been aware of the deep divide between the old settlers and the new arrivals in Palestine. With thousands of European refugees landing every day, the existing Jewish community there, the Yishuv, felt in danger of being flooded. By 1948 there were more than 350,000 Holocaust survivors in Israel. The Yishuv wished to maintain its hard-won image of itself as a distinct, proud, uncompromising people belonging to this land through history and love—unlike the frightened, beaten Holocaust survivors who kept arriving and claiming their share of a common future. Most of them came as refugees from death camps, not as the idealists who had chosen to settle in Palestine in earlier times. As the author Yehudit Hendel put it in a speech on Israeli television, "I was taught that the basest thing is not the Exile but the Jew who came from there." Perhaps the nastiest insult to the new arrivals was the slang term *sabon*, or soap, that came into use as a short form for "Holocaust survivor"—a reference to the Nazis' alleged practice of making soap from the boiled bodies of their victims.[4]

When poet Leah Goldberg spoke at a meeting of Ben-Gurion's Labor Zionists, she, too, made derogatory remarks about the Holocaust survivors: "This people is ugly, impoverished, morally suspect . . ."[5] The Yishuv regarded the Jews of the Exile not only as a sad and bedraggled lot but, worse, as having let themselves be "herded like sheep," without a fight, into ghettos and concentration camps. There was no sympathy for them. They were put to work with shovels and pickaxes to till the land and help create the new Jewish dream. There was little room for the doctors and lawyers, accountants and shopkeepers of the old world.

Adam Heller, who had been with his family on the Kasztner train, was only twelve years old when he left Switzerland for Palestine. Once there, he was quick to hide his identity as a Holocaust survivor. Only twenty-three years later did he finally accept his survival and put to rest his own sense of guilt for the slaughter.[6]

The young were enlisted immediately. A couple of weeks after the Second World War ended, Haganah commanders had gone to displaced persons camps in Europe to sign up young men for military training. The quasi-governmental Jewish Agency was not interested in immigration for the sake of the survivors; rather, as Ben-Gurion said, it wanted "people from the ages of eighteen to thirty-five" to help win the war and to build a country.

When Ben-Gurion declared the "establishment of a Jewish state in Palestine, which shall be known as the State of Israel," on May 14, 1948, both U.S. president Harry Truman and the Soviet Union's Joseph Stalin rushed to accord it immediate recognition. But the celebrations were short-lived. The day after the last of the British soldiers left, a massive force of Arab nations gathered to destroy the new state. Israel was invaded by 10,000 Egyptians, 7,000 Syrians, 3,000 Iraqis, 3,000 Lebanese, and the British-trained Arab Legion of Transjordan. The Jews were outgunned and outnumbered. Their army, including the untrained new arrivals from concentration camps, numbered only about 30,000 men and women. They lacked aircraft and heavy guns. Azzam Pasha, the secretary general of the Arab League, declared: "This will be a war of extermination and a momentous massacre."

But the Jews had experienced enough exterminations and massacres. The Czech government, under Soviet influence, began to airlift weapons to Tel Aviv, and Israel not only beat back the invaders but conquered new territories. Around 20,000 Holocaust survivors—one out of every five soldiers—fought in the war. Most of them didn't speak Hebrew and barely understood their orders. It is not surprising that a majority of the casualties were survivors from the concentration camps.[7]

Kasztner volunteered for the army but, at the age of forty-two, was too old to be accepted, despite his assertion that he had trained young halutzim in Transylvania to fight. He boasted that he and his

colleagues would have fought the enemy in hand-to-hand combat in
Hungary, but they didn't have a chance. "Here, we could have
looked the enemy in the eyes and known where to aim." Hansi, he
was fond of telling those who would listen, had wanted to pour
boiling oil on the heads of Wehrmacht soldiers when they paraded
through the streets of Budapest.

By the end of 1948, the Israeli army was 100,000-strong and well
equipped with Eastern European arms and armor. Through successive victories, it had gained confidence as a fighting unit and
occupied about 80 percent of what the United Nations had designated as Palestine. Peace negotiations began in January 1949 and
ended, on July 20, with Syria signing an agreement. Although not all
the Arab states signed on to the peace, the war was over. There was a
sense of optimism, of hard-won security in Israel. A new flood of
more than half a million Jewish refugees from surrounding Arab
countries did not stanch the sense of victory. Some 656,000 Arabs
fled from the Palestinian territories now occupied by Israel, making
room for the new exiles.[8]

Kasztner, as he declared in *Új Kelet*, was sure the Arab states
would refrain from further attacks. As a family, Rezső and Bogyó
were becoming more comfortable with life in the new country. A
group of friends, led by Dezsö Hermann, collected £320 for them,
enough money to pay for a two-room rental apartment above street
level on Amsterdam Street. Zsuzsi remembers the parties, the living
room full of cheerful Hungarian talk, jokes, laughter, music spilling
out onto the balcony—1940s jazz and schmaltzy songs—and dancing until the sun rose. Kasztner decided to run as one of
Ben-Gurion's Mapai Party candidates in the election for the First
Knesset (parliament) in January 1949. A lifelong Labor Zionist, he
felt he already knew this land. He certainly understood the major
issues and had the necessary credentials. But because he was fifty-ninth
on the party's slate, he had no chance of being elected. Undeterred, he
told friends he would be ready for the next time. His Hebrew would be
fluent by then, he spoke six other languages, and he had studied
ancient, biblical Hebrew as a child.

In 1949 he was appointed communications director and

spokesperson for Dov Yosef (Joseph), who held a number of ministries in the government. Yosef, a hero of the War of Independence and a former governor of Jerusalem, lacked the skills of a politician. He was uncomfortable in crowds, did not know how to handle personal appeals, and tended to be gruff when confronted by the media. Kasztner's job was to soften the minister's edges, glad-hand the public, receive visitors, accept petitions, and review requests. He had learned how to show patience and amiability in the company of tougher crowds than these, after all, and he had charm, particularly with women, and a cutting sense of humor that he could use to advantage with his minister's political opponents.

Kasztner tried again for the Knesset in 1951. This time he was fifty-third on the Mapai slate, so again was not elected. He was now director of public relations in the Ministry of Commerce and Industry. He continued to write for *Új Kelet* and to produce radio programs. He was a superb journalist, and coworkers remember him as quick-witted, often at the expense of others, and self-confident to the point of arrogance about his own accomplishments. Bogyó thought Rezső was becoming his old self again. He was full of hope and ambition and had almost stopped talking about the Nazi occupation of his homeland.

Zsuzsi at three years old had attended a local nursery school. She learned Hebrew so fast that she could not be identified as a Diaspora Jew. Except when she was at home, she was a tiny sabra, a native of Israeli. Rezső proved to be an attentive and loving father, never too busy for her, and always proud of her achievements.

The Brands also ended up in Palestine. "My father was so involved with the past that he could not handle the present or the future," Dani Brand remembered. Joel wrote a few articles and tried to make some money. He worked on his memoirs, but he could not finish the book or find a publisher. Finally, he gave his notes to Alex Weissberg, a journalist, who reconstructed the story—or, as both Hansi and Joel claimed, parts of the story—and had it published in 1958 as *Advocate for the Dead: The Story of Joel Brand*. Joel was never happy with Weissberg's version of his life and began, immediately, to work on another autobiography. He became increasingly depressed, started drinking heavily, and accused the world, especially former Jewish Agency politicians, of having let the Hungarian Jews die.

For a while, Hansi worked on a kibbutz near Haifa. She was, as she told Rezső, amazed at everyone's indifference to what had happened during the Holocaust. Even survivors seemed embarrassed to discuss their experiences. The Yishuv certainly did not want to hear about them. At kibbutz dinner tables, they talked about the success of new crops, the irrigation plants, and their fear of renewed hostilities with the Arabs. "Do you know," Hansi once asked Rezső, "how hard it is to evince the right amount of sorrow at the fate of chickens killed in a sniper attack when your mind is still full of the people we lost in Hungary?" She was fond of repeating what an Israeli journalist said to her when she remarked on the total lack of interest in Israel in what she had done during the war: "If you had arrived in a coffin," he told her, "we would have given you a reception worthy of a heroine."

The feud between Joel and Rezső was now well known in the Hungarian exile community. Kasztner blamed Brand for mishandling the mission to Istanbul and told everyone what he would have said to Chaim Barlas, the British and the Americans, had he been chosen to carry Eichmann's message. Some who continued to blame Kasztner for their family's financial losses sought out Brand, in the hope of hearing damaging information. Although Brand was bitter and angry with Kasztner, he refused to cooperate in their schemes.

Despite her earlier resolution, Hansi and Rezső met more often after Hansi moved to Tel Aviv. She bought a knitting machine and, as in Hungary, began to make gloves and scarves. Before long, she hired other women to knit for her burgeoning piecework enterprise. Dani Brand remembers his mother as a woman who was always busy with her hands. She demanded very little of life—and life, as it happened, was true to her expectations.

CHAPTER 30

The Prince of Darkness
Is a Gentleman

Ilana Dayan: Mr. Becher, is there anything you regret?

Kurt Becher: If I regret anything it is that Rudolf Kasztner and I did not achieve more than we did. In rescuing people.

Dayan: Would you say that you acted as a German patriot?

Becher: As a human being. You are smiling. That is the truth. You do not need to smile.

Dayan: You were part of the biggest murder machinery in history. You spoke about Jews as stück—pieces. You sold Jews for money. That is why I asked you whether you regret anything.

From an interview with Kurt Becher
by Israeli television journalist Ilana
Dayan on December 22, 1994

The Nuremberg trials were over, the sentences handed down, the executions carried out. Kurt Becher, having provided lengthy statements about his own good deeds and some critical comments about a number of his former colleagues, was a free man by late 1948. His path to respectability began immediately. He went back to Hamburg, seemingly penniless, but before the end of that year he suddenly gained access to a substantial sum of money. Where it came from remains unclear to this day. The Oppenheims, whose horse-breeding operations he had acquired on behalf of Himmler, showed their gratitude for being alive by having their bank invest in Becher's new venture. They even invited him to the bank's 200th anniversary celebrations in 1989,[1] but they did not, in the late forties, give him the kind of money he needed to buy himself a new business. Yet that is what he did: he bought out a fodder and agricultural products wholesaler in Bremen,[2] where he proceeded to enjoy a successful career as a wealthy grain merchant and importer-exporter.

There is some correspondence between Becher and Dr. Chaim Posner of the Israeli Ministry of Finance to suggest that he was involved in arms purchases for Israel in 1948,[3] but he traded mostly with the Communist bloc, particularly Hungary. He imported Hungarian specialties—sausages, honey, pepper—to the Federal Republic of Germany (West Germany), but he never visited the country again. He had reason to fear that someone would recognize him and bring him to the attention of the Justice Ministry, which, despite his commercial dealings with the country, still had an outstanding warrant for his arrest. He was, after all, the man who had stolen most of Hungary's wealth in 1944.

He divorced his first wife and married Hermine von Platen, the lovely countess who had so much enjoyed her life in Budapest. After Hermine died, he married twice more, always choosing good horsewomen.

There were various attempts to try him as a war criminal. In 1962–63 the Zurich magazine *Sie und Er* published a series of articles by Kurt Emenegger about Kurt Andreas Ernst Becher, Himmler's trusted economic envoy. In 1964, when Becher testified at the trial of ss cavalry officer Franz Magill, he claimed that he heard for the first time there about the massacres of Jews in the Ukraine and Russia. He stated that his task had been to "ensure the maintenance of communications between the brigade and staff officers."[4] Later he testified at the trial of ss Major General Gustav Lombard. The charges in both trials were in connection with the murder of the Jewish population of the Pripet Marshes in 1941. Becher seemed to suffer from a complete memory lapse when he was asked about his orders to "cleanse" the area of Jews, and the charges against him were abandoned for lack of reliable evidence and witnesses. Becher claimed on both occasions that he had known nothing about the killing of innocent civilians until he came into contact with Rezső Kasztner and became his accomplice in saving lives. As for the word *Endlösung*, Final Solution, he heard the expression for the first time from his American interrogators before the Nuremberg Trials.

Becher sent his written testimony to Eichmann's trial in Jerusalem in 1961. Understandably, he would not attend in person because he was worried about being charged under Israel's Nazis and Nazi Collaborators (Punishment) Law of 1950. He may also have been concerned about the people who hoped to repossess their valuables once they escaped, such as the fifty extra passengers he had placed on the Kasztner train at an average fee of $25,000 each.

In May 1982, after the publication of Karla Müller-Tupath's book *Reichsführers gehorsamster Becher* (The Reichsführer's Most Obedient Becher: A German Career), the Bremen state prosecutor launched a judicial inquiry into Becher's possible participation in mass murder. The prosecution based its case on the testimonies of two witnesses, one of whom, a member of the ss cavalry, said that the regiments had been ordered to liquidate the Jewish population in the Pripet Marshes area of Mosyr, Bobruysk, and Rietschitza, in Russia. Both witnesses accused Becher of having planned and led the massacres under the command of Hermann Fegelein. Luckily for Becher, both witnesses died before the case could proceed to trial. Becher insisted that he had had nothing to do with and no knowledge of any planned measures to annihilate Jews. He admitted only to having been aware of a few cleanup operations against partisans.

Müller-Tupath contended that Becher's sudden wealth came from valuables he acquired in Hungary, including blood money from the persecuted Jews, and that he had had ample opportunity to hide this hoard in Swiss banks while he was in Switzerland negotiating with Saly Mayer. Becher consistently denied all personal financial gains from his trading in lives on behalf of the ss.

Becher achieved national and international renown in the business world when he was nominated in 1982 to the board of directors of Hapag-Lloyd, a giant German shipping company resulting from the merger of Lloyd of Bremen and Hapag of Hamburg. He had already sat on an advisory board for the company, and, because his business involved extensive shipping contracts, he was an obvious choice. He also sat on the board of a German bank. However, when several employees of the shipping company decried the appointment of a former highly placed ss man, critical articles appeared in newspapers in Germany and abroad. Becher refused to comment on the accusations and claimed that Müller-Tupath's book and those articles were untruthful and of no importance. For that reason, he said, he did not bother to sue the authors for libel.

The Bremen prosecutor's judicial inquiry continued while Becher and the board deliberated. At the end of July, Becher declined the board position in a carefully worded letter from his lawyer to avoid "unnecessary dissension" and strictly in the interests of Hapag-Lloyd. The chairman of the board acknowledged and accepted Becher's position "with understanding and regret." The Bremen state inquiry ended with all charges dropped, for lack of evidence, and the Becher file was closed.

By the early 1980s, Becher was a close associate of the political establishment and an occasional dinner companion of Chancellor Helmut Kohl and others in the upper echelons of West German business and society. Whether he had managed to secrete away a substantial portion of the infamous "Becher Treasures" is still not known. Sixty years later, their true value and their rightful ownership were still being debated.

When Ilana Dayan interviewed Becher on December 22, 1994, for an Israeli television program called *Fact*, Becher, as usual, presented well: he was an elegant gentleman with impeccable manners. Dayan, in contrast, seemed rough, overly persistent, a tough journalist and Yale-educated lawyer seeking truthful answers to her questions. After she introduced the name of Rudolf Kasztner (she called him by his German name), she asked Becher if they were friends.

"We were friends," he replied. "We addressed each other as *du* [the familiar "you"]. I called him Rudolf."

"Did he also address you by your first name?"

"Yes, of course."

Kurt Becher died in his bed in 1995 at the age of eighty-five.

Ernst Kaltenbrunner, the chief of the Reich Main Security Office, was executed in Nuremberg on October 16, 1946. His last words were, "Good luck, Germany."

Dieter Wisliceny, after first testifying at Nuremberg, was extradited to Czechoslovakia in 1947, tried, and convicted for his leading role in the murder of the Jews of Slovakia, Greece, and Hungary. He was hanged in Bratislava on May 4, 1948.

Captain Josef Kramer, "the beast of Belsen," was condemned to death by a British military court and hanged in Hameln, Germany, on December 13, 1945.

László Endre, László Baky, and Ferenc Szálasi were hanged; Döme Sztójay, László Ferenczy, Andor Jaross, and Peter Hain were tried in Budapest and executed by firing squad in 1946.

Edmund Veesenmayer was sentenced to twenty years' imprisonment in April 1949. He was granted clemency and freed after serving only three. He returned to civilian life in Darmstadt, Germany.

Hermann Krumey was tried in 1960 and condemned to five years of hard labor. On appeal, he was sentenced to life imprisonment.

Otto Hunsche, who was arrested and tried in 1960, was sentenced to twelve years.

Miklós Horthy died of old age in Portugal in 1957. To the end of his life, he enjoyed financial assistance from the Chorin family. Miklós Horthy Jr. died in Portugal in 1993.

Alois Brunner, the man who had Gizi Fleischmann and some

twenty thousand Slovak Jews murdered, the man who had been fond of saying "it is more important to kill Jews than to save German soldiers," was last seen in Damascus, Syria. He worked for the American Central Intelligence Agency after the war. In 1985 he was interviewed by a journalist working for the German newspaper *Die Welt*. At the time, Brunner was busy with arms trading and exports to the Orient.[8]

Why did Kasztner go out of his way to help Becher? Bogyó thought the simple explanation was that Rezső always kept his word. He had promised Becher his help at a time when survival depended on the currency of his word being accepted. Bogyó fully accepted that Becher was the one "angel" in the ss, the man who risked his life for others.[5] Hansi had a different explanation. In an interview in Tel Aviv in the 1970s, she said that Rezső had fallen for Becher's lovely countess and that it was she who had begged him to testify. Indeed, Hermine von Platen was in Nuremberg for the duration of Kasztner's testimonies. "Rezső never could resist a pretty woman," said Hansi.[6] As likely as that lighthearted remark might be, another explanation is supported by documents and letters: Kasztner was hoping he could help Israel recover some of the lost treasure of Hungary's Jews.

Hansi remembered receiving a letter from Krumey's wife, asking for money and "care packages." She ignored the requests. But she said that for Rezső, it had been a matter of honor. He had promised help, and he delivered on his promise to Krumey. Another explanation, and a more logical one, could be that the Jewish Agency Executive believed Krumey was another conduit to some of the lost treasure and that he had information about Eichmann's escape route.[7]

On May 2, 2005, the Paris-based newspaper *International Herald Tribune* ran an advertisement calling on "Jewish Hungarian victims of Nazi persecution and their heirs" to be part of the class-action lawsuit *Rosner et al. v. United States of America* to regain property seized by the Hungarian government in 1944 and spirited out of the country on the Gold Train. A settlement of $25.5 million was approved by the District Court of the Southern District of Florida on September 30, 2005. After deducting legal fees, approximately $21 million was distributed worldwide to social service organizations for programs benefiting the victims themselves.

CHAPTER 31

Letters to Friends in the Mizrachi

Is not the flight from responsibility merely another kind of betrayal? And if I take this upon myself, what is the line that I should never cross? . . . Common sense is almost incapable of drawing the line between self-sacrifice and betrayal . . . to judge the Judenrat [Jewish Council] after the fact, on the basis of testimonies, documents and sources—this is a task that is beyond the capacity of any human tribunal.

Rezső Kasztner, *Der Kasztner-Bericht*

In August 1952 Malchiel Grünwald, an elderly pamphleteer and stamp collector who owned a seedy downtown hotel in Jerusalem, launched a personal attack against Rezső Kasztner in a mimeographed newsletter called *Letters to Friends in the Mizrachi*. Grünwald had lost some of his family to the Holocaust, and a son in the 1948 Arab-Israeli War. He was described as a disappointed, angry old man whose one ambition had been to become a journalist. When he failed to find employment in the media, he launched a newsletter that he wrote, printed, and delivered to the post office himself. It had negligible circulation even among the Mizrachi, or religious Zionists, for whom it was intended. His mailing list of a few hundred included some journalists and politicians, Hungarian and Austrian community leaders in Israel, and heads of religious families. Few people took Grünwald or his frequent outpourings of hate seriously. He was particularly hysterical in his attacks on the ruling Labor Party, on government officials, and members of the Knesset—everyone he considered to have benefited from the trappings of power.

In his *Letters to Friends in the Mizrachi*,[1] he wrote: "Beloved Friends! I smell rotting carrion! What a first-rate burial we are going to have! This Rudolf Kastner has to be finished off! For three years I have waited for this moment. The smell of rotting carrion fills my nostrils. It will be a funeral of the very best kind! Dr. Rudolf Kastner must be liquidated. I have waited for this moment to bring to justice this careerist, who benefits from Hitler's theft and murder."[2]

He accused Kasztner of collaborating with the Nazis in the mass murder of millions of Jews for personal financial gain and of having saved his friend, Kurt Becher, from the punishment he deserved in order to prevent him from telling the truth about their business transactions. He went on to accuse Kasztner of saving fifty-two members of his own family at the expense of the thousands he had left to die, thereby participating in the murder of Hungarian Jewry. And he accused David Ben-Gurion's Labor Party of complicity in these actions.

A copy of *Letters to Friends* landed on Kasztner's desk at *Új Kelet*. Another found its way to him at the Ministry of Commerce. His first instinct was to ignore the tirade. He had been attacked before, though with less vitriol. That evening, he showed the newsletter to Bogyó, who turned pale and started to cry. It wasn't just the accusations but the choice of words that distressed her. When family and friends rallied around the Kasztners, they tried to reinforce Rezső's initial instinct to ignore Grünwald's rants. His newsletters were rarely read, they said. His allegations were always libelous. He was personally loathsome. His attacks were never backed up with facts. Even the Mizrachi ignored him. Few people wanted to hear what had happened in the Holocaust, and fewer still paid the slightest attention to these amateur pamphlets.

Only one newspaper bothered to mention the matter, and it did not even name Kasztner. But it posed the question: Why didn't the man accused exonerate himself?

Chaim Cohen, the attorney general in Ben-Gurion's government, agreed with this sentiment. Grünwald had demanded that Kasztner be charged under the Nazis and Nazi Collaborators (Punishment) Law, and Cohen felt compelled to do something. He called at the Kasztners' apartment and told them that the government on Kasztner's behalf should sue Grünwald for malicious libel.[3]

A tall, bald man, Cohen was an old-world lawyer, a gifted orator with a highly theatrical style. He outlined the government's and Kasztner's case to the couple with such vehemence that he left his reluctant audience with a sense that if Rezső did not agree to the suit, he would be admitting his guilt. To make sure of Rezső's agreement, Cohen wrote to Kasztner's boss in the Ministry of Commerce. Dov Yosef had not seen Grünwald's article and was not much interested in reading it. In his view, it required no action, and the nonsensical tirade would certainly not affect Kasztner's job with his ministry. Cohen, however, wrote: "We cannot remain silent about this publication. If there is an iota of truth in the accusations, it is incumbent upon us to investigate them. If, as I presume, there is no truth in them, the man who printed them must be put on trial."

Hansi was not persuaded. Nor was Bogyó. When Cohen said that Kasztner would have to resign his position at the ministry if he did not agree to launch a suit, Bogyó advised Rezső to resign. A trial would bring back all the terrible memories; it would force him to relive times best forgotten. It could become a public circus. So many had been lost in the Holocaust. There was so much pain, so much hatred walking the streets of Israel. "You didn't save everyone. Look at Palgi," Bogyó told him. "You thought he was a friend, but he has never forgiven you for the loss of the other two parachutists."[4] Palgi had been making some strange speeches recently, unable to forgive himself for being viewed as a hero in Israel when his friends had been murdered in Budapest.

"What more could I have done?" Rezső pleaded. He always became angry and defensive when someone mentioned Hanna Szenes and Ferenc Goldstein. "They came on a fool's errand. They endangered all our lives. And look at Palgi strutting around, being the hero. He saved no one. Not even himself. And Hanna . . . ," he waved his hand as if shooing away a pesky fly. "A lovely young poet. She should have stayed at home. But then, she couldn't have become a hero, could she?" Hanna's slim volume of poetry was a best-seller; her work was taught to schoolchildren. "She died. Many died, and they are not heroes . . . only these idiots and the sacrificial lambs of the Warsaw ghetto."

Bogyó was used to these ravings. Her husband had been deprived of the one thing more he craved—recognition.

"If I had been shot," he said, "do you think they would learn about me in their schools?"

Bogyó said a trial would bring out all those whose relatives were murdered by the Nazis. There would be accusations. Someone from Kolozsvár had appeared at several Mapai rallies, interrupting Rezső's speeches and accusing him of collaborating with the Nazis to save his own family. He had even been questioned by the police once about his dealings with the ss, but no action followed. They had their daughter to consider. Later, Bogyó would tell an interviewer that Rezső had been forced to sue, that he had been threatened with the Nazis and Nazi Collaborators Law. "Imagine," she shuddered. "My husband charged under the same law as Eichmann!"[5]

"No one," Cohen told Kasztner, "can be allowed to say that a senior government official collaborated with the Nazis."[6] Born in Germany, Cohen had immigrated in 1930, long before Germany's Final Solution, but his brother had been murdered by the Nazis, and he felt guilty for surviving in the relative safety of Palestine. He could not imagine a more heinous charge than that of Nazi collaborator, and he was not about to allow someone as prominent as Kasztner to ignore the accusations. He was determined to proceed against Grünwald. There is no jury system in Israel; judges sit either as a group or, in less complicated cases, singly. As it was assumed that this trial would be quick, a sole judge was appointed.[7]

Kasztner recognized the choice he faced: he would either have to allow the suit to go forward or abandon his political aspirations. He would not be able to serve in any senior position with "such a stain upon his name and the suspicion that he collaborated with the Nazis," as Cohen had stated; this "was, simply, unthinkable."

The fact that not even his own party took Grünwald seriously had no effect on Cohen's determination. Dov Yosef openly opposed the government's action, as did several Mapai members of the Knesset. But Cohen remained adamant.

Hansi advised Rezső that he should not testify himself.[8] An innocent man should not take the trouble to prove his own innocence. Rezső disagreed. If the suit was going to proceed, he said, he would take the stand. Here was his chance to dissolve the rumors that had circulated around him, to tell the true story of what he had done. As a lawyer, he insisted, he knew how to present a case. Did Hansi imagine that a man who could talk Eichmann into letting thousands of Jews evade the gas chambers would now have trouble with a fool like Grünwald? Why should he cower before his accusers? He had nothing to be ashamed of—and neither did Hansi. They had done their best in times when others had wavered, when few had dared raise their voices.

Seeing his determination to proceed, Hansi assured Rezső that many survivors would bear witness to his actions. She had called Sam Springmann, Moshe Schweiger, and Dezsö Hermann; they would certainly testify. Lea Komoly, Ottó's daughter, now married and living in Israel, would tell the judge about her father and the Rescue Committee. Then there were the halutzim—Peretz Révész, Rafi Benshalom, and the others. Rezső would not be alone. She, too, would testify. She had always stood by him, and always would.

Hansi believed the chance to shine a light on his actions was the real reason he chose, finally, to give in to Cohen's persistent urging. "He had always loved the limelight. He had grown used to it in Hungary and later in Austria. Here, he was nobody, a spokesman for a minister. Hired help. Rezső knew he was better than that."[9] He craved recognition. He wanted people to see him as he saw himself. But Hansi feared that those he had saved had started new lives. She was worried that many of them would not volunteer to help, as so few had come forward when the Kasztners arrived destitute. "Nobody likes to remember that he was saved. Nobody wants to be grateful for his life. It's a terrible feeling to owe someone your life," she said in an interview after the trial.

At the last moment, his old school friend from Kolozsvár, Dezsö Hermann, advised him to withdraw. "No one," he reasoned, "can emerge lily-white from such a catastrophe as the events in Hungary." As a practicing lawyer in Israel, Hermann viewed the case as one in which both sides would lose.[10]

Hansi tried to persuade Rezső to ask for an interpreter. He had learned Hebrew, he was fluent, but he did not speak it as well as he did other languages. His Hebrew lacked nuance, the extensive vocabulary, the quick wit, the elegant phrasing he had retained in both Hungarian and German. Yet Kasztner insisted the trial be conducted in Hebrew. "It's the language of my people," he said. "These are the people I fought for. They will understand."

Grünwald was represented by Shmuel Tamir, who was thirty-one years old, born in Jerusalem, a graduate of Hebrew University's Law Faculty, an eloquent speaker, a passionate opponent of the ruling Mapai (Labor) Party and its antecedent, the Jewish Agency, and bitterly antagonistic to everything he believed David Ben-Gurion and Moshe Sharett represented. He was against compromise and against negotiating with the enemy—to him, the enemy had been both the Germans, who had murdered the Jews of Europe, and the British, who had controlled the borders of Palestine. He judged Ben-Gurion's negotiations with the British to be on a par with Kasztner's negotiations with the Nazis. Tamir had been a member of the right-wing Revisionists and was one of the founders of its successor, the Herut [Freedom] Party, itself the chief adversary of the Mapai. As a deputy commander in the Irgun's Etzel force, the armed forces sponsored by the Revisionists, he had been arrested by the British, jailed, and deported to Kenya.

A few months before the Grünwald trial, Tamir wrote an article in *Herut*, the party's newspaper, accusing Ben-Gurion of partnership in the extermination of Jews in Europe, an attack occasioned by the government's contentious deliberations about whether to establish diplomatic relations with West Germany.[11] Tamir prided himself on being a sabra, "one who was never in the Exile," and was contemptuous of the jetsam that Europe sent to his land. He was handsome, ambitious, uncompromising, an attractive man with a dark tan, black hair, a high forehead, a long, aquiline nose, a jutting jaw, and eyes that were, as one journalist remarked, like basalt: black and sharp. He craved the fame and glory that goes with political power. He frequently attacked Menachem Begin as too soft and too old to lead the Herut Party, and he gathered support to replace him. "Why is the word 'resign' in the dictionary?" he had bluntly asked his party's leader at their last convention.

On the surface, Tamir and Kasztner had much in common. They were both idealistic Zionists; witty and brilliant intellectuals who lacked tolerance for opposition; ambitious men who were contemptuous of stupidity; debaters who excelled at argument. In this contest, Israel's longest and most discussed libel trial, they were destined to become deadly enemies.

The judge, Benyamin Halevi, was from Germany, a *yekke*, as the Israelis called the early German arrivals. He had trained under the same Jerusalem lawyer as Shmuel Tamir, and he had his own grudges against the Labor government. Perhaps because of his reputation as an unusually severe judge, he had twice been overlooked for an appointment to the Supreme Court in favor of others with less experience. He had written, in vain, to Ben-Gurion to intervene on his behalf. In 1954 he was in his prime. Disappointed with his lack of rewards, he saw this trial as an opportunity to demonstrate that he was worthy of the highest court.

From the beginning, Tamir's plan was not only to prove that Grünwald's claims were true but to go one huge step farther—to drag down the government with Kasztner. He realized that Malchiel Grünwald would not be able to pay his fee. As he recalled in his memoirs, all the old man could offer him were some stamp collections of questionable value. But he recognized that he had a chance, through Grünwald's article, to attack those people who he considered had failed the Yishuv. He told Grünwald he would take the case on one condition: it would

become "the trial of Jewish leadership during the period of the Holocaust," and, as attorney, he would have "absolute power" to proceed as
he saw fit. There would be no client-attorney consultations, no
second-guessing his approach.

The Grünwald trial, *The Attorney General of the Government of Israel
v. Malchiel Grünwald*, opened on January 1, 1954, a cold, wintry
day, in Jerusalem District Court, in a large, airy room with dark pan-
eling, high french windows that let in the afternoon sun, and two
enormous ceiling fans. For the first time, the Yishuv were forced to
confront the events of the Holocaust. The trial shook the government, created two notable careers, and destroyed a man.

During the first months, Amnon Tel, the assistant attorney for the
Jerusalem District, represented the prosecution. His modest expertise
was in civil law. He knew little about the laws of libel and, unlike
Tamir, had scant courtroom experience. His Hebrew was poor. When
Rezső's brother Gyula found out the identity of the prosecution
lawyer, he warned the family about Tel's incompetence, but Rezső felt
confident that he would be able to handle anything they threw at
him.

The star witness for the prosecution was Israel (Rezső) Kasztner.
He strode into the courtroom, confident, cheerful, radiating a sense
of well-being that he had not felt since before those dark days in
Budapest in 1944. He looked, once more, like the young, successful,
aggressive lawyer-politician who had seemed invincible in his hometown of Kolozsvár even after the German persecutions had begun.
Hansi and Bogyó sat in the courtroom. Both had advised him not to
take the stand, but, once in court, they were mesmerized by their
man's performance. Only Hansi would have the courage to tell him
that first evening that his testimony must be cut short, that he had to
stop looking as though he was strutting when he entered the courtroom, that in Israel his manner could work against his case.

Kasztner loved the attention. Although there was little newspaper
coverage of the proceedings at the beginning of the trial, there were
always cameramen and journalists in the back of the room, lights

flashing as he entered and left. He testified for three weeks, at first almost uninterrupted by judge or counsel except for the prosecution's helpful requests for explanations. He had an attentive audience, and the formal trappings in the courtroom provided just the right respectful surrounding.[12]

He described the Rescue Committee's efforts to help refugees in Budapest before the German invasion, and his dealings with Eichmann and his Sonderkommando afterward. He mentioned the Eichmann offer of trucks for lives and spoke of Joel Brand's failed mission. At length, he talked about his own dealings with Eichmann, the "Kasztner train," and the "Jews on ice" in Austria. He described the selection process for the train passengers, and the arrival of the three young parachutists from Palestine and the dilemma Ferenc Goldstein faced before he turned himself in. He talked about the negotiations on the Swiss border and referred to Kurt Becher as a Nazi officer he had dealt with at the time. He mentioned his affidavit in London about Becher, and his later evidence at the trial of Edmund Veesenmayer. He reported on the so-called Becher Deposits and his efforts, on behalf of the finance minister, to regain them for the State of Israel. As for drawing financial benefit from his dealings on behalf of the Jews he saved, he remarked with a self-deprecating chuckle that he had no property, no money, only debts.

Kasztner was pleased with the initial press notices. One editorial called him a man of steel nerves, iron logic, and profound vision. He told Bogyó several times that his judgment in choosing to tell his story had been the right one. When Hansi reminded him, again, that he should give more credit to the other members of the Rescue Committee, that a more modest presentation would gain him friends, he laughed. "Don't you remember, Hansi? I did most of the talking, and it worked in our favor, then." She was renting a room from a friend in Jerusalem so that she could stay close to the trial. He bought her flowers at the market and presented them with a flourish, just as he had, at times, during that long summer in Budapest. "Do you want me to tell them that you did all the thinking?" he needled.[13]

"Perhaps you should," she said. At the very least, he should have

Sam Springmann and Moshe Schweiger testify. They both knew a great deal about what had happened, and both would back up his statements. In Hansi's view, the committee had acted as a unit—each person had a function and no one, not even Rezső, was a boss.

Kasztner said he didn't think that would be necessary. The case would be over in a few days.

Bogyó didn't ask where he had been at night. She knew he had to talk to Hansi to help him remember and relive what had happened and in what sequence, and also to keep control of his emotions, much as she had helped him when he was dealing with the Nazis. During the first three weeks, while Kasztner preened for the cameras, while he steepled his long, elegant fingers in concentration as he told his stories of how he had outwitted the Germans, Bogyó had been watching Shmuel Tamir. The expression on his lean, unlined face was never uncertain, never confused. He took notes and seemed to smile when Kasztner presented his analysis of the cast of characters, his riveting descriptions of his high-level meetings with the Germans. Bogyó understood that her husband would need Hansi's presence for the difficult times to come.

Kasztner was so cheerfully confident in those first few weeks that he approached Tamir, as one lawyer to another, in the cafeteria of the courthouse and suggested that the two of them compare notes over a glass of wine when all this—he waved his hand dismissively toward the courtroom—was over. Tamir smiled and retreated with his tray.

The tide began to turn when Tamir started his cross-examination. He questioned Kasztner's inability to convince others of the truth of the death camps. He accused him of keeping Rudolf Vrba's and Alfréd Wetzler's report, the Auschwitz Protocols, from the Jewish councils in both Budapest and Kolozsvár. From here on, the specter of Jews going "like sheep to the slaughter" while Kasztner negotiated for the safety of a select, privileged few would haunt all the testimonies.

Tamir insisted that the "VIP train" carrying Kasztner's relatives and friends, his fellow Labor supporters, had been his reward for keeping silent about the extermination camps. He kept asking Kasztner when he had first learned of the extermination camps and when he

knew for sure that all the Hungarian Jews were being sent to
Auschwitz-Birkenau. When Kasztner answered that he had known
about them even before the Vrba-Wetzler report, Tamir countered
with a question: Why hadn't he warned everybody?

Worse, when Kasztner was first asked by Tamir about his relationship with Nazi officers, he denied that he had become friendly with
Becher. He denied that his own statement had saved Kurt Becher
from criminal prosecution at Nuremberg. He said he had testified
"neither in favor, nor against Becher. I tried only to tell the truth."
Tamir produced the letter Kasztner had written to Eliezer Kaplan,
the finance minister, claiming that "Becher was released thanks to
my personal intervention." Surely that provided proof of close cooperation between an ss officer and a Zionist leader and that Kasztner
believed his testimony had saved Becher's life?

"Do you admit that you wrote this letter?" Tamir asked.

"Yes—"

"You said in this courtroom that it was a lie that Becher was
released through your intervention. Was that a lie?" The young
attorney had moved close to the witness stand, a piece of paper in his
fingers.[14]

Kasztner lost his composure. He looked to Tel for help, but none
came. Tel had not advised him before the trial that the letter Tamir
held between his fingers had been part of the documentary evidence
provided to the defense before the trial. "I stand by what I said,"
Kasztner said, his voice suddenly very quiet.

Tamir kept snapping at him for hours, demanding to know which
time he had lied: When he took credit for saving Becher's life? Or
when he denied having done so?

Judge Halevi, who had shown early indications that he thought
Grünwald should apologize to Kasztner, pay a fine, and stop writing
scurrilous articles about people, now began to give Tamir leeway to
badger and shout, to demean Kasztner's every statement, interrupt
his replies, and make remarks of his own about the character of the
"Jews of the Exile."

Before the end of his cross-examination, Tamir produced the document, signed by Kasztner and submitted to the Denazification

Court, attesting to Becher's good works and his saving of Jewish lives. He produced the affidavit signed by Walter Rapp, legal officer of the U.S. State Department and counsel at Nuremberg. According to Rapp, Kasztner had arrived as a "voluntary witness on behalf of ss Colonel Becher" and his endeavors had proved to be the reason for Becher's release.

Kasztner pleaded that he had misunderstood the initial question, that he meant the testimony had not been presented at Nuremberg,[15] and that he had merely stated the facts about Becher, as far as he knew them. But the damage was done.

That night, Rezső knocked on the door of the Brands' apartment and asked to speak, alone, with Hansi. "Why?" Joel demanded. "Didn't you have time enough for that in Budapest?" He didn't want to hear Rezső's explanation that he needed her advice about the next day's cross-examination. He said he knew what Rezső wanted.[16] Rezső replied that in the last months of the Nazi terror, when Joel was in Turkey or Syria or wherever, when Eichmann was ready to murder all the remaining Jews in Hungary, there had been only the two of them left—Hansi and Rezső—to sort through the German lies, the deceit, to endure the sight of their friends being deported or marched to their deaths along the Budapest–Vienna highway. Only they could know how it had felt.

"Why haven't they asked me to testify?" Joel shouted. "I would tell them who was responsible. I know who condemned the last million Jews to death! That's why Tel isn't calling me, and you know it!"

Hansi shook her head sadly and asked Joel to leave them. "He is dreaming again," she told Rezső, and she poured the rest of Joel's whiskey down the drain so that it wouldn't be waiting for him when he returned.

She held Rezső's hands and soothed him as she had done in Budapest. The document Tamir had flourished in court was nothing Rezső should be ashamed of. He had saved Becher because he—they all—owed Becher their lives. "Just tell the truth, Rezső, tell them. You have nothing to hide."

But Tel had specifically advised him not to repeat his endorsements of Becher, and now he couldn't bring himself to admit he had saved a Nazi officer's life—or that he hadn't, but claimed to have done so.

"Being boastful is not a sin, but lying in court is a sin. Tell them," Hansi urged.

It was too late. Tamir shouted at him, kept asking the same questions over and over, and the judge allowed it to go on day after day. Kasztner grew pale, tired; his hands shook when he raised a glass of water to his lips, and once he slumped over the witness lectern, his face bathed in sweat, his fist clenched against his chest. Tel's repeated requests that Halevi stop Tamir's badgering went unheeded.

To counter Kasztner's claim that he had saved the majority of those who were sent to camps in Austria via Strasshof, Tamir produced a letter from Ernst Kaltenbrunner's Nuremberg trial: in it, Karl Blaschke, the ss mayor of Vienna, had requested laborers for farms and for clearing rubble from the streets of the city. Eichmann had fooled Kasztner, the too-willing accomplice, Tamir said. When Eichmann set the price of $100 a head for the "exchange Jews," when he demanded that the Va'ada pay for their food and clothing, he had already committed them to slave labor in Austria. Kaltenbrunner had promised them to his fellow Nazi in Vienna, and no matter how much Eichmann would have wished them all to be sent to Auschwitz, he had to obey his superior officer. The Va'ada's deal was a sham, Tamir told the court.

"But they stayed alive!" Hansi yelled from the back of the courtroom. "Without us, they would all have died."

Judge Halevi told her to keep quiet or she would be removed from the court. Only the witness was allowed to answer the questions. When Kasztner tried to explain that the Strasshof group included old men and women, young children as well as the able-bodied Blaschke had requested, Tamir did not allow him to finish speaking. And Tel did not rise to object.

Tamir took Kasztner back to his earlier statements about the infamous death march. "You said you met ss Colonel Höss?" Tamir asked.

"Yes. I met Colonel Höss in the Budapest office of Dr. Billitz, one of Colonel Becher's aides."

Halevi, who, like most people in Israel, had heard of Höss, the notorious commandant of Auschwitz, asked the next question. "What did you talk about?"

"We talked about the death march."

"What did Höss say about the death march?" Halevi asked.

"Höss said he thought the whole thing was swinish. He thought the things he saw happen along the road from Vienna to Budapest were utterly swinish," Kasztner replied. "I provided him with the details of how many had died, and he stated he would take steps to have the march stopped."

Hansi remembered later the terrible hush over the courtroom. This man was the same Höss who had admitted to slaughtering women and children, to hearing the mothers scream as they went mad cradling their dead babies in their arms. At his own trial he had testified how gold teeth had been extracted from the bodies, how surplus fat had to be drained, how the dead had to be turned over so the draft would fan the flames. "And what was Colonel Höss's job?" Halevi asked.

"He was the commander of Auschwitz."

"The commander of the death chambers?"

"Yes. It was he."[17]

When Kasztner left the courtroom, not even Hansi was waiting for him. She could not bear to watch his suffering any longer.

Kasztner went to see David Ben-Gurion, whom he had consulted before going to Nuremberg to testify on behalf of Becher and Krumey. He told his brother Gyula later that Ben-Gurion had been cordial but had not offered any assistance at the trial. He did, however, promise that one day he would help clear Kasztner's name. Yet when Gyula wrote to Ben-Gurion asking him to make a statement on Kasztner's behalf, he refused. He agreed that what had been said about Kasztner was appalling, but he claimed he could not effectively interfere, that other former members of the Jewish Agency Executive were "better informed" about the efforts to save European Jewry.[18]

The other witnesses failed to change the direction the trial had taken. Tel did not call former members of the Rescue Committee in

Budapest or the halutzim who had worked with Kasztner and could have testified to his gargantuan efforts there. Instead, he called several people who could testify to Kasztner's good character but had no personal knowledge of what he had done in Budapest. They were highly regarded and spoke well, but they had never been in Hungary. Worse, Tel called Yoel Palgi. His book was still a best-seller, and he had become a national hero as well as a senior executive with the Israeli airline company, El Al. Tel hoped that this man, who had written glowingly about Kasztner's fearlessness and self-sacrifice, would now be able to save his former teacher's tattered reputation. But Palgi, as Bogyó had feared, had become ambivalent about Kasztner. He was haunted by the death of his parents in Auschwitz, by the thought that Kasztner could have saved them on his train, and by the fate of his two companions, both of whom had perished after Rezső and Hansi had concocted a story about their being Jewish Agency emissaries.

Now, in the courtroom, Tamir did not spare Palgi: he had become contaminated by Kasztner, Tamir implied; he, too, had become a collaborator. When Tamir confronted him with different versions of the events in Hungary from those in his own book, Palgi claimed that his account was fiction. He had written a novel based on the events, and he felt no need to tell the whole story. Before he was through with him, Tamir had created the impression that this tarnished hero had been in the service of the Germans and had left his two companions to die.

In the course of his questioning, Tamir continually extended the net to the Jewish Agency, now Mapai, leaders. Both Palgi and Kasztner were Labor supporters, he insisted, and they had been controlled by the people now in power in Israel. They were all inclined to negotiate rather than to stand and fight. Negotiations had kept the Jewish Agency busy all during the war years, and the Mapai was merely the successor to the Jewish Agency.

Tel called Menachem Bader, a former member of the Jewish Agency's delegation in Istanbul. Bader talked about the blood-for-goods mission, about the way the Agency had tried to save the negotiations after the British objected to any deal with the ss. Tamir accused him and his colleagues Ehud Avriel, Teddy Kollek, and Moshe Sharett, then the prime minister of Israel, of working for British Intelligence. Had they not lured Brand to Aleppo in Syria to hand him over to the British, who then, predictably, advertised their rejection of the ss offer in the press? The British, after all, did not want any more Jews in Palestine. Bader stood his ground. The charges were preposterous, he said, no matter how often Tamir repeated them. Avriel was equally unhelpful to Tamir. He explained patiently that Brand could not have remained in Turkey without the required papers and that the Agency had tried to obtain an extension of his visa but to no avail. He presented a picture of Brand as an irrational, hysterical man who was no longer able to make his own decisions. The only reason he, Avriel, had accompanied Brand to Syria was their anxiety over leaving him alone. The British had assured the Agency's men in Istanbul that they would not arrest Brand. They had all been betrayed.

The prosecution called Eliahu Dobkin, a member of the Jewish Agency Executive who had dealt with Kasztner at the end of the war about the return of the Becher Treasures. Once on the stand, however, he denied all knowledge of Becher or the treasures. He claimed he had never even heard the name Becher before the Grünwald trial, and he seemed unaware that Kasztner had been acting on behalf of the Executive when he offered to testify on Becher's behalf at the preliminary hearings before Nuremberg.[19] Kasztner realized too late that Dobkin was going to deny his part in the negotiations to reclaim the treasures and that his testimony was intended to protect the Mapai leadership at a time when any negotiations with the Nazis, however well intentioned, would land the party in electoral hell. When Kasztner tried to let Judge Halevi know of Dobkin's bias, he was accused of interfering with the legal process.[20]

By this stage in the trial, the newspapers were filled with reports about the testimonies. The accusations against the ruling party made headlines, as did Tamir's contentions that the Jewish Agency knowingly hid news of the murder of Europe's Jews from the Yishuv. Although even a cursory examination of the evidence would have proved the opposite, the papers happily carried these banners.[21]

When Fülöp von Freudiger (by then known as Pinhas Freudiger) was called, he admitted that he had bought the lives of his family and friends from Dieter Wisliceny in late 1944 and escaped through Romania, leaving his Orthodox congregation behind to face the renewed deportations and the death marches. But Freudiger used his chance on the witness stand to provide a sense of the horrific times they had faced, the daily killings in the streets, the humiliations of the women, the deaths of the children. How could he not have tried to escape?

Freudiger, like Kasztner and the others, had thought the war would end in a matter of weeks. By 1944 the Allies had landed in Europe and were fighting their way to the heart of the Reich. Who could have imagined that the Hungarian Nazis would assist the Germans in killing Jews at such a time? Who had reckoned with the uncontrolled violence of the Arrow Cross?

Tamir asked Freudiger the same question he had asked Kasztner: "Why did you cooperate in the destruction of your own people?" During his response, people in the audience started screaming in Hungarian and Yiddish, accusing Freudiger of abandoning his post as a leader of the Orthodox Community. It was a devastating scene. Freudiger tried to explain that by saving himself, he had not caused the deaths of others, that he had not withheld any information. "What more could we have done?" he kept repeating, his voice breaking, his shoulders hunched, sobbing by the time Tamir finished with him. Continually stretching to include what he viewed as the cringing masses of European Jewry, Tamir repeatedly asked about the wretched mentality of the "Jews of the Exile" versus the exemplary character of the fighting sabra; the European Jews' resorting to bribery and pleading versus the Yishuv's mentality of proud resistance.[22] He left no doubt about where the Mapai leadership under Sharett and Ben-Gurion belonged. Judge Halevi did not interfere with the showmanship of the defense attorney or accept the prosecution's objections. Frequently he added questions and comments of his own, making it clear that he found Tamir's approach entirely acceptable.

Hansi had tried to dissuade Joel from testifying. She told him that whatever he said, his words would be turned against him. His notion that he could help Kasztner was mere sophistry. "If I do not testify, it will seem I have something to hide," Joel argued. "Perhaps you do," Hansi said. "Perhaps there are reasons why you did not return that have nothing to do with Sharett and the British. Perhaps you were afraid, Joel."

She had heard his long, often incoherent monologues about Rezső dealing with the Sonderkommando when he, Joel, had initially been the one chosen by Eichmann, and he had denied Eichmann the pleasure of choosing whom he would save. He had faced the devil alone. He had taken the message to Istanbul, and he was not going to allow Rezső to be the only one whose name would go down in history.

He had already told Tamir of his arrest by the British in Aleppo, his interrogation by Sharett, his long imprisonment in Cairo, his endless efforts to reach Ben-Gurion, Weitzmann, and Sharett once he arrived in Tel Aviv, his sense of hopelessness and betrayal by his own people, his belief that, if only the Jewish leadership had taken his story seriously, Hungary's million Jews would have been saved.

When he took the stand, Joel tried to share Rezső's glory and his blame. Tamir asked him questions intended to prove the Jewish Agency's guilt, but he failed to shake Brand's version of events in Budapest. Tamir seemed sure that if he kept battering at the same points over and over, he would be able to force Prime Minister Sharett, or at least Teddy Kollek, into the courtroom in self-defense. Sharett was so outraged by what he read and heard about the trial that he would have testified had the party leadership not dissuaded him. He insisted that Chaim Cohen, the attorney general, should take over the prosecution from the inexperienced Tel and try to control the damage.[23]

Kasztner's brother Gyula wrote to the Szatmár rabbi who had been on the Kasztner train with his large family and several follow-ers. He was one of the most highly respected Jewish religious figures, and Gyula was sure his testimony would help, but he refused. He had been saved by God, he insisted, not by another human being—and, least of all, by a Zionist.[24]

By now the trial had aroused so much emotion and interest that the judge decided to move it to a larger courtroom with more space for spectators and the media. Even the *New York Times* began to cover some of the key testimonies, and there was a lineup in front of the doors before they were opened for the day's proceedings.

When Tamir called Katherine Szenes to the witness stand, there was no doubt in anyone's mind that her role was to further vilify Kasztner, a job she accomplished with quiet dignity and great sadness. A widow of small stature and with a deeply lined face, she spoke as if it hurt her to have to tell the judge how Kasztner would not meet her when she sought his help in Budapest, and how her daughter Hanna—now a legendary martyr—was tortured and executed while he dashed in and out of his busy office. Hansi, she stated, had lied that he was not at home, and his secretary would not even accept her meager food parcel to hand to her imprisoned daughter.

Malchiel Grünwald had stopped attending his own trial, and no one remarked on his absence. When one day he returned, he was barred from entering the courtroom. No one had recognized him. Every seat was taken, and people were standing at the back, taking notes for the newspapers. Television crews were crowded outside, trying to catch glimpses of the witnesses. "But I am the defendant," Grünwald declared, somewhat offended. "My seat is with Shmuel Tamir."

The trial had long since ceased being a simple libel action. It was now "the Kasztner trial."

CHAPTER 32

The Price of a Man's Soul

Dr. Israel Kasztner acted with courage and resourcefulness for over a year as intermediary between Becher of the SS and Mr. Mayer . . . Aside from regularly securing a great deal of invaluable information from Dr. Kasztner concerning the progress and plans of the Nazi-Hungarian operations against the Jews, the tangible results of these negotiations can be summed up as the following:

1. The bringing to Switzerland of the two groups of Jews from Hungary via the concentration camp of Bergen-Belsen: on August 21, 1944, 318 persons, and on December 6, 1944, 1355 persons.[1]

2. The avoidance of the deportation of upwards of 200,000 Jews remaining in Budapest on August 25, 1944, when Eichmann's organization had 66 trains ready.

3. The exemption . . . of elderly and sick persons and children (Becher's orders had been no one under 16 and no women over 40 or men over 60) from the forced evacuation on foot of Jews from Budapest in November 1944.

4. The diverting of transports of some 17,000 Hungarian Jews to Austria rather than to Auschwitz in June 1944.

5. Tacit ss *agreement that the International Committee of the Red Cross be permitted in Budapest and environs to shelter some 3000 Jewish children in homes under the Committee's protection (August through December 1944).*

6. Facilities for the procurement and distribution of foodstuffs and clothing to some 7000 Jews in labor camps in Vienna region (January 1945).

7. The release and arrival in Switzerland of 69 prominent Jews from Slovakia and Hungary on April 18, 1945.

Although this cannot be definitely listed as a result obtained by Becher, he claimed during his last conversations with Mr. Mayer in April 1945 . . . that he had been instrumental in "neutralizing" and arranging the surrender of the camp of Bergen-Belsen to the advancing British forces. Kasztner was there with him at that time.

Roswell McClelland, *Report on the Activities of the War Refugee Board from March 1944 to July 1945*[2]

It is forbidden to save one man by spilling the blood of another.

Judge Benyamin Halevi, Jerusalem, 1955

Shmuel Tamir called Moshe Krausz, Kasztner's old adversary from Budapest, to the stand. Krausz had not done well since the end of the war. Although he had anticipated that he would be applauded for his actions during the Nazi occupation, the Jewish Agency had brought in a new man over his head and suggested that he consider retirement. He had clung tenaciously to his position and refused to vacate his office and his desk, let alone hand over his papers and files. In the end, the Agency had relented and appointed someone at the same level as Krausz but not, strictly speaking, above him.

Kasztner was convinced that Krausz, still pursuing his private vendetta for slights he had endured at Kasztner's hands, had been behind Grünwald's accusations. Tel had been quick to point out to the judge that Krausz's hand was clearly visible throughout the trial: Grünwald had been the bullet, but Krausz was the gun.

The little man had visibly aged during the previous ten years. His body had shrunk, his shoulders sagged forward, and his unusually large head, now sparsely covered with gray hair, sat precariously on his thin neck.[3] Dressed formally for the occasion, in a black, shiny suit and felt hat, his head barely bobbed above the witness stand when he faced Kasztner with a half smile of acknowledgment.

Krausz testified to his conviction that the only force driving Kasztner had been vanity: the belief that he, alone, could save the Jews, that his "German line" was the Jews' only hope. He, Krausz, even now unappreciated, uncelebrated, demoted by the Jewish Agency he had so faithfully served, had been the one backing the "Hungarian line," the one that might have worked. He was the one with the unique vantage point from the Swiss Consulate and the Glass House.

Krausz said that he had lodged a complaint against Kasztner at the 1946 Zionist Congress. He admitted, on cross-examination, that he had believed the Kasztner train was going directly to Auschwitz, and he had worked assiduously to discourage everyone from taking a chance on Kasztner's German connections.

Hansi Brand, watching Krausz on the witness stand, could feel the man's desperation, his hatred, his need to feel unblemished by the horrors they had all survived. Afterward, though, when he again took his place with the spectators, he must have known that nothing had changed for him, that bringing Kasztner down had not been the answer after all. She saw his haunted look, the agony of a life that, with so many dead, he felt unjustified in living. When he left the courtroom, he did not look at her.

Tamir used every chance in the trial to extol the virtues of his fellow fighting sabras and to denigrate the Diaspora Jews of Europe. To further his own political ambitions, he talked about his part in the War of Independence and made long speeches, virtually uninterrupted by the judge, about the heroic battles. He questioned witnesses from the Holocaust about what they knew of the Yishuv's resistance to British forces. He lectured them about the betrayal of the Yishuv by the Agency's organizations, headed by those same leaders who headed the government now. He submitted to the court newspaper accounts of the Haganah's battles with the Revisionist armies, of the betrayal of the Irgun by the Jewish Agency.

When Bandi Grosz was called to the witness stand and claimed that he had been chosen to accompany Joel Brand to Istanbul as Heinrich Himmler's personal representative, the spectators laughed at the small, ugly, balding, toothless old man claiming that he had been chosen to represent the ss Reichsführer. When Grosz testified that Brand's mission was merely a cover for Himmler's real intentions of negotiating peace with the Allies, even Judge Halevi smiled. Tamir was able to extract some sort of admission from Grosz that he was living in a room in Tel Aviv at someone else's expense. Perhaps that someone, he suggested, was the ruling Mapai Party?

Tel had ignored repeated pleas from several would-be witnesses who could have helped Kasztner in the early days of the trial. Hansi said later that a few of those she had asked to speak for the Rescue Committee had gone to Jerusalem specifically to testify and had waited, hoping they would be called. Sam Springmann had traveled from Europe at his own expense and stayed in Jerusalem for a couple of months. He was appalled at the way Tel handled the trial and offended that Kasztner did not insist that he should appear as a witness.[4]

"Rezső and I had very few real fights," Hansi said later, "but we did fight about Sam. The man was an old Zionist. He had run errands for the Agency and the Istanbul committee to Poland, he had been a member of our committee, he had known everyone." But "Sam was this little guy. Looked like a jockey. He had big ears, a prominent Adam's apple. He didn't look good. I think Rezső didn't want someone like that in his corner."[5]

Tel neither challenged nor cross-examined witnesses who claimed that Kasztner had left them in the dark about Auschwitz. He did not rise when some of those left behind in Kolozsvár claimed they would have crossed the border and escaped with their families had they known; he didn't object to testimony that they had not heard of the gas chambers from the hundreds of refugees in their midst; he did not question them when they said they would have resisted had they known. He allowed their silent accusations to stand and be remembered in the next day's papers.

Judge Halevi took part in questioning a few of the witnesses himself. When Kolozsvár Jewish Council member Hillel Danzig was on the stand, Halevi inquired what he would have done with regard to his family and himself had he known about Auschwitz. "I don't know, Your Honor," he replied, honestly. "I can think about it today and give you an answer. But that has no connection with those circumstances . . ."[6] When he heard the man's reply, Halevi shook his head in disbelief.

By this stage of the trial, Tamir was openly accusing Kasztner of having sacrificed the majority of Jews from his hometown of Kolozsvár to save a few he considered worth saving. He accused Kasztner of willfully hiding the truth about Auschwitz and helping to spread the fiction that everyone would be put to work in some other part of Hungary. Witnesses testified to the terrible loss of their families, their conviction that Kasztner had misled them all. No one mentioned what fate had befallen those Jews who resisted. In 1941, for example, when Dutch Jews attacked the ss in Amsterdam, four hundred were arrested and tortured to death.

After Chaim Cohen himself took over the prosecution from Tel, five months after the beginning of the trial, he called Kasztner's friend and former colleague in Budapest, Moshe Schweiger, wishing to establish that all the money and valuables handed to Becher had been transferred to Schweiger in Bad Ischl, Austria, and all had been accounted for when he gave the suitcases to the Americans. But it was too late. Tamir hammered away at Schweiger's testimony and, when he failed to make him stumble, he declared he would prove that much of the treasure had been stolen before it was given to Schweiger. He would prove, he insisted, that Becher and Kasztner had been in cahoots all along, knowingly defrauding Hungary's Jews of over $2 million. Tamir had begun to refer to Kasztner and Becher as a pair of criminals, with nothing to choose between them. The judge, despite earlier testimony to Kasztner's strained circumstances, allowed these statements to go unchallenged. He was, by now, openly biased in Tamir's favor.

Newspaper headlines, with very few exceptions, shouted their accusations of collaboration with the Nazis. *Herut's* July 12 issue, for example, stated that Becher was connected with a German firm that dealt with the Israeli Purchasing Delegation in Koln. Massive headlines announced the "terrible revelations" of the day, Tamir's accusations against the leadership of the Mapai, and demands that the prime minister explain his actions during the Holocaust. Israel's leading intellectual magazine, *Haolam Hazeh* (This World), under Uri Avneri's editorship, conducted an open vendetta against Kasztner and the Mapai. It accused the Jewish Agency of collaboration with war criminals. It painted the Yishuv's Tamir as admirable and fearless, and the Exile's Kasztner as a cringing functionary ready to make any deal so long as his own life was safe. There was no question, in its biased reporting, which one of these two would build the ideal land of the Hebrews. In some of his editorials, Avneri claimed that the truth of the Holocaust had been carefully hidden not only from the "sheep" of Hungary but also from the Yishuv in Israel. "As if the Hebrew papers hadn't reported on the killings," Hansi said, "as if they hadn't carried the news about the death camps. Everyone had known what was the fate of the Jews in Hitler's Europe."

When one of the men from Kolozsvár testified that he and his friends "would have killed the Hungarian police if we had known we were being taken to Auschwitz for extermination," Hansi was the only one shouting: "What would you have used? Kitchen knives?" And she was the only one who kept jumping to her feet during the parade of tragic witnesses, all anxious to appear as though they would have defended themselves, that they were not "sheep for the slaughter," that they were worthy of this new country. "They need someone to blame," she told Rezső after another day of painful testimony.

The last weeks of the trial attracted journalists from New York and London, from Paris and even Berlin. The international media were interested not so much in the party politics of the new state as in the fact that, somehow, this court had managed to put the victims of the Holocaust on trial. Ben Hecht, the American scriptwriter, journalist, and author, wrote a book about the trial and titled it *Perfidy*. It is an openly biased accusation against all those who made deals with the Nazis. For a long time, it was the only English-language version of the events of the *State of Israel v. Malchiel Grünwald* trial.

Rezső Kasztner returned to the stand on June 4, five months after the trial had begun.[7] He was a changed man, pale, soft-spoken, lethargic. He walked slowly and responded to Tamir's questions in a low voice. Several times the judge had to ask him to repeat, louder, what he had already said. When Halevi asked him why he had not informed everybody about the deportations, Kasztner's response was so faint that only those in the front rows could hear: "I had no definite knowledge. I heard rumors in Budapest . . . We all tried to check those rumors."

"Every day a train left after the middle of May—sealed trains that went to Auschwitz," Halevi said. "Did you know that?"

"Yes. After the middle of May I knew that as a fact."

"Did you inform the Jews of Kolozsvár of what you knew?"

There was a long silence while Kasztner tried to collect himself. He had been leaning over the stand, his face in his hand, his forehead bathed in sweat. How could he explain to this court what it was like in Hungary during those months?

"I want to hear your answer, Doctor Kasztner," the judge repeated, with apparent sarcasm. Perhaps he was already thinking of Doctor Faustus, to whom he would later compare Kasztner.

"I told them everything I knew," Kasztner replied, faintly.

"Then why didn't the Jews of Kolozsvár know about all that?" the judge persisted.

"Your Honor asks me . . ." It took him a long time to pull himself together. His breathing was ragged, his shoulders slumped.

The judge ignored Cohen's intervention. He would not allow Kasztner the reprieve of an adjournment.

After a few moments of silence, Kasztner said: "I am sorry to say that the witnesses from Kolozsvár who testified here . . . they don't represent the true Jewry of Kolozsvár."

The sound of Hansi's anguished cry broke the silence that followed.

"Why didn't you say that you *had* told them in Kolozsvár, that they all knew?" Hansi demanded afterward. "And why didn't you tell them you couldn't have persuaded people to flee or to fight, that it was impossible, that no one had weapons, that no one believed in Auschwitz, that they couldn't . . . Why do you have to take the responsibility for everything, Rezső? Why?"[8]

He was silent. He had started to march up and down the hotel room, just as he had done in preparation for those terrible meetings with Eichmann.

"Why did you let them think that you were ever in control of anything? That anyone cared what this one small Jew from the provinces said or did? You played right into that man's hands." Hansi would always avoid mentioning Tamir by name. They knew, they had all known about Auschwitz. They had listened to the refugees from the rest of Nazi-occupied Europe. How was Rezső to tell them what they already knew? As for the rest of the Jews in Hungary, what was he supposed to do, take out an advertisement in a Nazi-controlled newspaper?

Tamir questioned him again about presenting himself as a representative of both the Jewish Agency and the World Jewish Congress when he provided Becher with his passport to freedom, and about his subsequent claim of having saved Becher in his letter to Eliezer Kaplan. Kasztner admitted to "errors in wording," to an overstatement of what he had accomplished, but he was sure he had been acting in the best interests of the State of Israel.

"Why didn't you tell them you felt you owed that man?" Hansi asked, referring to Becher. "There was that thing he wore on his ss belt: something about valor and loyalty. Tell them that we'd be dead without him. Why didn't you say that you felt you represented the Joint and the Agency when you signed that affidavit? You did, you know, that's what you did. All along, that's who we thought we were." She blamed Rezső's so-called friends who had encouraged him to testify and then, when they were on the stand, had lied that they had no idea about the exterminations, that they would not have gone into the trains had they known.

"Everyone needed a Judas goat," she said, years later. "In a country that prides itself on bravery, how could they admit that they were sheep for the slaughter? Was it not easier to let Rezső take the blame?"[9] When she was asked why Kasztner had not told the judge that his friends were lying, Hansi replied that he was a man who was used to assuming responsibility for others. "He couldn't admit that he had no control over events," she said. "That we were all victims." Both the resisters and the compliant had died in the Holocaust. What the Budapest Va'ada proved was that there was a third way, as one of the Kasztner train's passengers put it: "Even if fraught with human frailty, self-interest and vanity, given self-sacrificing heroism, money, brains and audacity, there was a third way to confront the murderers."[10] Kasztner had found that way.

When Kasztner made his final statement in court, he was quiet, dignified, restrained, a man who had come through fire—again. There was no showing off, no attempt to gain favor with a judge who he knew had turned against him. "Within our limited possibilities," he said, "we did our best. Compared to the dimensions of the catastrophe, that was very little."[11] Then he added that he hoped, one day, there would be time to reevaluate the whole tragedy and the part he and his colleagues had played.

When it came to his summing up for the prosecution, Cohen added fuel to Tamir's fire by stating that if, indeed, Kasztner was guilty of collaboration and profiting from his crimes, he must be sentenced to death. After that, Cohen's denials of the charges were pallid, his belated attacks on the defense witnesses thin, and his arguments about the apparent contradictions in Tamir's marshaling of the case unconvincing.

Tamir's summation, by comparison, was passionate, scathing, abusive, and rhetorical, as was his attack on the leaders of the Mapai. He accused them of deceit, of working with the Germans as they had worked with the British. He lashed out at them for concluding a reparations deal with Germany. "Our land has given in to forgetfulness and perfidy," he charged. "The bones of the slain millions of

Auschwitz had been plowed into German soil as fertilizer. And now these plowmen . . . [have become] the new leaders of Germany . . . In payment for Jewish blood, money has been offered and accepted." He accused the former Jewish Agency chiefs of "criminality and cowardice." He charged all the prosecution witnesses with lying to protect their political party. Directing his words not to the judge but to the Israeli public, he demanded that Kasztner be placed on trial by the state under the Nazis and Nazi Collaborators Law.[12]

The long trial had drawn public attention to the role played by all those who had failed to offer safe haven for the Jews. It examined the parts played by the Allies, the Jewish Agency, the Joint, and the leaders of the new nation of Israel, and it focused on the Zionists' determination of the selection process to find the "right" kind of immigrants for the new country, to the detriment of others.

Judge Halevi retired to write his judgment.

Public attention moved to the 1955 elections. Kasztner, at the request of his Mapai party, agreed to withdraw his candidacy for the government's slate. It was a bitter and deeply distressing decision but one he felt he had to make. He did not wish to be an issue during the coming elections. He lost his job at the Tel Aviv radio station; the reason given was that it was relocating the Hungarian service to Jerusalem. He had become a controversial figure in the Hungarian refugee community. His daughter, Zsuzsi, was snubbed and shouted at on her way to school. Her friends were no longer allowed to play with her. One of her teachers treated her as though she had become invisible in his class. Some shops refused to serve Bogyó. Tenants in the apartment building pretended not to see the Kasztners when they met in the stairwell or in the corridor. A northern kibbutz, where many of the Hungarian halutzim lived, invited the family to live there to escape unwanted attention in Tel Aviv, but Kasztner decided to stay; going to a remote kibbutz would have felt like running away, he explained to Bogyó. The apartment had grown quiet. "There were no more parties, no more laughter," Zsuzsi recalled. Her father marched up and down in the small space of the living room, his face set, his shoulders hunched, often examining sheets from the trial transcripts. He didn't understand how things had gone so terribly wrong.

He analyzed Shmuel Tamir's tactics, his relentless contrasting of the new Jew with the purportedly morally abhorrent "Jew of the Exile." There was no doubt that the judge agreed with Tamir.

"How can someone who never faced the Nazis judge those who did?" Kasztner asked. When Hansi inquired why he had not told the court that everyone, except perhaps the smallest children, had known but didn't want to know about the extermination camps, Kasztner shook his head. Surely people understood that the simplest and most prevalent attitude was to deny what you knew; that it would have been impossible to live another hour had you acknowledged what you knew; that many thousands had committed suicide because they couldn't avoid "knowing." How could he have made his inquisitor understand that the old, the women and children—all those not in the labor companies—had no means to resist?

More than six months after the testimony had been heard, Judge Halevi announced that he was ready to deliver his ruling. He returned to the courtroom at 8 AM on June 22, 1955. Once again the place was packed, the chief witnesses were present. Grünwald was in a cheerful, almost expansive mood, wholly uncharacteristic of his former dour self. Several of Kasztner's colleagues, the halutzim from the time of the German occupation, and some of his friends and family were there.

Hansi and Rezső had spent the day before the verdict in a small hotel near Salameh Square in Jerusalem. He had been morose and quiet, getting up from his chair only to pour himself more coffee or to stare out the window, with a freshly lit cigarette in his hand. He had not slept for several nights now. He was listless and pale, and he had lost so much weight that his suit hung from his shoulders as though he had borrowed another man's clothes. Always nattily dressed, he now looked ill and unkempt, his shirt collar too wide for his neck. On the day itself, some of his friends stayed with him, waiting; others went to the courtroom, to leave only after they were already certain of the negative outcome. Kasztner did not go. He knew what the verdict would be.[13]

Hansi was the last to return to the hotel. She would say later that she wanted to wait till the end because she had still hoped that Halevi would reverse the trend of his judgment. But in her heart she knew that she had delayed because she was dreading the moment when she had to tell Rezső the verdict.

When she entered the room, Rezső rushed to meet her. Holding her at arm's length, he demanded to know what had happened. When she tried a few circumlocutions, ways of softening the blow, he shouted at her, "What happened, Hansi? What happened?"[14]

Then she told him.

She had expected an outburst, but he did not react. It was as though the air had gone out of the man, as though he had suddenly become hollow. Nor did he say anything on the drive home to Tel Aviv. When he reached the apartment, he merely told Bogyó that the news would be bad in the papers. "The judge," he said, "has found in favor of Grünwald."

He wanted to prepare her for the next day, which he knew would be terrible for his wife and his child. But he didn't have the energy to talk. All he said was that Zsuzsi should skip school for a few days.

Then he went for a long walk, alone.

Judge Halevi had not disappointed Shmuel Tamir. He blamed the Jewish leadership in Hungary, particularly Rezső Kasztner, for not warning the Jews that the deportation journey would be their last, for not giving them a true account of what awaited them in Auschwitz-Birkenau, for not pushing them to escape or to mount an effective resistance. Further, he concluded that Kasztner had traded the lives of the majority of his fellow Jews for the lives of a privileged few.

He accepted Moshe Krausz's testimony and blamed Kasztner for working against Krausz, rather than with him. He stressed that Kasztner had perjured himself when he was first asked about Becher, and said Kasztner had testified on Becher's behalf in full knowledge that Becher was a war criminal. In Halevi's view, Kasztner had exonerated Becher in order to justify his own actions. Though, in the end, the judge did not allow the comparison to extend to the ruling Mapai Party, the notion of odious compromise, rather than pure opposition, was at the core of the judgment.

He blamed Kasztner for accepting the patronage of the Nazis and, in a deft reference to Virgil, he accused Kasztner of falling into the Germans' trap: "Timeo Danaos et dona ferentes [I fear the Greeks bearing gifts]." This idea was central to his judgment of Kasztner. In accepting the gift of some privileged lives from the Germans, the judge held, Kasztner had abandoned the vast majority of his fellow Jews. In a second literary reference, Halevi compared him to Faust, Goethe's anti-hero, who made a deal with the devil.[15] In Halevi's opinion, Kasztner "had sold his soul to the devil" in order to save the few. The only accusation that Halevi found unproved in his courtroom was that Kasztner had shared in Becher's booty. For that bit of libel, he ordered Grünwald to pay a fine of one pound.

The verdict made the headlines. Most newspapers accused Kasztner of being a Nazi collaborator, of assisting in mass murder. His photograph appeared on the front page of one paper under the caption "Eichmann's partner." The attorney general's office announced that it would appeal Halevi's verdict to the Supreme Court.

Kasztner issued a statement to the media the same day. He compared his case to that of Alfred Dreyfus, who, like himself, had fallen victim to a terrible injustice.[16] "History and all those who knew what happened during those woeful times will bear witness for me," Kasztner said. "Now that those dreadful years have passed, during which I tried, not without success, to serve my people and to rescue at least some of my brethren who were condemned to death by the Nazis, I will do everything to clear my name."[17]

A *New York Times* headline read "Quisling Charge Stirs All Israel." The article below it said that "the man branded by a Jerusalem judge as a quisling with 'collaboration in the fullest sense of the word' . . . was a candidate for the dominant Mapai party in two previous parliamentary elections and a high official in several Mapai-controlled ministries."[18] Prime Minister Sharett stated that the government would not comment on the matter while it was under appeal.

Opposition parties, led by the Herut, accused the Mapai of covering up for Kasztner, and some members of the Knesset described the judgment as a general indictment of the ruling party. In an emotional speech on July 5, Sharett defended Kasztner and charged that not many of the thousands he had saved had been asked to speak at the trial. He said that the Jewish Agency, though it doubted the veracity of the blood-for-goods offer, had continued negotiations with the ss in order to gain time.

Kasztner's world had turned inside out. He was ashamed and confused; his sense of self-assurance was gone and his ability to deal with the problems of everyday life challenged. The simple tasks of going to a store, of helping his daughter with her daily trials, of comforting Bogyó, who was too depressed to get out of bed in the mornings, were proving too much for him.

Zsuzsi's memories of those days are surprisingly clear, though she was not yet ten years old. Her classmates would run after her in the street, throwing stones. Her beloved father, of whom she had been so proud, was labeled a Nazi, and she herself the daughter of a Nazi. She felt abandoned, friendless, and afraid to confide her fears to anyone. Dreadful graffiti appeared on the outside walls of their apartment building; an upstairs tenant threw garbage onto their balcony. Children in the street called her a murderess.[19]

Not a single sentence in all of the 274 pages of the verdict offered a refuge, a consolation. The entire document was a lethal attack on Kasztner. Several papers and some Knesset representatives were demanding that he be charged under the Nazi Collaborators Law.

Kasztner stopped going to coffeehouses, concerts, and parties, and he left the apartment only to work or when he was meeting Hansi. His friends treated him with exaggerated care, as though he were suffering from a terminal illness; they spoke softly in his presence, avoiding any mention of the case.

On July 7, Tamir filed a charge of perjury against him in Jerusalem District Court on the grounds that he had denied filing an affidavit on behalf of Becher at Nuremberg. A few timid pieces appeared in Kasztner's defense, but there were scant words of outrage at the injustice of the verdict. Only the former members of the Hungarian, Slovak, Polish, and Czech halutz underground movement rose to defend Kasztner. Many of them had worked with the Va'ada in Hungary and had witnessed Kasztner's courage and fortitude. The verdict had, they believed, besmirched not only one man's honor but also that of the whole movement. Alex Barzel's articles expressed their feelings most clearly. He defended Kasztner and those who had stood with him. His motives were "pure and sincere," he wrote. "The period was sullied and tragic . . . The verdict was a terrible injustice to him personally and to all of us."[20]

Humbled and lonely, without sufficient funds to be able to withdraw from public scrutiny, Kasztner continued to work long hours at the *Új Kelet* offices, venturing home only after dark.

CHAPTER 33

The Consequences

*The affair of the Judenrat (and perhaps also the Kasztner case)
should, in my view, be left to the tribunal of history in the coming
generation. The Jews who were safe and secure during the Hitler
era ought not to presume to judge their brethren who were burned
and slaughtered, nor the few who survived.*

David Ben-Gurion[1]

On Wednesday, June 29, 1955, the *New York Times* reported
that "Premier Moshe Sharett will force the resignation of
the Israeli cabinet," then "attempt to form a new government. These actions follow a tense session yesterday of the Knesset
concerning the Kaszner–Greenwald [sic] case ... there was a
motion of no confidence in the government in connection with the
case."[2] Sharett resigned, presented his new coalition, and then let the
government fall. He had no choice but to call a new election.
The Kasztner case haunted the halls of the Knesset, though most of
the Mapai's representatives made no overt mention of it. Only
Sharett dared state that the court's decision dealt with something

almost beyond judgment, with the tragedy of a whole people. Menachem Begin and his Herut Party continued to charge the Mapai with collaboration. One of their slogans read, "When you vote for Mapai, you vote for a Jew who turned Jews over to the Gestapo."[3] In their newspaper, *Herut*, they accused the Mapai of willingly handing Joel Brand over to the British, and Kasztner of preventing armed resistance to the deportations. A July 25 *Herut* headline read, "Betar Groups in Nazi Hungary Planned and Demanded an Armed Uprising—Kasztner Destroyed These Plans."

The *New York Times* reported that the judgment stirred all Israel, that "the question of how Jews should have behaved in Nazi-occupied Europe in 1944 on the brink of disaster was of such tremendous historic importance that it should not be adjudicated by a lone judge sitting in Jerusalem eleven years later."[4] Moshe Karen of the Tel Aviv newspaper *Haaretz* was one of the few journalists in Israel who dared criticize Halevi's judgment. "The judge explicitly admits that there was no hope of organizing a Jewish resistance . . . and if that is the case, what does he want?" he asked.[5]

The word "Kasztnerism," meaning duplicitous collaboration with the enemy, began to appear in speeches and in newspapers. Sharett was drawn into the fray, charging his enemies with base opportunism. He was forced, again, to defend his actions during Brand's mission and made much of his efforts to induce the Allies to bomb the train lines leading to Auschwitz, yet he was trapped into admitting that he, too, had been in favor of negotiating with the Nazis. As Karen of *Haaretz* wrote, "The repercussions of the Kasztner trial will continually poison the air we breathe," at least until the air could be cleared by a new judgment.[6]

At one Mapai meeting, Yoel Palgi suggested that the party adopt the proposal that, if Kasztner was a collaborator, he must be sentenced to death. No one was willing to make that statement in public—or not yet. There was some hope that the court appeal would help both Kasztner and the party.

In the July 1955 elections, the Mapai lost five seats in the Knesset, and its major opposition, Begin's Herut, doubled its seats. David Ben-Gurion returned as prime minister. Unlike Sharett, Ben-Gurion had managed to distance himself from the whole Kasztner trial. He claimed he did not even bother reading the verdict.

Kasztner, determined to clear his name, spent many hours with lawyers, planning the appeal, working on the details. He told an interviewer that he was now sorry he had allowed the attorney general's office to handle the case before Halevi, that too many witnesses who would have painted a true picture of events in Budapest had not been called. Afraid of making enemies of his former colleagues, he did not wish to stress that he had acted on behalf of the Jewish Agency. He felt honor-bound to resist hiding behind the Mapai leadership; in truth, he agreed with both their motives and their actions. Even his testimony on behalf of Wisliceny—though this story had not come up during the trial—had made sense because Wisliceny knew where Eichmann was hiding, and finding Eichmann and bringing him to trial was more important than seeing Wisliceny hang.

The judge had become a tool of Grünwald's defense, allowing Tamir's harassment, badgering, and endless speeches that served no purpose other than to bolster the counsel's own ego. Kasztner had been afraid to make this point publicly at the time, as had most Israeli critics of the trial, but one or two independent observers from the United States had made the same observations.

At no time had either Chaim Cohen or the judge taken into account the point that Kasztner's primary objective had been to gain time, to keep negotiating till the war was over, to delay the Nazis' murder machine for as long as possible. The evidence of those saved through the Strasshof scheme was ignored. Halevi had disregarded history.

The appeal was filed on August 21 over the signature of the attorney general. It was brief. It took issue with all of Halevi's conclusions and petitioned the Supreme Court not only to reverse the decision but to find Grünwald guilty of the original charge of criminal libel.

As Kasztner's despair deepened, his anger grew. His few interviews, now, were carefully planned, or so Hansi thought. She was the only adviser he accepted, the only person who was welcome to call on him at any time. The others, even Dezsö Hermann, felt they were no longer wanted. Hermann, who had appeared as a witness for the prosecution, had never explained why he claimed on the stand that he had never heard of Auschwitz-Birkenau from Kasztner or from anyone else.[7]

Kasztner sometimes spent the night with Hansi, arriving home in the early hours of the morning or going directly to his office from her apartment. Joel, guilty about his part in the verdict, absented himself on these occasions. He would leave with his package of cigarettes, his jacket flung casually over his shoulder, nodding at Kasztner as he left, banging the door behind him. Understanding Kasztner's state of mind, even Bogyó thought it was wise to let them be together, hoping Hansi could help persuade him to leave Israel, or at least Tel Aviv. Kasztner had received and refused an invitation from former Hungarian halutzim, suggesting that the Kasztners go to live on their kibbutz near Haifa until the Supreme Court reached its decision on the appeal.

"What would we do on a kibbutz?" Rezső always asked.

"I could work in the kitchens—," Bogyó ventured.

"You have no idea how to work in a kitchen," Rezső told her. She had learned how to do a lot of things since she had arrived in Palestine, and he had never criticized her before. "And I suppose I would dig potatoes?" he suggested.

It was typical of him, she said later, that he would never run from danger, that he always looked it in the eye, daring it to approach. The danger was so real that the government assigned two bodyguards to watch over the apartment and to follow him at a discreet distance when he ventured outside.

In March 1956, the chief magistrate in Jerusalem dismissed the charge of perjury against Kasztner. He agreed with Kasztner's contention that the affidavit had been filed at the Denazification Court. Tamir raged that he would take the matter to a higher court, but the year presented greater challenges than a retrial of the perjury case.

On October 29, 1956, the Israeli army invaded Egypt and occupied the Sinai Peninsula. It was a pre-emptive strike at the heart of Egypt's occupation of the Suez Canal. The invasion's chief achievement, as far as the Israelis were concerned, was that it signaled to the surrounding Arab states that Israel could preserve its security against its enemies. Headlines in Israeli papers were occupied with news of the victory and the ensuing peace negotiations. Kasztner was no longer in the headlines. The government canceled his protection.

He continued to work for *Új Kelet* and coproduced some radio programs. He took on some freelance work as a translator. Sometimes, there were flashes of the old Kasztner, the man who could make the women in the office smile when he walked by their desks. Tomy Lapid said that Kasztner seemed aware of his life being in danger. "He became a hunted man," Lapid said. "And he knew it."[8] Kasztner now looked along the street carefully before he stepped out of a doorway; he hesitated when he turned corners; once, when a car backfired, he ducked into a store; he stayed close to walls; he had seemed nervous even while the government-appointed guards followed him. There were so many abusive, threatening calls that he stopped answering his phone at the office. At home, too, he disconnected the telephone. He didn't want his wife or daughter listening to deranged ravings about how his life was to end.

Late one evening he called Zsuzsi to him, put his arm around her, and told her that no matter what happened, she had to remember that her father had done his best to save human lives. "There are two kinds of people in this world," he said, "menschen [good human beings] and the others who are not menschen." "He himself was a real mensch," Zsuzsi says, "and he wanted me to be the same." In hindsight, she realized that her father believed he would not live much longer.

On March 3, 1957, Kasztner was working the night shift at the editorial offices of *Új Kelet*. He drove a colleague and his longtime boss, Ernő Márton, home. A few minutes after midnight, Kasztner parked his car in front of his apartment building at 6 Sderot Emanuel Street. While he was still in the driver's seat, he was approached by two young men. A third, he saw, was standing in the shadows of the building. One of the men asked if he was "Doctor Kasztner." When he replied that, yes, he was, the man drew a gun, but it misfired. Kasztner opened the car door, pushing his assailant aside, then ran toward the entrance of the building. The man fired, again, twice in quick succession. This time the bullets found their target. Kasztner ran a few more steps, then collapsed. He shouted for help as the three assailants fled. He saw the gunman run to a jeep and speed off.

He was still conscious when the first person from the building arrived at the scene and tried to administer first aid. A woman who had gone to her balcony when the shots rang out ran to wake Bogyó. Another man heard Kasztner say that the assailant had gone in a jeep; that neighbor jumped on his bike and gave chase. Two men emerged from the jeep near the city zoo, where their pursuer, a former army man, found a phone booth and called the police.

A crowd gathered around Kasztner. Someone had called an ambulance. Bogyó, a neighbor reported later, seemed strangely calm when she saw that Rezső had been shot. Perhaps she, too, had been expecting something like this to happen. She knelt next to her bleeding husband, put a pillow under his head, covered him with a blanket, stroked his forehead, and whispered to him.

The ambulance took Kasztner to Hadassah Hospital. He remained conscious while the doctors examined him. He asked for the police to attend while he was X-rayed to determine where the bullets had entered. His statement to the police was detailed, cogent, precise. He tried to console Bogyó as he was wheeled into the operating room.

Friends and a few passengers from the Kasztner train went to the hospital with flowers. There were hundreds of telegrams with good wishes for a speedy convalescence. Strangely, there was even a telegram from Malchiel Grünwald, wishing him a complete recovery despite "our fundamental disagreements." Shmuel Tamir expressed shock and disgust at the attack on the man he had worked so hard to destroy. Zsuzsi sent her father a note with her warm kisses. Yoel Palgi sent flowers. Newspapers that had denounced Kasztner now shouted in headlines that the attackers had aimed at the heart of the nation of Israel.

Kasztner's room was guarded by two policemen. He was conscious but spoke little. He wished to see no visitors except his immediate family and Hansi. Bogyó had intended to bar Hansi from the room, but she managed to plead her way in. At one point he asked her, "Why did they do this to me?" Hansi was with him on March 12 as his condition began to deteriorate.

On March 15, at 7:20 AM, Rezső Kasztner died.

CHAPTER 34

The Aftermath

I cannot refrain from expressing again my sorrow over the impression which may have been made in some people regarding the phrasing of my testimony about Becher, and the result of it. Neither I nor my friends have anything to hide in this whole affair, and we do not regret that we acted in accordance with our conscience, despite all that has been done to us in this trial.

Rezső Kasztner, from his statement after the Grünwald trial

We shall not rest nor shall we remain silent until your name is cleared.

Alexander Rosenfeld, at Rezső Kasztner's funeral

On Sunday, March 17, 1957, Rezső Kasztner's coffin was set up in front of the Hadassah Hospital in Tel Aviv[1] to provide his many admirers with an opportunity to pay their respects in public and to show their solidarity with the family. His mother, his two brothers, Bogyó, and Zsuzsi stood next to the coffin. Though neither David Ben-Gurion nor Moshe Sharett came, the Mapai were represented by Attorney General Chaim Cohen and State Secretary Teddy Kollek. Some of his old colleagues from Budapest and Kolozsvár, and the halutzim who had worked with him paid their respects. Hansi stood near the coffin but out of Bogyó's immediate circle. Yoel Palgi was there, as were many of the passengers from the Kasztner train. At the Bilu Synagogue, Rezső's brother Gyula, his voice breaking as he read the words, recited the Kaddish, a prayer for the dead. Zsuzsi sobbed throughout the service.

Kasztner was interred at the Nachlat Yitzhak Cemetery in Givataim, on the outskirts of Tel Aviv, amid numerous declarations of friendship and tears. Most of the speakers vowed to continue the struggle not only to clear his name but also to enshrine it among the heroes of the Holocaust. Those he had helped to survive promised to take care of his family.

Új Kelet published a moving obituary written by Ernő Márton. He praised Kasztner's capacity for wit and erudition and his obsession with saving Jewish lives, his death-defying courage, his self-sacrifice, and his ambition to do something great, something "eternally significant for his people."[2]

Within days of the murder, the police arrested twenty-four-year-old Zeev Eckstein, who admitted his guilt during interrogation. Based on his confession, Joseph Menkes, a former member of the terrorist Stern Gang, was then arrested, as was, later, Yaakov Cheruti, a lawyer. The police found a large cache of guns and ammunition at Eckstein's and Menkes's homes. In a prepared statement, the police claimed to have discovered an organized underground with plans for further terrorist acts against the government, but, even at the time, there were serious doubts about this version of events. A year before the murder, Eckstein reputedly had worked for Shin Bet, the government's security service of the day. He had been used as an undercover agent in the right-wing underground. Some journalists suggested that the government, finding Kasztner an embarrassment, had been complicit in his murder. Adam Heller, who had been in a Boy Scout group with Eckstein, remembers him as somewhat slow-witted and craving acceptance, eager to show that he could do everything everyone else did, and better. He could not have been the man who planned the assassination.[3]

Uri Avneri, the journalist who—long before Halevi's judgment—had accused Kasztner of complicity in the murder of his fellow Jews, stated that Shin Bet silenced Kasztner at the ruling party's behest. Menachem Begin wrote in *Herut* that the assassins' bullets prevented Kasztner from revealing secrets he knew about the governing party, secrets that would have damaged its standing with the people of Israel. He also hinted that the timing of Kasztner's murder had the desired effect of deflecting attention from the Israeli army's withdrawal from the Sinai Peninsula, a controversial issue at that time. No evidence has ever been found to justify this accusation,[4] though the rumors continued. Ben-Gurion's personal interest later in the early release of the convicted killers added fuel to the speculation.

The three men were tried, convicted of murder, and sentenced to life imprisonment on January 7, 1958.

A week later, the Supreme Court, in a four-to-one decision, exonerated Rezső Kasztner. The five judges' words were read into the record on January 15. Justice Shimon Agranat noted that Judge Halevi had erred about the circumstances of the Rescue Committee in Budapest in 1944–45; that he had based his decisions on "knowledge gained from hindsight," and that Kasztner had acted in what he believed to be the best interests of all the people, not only those he had managed to save. He refuted Halevi's statements point by point, including his wholehearted reliance on the testimony of Moshe Krausz. The only point on which Agranat agreed with the original judgment concerned Kasztner's confounding affidavit on behalf of Kurt Becher. Two of the other four judges concurred with Agranat in rejecting Halevi's verdict. They were sharply critical of the way in which the original judge had conducted the trial; the fourth judge, while agreeing with Halevi that Kasztner had become an unwitting ally of the Nazis, stressed that the man had firmly believed that he was achieving vastly more than the rescue of the few and had been working on a much larger plan, but that time was, in the end, not on his but on Eichmann's side. The fifth judge, Moshe Silberg, wrote a dissenting opinion. He still believed that the Nazis could not have carried out their deportation program in Hungary with the speed and ease they did had the Jews been aware of where the trains were going and what awaited them at the end of the line.

In the key matter of collaboration with the Nazis, the majority accepted the attorney general's appeal and convicted Malchiel Grünwald of libel. In recognition of his advanced age, they handed him a one-year suspended sentence and a fine of £200.[5]

In the midst of the joys of vindication that followed the Supreme Court's decision, notes of doubt and of unrelieved sadness remained. The doubt was voiced by several journalists who kept on criticizing the man they claimed had sold his soul; the deal with Becher continued to haunt Kasztner's memory. The profound sadness was expressed by his widow and his daughter: the new verdict had come too late to save his life.

Judge Halevi was on the tribunal for the 1961 trial of Adolf Eichmann and was, finally, appointed to the Supreme Court of Israel in 1963. He left the bench in 1969 to be eligible for election to the Knesset on the Herut ticket. At the time, he told a journalist at the Tel Aviv newspaper *Ma'ariv* that his words about Kasztner had been misinterpreted by the media and that, on reflection, perhaps he should have chosen them more carefully. It had not been necessary to bring Satan into the verdict, he said; the facts of the case and his own two hundred carefully composed conclusions spoke for themselves. Contrary to his own high expectations, in the Knesset he became an indifferent, largely ignored backbencher, a considerable comedown from his days in the limelight of the two biggest trials in Israel's history.

* * *

Uri Avneri, whose columns had contributed to the atmosphere of hate and repugnance created by the Kasztner trial, had a chance in the late 1950s to reconsider his words: "Kasztner was caught up in events which were so much bigger than an ordinary—or even an extraordinary—person could handle," he wrote in his own magazine, *Haolam Hazeh*. "How can we judge what was right and wrong in such a situation? In the end I must say I tend toward Kasztner. I don't believe he was a traitor." That fine summation of where Avneri stood would have been welcome a couple of years earlier. Now it hardly registered.

Bogyó Kasztner, deeply depressed after her husband's murder, tried to start a new life with her daughter, but few job opportunities presented themselves. Her early education in ancient history was not useful in the Israel of the 1960s. She had no work experience and no idea how to acquire the necessary skills to support them both. A few of Kasztner's friends put a small fund aside, but it was never enough. Teddy Kollek,[6] who remained an occasional visitor to the Kasztner home, wrote to the president of the World Zionist Organization that Kasztner's widow had been left with money insufficient even to pay the meager rent on their apartment. Sharett and other members of the Mapai offered no assistance. Bogyó's claim for work-related insurance on the death of her husband was turned down: it was deemed that Kasztner had not died in the course or as a result of his work. In the end, she was given the opportunity to open a national lottery stall.

She never allowed anyone to call her a "widow" before she died in 1973. For Bogyó, as for Hansi, Rezső had not really died.

When Zsuzsi Kasztner was approached by Ben-Gurion in 1963 about the release of Menkes, one of the three men convicted of murdering her father, she said she felt nothing about his release. His serving the full sentence would not return her father to her, and at least she could return Menkes to his own children. She was not consulted about the release of the other two men. All three were set free six years after their arrest. When Eckstein was interviewed by Israeli television, he said he still believed he had done the right thing in murdering Rezső Kasztner.[7]

Zsuzsi Kasztner-Michaeli met Eckstein shortly before I spoke to her in April 2006. Her own impression from that conversation was that her father's murderer now regretted his hasty action. Zsuzsi lives today in a modest apartment in one of the outlying suburbs of Tel Aviv. She is divorced. She works as a nurse, six days a week. A dark-haired woman with a thin, intense face, she has her mother's long, aristocratic fingers and her father's keen, intelligent questioning of the obvious. She has learned not to be trusting.

She cares for five cats and a crippled dog. In her living room there is a large oil painting of her grandfather, József Fischer. There are photographs of her mother, Bogyó, smiling, looking exceptionally beautiful with her hair pulled back, her dark eyes challenging the camera. In a back room there is her father's old Remington type-writer and his desk lamp. She plays me a disk of her father and mother chatting and singing in Hungarian, her own childish laugh-ter in the background. It is a faked radio broadcast Rezső made for some family occasion. He jocularly interviewed his wife and daugh-ter as if they were famous personalities, and then they sang some Hungarian songs together. She has nurtured their memory and will continue to do so till the end of her life.

"My father taught me Shakespeare," she says. "I could recite Hamlet's famous soliloquy when I was ten years old. Ironic that he loved that . . . 'To be or not to be / That is the question.' " She met Kurt Becher for the first time when he was already eighty-five, still handsome, still a commanding presence. "He referred to me as *Die Tochter von meinem guten Freund, Rudolf,* 'the daughter of my good friend, Rudolf.' "

Afterward, she visited Becher several times in Germany. He was proud of what he and Kasztner had done during the war. When she asked him why he had not offered to testify on behalf of her father in Jerusalem, he said anything he did on behalf of Kasztner would have hurt his friend's chances of a fair trial. Only at Zsuzsi's urging did he agree to the 1994 interview with Ilana Dayan. During that inter-view, Becher characterized the Kasztner trial as a crime. "He was the only man who was really successful in doing something for the Jew-ish people in that situation, at that time," Becher said.

One of Zsuzsi's daughters, Mayrav, has become a celebrated televi-sion interviewer in Tel Aviv. She has the opinionated, direct style that was so characteristic of her grandfather—but now it is more fashionable to show off one's intelligence.

Moshe Krausz, the indefatigable bureaucrat, continued to blame everyone who had overstepped the bounds of his own limitations back in Budapest. As late as 1971, he wrote to Carl Lutz protesting angrily that what Lutz had done in 1944 with his, Krausz's, covering letter had been illegal and unauthorized. The package containing the Auschwitz Protocols that should have gone to Chaim Posner of the Jewish Agency had been readdressed. The fact that the actual recipient, George Mandel-Mantello, by publicizing Rudolf Vrba's report may have saved thousands of Jewish lives did not matter to Krausz any more in 1971 than it had in 1944.[8]

* * *

Joel Brand spent years working on his story but somehow couldn't get it finished. When Alex Weissberg offered to help him, Joel didn't realize he would become a character in someone else's book. He complained, his son Dani said, that some people had pressured Weissberg not to tell the whole story—that it could be damaging to the former Jewish Agency people.

Dani said that Joel moved to Germany after the Kasztner trial; he had a job there with the Israeli Consulate. In the summer of 1955 he went to see Becher in Bremen. He was interested in hearing about the German side during their negotiations with the Va'ada. Joel and Hansi wrote a book later, after the trial, after Joel returned from Europe.

Joel Brand died in 1964.

Hansi Brand continued to work and live modestly, as she always had. Her gloves operation supported her and her sons. Later, when the boys had grown up and she retired, she worked at an orphanage. "There were a hundred and twenty children in the home and they all called her 'Mom,' " recalled her friend Eva Carmeli. "She always remained more interested in other people than in herself. Toward the

end of her life, with both hips gone and barely able to walk, she continued to deliver chocolates to the homeless."[9] Hansi had many
friends and admirers, some from the early days in Hungary when she
had selflessly given whatever she had to refugees. "I think the most
important thing was not to be a hero but to survive," she told an
interviewer. "No one who was not there, least of all the judge in that
shameful trial, had any notion what it was like to live in Hungary in
those days. We acted according to our consciences."

One of her friends said that Hansi continued to love Rezső even
after he died. She never stopped thinking and talking about him. In
one of her last interviews she compared him to a butterfly that had
flown too close to the flame—the flame fed by the fires of
Auschwitz. As for the judge's metaphor, she said, Rezső in his
supreme self-confidence had indeed thought he was dealing with the
devil on an equal footing. And yes, he would have sold his soul to
save the lives of others.

Hansi died on April 9, 2000.

Shmuel Tamir was elected to the Knesset in 1967. He had tried to
have the matter of the Mapai's purported culpability in the Holocaust reopened after the Eichmann trial, using Eichmann as a key
witness, but failed. After donning the colors of several parties, he
made it to the position of minister of justice. Late in life, he returned
to the practice of law. He went to the media every time there was an
event or memorial to Rezső Kasztner. His vilification of the man
never let up. His memoirs reveal, perhaps unintentionally, that the
Kasztner trial was the highlight of his life and career. It is, certainly,
the largest chunk of a very thick two-volume work. A few weeks
before he died in 1987, he gave an interview criticizing a radio play
that had spoken of Kasztner as a victim.

Late in life Tamir faced what one of Kasztner's admirers referred to
as a "Kasztnerian dilemma" when, in May 1985, he represented
Minister of Defense Yitzhak Rabin at negotiations for the release of
Israeli prisoners in the Lebanon war. He agreed to the exchange of
1,100 terrorists for only three Israeli soldiers.

CHAPTER 35

The Banality of Evil

Justice insists on the importance of Adolf Eichmann, son of Karl Eichmann, the man in the glass booth built for his protection: medium-sized, slender, middle-aged, with receding hair, ill-fitting teeth, and nearsighted eyes, who throughout the trial keeps craning his scraggly neck toward the bench (not once does he face the audience), and who desperately and for the most part successfully maintains his self-control despite the nervous tic to which his mouth must have become subject long before the trial started.

Hannah Arendt, *Eichmann in Jerusalem*[1]

Otto Adolf Eichmann, former lieutenant-colonel of the German Reich, was captured in Buenos Aires, Argentina, on May 11, 1960, by Israeli agents. He was transported to Tel Aviv and brought to trial under Israel's Nazis and Nazi Collaborators (Punishment) Law in Jerusalem District Court on April 11, 1961. He spent over a month on the stand, testifying about his participation in the Final Solution.

He was still proud of his wartime "idealism." Unlike the

"businessmen" of Kurt Becher's kind, he maintained his full belief in the cause of making Europe free of Jews. In the beginning, his idea had been to help them emigrate. He had, personally, simplified the emigration system for Austrian Jews. Until he arrived, he said, as a mere second lieutenant in 1938, there had been nightmarish difficulties with the paperwork. Without his dedication, it would have taken years to "cleanse" the country of its Jews. He, alone, took credit for devising a system that fed people in at the entrance to a building, where they could hand over their property and their citizenship and walk out through the exit the same day, their departure visas and entry permits for Palestine in hand. His successful system would have been extended to the rest of Europe, he claimed, had the Allies and the neutral nations agreed to take more Jews.

When the supply of exit visas to Palestine dried up—Eichmann said it was the British who caused the difficulties, not the Germans—he pioneered the concept of a homeland for Jews in the Radom district of Poland and, later, in Madagascar. Eichmann himself had visited the Nisko area near the San River in Poland and found it highly suitable, but Hans Frank, Hitler's appointed governor of occupied Poland, destroyed that plan. Madagascar, situated off the east coast of Africa, was difficult to reach when the Allies were interfering with sea routes. Eichmann said it was only after his unappreciative superiors—Himmler, Hitler, Heydrich—had nixed the various "geographic solutions" that he reluctantly agreed to follow Hitler's directive for a "physical solution."

Eichmann was still disappointed that his ideas had been ignored and bitter that he had not progressed beyond the status of lieutenant colonel while others, less dedicated and less hardworking than he, had been rewarded with higher ranks. Becher, for example, was made a full colonel before the war ended. "Himmler had sent his own man to Budapest," Eichmann said. "Becher dealt with Jewish emigration."

After Hitler's attack on Russia in June 1941 Lieutenant General Reinhard Heydrich, chief of the Reich Security Office, had instructed Eichmann to proceed with the implementation of a "Final Solution to the Jewish problem in Europe." By that time, practically all Jewish emigration had ceased, because of Britain's position on its Palestinian protectorate and because of Hitler's friendship with the Grand Mufti of Jerusalem. Eichmann confirmed Wisliceny's Nuremberg testimony that the Mufti "constantly incited him to accelerate the extermination measures."[2]

Eichmann testified that he had been baffled by Heydrich's speech at the Wannsee Conference in January 1942. At first he had not understood what "Final Solution" meant. To elucidate the matter, Heydrich explained that "the Führer has ordered the physical extermination of the Jews." Eichmann told the Israeli court that he and his fellow officers had sat in silence for a few minutes while they absorbed the meaning of that phrase. Strangely, that may have been the last time those words were spoken openly. Afterward, all discussions and conversations employed euphemisms for mass killings: Final Solution, special treatment, labor in the east. At his trial, Eichmann made no effort to use the softening language.

He recalled with convincing horror how mobile gas trucks had been used in the east, how hundreds of Jews—women and children, young and old—had been ordered to strip before being packed into trucks, where they were killed slowly and agonizingly by gas. He remembered the trucks being opened after the shrieking had died down and the bodies being thrown into ditches. In Minsk he had witnessed a troop of Sonderkommando shoot hundreds of huddling, naked people and throw them into ditches. In Treblinka he had observed a column of naked women and children being marched into a large hall to be gassed. He had refused to watch through the special peephole that made it easy for the shift workers to note when the doors could be opened again and the bodies removed for burning.

Eichmann had been disgusted by what he had seen, he testified at the trial. He was repelled by the dreadful acts that young German recruits were forced to commit, and he felt sorry for the untrained boys who were given such orders. If he felt anything for the dying Jews, he did not say so. Personally, he had never killed a single Jew, he said.

As a fellow idealist, he said he had no difficulty in understanding Rezső Kasztner and Joel Brand, but he never had his heart in the "trucks for lives" or the "blood for wares" deal he had instructed Brand to take to Istanbul. It had been Himmler's idea. As an idealist, he justified it to himself with the belief that the German army needed whatever was on the list, even if it turned out to be fewer trucks and more coffee. In a small way, the exchange had worked; in a larger sense, though, he said bitterly, it had guaranteed the safety of some of the "gentlemen" soldiers, men such as Kurt Becher. Eichmann did not hide behind any pretense of humanity.

Eichmann talked of Kasztner as a like-minded person. "Kasztner smoked cigarettes as though he were in a coffeehouse. While we talked, he would smoke one aromatic cigarette after another, taking them from a silver case and lighting them with a little silver lighter . . . With his great polish and reserve, he would have made an ideal Gestapo officer himself." Eichmann claimed that Kasztner had "agreed to help keep the Jews from resisting deportation if I would close my eyes and let a few hundred or a few thousand young Jews emigrate to Palestine . . . He wanted only biologically valuable material. It was a good bargain."

When Hansi Brand heard this part of Eichmann's statement, she said that the prosecutors could discount everything that Eichmann had said.[3] The facts were that only a very small proportion of those the Va'ada saved were young. As for Eichmann's contention that Kasztner had been keenly interested in "biologically valuable material," that was language used only by the Nazis. In her own testimony, she detailed how Eichmann had frequently talked about "positive biological material." He viewed Jews from the Carpathians as "positive" because "they were Jews in body and soul." How could one tell the difference between a biologically valuable Jew and an intellectually valuable one? And how could Kasztner have kept order in the ghettos? Who asked him? His only trip outside Budapest had been to his hometown, she said, and even there no one believed him about the death camps. In a later interview with Randolph Braham, she said most of the Jews in Kolozsvár knew what the deportations meant. They had heard about Auschwitz from Polish refugees.

Eichmann remembered Hansi and smiled at the memory. "She was the smart young woman who was there with Kasztner," he said.

Eichmann thought she was smarter than Kasztner—at least, she knew more than he did.

Throughout the Eichmann trial, the prosecution made every effort to avoid letting the Kasztner trial proceedings seep back into the courtroom and thence into the headlines. In this objective they were largely successful, despite Shmuel Tamir's insistence that the matter of Malchiel Grünwald's conviction be re-examined in light of Eichmann's testimony and that Eichmann be asked more questions about his dealings with Kasztner.

André Biss, who had worked with Kasztner in Budapest and therefore knew Eichmann, was not called to testify, because chief prosecutor Gideon Hausner discovered that he was going to use the opportunity to defend Kasztner's actions. As Biss later recalled of Eichmann's trial, "102 witnesses for the prosecution were heard, [and] at least 90 of them had not only never met Eichmann but, until the end of the war, had never even heard his name." Biss had traveled to Israel fully expecting to be called, but after he told the prosecutor that he would not give evidence unless he was free to tell the truth and that the truth involved testimony on behalf of Kasztner, Hausner dispensed with him as a witness.[4]

In an interview he gave *Life* magazine, Eichmann described Kasztner as "an ice-cold lawyer and a fanatical Zionist." He claimed that they had "negotiated entirely as equals. People forget that. We were political opponents trying to arrive at a settlement and we trusted each other perfectly."

The difference was, as Hansi remarked when she saw the article, that only one of them could have sent the other to the gas chambers. How could this murderous criminal compare himself with Kasztner, whose sole interest in those meetings had been to save lives? And why would the media repeat these ravings? Nevertheless, the portrait of Kasztner that Eichmann presented was a testimonial of its kind. It demonstrated how well Kasztner had played the life-and-death roulette game, and how well he had fooled this notorious architect of the Holocaust into believing that they had been equal partners.

In his concluding statement, Eichmann said: "I am not the monster I am made out to be. I am the victim of a fallacy." He did not elaborate on the meaning of "fallacy," but it can be assumed that he meant the murder of Europe's Jews had been based on some fallacious beliefs, though he never articulated which ones. Four years before the trial, in an interview with Willem Sassen, a Dutch journalist, he had said without reservation: "There is nothing I have to regret. Had we killed eleven million Jews as contemplated, however, I would have been happier." The eleven million referred to all the Jews of Europe, Great Britain, Ireland, and Switzerland—a number that Eichmann had calculated would fall into his hands once the war was won.[5]

On December 15, 1961, Adolf Eichmann was sentenced to death. On March 29, 1962, after one week of deliberation, the Court of Appeal confirmed the judgment.

On May 31, 1962, after all appeals had been exhausted, Adolf Eichmann was hanged. His body was cremated and his ashes scattered outside the borders of Israel.

CHAPTER 36

Other Lives

We are not dealing here with something that is dead and buried;
we are not taking scrap metal from the stores of history. Not one of
the survivors will ever be the same as before; nor will human soci-
ety again be able to be what it was.

Gideon Hausner, chief prosecutor at the trial of Adolf
Eichmann

When she smiled, you could still see that Olga Munk had
been a very beautiful woman. She sat on a white armchair in the driveway of her home near a synagogue in
the west end of the city of Toronto, Canada. Her hands rested in her
lap. She wore a chiffon scarf over her hair, loosely tied, so you could
see the way the strands of hair were still thick and perfectly arranged.
She wore heavy baize stockings despite the heat. "It's arthritis, you
know," she said. Otherwise, she felt comfortable with old age.

She remembered the side slats of the cattle cars, the way people sat
on the floors, the smell of unwashed bodies, the one waste bucket
they all shared. "There was no chance of modesty now." She

remembered Auspitz, and the German guards laughing when the
women stripped naked.

In Bergen-Belsen her six-year-old son, John, had thought it amazing that his mother was in charge of cleaning the latrines. She had
always been so fastidious.

John Brunner remembers sitting next to his mother's drawn-up
knees, watching the sunlight race through the slats of the boxcar;
lying in a field, the wheaty smell of the July heat; the persistence of
the mosquitoes during the night. In Bergen-Belsen when the bell
rang for meals, he was already waiting, his bowl outstretched. He
remembers the hunger.

He is now a barrister in Toronto. His wide-set windows give onto
the financial core of the city. He had never even heard of Rezső
Kasztner until the 1996 Toronto International Film Festival presented an Israeli television movie about the notorious libel trial in
Jerusalem.[1] His stepfather, Louis Munk, hadn't wanted to see it, but
Olga persuaded him. Afterward, Louis didn't want to discuss the
film.

"I think that's when I became interested in the story," John said. "I
started reading about it."

Egon Mayer was a professor at the Brooklyn College and a director
of the Center for Jewish Studies at the City University of New York
when I met him in 2001. He was the author of numerous articles
and books about interfaith marriage, but he had a special interest in
the history of the Holocaust and, in particular, the Kasztner train.

A small, quiet man, wrapped in an English raincoat, he had spent
years studying what Kasztner had done, accumulating documents
and translating key items from the archives. He became increasingly
animated, his voice rising in outrage when he talked about the terrible injustice of Kasztner's fate. He paid to have *Der Kasztner-Bericht*
translated into English; he worked with an editor on a translation of
Peretz Révész's autobiography. He set up a Kasztner memorial Web

site,[2] and some of the men and women on the train had contacted him to tell their stories.

Mayer's parents had rented a villa in the Buda Hills for their honeymoon in February 1944. The wedding gifts were still in storage in Pest when the Germans occupied the city. Mayer's grandfather ran an Orthodox soup kitchen for refugees, and that's how he first heard of the train. The family bought their lives with cash, jewelry, and the wedding gifts. Egon Mayer was born in Caux six weeks after the second transport from Bergen-Belsen arrived in Switzerland.

He was anxious to point out that the train was hardly Kasztner's greatest achievement, emphasizing what a formidable feat it had been to have those Jews put "on ice" in Austria. "People will tell you Kasztner neither caused nor aided in the saving of the Strasshof few, that Eichmann and Kaltenbrunner would have sent those eighteen thousand people to work in Austria with or without him, that they were responding to an urgent demand for workers in essential war industries. This is not true. Look at how Eichmann handled the transport of workers to build fortifications outside Vienna. He didn't care that most of them died" on their forced march. Strasshof was, in Mayer's opinion, reason enough for Kasztner to help Krumey. Mayer's father testified at Krumey's 1964 war-crimes trial, remembering him as one of the ss officers who had collected the payment for Kasztner's train. Afterward, he told Egon, he had been made to feel like a criminal even by his friends because he had given money to the Germans to save the family's lives. "I guess they would rather we had all died," he said.[3]

In Mayer's view, Kasztner succeeded with the ss because of the way he determinedly presented himself. He was focused, deliberate—a businessman, someone dispassionate who offered a reasonable sum for a reasonable favor. He claimed that he represented powerful Jewish overseas interests and promised additional payments. Maybe he had begun to believe his own myths. Maybe that's what gave him the courage he needed in Budapest.

Mayer said that Hansi Brand helped Kasztner to trust that the gamble would pay off. Had she not been there, Mayer believed, he himself would not be sitting in New York. He smiled when he thought about the chance of never being born. For over sixty years, he said, he had lived in a past he did not remember. His mother, who did remember, never talked about the Holocaust or the Kasztner train.

Egon Mayer had helped to organize a special event in New York in the winter of 2000 in honor of the English-subtitled release of Motti Lerner's film *The Kastner Trial*. Shlomo Aronson, the author of the book *Hitler, the Allies, and the Jews*, gave the keynote address. Egon moderated a panel that included the respected scholar Randolph Braham and Zsuzsi Kasztner-Michaeli, who had flown in for the occasion with her TV-celebrity daughter. When the film was over and the speeches were finished, some two hundred elderly men and women argued over the events of the Kasztner trial. Voices were raised. When one young man challenged all the speakers and denounced Kasztner as having "sold his soul to the devil," several people left in disgust. Shlomo Aronson asked the protester to justify his belief. He replied that he had read Ben Hecht's *Perfidy*, and he didn't need another source.

Perfidy, Mayer told me, was the most biased, least researched book he had ever read on the subject. The Academy Award–winning American screenwriter and journalist covered the Kasztner trial, and he went on to write hate-filled articles and this terrible book, Mayer said. Hecht was a supporter of Vladimir Jabotinsky's Revisionists and the Stern Gang, he was to the right of Menachem Begin, and he took Shmuel Tamir's side in everything. How could anyone seriously interested in what happened in Hungary during 1944–45 read only Ben Hecht? Mayer asked. And he posed another idea as one worth investigating: "The most enduring question asked about Oskar Schindler is why he bothered to save any Jews. By contrast, the most damning question asked about Kasztner is why he didn't save more."

As for the affidavit supporting Kurt Becher, Mayer believed that Kasztner owed the ss colonel a debt, and, he said, an honorable man delivers on his promises.

Egon Mayer died in 2004.

"No question," said Hansi's friend Sári Reuveni, "theirs was a real and enduring love, and it lasted till Hansi's death. Ten years after Kasztner had been murdered, Hansi still thought about him every day. Life had been hard for her. At the end of the war, she was there with two traumatized children; Joel still trying to figure out the past. By then he drank too much. An angry, disappointed man who never found his place in the world. Sunk into self-pity."

Sári worked in the Hungarian Archives at Yad Vashem in Jerusalem, the official Israeli memorial to the victims of the Holocaust. She was a vision in pink and light blue, her soft, rainbow dress flowing around her as she walked along the long corridor to her small office near the back elevators. She looked as though she had just stepped out of an elegant café on Váci Street in the heart of Budapest.

She had spent a year in Auschwitz.

"Every day during the trial," she said, "Hansi would be there, and most evenings Rezső went to her. She was there to comfort him, she told me, but it was more than that. She gave him the strength to go on. She made him realize that what he had done was, in those days, at that time, more than anyone else could have done. He had really saved lives. No one who was not there could imagine what it was like. Not the judge, not the press who condemned him, not the jackals of the prosecution. Hansi knew.

"She was here what she had been there—his soul."

Dani Brand, the older of Hansi's two children, lives in Tel Aviv with his family. He remembers a little about arriving in Palestine with his father, a gregarious, red-haired, friendly man, a great poker player—Joel's nickname was "Fox." When Dani and his brother, Michael, were in the kibbutz Givat Chaim after they arrived in Palestine, it was Joel who visited them every week. Dani hated the regimented life of the kibbutz. He was a little kid, but he had grown used to being treated like a small adult. They had been through so much. Hansi believed in life, Dani said, in our future. Once, he said, she told him: "I think the most important thing is not to be a hero but to survive."

*   *   *

Peretz Révész lived on a kibbutz near Haifa in 2003. He was a small,
wiry man, with thinning, curly hair still showing its original rusty
color but mixed now with white. His tanned face displayed a red-
head's freckled resistance to the sun. He and his wife, Nonika, shared
a small, white house surrounded by roses.

Peretz was proud of his friendship with Rezső and Hansi. He met
them for the first time in 1942 when he first escaped from Slovakia.
Hansi offered him a place to stay, clothes, and fake identity papers,
which allowed him to move about in Budapest. Like Kasztner, he
had been a young Zionist. There had never been any doubt in his
mind that, should he survive the Germans, he would live in Israel.

No one in Israel who had not been there, he said, could imagine
the horrific confusions of that time in Hungary. There had been an
assumption during the trial that events progressed in some orderly
fashion, that there were moments when alternative decisions could
have been made, when Kasztner could have assembled the Jews of
Kolozsvár or of Budapest to shake them out of their collective
lethargy, their belief that "it could not happen here." But, Peretz
said, "no such time existed. And when we tried, we were shouted
down; after all, the Jews had lived in peace in Hungary for over a
thousand years."

"A notion of an uprising, like the one in the Warsaw ghetto?
Ridiculous! The young men were in the labor service. A revolt of the
women and children, the old and the sick?"

Despite Kasztner's air of commanding certainty, Peretz thought
that he had been as uncertain and terrified as everyone else. He was
not a mythical David locked in battle with the German Goliath, but
a determined fighter for human lives who risked his own life every
day.

Peretz remembered Kurt Becher as "handsome, polite, dapper, in a
freshly ironed jacket." When they first met in the late summer of
1944, there had still been some faint hope that the remaining Jews of
Slovakia, including Peretz's parents, could be saved. "I offered to trade

some twenty thousand barrels of fuel I did not own. Both of us—Becher and I—knew that the deal existed only on paper, but he carried on with the negotiations. He pretended the oil was really there. He did not want to inform Himmler that the Jews could not meet their business obligations." The pretense served Becher well. Himmler would assume Becher was gainfully employed in the service of the Reich, and, if Germany lost the war, he would be able to present himself as a man who had helped the Jews.

"Of course, Kasztner knew this, but it did not matter. So long as Becher helped us, why would we take the trouble to examine his motivations? What difference did it make if he was using us to build his alibi? We were using him to survive.

"After the second Kasztner transport reached Switzerland, Kasztner could have stayed there, but he chose, instead, to return. We were busy, then, with placing orphans in what we thought would be safe Red Cross houses. Hansi was responsible for the organization of the various homes, finding new places when we feared we had been betrayed. As the Arrow Cross rounded up the adults, more and more of the children came. I remember the wife of a former Hungarian prime minister who ran a home in Buda for over two hundred babies.

"I remember when an Arrow Cross gang burst into the Teleki Square children's home. They were ready to kill all the children. A German soldier who had been billeted in a nearby apartment stopped them. There must have been at least fifty Arrow Cross men, but one German soldier could intimidate them by shouting orders."

When Peretz asked the soldier how he could reward him, the man asked for a silver cigarette box engraved with "To Kurt Neumann as a token of my thanks." Peretz fulfilled his wish the next day.

"We had long ago run out of Red Cross protection papers and had started to manufacture our own copies. When I showed one of our copies to a Red Cross official, he could not tell the difference between ours and theirs. We had become highly professional. But that was in late '44. In the beginning, when we were making fake schutzpässe for the refugees, they were so amateurish anyone would have known."

At the trial, Kasztner claimed that the Rescue Committee had saved about three thousand Jews by printing passes and Christian identity papers. Peretz Révész had been one of many instant Christians. "And there were a great deal more than three thousand," he said. "There were twenty-five hundred from Poland alone. Thousands of children whose parents had been murdered. Kasztner, for once," he chuckled, "was uncharacteristically modest."

Révész's memoir will be dedicated to those who helped to save the children. Both Rezső Kasztner and Hansi Brand will be included among the names of the brave.

Eva Zahler Berg lives in an airy apartment in downtown Toronto. She is a beautiful woman with big, brown eyes that dance with delight when she talks about her life. Sure, they were not easy years when she finally reached the "Promised Land," nor was she ever much good at agricultural work, but she managed to have some fun. Her mother, Elizabeth, had finally become an actress again, appearing in parts she had only dreamed of during the fascist years. Elizabeth remained Bogyó's friend during the trial and shared her anxiety and later her mourning. She helped at the lottery kiosk where Bogyó sold tickets to make ends meet.

Eva remembers Rezső Kasztner as a warm, fun-loving man, always a friend, always reliable. He was thoughtful and kind to her, ready with advice. He wrote to her on the occasion of her marriage to an older man, a letter full of steadying advice, telling her how it is time she put her life in order. Bogyó sent the traumatized Zsuzsi to her after Rezső was murdered in Tel Aviv.

Esther Miron lives in a comfortable, spacious apartment near the Great Jerusalem Synagogue. Her living room is overflowing with books on wide shelves, on tables, on the window ledge, some larger volumes leaning up against the sides of bookcases.

"I remember the trial," she said. "I knew Mrs. Szenes. Kati. Hanna's mother."

Hanna had moved to Israel from Hungary in 1939. Kati had no

idea how her two children had become interested in Zionism—the family viewed themselves as Hungarian first, and her husband was a successful writer. They didn't discuss politics at home.

In June 1944 Kati Szenes was arrested in Budapest and taken to the military police headquarters. She was interrogated about the whereabouts of her daughter. She had thought, then, that Hanna was still on a kibbutz near Haifa. She almost fainted when four uniformed men dragged Hanna into the room. Her daughter's lovely blond hair was shorn, her face was swollen, the area around her eyes was black, and one of her front teeth was missing. Hanna wept when she saw her mother.

For a few days, mother and daughter were in the same prison, where both were interrogated. After Kati was released, she spent several weeks trying to find out what had happened to Hanna. She haunted the offices of the Hungarian police, prison officials, lawyers' chambers, government buildings, and the Sip Street offices of the Rescue Committee. She waited for hours to speak with Kasztner, to ask for his help to intercede with the ss.

"Did you know that Kasztner wouldn't even speak with her?" Esther Miron asked. Kati Szenes was not even allowed to attend her daughter's funeral. Jews were not permitted to be at one another's funerals.

As dusk gathered in the shadows of the apartment, the Great Jerusalem Synagogue announced the start of the Sabbath with the long, plaintive sound of the shofar, the ram's-horn trumpet. Esther lit the candles at the dining room table and paused. "I am still trying to decide whether to forgive God," she said.

* * *

"Béla Marross" is not his real name. Since the war he has changed his name twice. No one knows where he lives. He is ninety years old. Over sixty years ago he was on the Kasztner train—and he is still apologizing for being alive. "I do not know why I was selected. Barely knew Kasztner. We were both Zionists, but he was at the top of the organization, and I was a nobody. I doubt if he would have recognized me."

"Unless you've seen Bergen-Belsen, you cannot imagine the size of it, the German shepherds the guards used, the morning roll calls—yes, every day, to make sure no one had escaped or tried to find relatives in the other parts of the camp. We had nicknames for the ss guards. One of them—we called him Popeye—brought a pair of shoes for a girl in our group. All our shoes were worn down. Hers had fallen apart; she was barefoot."

After the war Dr. Marross returned to Budapest to find the rest of his family. His brother and sister had been murdered. They hadn't wanted to risk the train.

Lea Fuerst, Ottó Komoly's daughter, lived in a tiny apartment in Tel Aviv. So much time had passed since the war, since her father was murdered by the Arrow Cross. He was, she said, a Hungarian patriot, proud that he had been decorated during the First World War. For the first months after the occupation, he refused to believe that Regent Horthy would not interfere on behalf of the Jews who had been faithful to him and his predecessors for centuries. Komoly wouldn't go on the Kasztner train, despite his position with the Va'ada; he thought he would be needed at home. He was, she said, the real hero of the Rescue Committee.

Had Ottó Komoly lived, she said, the Kasztner trial would have gone differently. It had been Komoly's decision that Kasztner should follow the "German line," because he was best qualified to act tough with the Sonderkommando. After only one visit to the Majestic Hotel, Komoly realized that he couldn't handle it himself. He lacked the ability to pretend.

Lea still mourned his death. "Is it possible ever to recover from the murder of one's father?"

György Vámos held out a copy of Ernő Szilágyi's book.[4] Vámos, who used to work for Hungarian Radio's documentaries section, is a Holocaust survivor. He looks after the Glass House in Budapest, the last refuge of some five thousand Jews as they hid from the Arrow

Cross. Szilágyi's book is at once a memoir and a philosophical con-
templation of various aspects of life; he was a scholar of the Bible and
of ancient history. He was a friend of Kasztner, and, more than any
other individual, he had been responsible for preparing the lists for
the train and for Strasshof.

He saw Kasztner as one in a long line of archetypes, the *stadlan*, the
"fixer" who tries to negotiate survival terms with successive overlords
bent on the annihilation of the Jews. Throughout the centuries there
had been such men, at the courts of Ferdinand of Aragon, Isabella of
Castille, Ivan the Terrible, and other Russian and Polish rulers. Once
the enemy was defined as the Nazis, Kasztner had assumed the role of
the *stadlan*. "One evening, after he had spent a day at the Majestic,
Kasztner turned to me," Szilágyi wrote. "His face was both terribly sad
and terribly proud: 'Believe me, this is how we have always done it.' "[5]

Ernő Szilágyi did not live to see his book published in 2002. It is
an extraordinary document, sometimes poetic, sometimes tough
minded, full of sharply observed detail. Perhaps he would not have
wanted to see it. He returned to Budapest from Switzerland with his
parents in 1948. He lived modestly until he died in 1970. A friend
and admirer suggests that Szilágyi condemned himself to death by
starvation.[6] Perhaps he never recovered from being one of those
charged with making the selections for the Kasztner train and the
Jews on ice: "He could not bear the memory of having been a judge
for the lives and deaths of others," Attila Novák wrote.

Adam Heller is a distinguished research professor at the University
of Texas, at Austin. His contributions to science are described in
more than 230 articles he has had published, and his contributions
to technology are recognized in 87 U.S. patents. He has received
enough awards and medals to cover several walls. He was a boy on
the Kasztner train.

In Kolozsvár Adam's father was very active in the Zionist movement, which would explain how his family was selected for the train.
But Adam thinks the reason may have been that the committee
preparing the list favored the families of labor service men; his

father, Ferenc, had just returned from a long stint in the Ukraine. Of course they knew about the deportations, he said. He remembers his mother returning home one day after she had delivered food for the Polish refugees. "What kinds of stories are people making up these days just to get more help from us!" she said. "Imagine, they were telling me that the Germans are murdering all the Jews!"

"We didn't want to know what we knew," Adam says. "And Dezső Hermann did not want to say that at the trial of his friend. He was a leading jurist. On the witness stand, when he said 'no one knew of the deportations to Auschwitz,' he meant that no one he knew had firsthand evidence."

In Israel, Heller says, the political leadership scrambled to dissociate itself from the "Jewish lambs." "The heroes were the paratroopers and the people who revolted in the Warsaw ghetto. Poor Rezső was an antihero. Who would stake his Israeli leader image on supporting a man who saved lives by negotiating with the Germans?"

Heller had been a friend of Zwi Hermann, Dezső's brother, who served with the Jewish Agency, and who told Heller: "Years later, when I met Eliahu Dobkin in Tel Aviv and asked him why the former Jewish Agency members didn't stand up for Kasztner in court, Dobkin looked at me with great sadness and said, 'I just couldn't.' "

Peter Munk, the founder and chairman of Barrick Gold Corporation, now presides over the world's largest gold producer.[7] He's also a great philanthropist, donating millions of dollars to hospitals and universities for facilities and research centers in his name.[8]

In 2006 he hosted a posh dinner party at the exclusive Toronto Club to welcome a former Hungarian president and his entourage to Canada. Munk and his partners in Budapest were looking at additional investments in central Europe. The Hungarian politicians and diplomats needed Munk's advice about doing business in North America.

His childhood friend Erwin Schaeffer oversees a real-estate company with Peter Munk, which has developed a new shopping and entertainment plaza in Poland. The Silesia City Center is the largest development in the region near Kraków. It is in an excellent location, just under one mile from the regional capital, Katowice, and just over a mile from the site of Auschwitz-Birkenau.

Munk and Schaeffer still do not talk about the Kasztner train.

The Kasztners and the Brands are buried in Nachlat Yitzhak Cemetery in Givataim, Tel Aviv.

A small forest has been planted in Rezső Kasztner's name near Ein Ayala, close to Haifa. The inscription on the marble tablet at the fork of a dirt road reads, "The Kasztner Forest."

There is another modest memorial plaque on the wall at 8 Váci Street in downtown Budapest, on the Pest side of the Danube, the pension where he rented an apartment in 1941. It reads:

> DR. REZSO KASZTNER 1906–1957
> DURING THE HOLOCAUST, AS A MEMBER
> OF THE BUDAPEST RESCUE COMMITTEE, HE RISKED HIS
> OWN LIFE TO SAVE THE LIVES OF MANY OTHERS.
> ERECTED BY THE KASZTNER MEMORIAL COMMITTEE 1998

The Spinoza Café is situated in the middle of the place where the Jewish ghetto used to be in Budapest. At the round, marble-top tables, young people gather, eating pâté or indulging in stylish coffees, teas, and wine. There is a piano and, in the evenings, live performances of comedy, music, and mime. Just around the corner a plaque commemorates the liberation of the ghetto on January 18, 1945. It is at the site of one of the gates where Arrow Cross guards stopped anyone who was trying to leave or enter, a few yards from the old wall that used to isolate the ghetto from the rest of the city, and only half a block from Klauzál Square, where mountains of frozen corpses were piled during the winter of 1944–45. The Spinoza is filled with laughter as a couple rehearses a cabaret song.

Outside, a group of tourists follows a woman with a red umbrella toward the Great Synagogue on Dohány Street. She is pointing to the high windows of older buildings, reminding everyone that they may not be able to see them again; several developers have been vying for the right to demolish these buildings, to make room for new condos and office towers.

In the café, a few of the guests are engaged in a lively debate about, on the one hand, the need for conservation and memory and, on the other, the desire to wipe the horror of the ghetto from the collective consciousness.[9]

The Great Synagogue has been restored to its prewar splendor. In its fenced-off courtyard—the one that connects the synagogue with the back of the old Sip Street Community Center—stands the sculpture of the weeping willow where Erwin Schaeffer first told me about the murder of his father. The area has been named Raoul Wallenberg Memorial Park to commemorate the Swedish diplomat "who saved the lives of thousands." Among the numerous plaques in honor of "the Righteous," there is a modest one bearing the name of Rezső Kasztner.

Acknowledgments

There are many people whose assistance I wish to acknowledge: Professor Randolph Braham, who read and commented on the second-to-last draft of this manuscript; Professor Adam Heller, who gave me his detailed notes; Professor Michael Marrus, who read two successive drafts without complaint and gave me the benefit of his wisdom on both of them; Yitzhak Katsir, who provided Kasztner family notes and photographs and drew my attention to the minutiae of Israeli law; Geraldine Sherman, who was the first to insist on extensive endnotes; Yehuda Lahav, who generously provided his notes and his book about a "wounded life"; George Jonas, who kept encouraging me to go on with the research even when it became obvious that many documents, books, and memories were contradictory; John Pearce, who is much more than an agent—he is a painstaking editor; Rosemary Shipton, my imaginative editor; Wendy Fitzgibbons, the most exacting copy editor anyone could wish for; Wendy Wright, who helped with the translation of Karla Müller-Tupath; Professor Yechiam Weitz, who allowed me to read the unpublished translation of his brilliant book, "The Man Who Was Murdered Twice"; Gabriel

Barshaked, whose taped interviews in the Yad Vashem Archives proved to be a most valuable source for mining Hansi's memories; Yitzhak Livnat, without whose assistance in Israel I would certainly have been lost in the archives, as well as in the city streets; and my intrepid Canadian publisher, Scott McIntyre, who stuck with this massive project till the end. I am grateful to George Gibson, my American publisher, for his consistently wise queries and his fierce editorial eye, and István Deak for his detailed comments for the American edtion.

I want especially to thank all the people I interviewed for this book, because without their help I could not have written it. Some I have described in detail in the text; others are presented here in alphabetical order by surname.

Shlomo Aronson, a historian with a vibrant sense of humor, was able to describe many of the people I wrote about.

Yehuda Bauer is an academic adviser to the Yad Vashem Archives. I found his book *Jews for Sale?* invaluable.

Eva Berg lent me her treasured copy of Robert St. John's book *The Man Who Played God*, but I appreciated more the hours we spent with her memories of Rezső and Bogyó Kasztner in the Váci Street pension, her stories about how she and her mother survived the Holocaust, their journey to Israel via Cyprus, and her continued relationship with Rezső.

George Bishop (Bischitz), age seventeen in 1944, carried messages for the Judenrat before entering the Kolozsvar Ghetto. He thinks his family was selected for Kasztner's train because his father was a decorated officer in WWI. In 1949, he volunteered for the Israeli Paratroopers, becoming an early parachute instructor with sixty jumps to his credit. He emigrated to the United States in 1955 and, as owner of Truflex-Pang Rubber Company, opened manufacturing joint ventures around the world.

Randolph Braham works in his sparse office at City University in New York, surrounded by books and manuscripts. He is the real dean of Hungarian Jewish history. His many books were of enormous help in marshaling the facts, and his two-volume work *The Politics of Genocide* proved to be my guide and checkpoint throughout.

Dani Brand and his wife were kind enough to invite me into their home in Tel Aviv and share with me their own stories about Hansi and Joel.

Eva Carmeli talked to me in her home in Tel Aviv and told me how her friend Hansi continued working with children until she was eighty-eight years old.

Dov Dinur has written his own book in Hebrew about Kasztner. He was one of the young halutzim in Hungary in 1944, and he remembers Rafi Benshalom and all the others in this book. I talked with him in Haifa, and we visited Peretz Révész together in 2006.

Margit Fendrich, Joel Brand's niece, greeted me in her elegant apartment in Tel Aviv. Her memories of the terrible times that followed her being left behind by the second Kasztner train to Switzerland, and her recollections of the Nuremberg Trials, have been of immense help in writing this book.

Lea Fuerst, Ottó Komoly's daughter, lived in Tel Aviv in a home for the elderly before her death in 2006. She had perfect recall of those years in Budapest.

Adam Heller, a scholar, professor and research scientist at the University of Texas, thinks his family was selected in Kolozsvár for the Kasztner train because his father had survived labor service in the Ukraine.

Zsuzsi Kasztner, Rezső and Bogyó's daughter, talked with me in Tel Aviv and sent more information after our meeting. She has three daughters: Mayrav, the TV and radio interviewer; Michal, a businesswoman, and Keren, who was completing her graduate work in international law and human rights.

Agnes Lantos, then a dressmaker, survived in hiding in Buda, helped by many of her clients. When the Soviet army arrived in Budapest, she made clothes for the women soldiers who could afford a bit of luxury. Agnes's sister, MAGDA LÉTAI, and her sister-in-law were on the death march to Vienna in late October 1944 and ended up in Ravensbrück concentration camp. Both of them survived because of Magda's determination not to give up.

Joe Lebovic shared his experiences of hiding in Budapest during the Arrow Cross's rule.

Yitzhak Livnat told his harrowing story of the foot march from Auschwitz to Mauthausen in January 1945, of the German soldier who told him he was too young to die, of the hastily constructed Gunskirchen concentration camp in March 1945, of the thousands who died of typhus and starvation. He found love and life in Israel.

Ron Lustig is director of the Memorial Museum of Hungarian-Speaking Jewry in Safed, Israel. The museum was founded by his parents, both Holocaust survivors, in early 1948. Situated in a place where no one would expect a museum—about one hundred miles from Tel Aviv and close to Lake Galilee—it is jammed full with memorabilia from centuries of Hungarian Jewish life. The museum's Web URL is www.hjm.org.il/.

Tom Margittai, a young passenger on Kasztner's train, went on to become co-owner of the Four Seasons, one of the most famous restaurants in New York.

Egon Mayer's Kasztner Memorial Web site is still available at www.kasztnermemorial.com/.

Agnes Pap, a journalist, has been studying and documenting the houses occupied by the ss and the Arrow Cross, as well as safe houses for Jews and other buildings of special interest to people studying the Hungarian Jewish catastrophe. She drove up Swabian Hill with me to the former Majestic Hotel, still an imposing building though with somewhat worn outer walls. The acacias and chestnut trees are still there, as is that wonderful view over the Danube. The footbridge that Rezső Kasztner, Hansi and Joel Brand used to cross for their meetings with Eichmann remains, as does the small enclosure that used to be the guardhouse. Little has changed inside the former hotel. Under the Communists, this building became a choice apartment complex for party members and their families. When we were there in 2005, the couple in Eichmann's former offices were renovating their new apartment. They had heard the stories about a bedroom where Göring had once spent a night as Eichmann's guest. Later, Agnes and I had a glass of wine in the Astoria Hotel bar, where not much has changed since the ss officers drank there in 1944. The interrogation and torture area of the basement has been transformed into a conference center.

Anna Perczel, an architect and historian, is still trying to save buildings in the former Budapest ghetto from demolition.

Baba Schwartz let me read her heartrending memoir about her last farewell to her father at Auschwitz-Birkenau. Baba lives with her husband, Andor, in Australia. Andor survived the Holocaust in the Glass House.

Rabbi József Schweitzer went into hiding with his aunt when the Germans occupied the Budapest Rabbinical Seminary in March 1944. He was picked up by the Arrow Cross in November and assigned to a work detail digging antitank ditches east of the city. Again he escaped, and he hid in the Glass House until January 1945; in March that year, he returned to his studies at the Rabbinical Seminary. I met him there, in his modest office, in 2005.

Szabolcs Szita is the author of several books on the Holocaust, including one on Kasztner and the Budapest Rescue Committee. When I asked how he became a historian of the Holocaust in Hungary, he told me this story: "I was researching a historical book, digging in Sopron [in Hungary], when we came across some human bones. When I asked the locals, they said the bones must have belonged to the Jews who dug trenches during the war. There are no Jews in the area now—just the bones." This is what propelled him to make sure those who had disappeared would not be forgotten.

Julia Vajda, a psychiatrist in Budapest, collects interviews with Hungarian Holocaust survivors.

György Vámos, former documentaries chief for Hungarian Radio, is head of the Carl Lutz Foundation in Budapest. György was only six years old when he and his mother were taken to the Danube by the Arrow Cross to be shot. They had been in the Glass House on Vadász Street. He does not know how they were rescued or why, but he does remember asking one of their captors, "Nyilas bacsi [How long do we have to stand here]?"

Paul Varnai, one of the Strasshof child deportees, is a retired professor in Ottawa, Canada.

Judy Young's parents did not make it onto the Kasztner train. Her father, George Balazs, was a biblical archaeologist of such high standing that he and his family were offered places on the Kasztner train. He declined at the last moment because, Judy thinks, he suspected that the train was just another German ruse. Judy's parents were deported to Auschwitz-Birkenau between July 6 and 8, 1944, from Ujpest, in one of the last deportations; she was almost one year old when her mother handed her to a relative to be cared for until they returned. They never came home again.

Notes

In citing sources, short titles are used to lead the reader to the accompanying bibliography. Page or chapter numbers of referenced works are not cited.

INTRODUCTION

1. Auschwitz-Birkenau, or Auschwitz II, was a second camp near the original concentration camp at Auschwitz in Poland, renamed Auschwitz I.
2. This is the figure reported by Edmund Veesenmayer, Reich plenipotentiary for Hungary, to his superiors; the number reported by Hungarian gendarmerie chief Colonel László Ferenczy was 434,351.
3. Schindler is the hero of Thomas Keneally's book *Schindler's Ark* (later retitled *Schindler's List*) and of the movie *Schindler's List*.
4. Schindler, *Ich, Oskar Schindler*.

PART ONE: THE JEWISH QUESTION

1. Attributed to Burke (1729–97), Irish philosopher and statesman. Possibly it is a distillation of the words found in his *Thoughts on the Cause of the Present Discontents* (1770).

CHAPTER 1: DESPERATELY SEEKING PALESTINE

For personal information I relied primarily on Rezső Kasztner's writings in *Új Kelet*; Dezsö Hermann's memries in Ofry, *Egy Évszázad Tanúja*; information provided by Yitzhak Katsir, Rezső Kasztner's nephew; and interviews with Adam Heller and George Bishop.

1. Information provided to the author by Yitzhak Katsir.
2. Ofry, *Egy Évszázad Tanúja*.
3. Kontler, *A History of Hungary*, and Lendvai, *The Hungarians*.
4. MacMillan, *Paris 1919*.
5. Gilbert, *The Holocaust*.
6. Herzl, *The Jewish State*.
7. Information from Yitzhak Katsir.
8. Ben-Gurion in 1948 became the first prime minister of Israel.
9. In parts of Europe, the social title "Dr." is bestowed on lawyers and other professionals.
10. Ofry, *Egy Évszázad Tanúja*. Dezsö Hermann was on the Kasztner train. He became a celebrated lawyer in Israel and spent the last years of his life trying to clear Kasztner's name.
11. Information from Yitzhak Katsir.
12. Ofry, *Egy Évszázad Tanúja*.
13. Information from Yitzhak Katsir.
14. Ofry, *Egy Évszázad Tanúja*.
15. The Ihud was formed in 1930 from two other leftist parties.
16. Chaim Weizmann in 1948 would become the first president of Israel.
17. It is now called the Babelplatz.
18. *Times* (London), September 17, 1935.
19. Information from Yitzhak Katsir.
20. *Hansard*, April 14, 1937.
21. Gilbert, *The Holocaust*.
22. Wasserstein, *Britain and the Jews of Europe, 1939–1945*.
23. Gilbert, *The Jews in the Twentieth Century*.
24. "Albion" is among the ancient names for Britain.
25. Born in Lithuania, Chaim Barlas had been a Zionist youth worker. He was director of the Agency's Palestine Office in Warsaw from 1919 till 1925, when he emigrated to Palestine. From 1926 to 1948, he was

stationed in Geneva, then Istanbul, as a director of the Jewish Agency's Immigration Department.

26. Porat, *The Blue and the Yellow Stars of David.*
27. Gilbert, *The Jews in the Twentieth Century.*
28. Levin, *The Holocaust.* The judge used these words at the trial of one of a few German soldiers.
29. Haganah membership was estimated at about sixty thousand; it undertook a range of missions, including assisting with illegal immigration.
30. Wasserstein, *Britain and the Jews of Europe, 1939–1945.*
31. In his *Memoirs*, Horthy did not see this pact as an affirmation of Hungary's commitment to Germany.
32. Braham, *The Politics of Genocide.*

CHAPTER 2: THE GATHERING STORM

For scenes in this chapter I relied on my interviews with Eva Berg, Zsuzsi Kasztner, Sári Reuveni, and Peretz Révész; Salamon, *Keresztény Voltam Európában* (I Was a Christian in Europe); *Der Kasztner-Bericht* (The Kasztner Report); Benshalom, *We Struggled for Life*; Horthy, *Memoirs*; Stern, *Emlékirataim*; Biss, *A Million Jews to Save*; Joel Brand's testimonies at the trials of Malchiel Grünwald and Adolf Eichmann; Hansi Brand's interviews by Dr. Gabriel Barshaked and her trial testimonies; and Szilágyi, *Ismeretlen Memoár a Magyar Vészkorszakról* (An Unknown Memoir about the Hungarian Holocaust).

1. Under the Jewish calendar.
2. Kádár and Vági, *Self-financing Genocide.*
3. Zweig, *The Gold Train.*
4. Eva Berg, interviewed by the author in Toronto in 2006.
5. Komoly, "What May Jews Learn from the Present Crisis?"
6. Benshalom, *We Struggled for Life.* When Rafi Benshalom arrived in the capital in January 1944, he was astonished at the open animosity among the various groups. The fact that this rivalry continued during the German occupation is difficult to understand.
7. Salamon, *Keresztény Voltam Európában*, and *Der Kasztner-Bericht.*
8. These *halutzim* (in the singular, *halutz*) were getting ready to emigrate to Palestine. During the war years, the word "halutz" had the additional romantic connotation of a revolutionary spirit.

9. Salamon, *Keresztény Voltam Európában.*
10. Ibid.
11. Kasztner, *Der Kasztner-Bericht.*
12. Braham, *The Politics of Genocide.*
13. Braham estimates that by 1943 there were fifteen thousand refugees in Hungary.
14. The committee had been set up in 1914 to help European Jews, with its headquarters in New York and branch offices in various countries in Europe. After 1942, it experienced difficulty in transferring funds to Europe because of U.S. regulations governing the transfer of funds to Nazi-occupied areas.
15. Salamon, *Keresztény Voltam Európában.*
16. Szilágyi, *Ismeretlen Memoár a Magyar Vészkorszakról.*
17. Horthy believed this to have been an unprovoked attack by the Soviets.
18. Weizmann had applied directly to Prime Minister Winston Churchill.
19. St. John, *The Man Who Played God.*
20. Gabriella Mauthner, interviewed by Lajos Erdelyi.
21. The Abwehr under Admiral Wilhelm Canaris had become a competitor to the Sicherheitsdienst (Reich Security Office, or SD) and the Gestapo when it came to information gathering. It had well-trained agents throughout the world. Springmann said both Hitler and SS boss Heinrich Himmler liked the idea of competition among the Reich agencies.
22. Friling, *Arrows in the Dark.*
23. Biss, *A Million Jews to Save.*
24. Hansi Brand's first meeting with Rezső Kasztner was described by Sári Reuveni and Peretz Révész in interviews with the author.
25. Joel Brand, in Weissberg, *Advocate for the Dead.*

CHAPTER 3: A QUESTION OF HONOR, LAW, AND JUSTICE

For some scenes I relied on *Der Kasztner-Bericht*; my interviews with Peretz Révész and Sári Reuveni; Egon Mayer's articles; Braham, *The Politics of Genocide*; Braham's three-volume *Hungarian Jewish Studies*; Joel Brand's testimonies at the trials of Malchiel Grünwald and Adolf Eichmann; Hansi Brand's interviews by Barshaked; Weissberg, *Advocate for the Dead*; and Schindler, *Ich, Oskar Schindler.*

1. Horthy, *Memoirs*.
2. Weissberg, *Advocate for the Dead*.
3. Lévai, *Fehér Könyv*.
4. *Der Kasztner-Bericht*.
5. According to Dov Dinur, Kasztner did not belong to a recognized, elected leadership group in Budapest. He was not a man of capital; he was from a distant, newly re-annexed province, and he lived off a small salary provided by the Jewish National Fund. Levai mentions him as "an uninvited guest."
6. Weissberg, *Advocate for the Dead*, and Brand's testimony at Grünwald trial.
7. Hansi Brand, interviewed by Dr. Gabriel Barshaked in 1995. The author also reviewed several filmed interviews with Hansi.
8. Weissberg, *Advocate for the Dead*.
9. Hansi Brand, interviewed by Barshaked.
10. Information provided to the author by Zsuzsi Kasztner.
11. None of them survived the war. Bauer, *Jews for Sale?*
12. Peretz Révész, interviewed by the author in 2005 and 2006.
13. According to Bauer, seven thousand to eight thousand Slovak and Hungarian Jews had fled Slovakia for Hungary by the early spring of 1942.
14. Porat, *The Blue and the Yellow Stars of David*.
15. Bauer, *A History of the Holocaust*.
16. Friling, *Arrows in the Dark*.
17. *Der Kasztner-Bericht*.
18. Much of this account is based on *Der Kasztner-Bericht* and on Barshaked's interviews with Hansi Brand; some descriptions here are from Keneally, *Schindler's Ark*.
19. Schindler, *Ich, Oskar Schindler*.
20. Gilbert, *The Jews in the Twentieth Century*.
21. Wyman, *The Abandonment of the Jews*.

CHAPTER 4: THE POLITICS OF GENOCIDE

Both here and in Chapter 5 I relied on several sources, including Vrba and Bestic, *Escape from Auschwitz*; Höss's statements at Nuremberg and his autobiography, *Death Dealer*; Rees, *Auschwitz*; and survivors' accounts, including those at Yad Vashem Archives and at the United States Holocaust Memorial Museum.

1. By this time, according to Yehuda Bauer, there were about 2,500 Polish Jews in Hungary. Other historians put the figure even higher.

2. Kontler, *A History of Hungary.*

3. Shirer, *The Rise and Fall of the Third Reich.*

4. Horthy, *Memoirs.*

5. Horthy, *Memoirs;* Bauer, *Jews for Sale?;* Stern, *Emlékirataim.* Buda Castle is also known as the Royal Palace.

6. Horthy, *Memoirs.*

7. Ibid.

8. Braham, *The Politics of Genocide;* in an interview, Adam Heller told the author of the current text that his own father was one of the few who escaped, clawing his way through the flames and the burning bodies.

9. Schindler, *Ich, Oskar Schindler.*

10. Szita, *Aki Egy Embert Megment* (He Who Saves a Single Life).

11. Bauer, *A History of the Holocaust.* She did not know that about 2.5 million of Poland's Jews were dead by the spring of 1943.

12. *Der Kasztner-Bericht.*

13. Wisliceny's testimony before the International Military Tribunal at Nuremberg, January 3, 1946.

14. Feig, *Hitler's Death Camps;* author's translation of the ss oath.

15. Hersh and Mann, *Gizelle, Save the Children!*

16. Horthy, *Memoirs.*

17. Shirer, *The Rise and Fall of the Third Reich.*

CHAPTER 5: BUDAPEST: THE BEGINNING OF
THE END

Several scenes in this chapter are based on Joel Brand's memoirs; Weissberg, *Advocate for the Dead*, Gabriel Barshaked's interviews with Hansi Brand; and *Der Kasztner-Bericht.*

1. Rees, *Auschwitz.*

2. Vrba and Bestic, *Escape from Auschwitz.*

3. *Der Kasztner-Bericht.*

4. *Der Kasztner-Bericht.*
5. Weissberg, *Advocate for the Dead*. As Brand said: "One of our most capable men, fit for any conceivable job—except that of army commander."
6. The clandestine army of the Yishuv from which Israel's army evolved after the creation of the State of Israel.
7. By 1944 there were about thirty thousand Jews in the British army.
8. Brand's recollection, in Weissberg, *Advocate for the Dead*.

PART TWO: THE KINGDOM OF THE NIGHT

The headline for this part is drawn from Elie Wiesel's *Night*.

CHAPTER 6: THE OCCUPATION

For scenes in this chapter I relied on Munkácsi, *Hogyan Történt?*; Szilágyi, *Ismeretlen Memoár*; Joel Brand's testimonies at the trials of Malchiel Grünwald and Adolf Eichmann; Hansi Brand's interviews by Barshaked; *Der Kasztner-Bericht*; Révész, "Against a Tidal Wave of Evil"; and my interviews with Peretz Révész.

1. It was revealed later that when Veesenmayer was shown the lists of those arrested, he did not think enough Jews had been imprisoned, so he ordered that the numbers be doubled.
2. *Der Kasztner-Bericht.*
3. Chorin and his brother-in-law, Móric Kornfeld, had actually gone into hiding at the Zirc Cistercian Abbey some sixty miles west of Budapest, but the Va'ada members did not know that at the time.
4. István Deak's personal recollection, told to the author in 2006.
5. Hansi Brand, interviewed by Gabriel Barshaked.
6. Szilágyi, *Ismeretlen Memoár*; Munkácsi, *Hogyan Történt*.
7. Munkácsi, *Hogyan Történt?*; Braham, *The Politics of Genocide*.
8. Krumey's testimony at Nuremberg and, later, at Eichmann's trial.
9. In his evidence at Eichmann's trial, Krumey said that he had not "taken the term 'special treatment' to mean extermination," though it had been established already that these words were a euphemism for murder. (At his trial in Nuremberg in 1946, Wisliceny would complain that the children created "difficulties" because the Chelmno camp to which they

were sent was not set up for unaccompanied youngsters.)

10. There are several accounts of this event. I relied most on Ernő Munkácsi's *Hogyan Történt?*

11. Munkácsi, *Hogyan Történt?*

12. Braham, *The Politics of Genocide.*

CHAPTER 7: OBERSTURMBANNFÜHRER ADOLF EICHMANN

The early biographical details in this chapter are based on Eichmann's pre-trial and trial testimonies and Wisliceny's testimonies at Nuremberg.

1. Von Lang, ed., *Eichmann Interrogated.*

2. Wisliceny's testimony at Nuremberg.

3. Among other things, Max Nordau wrote a paper for the First Zionist Congress; Moses Hess wrote *Rome and Jerusalem: The Last National Question.*

4. Wisliceny's testimony at Nuremberg.

5. Kádár and Vági, *Self-financing Genocide.*

6. Carpathian Ruthenia and northeastern Hungary were designated Zone I, and northern Transylvania—including Kolozsvár—was Zone II in the agreed order of ghettoization and deportation. Northern Hungary was designated Zone III; the southeast was Zone IV; the southwest, Zone V; Zone VI, the last, was to be Budapest. For details, see Braham, *The Politics of Genocide*, vol. I.

7. Braham, *The Politics of Genocide*, vol. 1.

8. Horthy, *Memoirs.*

9. Wyman, *The Abandonment of the Jews.* In his March 24, 1944, statement, Roosevelt referred to the events in Hungary as "one of the blackest crimes in history."

10. This meeting is recorded in Szilágyi, *Ismeretlen Memoár.*

11. Kasztner was referring to the deals the Germans had made with various Jewish leaders to allow the exit of large numbers of Jews to Palestine.

12. This section is based on the memoirs of Carl Lutz; on Benshalom, *We Struggled for Life*; and on *Der Kasztner-Bericht.*

13. Sources for information about this meeting include Braham, *The Politics of Genocide*; Munkácsi, *Hogyan Történt?*; Komoly, "The Diary Of Ottó

Komoly"; Stern, "A Race against Time."

14. Munkácsi, *Hogyan Történt?*
15. Braham, *The Politics of Genocide.*
16. Ibid.

CHAPTER 8: IN THE ANTEROOM OF HELL

This chapter is based on *Der Kasztner-Bericht*; Weissberg, *Advocate for the Dead*; Hansi Brand's interviews with Gabriel Barshaked, and Szilágyi, *Ismeretlen Memoár.*

1. *Der Kasztner-Bericht.*
2. Munkácsi, *Hogyan Történt?*
3. Stern, *Emlékirataim.*
4. Interview with Eva Zahler.
5. Elizabeth Zahler never recovered the pension, nor the loan she had given the manageress.
6. Kádár and Vági, *Self-financing Genocide.*
7. Zeev Hadari (Venia Pomerantz) reported to his superiors in Jerusalem that all the payments were funded by "local resources." Hadari, *Against All Odds.*
8. Kasztner, "A Nagy Embervásár" (The Great Trade in Lives).
9. *Der Kasztner-Bericht.*
10. Braham, *The Politics of Genocide.*

CHAPTER 9: BARGAINING WITH THE DEVIL

This chapter is based on Weissberg, *Advocate for the Dead*; Joel Brand's testimonies at the trials of Malchiel Grünwald and Eichmann; *Der Kasztner-Bericht*; Tschuy, *Dangerous Diplomacy;* Hansi Brand's interviews with Gabriel Barshaked and Randolph Braham; and Wisliceny's testimonies at Nuremberg.

1. The Nazis referred to the ghettoization and deportation of the Jews as "the *Aktion.*"
2. Brand's testimony at Eichmann's trial.
3. Bauer, *Jews for Sale?*
4. Salamon, *Keresztény Voltam Európában.*

5. Stern, *Emlékirataim.*

6. Tschuy, *Dangerous Diplomacy.*

7. Szilágyi, *Ismeretlen Memoár.*

CHAPTER 10: THE AUSCHWITZ PROTOCOLS

1. Vrba and Wetzler, "Auschwitz Protocols."

2. Though acknowledged as providing the first credible information about mass murder at Auschwitz, Vrba's accounts of events in general caused ongoing controversy.

3. This meeting and conversation are based on Brand's recollections in Weissberg, *Advocate for the Dead*, and his testimonies at the Grünwald and Eichmann trials.

CHAPTER 11: THE REICHSFÜHRER'S MOST OBEDIENT SERVANT

1. The conversations between Brand, Klages, and Eichmann are based on Brand's recollections in Weissberg, *Advocate for the Dead,* and his testimonies at the Grünwald and Eichmann trials. Becher's personal history is based on Müller-Tupath, *Reichsführers gehorsamster Becher*, on his Nuremberg testimonies, and on Kádár and Vági, *Self-financing Genocide.*

2. Becher's interrogation at Nuremberg.

3. Gabriella Mauthner, interviewed by Lajos Erdelyi.

4. This information is based on Tschuy, *Dangerous Diplomacy.* Several other writers question the timing indicated by Tschuy for Kasztner's receipt of the Auschwitz Protocols and his subsequent actions.

5. Kádár and Vági, *Self-financing Genocide.*

6. Ben-Tov, *Facing the Holocaust in Budapest.*

7. *Der Kasztner-Bericht.*

8. Braham, *The Politics of Genocide.*

9. To this day there are emotional debates about who made the final list, how many people were involved in the selection, and why some were excluded. For example, see András Gáll, "Volt Egyszer Egy Huszadik Század" (Once There Was a Twentieth Century).

10. Braham, *The Politics of Genocide.*

11. I have a copy of a notarized statement (18 Nov. 1994) from Susan Gal (Fried) testifying that her Zionist father had tried to warn the Jewish congregation of Szatmar to escape to Romania. The rabbi, Joel Teitlebaum, warned him not to panic the people or he would face "excommunication."

12. Kasztner, "A Nagy Embervásár."

13. Moshe Shertok later changed his name to Moshe Sharett.

14. *Der Kasztner-Bericht*; Porat, *The Blue and the Yellow Stars of David*.

CHAPTER 12: MISSION TO ISTANBUL

The Istanbul scenes in this chapter are based on Weissberg, *Advocate for the Dead*; Joel Brand's testimonies at the Grünwald and Eichmann trials; Friling, *Arrows in the Dark*; Porat, *The Blue and the Yellow Stars of David*; Bauer, *Jews for Sale?*; Hadari, *Against All Odds*; and Grosz's testimony at the Grünwald trial.

1. Weissberg, *Advocate for the Dead*.

2. After the annexation of former Hungarian territories in Czechoslovakia, Romania, and Yugoslavia, the Jewish population of Hungary was estimated to be 800,000, including converts to Christianity, who, by Nazi definition, were also Jewish.

3. Porat, *The Blue and the Yellow Stars of David*. Formed in 1942, shortly after Yishuv leaders learned of the planned annihilation of three to four million Polish Jews, the committee's formal name was "Committee for the Jews of Occupied Europe." Initially, it represented all factions of the Yishuv.

4. Friling, *Arrows in the Dark*; Porat, *The Blue and the Yellow Stars of David*.

5. Hadari, *Against All Odds*.

6. Ben-Gurion was chairman and Shertok was head of the Agency's Political Department.

7. Porat, *The Blue and the Yellow Stars of David*.

8. Peretz Révész, interviewed by the author.

9. Hansi Brand, interviewed by Gabriel Barshaked.

10. Braham, *The Politics of Genocide*.

11. The first and subsequent meetings are reported on in *Der Kasztner-Bericht*; Biss, *A Million Jews to Save*; Bauer, *Jews for Sale?*; and Hansi Brand's interviews with Barshaked.

12. Hans Frank had been named governor general of the General Government of Nazi-occupied Poland, after the annexation of the western provinces by the Reich.

13. Rees, *Auschwitz*.

14. Hajj Amin el Husseini was a leader of the Arab revolt against the British mandate and against Jewish immigration. His enthusiasm for Nazism was well known, as was his support for the extermination of Jews.

15. The Bermuda Conference between Britain and the United States opened on April 19, 1943, in Hamilton, Bermuda. All suggestions that the Allies accept the unlimited emigration of Jewish refugees were rejected there. Ian Henderson of the British Foreign Office minuted: "We have already opposed the idea of a general appeal to the German Government suggesting that they should unload all Jews under their control on the Allies. German acceptance would raise insuperable difficulties connected with transport, supply, passage through neutral countries . . ."

16. Hansi Brand, interviewed by Barshaked.

17. *Der Stürmer*, a rabidly anti-Semitic Nazi weekly published by Julius Streicher, had but one purpose: to vilify Jews and urge actions against them.

18. Eichmann denied this story at his trial.

19. Salamon, *Keresztény Voltam Európában*.

20. Stern, "A Race against Time."

21. The real investigation, of course, did not happen until long after the end of the war.

22. Wisliceny's testimony at Nuremberg.

23. July 7, 1947, and March 2, 1948.

CHAPTER 13: A MILLION JEWS FOR SALE

The Istanbul parts of this chapter are based on Weissberg, *Advocate for the Dead*; Joel Brand's testimonies at the Grünwald and Eichmann trials; Friling, *Arrows in the Dark*; Porat, *The Blue and the Yellow Stars of David*; Bauer, *Jews for Sale?*; Hadari, *Against All Odds*; and Grosz's testimony at the Grünwald trial.

1. Weissberg, *Advocate for the Dead*.

2. Grosz's testimony at the Grünwald trial.

3. Bauer, *Jews for Sale?*

4. Weissberg, *Advocate for the Dead*.

5. Munkácsi, *Hogyan Történt?*

6. *Der Kasztner-Bericht.*

7. Becher testified at Nuremberg that Himmler's instructions had been: "Get out of the Jews everything that can be got out of them . . . As to what promises we'll keep, we'll just have to see."

8. *Der Kasztner-Bericht.*

9. Szita, *Aki Egy Embert Megment.*

10. Tschuy, *Dangerous Diplomacy.*

11. In his book *Against All Odds*, Zeev Venia Hadari (formerly Pomerantz) writes about repeated warnings to Jews in the ghettos about the deportations.

12. In his written testimony from abroad for Eichmann's trial, Becher claimed he and Kasztner had been "introduced by Dr. Billitz."

13. Born in Galicia, Bader had been a leader of Hashomer Hatzair, the Histadrut Jewish trade union, and the Zionist Action Committee.

14. This account is based on *Der Kasztner-Bericht;* Biss, *A Million Jews to Save;* and Hansi Brand's interviews with Gabriel Barshaked.

15. Braham, *The Politics of Genocide.*

16. Bauer, *Jews for Sale?*

17. Weissberg, *Advocate for the Dead;* Bauer, *Jews for Sale?;* Brand's testimonies at the Grünwald and Eichmann trials.

18. Kollek, *One Jerusalem.*

19. Hadari, *Against All Odds.*

20. Weissberg, *Advocate for the Dead.*

21. Braham, *The Politics of Genocide.*

22. Ibid.

23. In 1949 the government of Israel established the Ha-Mossad le-Modiin ule-Tafkidim Meyuhadim, the Institute for Intelligence and Special Operations. It is this incarnation of the Mossad that today is known worldwide.

24. Bauer, *Jews for Sale?*; Porat, *The Blue and the Yellow Stars of David.*

25. Avriel had been involved in negotiations for the escape of five thousand Jewish children and accompanying adults from Europe in 1943.

26. The right-wing Zionist Revisionist movement, active in eastern Europe, advocated the establishment of a Jewish state and an armed struggle to achieve its goals. Its youth wing was known as Betar, and in Europe a number of Betar members took part in the resistance movement against the Nazis.

CHAPTER 14: A GAME OF ROULETTE FOR
HUMAN LIVES

Various scenes in this chapter are based on *Der Kasztner-Bericht*; Wisliceny's testimonies at Nuremberg; Hadari, *Against All Odds*; and Joel Brand's testimonies at the Grünwald and Eichmann trials.

1. Tschuy, *Dangerous Diplomacy*.
2. Ibid.
3. *Der Kasztner-Bericht*.
4. Bauer, *Jews for Sale?*
5. Hadari, *Against All Odds*.
6. Porat, *The Blue and the Yellow Stars of David*.
7. Bauer, *Jews for Sale?*
8. The War Refugee Board had been established in January 1944 in response to the European refugee crisis.
9. Wisliceny's testimony at Nuremberg.
10. Lowy, *A Kálváriától a Tragédiáig*.
11. Dinur, *Kastner*.
12. Information from Zsuzsi Kasztner.

CHAPTER 15: ROLLING THE DICE

1. Author's translation.
2. *Der Kasztner-Bericht*.
3. Bauer, *Jews for Sale?*
4. *Der Kasztner-Bericht*.
5. Hansi Brand, interviewed by Gabriel Barshaked in Tel Aviv.
6. *Der Kasztner-Bericht*.
7. Braham, *The Politics of Genocide*.
8. Hansi Brand, interviewed by Gabriel Barshaked in Tel Aviv.
9. Freudiger, "Five Months."
10. Braham, *The Politics of Genocide*.
11. Braham, *The Politics of Genocide*.
12. Kádár and Vági, *Self-financing Genocide*.
13. Braham, *The Politics of Genocide*.
14. Schiller has the number as 5,239.

15. According to Schiller, in *A Strasshofi Mentőakció* (The Strasshof Rescue), the number registered on arrival was only 14,700. Argermayer's numbers have been debated by several historians; some have put the figure as low as 14,000, others as high as 25,000. I have chosen to stay with the Argermayer estimate because this is the one that Kasztner received.
16. There were 6,641 from Debrecen, 2,567 from Szolnok, and 564 from Baja.
17. Braham, *The Politics of Genocide.*
18. Kádár and Vági, *Self-financing Genocide.*
19. *Report on the Activities of the Red Cross in Hungary, 1944–45.*
20. In his *Memoirs*, Horthy claimed he had not seen the Auschwitz Protocols until later.
21. Kasztner, "A Nagy Embervásár."
22. *Der Kasztner-Bericht.*
23. Jaross's people convinced Serédi that the government was already taking action on the matter of the converted Jews. It was not.

CHAPTER 16: BLESSINGS FROM HEAVEN

My sources for scenes and dialogue include Kasztner's and Palgi's testimonies at the Grünwald trial; Hansi Brand's interviews by Barshaked; Palgi, *Into the Inferno*; Biss, *A Million Jews to Save*; and notes from Kasztner's secretary, Lily Ungár.

1. Interviewed by Gabriel Barshaked.
2. Since 1941, Yishuv leaders had pressured the British to establish a special Jewish squadron. David Ben-Gurion had been assured that the United States would be onside for at least elite commando units of the Haganah to be used against the Reich. In 1942 Moshe Shertok had asked if they could be used in Poland or Bulgaria. His proposals were rejected.
3. Porat, *The Blue and the Yellow Stars of David.*
4. Schur, *Hannah Szenes.*
5. Kasztner discovered later that he was in Mauthausen, a concentration camp in Austria.
6. Hansi Brand, interviewed by Barshaked.
7. Ibid.

CHAPTER 17: STRASSHOF: THE JEWS ON ICE

Some information in this chapter is based on Braham, *The Politics of Genocide*; Szita, *Aki Egy Embert Megment* and *Utak a Pokolból*; Schiller, *A Strasshofi Mentőakció*; and *Der Kasztner-Bericht*.

1. Braham, *The Politics of Genocide*.
2. Szita, *Aki Egy Embert Megment*.
3. Most of these were systematically beaten to death by the guards, and they lie buried in mass graves in Strasshof.
4. Letter from Kaltenbrunner to Blaschke, June 7, 1944.
5. Paul Varnai, interviewed by the author in Budapest in 2006.
6. Hargittai, *Our Lives*.
7. During the years of Nazi terror, over 100,000 Austrian gentiles were incarcerated and almost 20,000 were murdered by the Gestapo.

CHAPTER 18: THE MEMORIES OF PETER MUNK
AND ERWIN SCHAEFFER

1. Interviewed by the author in Toronto in 2003–04.
2. Interviewed by the author in Budapest in 2003–04 and 2007, and in New York by phone.
3. Katharina Munk survived Auschwitz and returned to Budapest. Eventually, she remarried and ended up in Toronto. She died in 1988.
4. To this day, Erwin is convinced that one of those men was Rezső Kasztner.

CHAPTER 19: THE JOURNEY

I read numerous accounts of this journey and the arrival at Bergen-Belsen and interviewed several people who were on the train.

1. According to André Biss, the number leaving Budapest was 1,300, and the other 200 clambered aboard at various stages when the train stopped.
2. Szita, *Aki Egy Embert Megment*.
3. In his memoir, "Five Months," Fülöp von Freudiger writes of how deeply he resented being given so few seats for the Orthodox, who, in his view, "constituted half of the Jewish population in the country," though

only 10 percent in Budapest.

4. Szita, *Aki Egy Embert Megment.*

5. Margit Fendrich, interviewed by the author in June and December 2006. The boy's name: Yitzhak Weinberg.

6. "Erőltetett Menet" (Forced March), by Jenő Kolb, is a diary of the train journey. I have relied on it for many details in this chapter.

7. Auspitz bei Brunn, in Austria.

8. Biss, *A Million Jews to Save.*

9. Braham, *The Politics of Genocide.*

10. Bergen-Belsen did not become a death camp where more than 100,000 people were murdered and where thousands died of typhoid, or dysentery, or hunger until much later, when other camps were evacuated as the Allies advanced.

11. Schiller, *A Strasshofi Mentőakció.*

12. Zsolt, *Kilenc Koffer,* author's translation.

13. Kolb, "Erőltetett Menet."

14. Ibid.

15. Ibid.

CHAPTER 20: THE END OF THE GREAT PLAN

1. Dated July 12, 1944, the letter was sent to Schwalb in Geneva.

2. Freudiger, "Five Months."

3. Bader would, from 1949 to 1951, be a Mapai member of the Knesset.

4. Friling, "Nazi-Jewish Negotiations in Istanbul in Mid-1944."

5. Weissberg, *Advocate for the Dead.*

6. Ibid.

7. Bauer, *Jews for Sale?*

8. Ibid.

9. Hirschmann, *Life Line to a Promised Land.*

10. Churchill to Eden, July 11, 1944, cited in Porat, *The Blue and the Yellow Stars of David.*

11. Churchill dismissed US State Department concerns over Soviet suspicions about the ss deal, which he referred to as "a naked piece of blackmail on threats of murder."

12. Weissberg, *Advocate for the Dead.*

13. Kasztner, "A Nagy Embervásár."
14. The coffee had been paid for by the Joint.
15. Hansi Brand, interviewed by Gabriel Barshaked in Tel Aviv.
16. Stern, "A Race Against Time."
17. *Report on the Activities of the Red Cross in Hungary, 1944–45*.
18. According to Komoly's diaries, he was now dealing with a range of people in all political parties. Discussions included his potential role in a postwar Hungarian government.
19. In his postwar book *We Struggled for Life*, Rafi Benshalom characterized the official leaders of Hungarian Jewry as a "particularly ugly lot," and charged Krausz, personally, with incompetence and willful obstruction of kalutz activities through his Palestine Office.
20. Stern, "A Race against Time."
21. Wisliceny's testimony at Nuremberg.
22. Cole, in *Holocaust City*, estimates the number of people deported between May 15 and July 8, 1944, as 437,402.

CHAPTER 21: STILL TRADING IN LIVES

1. Bauer, *Jews for Sale?*
2. Braham, *The Politics of Genocide*, vol. 2.
3. Brand's testimony at the Grünwald and Eichmann trials. Hecht, in *Perfidy*, says: "His Lordship had already tried the bottom of the Mediterranean for the Jews on the refugee ships," a reference to the sinkings of the vessels *Struma*, *Patria*, and others.
4. *Der Kasztner-Bericht*.
5. Braham, *The Politics of Genocide*.
6. *Der Kasztner-Bericht*.
7. Kasztner, "A Nagy Embervásár."
8. Biss, *A Million Jews to Save*.
9. *Der Kasztner-Bericht*.
10. Braham, in *The Politics of Genocide*, says that only seven thousand people held these emigration certificates, but Porat, in *The Blue and the Yellow Stars of David*, claims there were eight thousand. Given that none of these would-be emigrants made it out of the country, this difference is of purely academic interest.

11. Porat, *The Blue and the Yellow Stars of David.*

12. Salamon, *Keresztény Voltam Európában.*

13. According to Ferenczy's testimony to the Hungarian State Police, the meeting was actually arranged by Petö.

14. Braham, *The Politics of Genocide.*

15. Kádár and Vági, *Self-financing Genocide.*

16. *Report of Roswell McClelland on the Activities of the War Refugee Board in Switzerland,* Dossier on the Saly Mayer Negotiations.

17. Wallenberg arrived on July 9, the day that the Hungarian countryside was emptied of Jews.

18. LeBor, *Hitler's Secret Bankers.*

19. Freudiger, "Five Months."

20. *Der Kasztner-Bericht.*

21. Wyman, *The Abandonment of the Jews.*

22. The effort included two volumes containing all the particulars and photographs of 2,200 people.

23. Telegram from the American Legation to the War Refugee Board, August 11, 1944.

24. Braham, *The Politics of Genocide.*

25. Porat, *The Blue and the Yellow Stars of David.*

26. Kasztner's notes from the meeting, dated July 15, 1944.

27. Eichmann told Kasztner he had been told to let about five hundred go, but he could use his judgment for the exact number. "It could be more or less," he said.

CHAPTER 22: THE BRIDGE AT SAINT MARGARETHEN

All the participants wrote, reported, or testified about the first meeting on the bridge and its aftermath. See also Bauer and Guttman, "The Negotiations between Saly Mayer and the Representatives of the ss in 1944–1945," and Dossier on the Saly Mayer Negotiations, Records of the War Refugee Board.

1. Bauer, *Jews for Sale?*

2. John Pehle of the War Refugee Board had written to U.S. undersecretary of state Edward R. Stettinius on August 17: "I feel strongly that we cannot enter into any ransom transactions with the German authorities in order to obtain the release of the Jews."

3. Cabled report on the meeting from the American legation in Bern.

4. George Bishop, interviewed by the author in New York.

5. Lowy, *A Kálváriától a Tragédiáig.*

6. Himmler's telegram is dated August 25, the date that had originally been set for the start of the deportations of Budapest's Jews. This telegram, document number K-214067 of the Nuremberg documents, is quoted by Dov Dinur as conclusive proof that Kasztner's dealings with Becher were responsible for the postponement and eventual cancellation of the deportations.

7. Hausner, *Justice in Jerusalem.*

8. *Der Kasztner-Bericht.*

9. The Bratislava Working Group was still convinced that all that stood between Slovak Jews and deportation was Wisliceny's greed.

10. Bauer, *Jews for Sale?*

11. Ibid.

CHAPTER 23: THE END OF SUMMER

1. Wisliceny's testimony at Nuremberg.

2. *Der Kasztner-Bericht.*

3. Ibid.

4. In his account, André Biss takes credit for sending Grüson into this meeting with Brunner.

5. Biss, *A Million Jews to Save.*

6. *Der Kasztner-Bericht.*

7. Ibid.

8. Biss, *A Million Jews to Save.*

9. Biss described him as "a member of the ss equipment section," one of the "moderate group of economists."

10. There are three versions of what was said at this meeting. I have chosen the one related by Wyler-Schmidt.

11. *Der Kasztner-Bericht.*

12. Ibid.

13. Davies, *Europe.*

14. Szita, *Aki Egy Embert Megment;* report prepared by Lily Ungár, Kasztner's secretary.

15. Kollek was born near Budapest but grew up in Vienna.

16. Weissberg, *Advocate for the Dead.*

17. Documentary film, *Alois Brunner: The Last Nazi.*

18. According to the Bratislava Working Group's estimates, there were between two thousand and three thousand Jews in hiding.

CHAPTER 24: THE DYING DAYS OF BUDAPEST

1. Braham, *Hungarian Jewish Studies,* vol. 3.

2. Keegan, *The Second World War.*

3. "The Diary Of Ottó Komoly"; *Der Kasztner-Bericht.*

4. In his *Memoirs*, Horthy claims that had the Allies followed his suggestion, the war would have ended several months before it did.

5. Biss's "gentleman soldier" Klages died of his wounds.

6. Braham, *The Politics of Genocide.*

7. Szita, *Aki Egy Embert Megment.*

8. Later, he changed his name to Yehuda Lahav and became a successful journalist and author in Israel. Despite his disagreement with this author's conclusions, he was an early and helpful critic of this manuscript.

9. Interviewed by the author.

10. *Der Kasztner-Bericht*, and Kasztner's typed records of meetings.

11. Geschke, as SD commander, had been directly responsible for the reprisals against the civilian population of Lidice following the killing of Heydrich by partisans.

12. Schwartz, *Living Memory.*

13. *Perlasca: An Italian Hero*, film by Rai Fiction and Focus Film.

14. Interviewed by the author in Toronto in 2006.

15. October 17 memorandum from Byron Price of the Office of Censorship, Washington, to John Pehle: "Transactions of this nature are clearly in violation of the 'Trading with the Enemy Act.'"

16. Cohen, "The Halutz Resistance."

17. Benshalom, *We Struggled for Life.*

18 Hausner, *Justice in Jerusalem.*

19. Interviewed by the author in Toronto in 2006.

CHAPTER 25: IN THE SHADOW OF THE
THIRD REICH'S FINAL DAYS

The dialogue in this chapter is based on both Kasztner's and Saly Mayer's recollections.

1. Mayer warned Becher to stop negotiating on the basis of a "trade in humans." Becher responded that the actual words used were irrelevant, but he agreed to say "performance" and "counterperformance" when he met McClelland the next day.
2. *Der Kasztner-Bericht.*
3. Kasztner, "A Nagy Embervásár."
4. Jüttner's testimony for Eichmann's trial.
5. Becher's testimony at Nuremberg.
6. According to the Kasztner Bericht, there were about 3,500 people at Columbus Street at this time.
7. Cohen, "The Halutz Resistance."
8. Schmidt, "Mentés Vagy Árulás?"
9. *Der Kasztner-Bericht.*
10. The total number of Jews sent on the "death march" is reported to have been between forty thousand and eighty thousand, about half of whom arrived alive.
11. Bauer, *Jews for Sale?*
12. Cole, *Holocaust City.*
13. The last murders by gassing in Auschwitz had taken place at the end of October. Whether Becher had anything to do with Himmler's change of attitude is doubtful. The crematoria in Auschwitz-Birkenau were demolished starting on November 25, and it would have taken a few days for them to be completely destroyed.
14. Margit Fendrich, interviewed by the author.
15. Biss, *A Million Jews to Save.*
16. *Der Kasztner-Bericht.*
17. Ibid.
18. Hansi explained in her taped interviews with Gabriel Barshaked that she had not agreed to his proposal but merely let it hang in the air, as they both waited for the atrocities to end.
19. Most of the money for medicines and food came from the Joint via the

International Red Cross.

20. According to Kádár and Vági, in *Self-financing Genocide*, eight hundred wagons and thirty barges carried Becher's loot out of Hungary.

21. According to István Deak, this figure is only "a popular legend."

22. Kádár and Vági, *Self-financing Genocide*.

23. Zweig, *The Gold Train*.

24. Musy, staunchly Catholic, initially had been an admirer of the Nazis.

25. Kasztner had to check in with Dr. Adolf Ebner, the Gestapo's second-in-command in Vienna, who instructed him to have no contact with Aryans and not to reveal to anyone at the Grand that he was a Jew.

26. According to Kasztner, the records showed 18,220 people.

27. Schiller, *A Strasshofi Mentőakció*.

28. Rees, *Auschwitz*.

29. According to Randolph Braham, approximately 440,000 people.

30. The first estimate, by the Soviet government, of the number of people murdered at Auschwitz was four million. Historians still disagree on the exact number: Hilberg's figure is one million, Gilbert's is two million, and Bauer's is 2.5 million for the Jews only. Numbers for the different nationalities vary as well. I have chosen to go with Kádár and Vági's numbers because they are among the most recent estimates.

31. Rees, *Auschwitz*. Piper, in his book *Auschwitz*, estimates that the number of dead could be as high as 1.5 million, but as the Germans kept no record of those murdered in the gas chambers immediately on their arrival, it is difficult to find the exact number.

32. International Military Tribunal, Nuremberg, 15 April, 1946.

33. Krumey's testimony for Eichmann's trial.

34. Szita, *Aki Egy Embert Megment*.

35. Wisliceny's testimony at Nuremberg.

36. *Der Kasztner-Bericht*; Wisliceny's testimony at Nuremberg.

37. Schiller, *A Strasshofi Mentőakció*.

38. Already, in 1943, he had told an ss audience that "it is now deplorable by reason of the loss of labor that the prisoners died in tens and hundreds of thousands of exhaustion and hunger."

39. Varnai, "Jaj a Gyermekkor Milyen Tündéri Szép Volt."

CHAPTER 26: BUDAPEST IN THE THROES OF
LIBERATION

1. On November 7 General Ottó Hátszegi-Hatz had defected to the Soviets with the complete Margarethen line defense plans, and on November 13 Major Ernő Simonffy-Tóth delivered the plans for the defense of the city.

2. Interviewed by the author in Toronto in 2006.

3. Lahav, *Sebhelyes Élet.*

4. Dani Brand, interviewed by the author in Tel Aviv in 2005 and 2006.

5. Ungváry, *The Siege of Budapest.*

6. Schwartz, *Living Memory.*

7. A photocopy of the certificate was displayed at the Citadel in Budapest in 2006 at an exhibition commemorating the siege. Jerezien is mentioned in Gilbert, *The Righteous,* his account of non-Jews who assisted the Jews during these terrible years.

8. Hansi Brand, interviewed by Gabriel Barshaked.

9. Shirer, *The Rise and Fall of the Third Reich.*

10. Nuremberg testimony, November 26, 1947; Ungvary, *The Siege of Budapest.*

11. Mendelsohn and Detwiler, eds., *The Holocaust,* vol. 15; Becher took the credit during his direct questioning by Kasztner at Nuremberg on July 7, 1947.

12. Kasztner, "A Nagy Embervásár."

13. At his trial, even Ferenc Szálasi claimed credit for stopping the destruction of the ghetto.

14. Salamon, *Keresztény Voltam Európában.*

15. Ungváry, *The Siege of Budapest.*

16. Ibid.

17. Davies, *Europe;* Keegan, in *The Second World War,* says the numbers were grossly exaggerated and estimates only thirty thousand.

18. Szilágyi, *Ismeretlen Memoár a Magyar Veszkorszakról.*

19. The deposit had been approved "for humanitarian purposes" on January 24. See also the letter from the American Joint Distribution Committee of February 16.

20. According to Szita, in *Aki Egy Embert Megment,* between November 28

and December 21 the money was deposited with Th. Willy, a Lucerne firm that used the cash to pay for sixteen tractors for a German firm. *Der Kasztner-Bericht* says the deposit purchased 122 tractors and 30 trucks. In addition, three truckloads of food were sent from Switzerland to the concentration camps.

CHAPTER 27: NAZI GOLD

1. *Der Kasztner-Bericht.*
2. Bauer, *Jews for Sale?*
3. This order, issued in October 1944, was submitted in evidence against Ernst Kaltenbrunner at Nuremberg on April 12, 1946.
4. Becher's testimony for Eichmann's trial; *Der Kasztner-Bericht.*
5. In March alone, 18,168 prisoners had died of hunger and disease.
6. Margit Fendrich, interviewed by the author; Hansi Brand, interviewed by Gabriel Barshaked.
7. The Allies established a "uniform legal basis in Germany for the prosecution of war criminals" with trials to be held in Nuremberg before the International Military Tribunal. Ernst Kaltenbrunner was tried and convicted by these proceedings. Twelve separate trials followed, known as the Subsequent Nuremberg Proceedings.
8. Kádár and Vági, *Self-financing Genocide.*
9. Szita, in *Aki Egy Embert Megment,* says the journey took twelve days.
10. *Der Kasztner-Bericht* reported that Wisliceny had, in fact, been appointed "inspector of Theresienstadt" and was traveling there in his new capacity.
11. Szita, *Aki Egy Embert Megment.*
12. When Kaltenbrunner was confronted at Nuremberg on April 12, 1946, with testimony given earlier by Ziereis, he denied having given such an order.
13. After Himmler was given a fierce tongue-lashing by Hitler, according to Bauer in *Jews for Sale?*
14. Kaltenbrunner's office was moved to Salzburg to avoid destruction by Allied bombings of Berlin.
15. Moshe Schweiger's Report, October 21, 1945.
16. Becher's testimony for Eichmann's trial.

17. Becher's and Kaltenbrunner's testimonies at Nuremberg.

18. Bauer, *Jews for Sale?*

19. Kádár and Vági, *Self-financing Genocide*.

20. Bauer, *Jews for Sale?*

21. According to Bauer, Wallenberg saved 4,500 Jews with his papers and his personal intervention with both the Arrow Cross and the Szálasi government operatives.

22. Bauer, *A History of the Holocaust*.

23. Paul Varnai's interview with István Domonkos.

PART FOUR: DEATH WITH HONOR

1. Segev, *The Seventh Million*.

CHAPTER 28: IN SEARCH OF A LIFE

For some scenes I relied on Szilágyi, *Ismeretlen Memoár*; my interviews with Tom Margittai, Eva Carmeli, and Margit Fendrich; Hansi Brand's interviews by Barshaked; and interviews in the Brubyak Studio film *Kasztner*.

1. Weitz, "The Man Who Was Murdered Twice."

2. Tom Margittai, interviewed by the author.

3. Novák, "Egy Ismeretlen Kronikája."

4. In Bill Jones's documentary film *Secret History*.

5. Tschuy, *Dangerous Diplomacy*.

6. In the English-language edition published in 2003, Palgi talks of the horror with which Kasztner received him and Goldstein in Budapest, particularly his consternation at the Yishuv's belated and completely useless rescue plan. But he also claims that Kasztner had promised to help all three of the parachutists escape from prison if he and Goldstein succeeded in convincing their captors that they had come as emissaries of the Jewish Agency on behalf of the blood-for-goods deal.

7. Information from Zsuzsi Kasztner.

8. The private Kasztner archive, consisting of three boxes of letters to family and friends, was donated to Yad Vashem on June 22, 2007. This is an excerpt from Kasztner's letter to his Kolozsvar friend Hilel Danzig on February 6, 1946. The translation is my own.

"You are probably familiar with these feelings of depression and shame, the strange malaise that we few survivors are experiencing when we think of the millions who died. This feeling is particularly overwhelming when we think not of the numbers and the geography but of the individuals, our friends, our comrades, whose lives are preserved only in our fading memories. I would have been shocked to learn of Ferenc Goldstein's death had he been one of the six million, but I knew him well, we grew up together . . .

"I am overcome with rage at the memory of our helplessness, our desperation, our efforts to fight for lives—and he offered up his own life with the natural grace of a true hero to help us . . . I believe that we were both driven by the same ideals, the same desperation, and we fought for the same cause, though with different weapons."

9. The Criminal Division of the Hungarian State Police held hearings to determine whether to prosecute members of the Budapest Va'ada, including Kasztner. Ferenczy gave a deposition on April 19, 1946 (the document is in the Hungarian National Archives) regarding his meetings with Kasztner and members of the Jewish Council. In November 1945, David Ben-Gurion noted in his diary that Kasztner believed he was accused of being a collaborator and was afraid to go to Palestine. Yechiam Weitz writes about the process adopted by the Jewish Agency Executive to determine whether formal hearings should be held, c.f. his book "The Man Who Was Murdered Twice."

10. Menachem Begin was from Poland, and most of his family and his village had been murdered during the Holocaust. He survived the Nazis and a Soviet slave camp. In 1943 he became the leader of the clandestine Irgun, the Revisionists' army. He was, from the beginning, against all deals and negotiations with the British—at least while they were ensconced in Palestine.

11. Central Zionist Archives.

12. Statement of Israel Kastner before the American Investigative Committee for War Crimes, Headed by Justice Jackson, Regarding the Jews of Hungary.

13. Barri, "The Question of Kastner's Testimonies on Behalf of Nazi War Criminals." The statements by Kasztner were made on September 13, 1945.

14. Zweig, *The Gold Train*.

15. The affidavit is dated October 21, 1945.
16. Information from Zsuzsi Kasztner.
17. Hansi Brand, interviewed by Gabriel Barshaked.
18. Eva Carmeli, interviewed by the author in Tel Aviv in 2006.
19. *Der Kasztner-Bericht.*
20. A short version of his report appeared in the Hungarian newspaper *Haladás* (Progress) on December 25, 1946.
21. Hansi Brand, interviewed by Barshaked.
22. Shoshana Barri's research on this change of attitude and the reasons for it can be seen in her articles "The Question of Kastner's Testimonies on Behalf of Nazi War Criminals" and "The Kastner Affair: Correspondence between Kurt Becher and Dr. Chaim Posner, 1948."
23. January 20, Central Zionist Archives.
24. Zweig, *The Gold Train.*
25. The sentences against the twenty-four defendants in the first of the Nuremberg Trials before the International Military Tribunal, the so-called Trial of the Major War Criminals, were handed down on October 1, 1946. The Subsequent Nuremberg Trials began on October 25.
26. Margit Fendrich, interviewed by the author.
27. Zweig, *The Gold Train.*
28. Wisliceny's testimony at Nuremberg.
29. Kasztner's statement at Nuremberg, August 4, 1947.
30. Kasztner's testimonies at Nuremberg. Transcripts of testimonies can be found in Trial of the Major War Criminals before the International Military Tribunal Sitting in Nuremberg, Germany . . . from the Official Transcripts and online through the Nizkor Project.

CHAPTER 29: THE JEWS OF THE EXILE

I relied for some scenes in this chapter on my interviews with Zsuzsi Kasztner, Adam Heller, and Dani Brand; information provided by Yitzhak Katsir; Hansi Brand's interviews by Barshaked; the Brubyak Studio film *Kasztner*; and Segev, *The Seventh Million.*

1. In a telephone interview with the author in December 2006.
2. Having failed to prevent another world war, the League of Nations dissolved itself in 1946. Its mandates were transferred to the United

Nations, founded in 1945 to replace the League and operate under a more effective structure.

3. In his testimony before the International Military Tribunal, Wisliceny had also credited Krumey with selling Eichmann on the idea of Kasztner's "Jews on ice" in Austria.

4. Segev, *The Seventh Million*.

5. Ibid.

6. Adam Heller, interviewed by the author in 2007.

7. Segev, *The Seventh Million*.

8. Johnson, *A History of the Jews*.

CHAPTER 30: THE PRINCE OF DARKNESS IS A GENTLEMAN

For details of Becher's life I relied on Müller-Tupath, *Reichsführers gehorsamster Becher*; Becher's testimonies at Nuremberg and for Eichmann's trial; and Kádár and Vági, *Self-financing Genocide*.

1. Kádár and Vági, *Self-financing Genocide*.

2. Bauer, *Jews for Sale?*

3. Barri, "The Kastner Affair: The Correspondence between Kurt Becher and Dr. Chaim Posner, 1948."

4. Müller-Tupath, *Reichsführers gehorsamster Becher*.

5. Zsuzsi Kasztner, interviewed by the author.

6. Interviewed by Gabriel Barshaked.

7. Barri, "The Kastner Affair."

8. *Alois Brunner*, Cinevision film.

CHAPTER 31: LETTERS TO FRIENDS IN THE MIZRACHI

I used as my main sources for scenes the Israeli Broadcasting Authority's miniseries *Mishpat Kastner*, written by Motti Lerner and based on his extensive interviews and the Grünwald trial's transcripts; Weitz, "The Man Who Was Murdered Twice"; Hecht, *Perfidy*; Segev, *The Seventh Million*; information provided by Yitzhak Katsir; and Hansi Brand's interviews by Barshaked.

1. No. 51 (August 1952).

2. Yechiam Weitz, "The Man Who Was Murdered Twice," and *Mishpat Kastner* film.

3. In a case of criminal libel, as this case would be, in Israel it is the government who lays the charges; the person allegedly libeled needs merely to cooperate.

4. Hansi Brand, interviewed by Gabriel Barshaked.

5. Ofry, *Egy Évszázad Tanúja*.

6. Segev, *The Seventh Million*.

7. Bilsky, "Judging Evil in the Trial of Kastner."

8. Yechiam Weitz, "The Man Who Was Murdered Twice," and *Mishpat Kastner* film.

9. Hansi Brand, interviewed by Barshaked.

10. Ofry, *Egy Évszázad Tanúja*.

11. The reparations and compensation agreements between West Germany and Israel were signed in September 1952 by Moshe Sharett and Konrad Adenauer. Throughout the long negotiations there were protests, including one assassination attempt, by Jews who disagreed with any deals with the murderers of six million Jews. At the end of the process, the German government committed to pay 3.4 million marks, partly in German goods, partly in fuel, and to compensate Nazi victims for lost property, imprisonment, and slave labor. Many Holocaust survivors viewed the appearance of German-made products in Israeli stores as disturbing reminders of the past; others found the bureaucratic maneuverings around the applications for restitution humiliating. However, the total positive effect of the financial gains on Israel's shaky economy was indisputable.

12. Hansi Brand, interviewed by Gabriel Barshaked, and *Mishpat Kastner* film.

13. Hansi Brand, interviewed by Gabriel Barshaked; *Mishpat Kastner* film; Segev and Weitz.

14. Ben Hecht, *Perfidy*; *Mishpat Kastner* film; Yehuda Bauer.

15. This, strictly speaking, was true.

16. *Mishpat Kastner* film.

17. Hecht, *Perfidy*.

18. Ben-Gurion to Yehoshua [Gyula] Kastner, February 2, 1958.

19. Barri, "The Question of Kastner's Testimonies on Behalf of Nazi War

Criminals"; Barri, "The Kastner Affair: Correspondence between Kurt Becher and Dr. Chaim Posner, 1948."

20. In a letter to Judge Halevi, Kasztner accused Dobkin of extraordinary forgetfulness.

21. Mosle Sharett's letter to the press, July 12, 1955, responds to accusations that he and the Agency did little to alert the Yishur to the murder of European Jews. He lists successive actions by himself and the Agency Executive.

22. Segev, *The Seventh Million*.

23. Yechiam Weitz, "The Man Who Was Murdered Twice."

24. Yitzhak Katsir, in a note to the author. Adam Heller's father went to see the Szatmár rabbi, personally, to ask him to testify. He refused.

CHAPTER 32: THE PRICE OF A MAN'S SOUL

For scenes at and around the trial I relied most on Israeli Broadcasting Authority's miniseries *Mishpat Kastner*; Weitz, "The Man Who Was Murdered Twice"; Hecht, *Perfidy*; Segev, *The Seventh Million*; information provided by Yitzhak Katsir; Hansi Brand's interviews by Barshaked; Zsuzsi Kasztner's recollections; Nagy, *A Kasztner Akció*; and coverage of the trial in the *New York Times*. Regarding the information from Kolozsvár, see also Tibori Szabó's thesis, "Az Erdélyi Zsidóság Identitástudatának Alakulása."

1. Numbers vary with the source. Szita in *A Humánum Példái* cites 1,552.

2. Records of the War Refugee Board, box 43, Franklin D. Roosevelt Library, Hyde Park, NY.

3. Krausz was described by Palgi, among others.

4. Yechiam Weitz, "The Man Who Was Murdered Twice."

5. Hansi Brand, interviewed by Gabriel Barshaked.

6. Segev, *The Seventh Million*.

7. Transcripts of the Kasztner trial.

8. *Mishpat Kastner* film; Hansi Brand, interviewed by Gabriel Barshaked.

9. Hansi Brand, interviewed by Barshaked.

10. Nagy, *A Kasztner Akció*.

11. Weitz, "The Man Who Was Murdered Twice"; transcripts of the Kasztner trial.

12. Ibid.
13. Weitz, "The Man Who Was Murdered Twice"; *Mishpat Kastner* film.
14. Ibid.
15. Ibid.
16. Dreyfus was a Jewish French army officer who in 1895 was wrongfully imprisoned for treason; he was officially exonerated years later.
17. *Haboker*, June 23, 1955; official statement for the Voice of Israel, the government's broadcasting service.
18. Gilroy, "Quisling Charge Stirs All Israel."
19. Information from Zsuzsi Kasztner.
20. Weitz, "The Man Who Was Murdered Twice."

CHAPTER 33: THE CONSEQUENCES

1. Weitz, "The Man Who Was Murdered Twice."
2. Gilroy, "Israeli Cabinet Asked to Resign." "Greenwald" is a variant of "Grünwald."
3. Segev, *The Seventh Million*.
4. Gilroy, "Quisling Charge Stirs All Israel."
5. Karen, *Haaretz*. June 24, 1955.
6. Segev, *The Seventh Million*.
7. *Mishpat Kastner* film.
8. Tomy Lapid, interviewed in the film *Kasztner*.

CHAPTER 34: THE AFTERMATH

1. Weitz, "The Man Who Was Murdered Twice."
2. Márton, *Új Kelet*. April 17, 1957.
3. Adam Heller, interviewed by the author.
4. Friling, "Nazi-Jewish Negotiations in Istanbul in Mid-1944."
5. Weitz, "The Man Who Was Murdered Twice."
6. Born in Vienna, Kollek emigrated in 1934. He was an emissary of Hechalutz in Europe, a member of the Jewish Agency's Political Department from 1940 till 1947, and a close friend of Ben-Gurion, and he had been chief of staff in the prime minister's office. He was elected mayor of Jerusalem in 1967, a position he continued to hold for a quarter of a century.

7. Shlomo Aronson, interviewed by the author in Tel Aviv in 2006.

8. Tschuy, *Dangerous Diplomacy*.

9. Eva Carmeli, interviewed by the author. She was proud to have been one of Hansi's friends.

CHAPTER 35: THE BANALITY OF EVIL

1. A German-born American journalist, editor, professor, and author, Arendt subtitled her book about the Eichmann trial *A Report on the Banality of Evil*. For some portions of this chapter I relied on her report but also on Eichmann's own testimonies; Hausner, *Justice in Jerusalem*; Reitlinger, *The Final Solution*; and Von Lang, *Eichmann Interrogated*.

2. Throughout the Eichmann trial, newspapers in Jordan, Syria, and Egypt voiced their sympathy for the accused and their regret that he had failed in his mission.

3. Hansi Brand, interviewed by Gabriel Barshaked.

4. Biss, *A Million Jews to Save*.

5. *Saturday Evening Post*, November 3, 1962.

CHAPTER 36: OTHER LIVES

1. The three-part 1994 television miniseries *Mishpat Kastner* (The Kastner Trial, or Kastner Family), written by Motti Lerner, was shown by Israeli television in 1995; the program renewed the debate about Kasztner's role in saving Becher's life and the issue of his dealings with the ss in 1944–45.

2. At www.kasztnermemorial.com/.

3. Mayer, "Jewish Holocaust Rescuer Murdered in Tel Aviv."

4. Szilágyi, *Ismeretlen Memoár*.

5. Ibid.

6. Novák, "Egy Ismeretlen Kronikája."

7. *Financial Post*, December 23, 2005.

8. *Toronto Star*, May 31, 2006.

9. Anna Perczel, an architect and historian I met in 2006 and 2007, explained the danger of losing buildings that still hold Hungarians' collective memory of the Holocaust and of the only ghetto in Europe that most people survived. She co-authored the book *Séták a Zsidóne-gyedben* (Walks in the Jewish Quarter), published in 2006.

Bibliography

BOOKS

Abella, Irving, and Harold Troper. *None Is Too Many: Canada and the Jews of Europe, 1933–1948*. Toronto: Key Porter Books, 2000.

Aranyi, Asher. *One Eye Cries While the Other Laughs*. Translated by Rochelle Mass. Kibbutz Dalia: Maarechet, 2002.

Arendt, Hannah. *Eichmann in Jerusalem: A Report on the Banality of Evil*. 1963. Rev. ed. New York: Penguin Group, 1994.

Aronson, Shlomo. *Hitler, the Allies, and the Jews*. Cambridge, UK: Cambridge University Press, 2004.

Barta, George. *Odyssey of a Survivor*. Toronto: Sigma, 1998.

Bauer, Yehuda. *The Jewish Emergence from Powerlessness*. London, UK: Palgrave Macmillan, 1980.

———. *The Holocaust in Historical Perspective*. Seattle: University of Washington Press, 1982.

———. *Jews for Sale? Nazi-Jewish Negotiations, 1933–1945*. New Haven, CT: Yale University Press, 1994.

———. *A History of the Holocaust*. Rev. ed. Danbury, CT: Franklin Watts, 2001.

Benedek, István, and György Vámos. *Tépd Le a Sárga Csillagot*. Budapest: Pallas Lap és Könyv, 1990.

Benshalom, Rafi. *We Struggled for Life: The Hungarian Zionist Youth Resistance during the Nazi Era*. Jerusalem: Gefen, 2001.

Ben-Tov, Arieh. *Facing the Holocaust in Budapest: The International Committee of the Red Cross and the Jews of Hungary, 1943–1945*. Boston: Martinus Nijhoff, 1988.

Biss, André. *A Million Jews to Save: One of the Most Startling Untold Stories of the Second World War*. London: New English Library, 1975.

Botting, Douglas. *The Aftermath: Europe*. Alexandria, VA: Time-Life Books, 1983.

Braham, Randolph L. *The Destruction of Hungarian Jewry: A Documentary Account*. New York: Pro Arte, 1963.

———. *The Hungarian Jewish Catastrophe: A Selected and Annotated Bibliography*. New York: Social Science Monographs, and the Institute for Holocaust Studies, City University of New York, 1984.

———. *Studies on the Holocaust in Hungary*. Boulder: Social Science Monographs; New York: Csengeri Institute for Holocaust Studies of the Graduate School and University Center, City University of New York, 1990.

———. *The Politics of Genocide: The Holocaust in Hungary*. Rev. ed. 2 vols. New York: Rosenthal Institute of Holocaust Studies, City University of New York; Boulder: Social Science Monographs, 1994.

———, ed. *Hungarian Jewish Studies*. 3 vols. New York: World Federation of Hungarian Jews, 1966–69.

———, ed. *Contemporary Views on the Holocaust*. Boston: Kluwer-Nijhoff, 1983.

———, ed. *Perspectives on the Holocaust*. Hingham, MA: Kluwer-Nijhoff, 1983.

———, ed. *The Tragedy of Hungarian Jewry: Essays, Documents, Depositions*. New York: Institute for Holocaust Studies, City University of New York; Boulder: Social Science Monographs, 1987.

———, ed. *The Tragedy of Romanian Jewry*. East European Monographs. New York: Rosenthal Institute for Holocaust Studies, City University of New York, 1994.

———, ed. *The Wartime System of Labor Service in Hungary: Varieties of Experiences*. New York: Rosenthal Institute of Holocaust Studies, Graduate Center of the City University of New York; Boulder: Social Science Monographs, 1995.

Braham, Randolph L., and Scott Miller, eds. *The Nazis' Last Victims: The Holocaust in Hungary*. Detroit: Wayne State University Press, in association with United States Holocaust Memorial Museum, 1998.

Braham, Randolph L., and Attila Pók, eds. *The Holocaust in Hungary: Fifty Years Later*. New York: Rosenthal Institute for Holocaust Studies,

Graduate Center of the City University of New York / Europa Institute, Social Science Monographs, 1997.

Braham, Randolph L., and Béla Vágo, eds. *The Holocaust in Hungary: Forty Years Later*. New York: Social Science Monographs, and Institute of Holocaust Studies, City University of New York and University of Haifa, 1985.

Brand, Joel and Hansi. *Satan and the Soul*. Tel Aviv: Ladori, 1960.

Brenner, Lenni. *Zionism in the Age of the Dictators*. London: Croom Helm, 1982.

Cesarani, David. *Eichmann: His Life and Crimes*. London: Vintage, 2005.

Chesnoff, Richard Z. *Pack of Thieves: How Hitler and Europe Plundered the Jews and Committed the Greatest Theft in History*. London: Weidenfeld & Nicolson, 2000.

Chorin Strasser, Daisy. *Az Andrássy Úttól a Park Avenue-ig: Fejezetek Chorin Ferenc Életéből, 1879–1964*. Budapest: Osiris, 1999.

Cohen, Asher. "The Halutz Resistance and the Anti-Nazi Movements in Hungary, 1944." In *The Holocaust in Hungary: Forty Years Later*. Edited by Rudolph L. Braham and Béla Vágo. New York: Social Science Monographs, and Institute of Holocaust Studies, City University of New York and University of Haifa, 1985.

Cole, Tim. *Holocaust City: The Making of a Jewish Ghetto*. New York: Routledge, 2003.

Davies, Norman. *Europe: A History*. Oxford: Oxford University Press, 1996.

Dinur, Dov. *Kastner: Giluyim Hadashim al Ha'ish U'poalo*. Haifa: Gastlit, 1987. An unpublished partial English translation attributed to László Devecseri and titled "Kasztner: New Light on the Man and His Deeds" was lent to the author by Peter Munk.

Dobos, Marianne. *Akkor is Karácsony Volt, 1944*. Miskolc: Bibor, 2003.

Eisenberg, Azriel Louis. *Witness to the Holocaust*. New York: Pilgrim Press, 1981.

Erdenyi, John. "Bad Old Times: The Nazi Years." In manuscript.

Feig, Konnilyn G. *Hitler's Death Camps: The Sanity of Madness*. New York: Holmes & Meier, 1981.

Fleming, Gerald. *Hitler and the Final Solution*. Berkeley: University of California Press, 1987.

Freudiger, Fülöp von. "Five Months." In *The Tragedy of Hungarian Jewry: Essays, Documents, Depositions*. Edited by Randolph L. Braham. New York: Institute for Holocaust Studies, City University of New York, 1987.

Friedlander, Sam. *Memory, History and the Extermination of the Jews of Europe*. Bloomington: Indiana University Press, 1993.

Friling, Tuvia. *Arrows in the Dark: David Ben-Gurion, the Yishuv Leadership, and Rescue Attempts during the Holocaust.* Vol. 1. Translated by Ora Cummings. Madison, WI: University of Wisconsin Press, 2005.

Gilbert, Martin. *Auschwitz and the Allies.* New York: Holt, Rinehart & Wintson, 1981.

———. *The Holocaust: The Jewish Tragedy.* London: Collins, 1986.

———. *William S. Churchill: Volume Seven: Road to Victory 1941–1945.* Oxford: William Heinemann, 1986.

———. *The Jews in the Twentieth Century: An Illustrated History.* New York: Schocken, 2001.

———. *The Righteous: The Unsung Heroes of the Holocaust.* Toronto: Key Porter Books, 2003.

———. *Churchill and the Jews.* New York: Henry Holt and Company, 2007.

Gutman, Yisrael, and Efraim Zuroff. *Rescue Attempts During the Holocaust: Proceedings of the Second Yad Vashem International Historical Conference, Jerusalem, April 8–11, 1974.* Jerusalem: Yad Vashem Institute, 1978.

Hadari, Zeev Venia. *Against All Odds, Istanbul 1944–1945.* Ministry of Defense of Israel, 1992. Parts of this book, dealing with Brand and Kasztner, were translated from Hebrew by Adam Heller for the author.

Handler, Andrew, ed. *The Holocaust in Hungary: An Anthology of Jewish Response.* Tuscaloosa, AL: University of Alabama Press, 1982.

Hargittai, István. *Our Lives.* Budapest: Akadémiai Kiadó, 2005.

Hausner, Gideon. *Justice in Jerusalem.* New York: Harper & Row, 1966.

Hecht, Ben. *Perfidy.* Jerusalem: Milah Press, 1961.

Heilper, Zwi. "From Bergen-Belsen to Caux via Lustenau." In manuscript.

Hersh, Gizelle, and Peggy Mann. *Gizelle, Save the Children!* New York: Everest House, 1980.

Herzl, Theodor. *The Jewish State.* 1896. Reprint, New York: Dover, 1989.

Hilberg, Raul. *Perpetrators, Victims, Bystanders: The Jewish Catastrophe, 1933–1945.* New York: HarperCollins, 1992.

Hirschmann, Ira A. *Life Line to a Promised Land.* New York: Vanguard, 1946.

Hitler, Adolf. *Mein Kampf.* Translated by Ralph Mannheim. New York: Houghton Mifflin, 1971.

Horthy, Miklós. *Memoirs.* New York: R. Speller, 1957.

Höss, Rudolf. *Commandant of Auschwitz: The Autobiography of Rudolf Höss.* London: Weidenfeld and Nicolson, 1959.

———. *Death Dealer: The Memoirs of the SS Kommandant of Auschwitz.* Edited by Steven Paskuly. Translated by Andrew Pollinger. Buffalo: Prometheus Books, 1992.

Ignotus, Paul. *Hungary.* New York: Praeger, 1972.

Issacson, Judith Magyar. *Seed of Sarah: Memoirs of a Survivor.* Champaign, IL: University of Illinois Press, 1990.

Johnson, Paul. *Modern Times, The World from the Twenties to the Eighties.* New York: Harper & Row, 1983.

————. *A History of the Jews.* New York: Harper & Row, 1987.

Kádár, Gábor, and Zoltán Vági. *Self-financing Genocide: The Gold Train.* Budapest: Central European University Press, 2004.

————. *Hullarablás, a Magyar Zsidók Gazdasági Megsemmisítése.* Budapest: Hannah Arendt Egyesület / Jaffa, 2005.

Kasztner, Rezső. *Der Kasztner-Bericht* (The Kasztner Report). Munich: Kindler, 1961. Originally published in 1946 as *Der Bericht des Judisches Rettungskommittes aus Budapest, 1942–1945.* The initial report was prepared for submission to the World Zionist Organization's 1946 meeting in Basel; it was subsequently published under the title *Der Kasztner-Bericht,* edited by Ernest Landau, and later as *Der Kasztner-Bericht über Eichmanns Menschenhandel in Ungarn.*

Keegan, John. *The Second World War.* New York: Penguin Books, 1990.

Keneally, Thomas. *Schindler's Ark.* London: Hodder & Stoughton, 1982.

Kertész, Imre. *Sorstalanság.* Budapest: Magvető, 1975.

Kollek, Teddy. *One Jerusalem: A History of Forty Centuries.* New York: Random House, 1968.

Komoly, Ottó. "The Diary of Ottó Komoly: August 21–September 16, 1944." In *Hungarian Jewish Studies.* Vol. 3. Edited by Randolph L. Braham. New York: World Federation of Hungarian Jews, 1966–69.

————. "What May Jews Learn from the Present Crisis?" In *The Holocaust in Hungary.* Edited by Andrew Handler. Tuscaloosa, AL: University of Alabama Press, 1982.

Kontler, László. *A History of Hungary: Millennium in Central Europe.* New York: Palgrave Macmillan, 2002.

Lahav, Yehuda. *Sebhelyes Élet.* Budapest: Makkabi, 2003.

Langlet, Nina. *A Svéd Mentőakció, 1944.* Budapest: Kossuth, 1988.

LeBor, Adam. *Hitler's Secret Bankers: How Switzerland Profited from Nazi Genocide.* New York: Simon & Schuster, 1997.

Lendvai, Paul. *Határátlépés: Az Üllői Útról a Nagyvilágba.* Budapest: Helikon, 2002.

————. *The Hungarians: A Thousand Years of Victory in Defeat.* Translated by Ann Major. Princeton, NJ: Princeton University Press, 2003.

Lévai, Jenő. *Fehér Könyv: Kulfoldi Akciók Magyar Zsidók Mentsegere.* Budapest:

Officina, 1947.

———. *The Black Book on the Martyrdom of Hungarian Jewry*. Zurich: Central European Times, 1948.

———. *Zsidósors Magyarországon*. Budapest: Magyar Téka, 1948.

Levin, Nora. *The Holocaust: The Destruction of European Jewry, 1933–1945*. New York: T.Y. Crowell, 1968.

Linnea, Sharon. *Raoul Wallenberg: The Man Who Stopped Death*. Philadelphia: Jewish Publication Society, 1993.

Lowy, Daniel. *A Kálváriától a Tragédiáig: Kolozsvár Zsidó Lakosságának Története*. Kolozsvár: Koinónia, 2005.

Lukacs, John. *Budapest 1900: A Historical Account of a City and Its Culture*. New York: Grove Press, 1988.

MacMillan, Margaret. *Paris 1919: Six Months That Changed the World*. New York: Random House, 2002.

Márai, Sándor. *Ami a Naplómból Kimaradt, 1945–1946*. Toronto: Weller Publishing, Toronto, 1968.

———. *Memoir of Hungary, 1944–1945*. Budapest: Corvina, in association with Central European University Press, 1996.

Matyas, Vince. *Korkepek 1938–1945*. Budapest: MTI, 2005.

Mendelsohn, John, and Donald S. Detwiler, eds. *The Holocaust: Selected Documents in Eighteen Volumes*. Vol. 15. New York: Garland, 1982.

Müller-Tupath, Karla. *Reichsführers gehorsamster Becher: Eine Deutsche Karriere*. Berlin: Aufbau, 1999.

Munkácsi, Ernő. *Hogyan Történt? Adatok és Okmányok a Magyar Zsidóság Tragédiájához*. Budapest: Renaissance, 1947.

Nagy, Péter S. *A Kasztner Akció, 1944*. Budapest: Rejtel, 1995.

Ofry, Dán. *Egy Évszázad Tanúja: A Dr. Hermann Dezsö-dosszié*. Budapest: Makkabi, 2001.

Palgi, Yoel. *Into the Inferno: The Memoir of a Jewish Paratrooper Behind Nazi Lines*. New Brunswick, NJ: Rutgers University Press, 2003.

Patai, Raphael. *The Jews of Hungary: History, Culture, Psychology*. Detroit: Wayne State University Press, 1996.

Piper, Franciszek. *Auschwitz: How Many Perished: Jews, Poles, Gypsies*. Oswiecim: Poligrafia, 2005.

Porat, Dina. *The Blue and the Yellow Stars of David: The Zionist Leadership in Palestine and the Holocaust, 1939–1945*. Cambridge, MA: Harvard University Press, 1990.

Rees, Laurence. *Auschwitz: A New History*. New York: PublicAffairs and BBC Books, 2005.

Reitlinger, Gerald. *The Final Solution: The Attempt to Exterminate the Jews of Europe, 1939–1945.* New York: A.S. Barnes, 1961.

Révész, Peretz. "Against a Tidal Wave of Evil." Translated from the Hebrew by Isabella Arad. In manuscript.

Rohmer, Richard. *Golden Phoenix: The Biography of Peter Munk.* Key Porter Books: Toronto, 1997.

Salamon, Andrew. *Childhood in Times of War: An Autobiography.* Toronto: SAS, 1995.

Salamon, Mihály. *Keresztény Voltam Európában: Pesti Riportregény a Nyilas Időkből.* Translated by György Vámos. Tel Aviv: Neografika, 2005.

Schiller, József. *A Strasshofi Mentőakció és Előzményei, 1944–1945.* Budapest: Cserépfalvi, 1996.

Schindler, Oskar. *Ich, Oskar Schindler: Die persönlichen Aufzeichnungen, Briefe und Dokumente.* Edited by Erika Rosenberg. Munich: F.A. Herbig, 2000.

Schur, Maxine Rose. *Hannah Szenes: A Song of Light.* Philadelphia: Jewish Publication Society of America, 1986.

Schwartz, Andor. *Living Memory.* Melbourne, Australia: Schwartz, 2003.

Segev, Tom. *The Seventh Million: The Israelis and the Holocaust.* Translated by Haim Watzman. New York: Hill & Wang, 1993.

Shirer, William L. *The Rise and Fall of the Third Reich: A History of Nazi Germany.* New York: Simon & Schuster, 1960.

Soros, Tivadar. *Masquerade: Dancing around Death in Nazi-Occupied Hungary.* New York: Arcade, 2001.

St. John, Robert. *The Man Who Played God: A Novel about Hungary and Israel, 1944–1956.* Garden City, NY: Doubleday, 1962.

Stern, Samu. *Emlékirataim: Versenyfutás az Idővel.* Budapest: Bábel, 2004.

Stern, Samuel. "A Race against Time: A Statement." In *Hungarian Jewish Studies.* Vol. 3. Edited by Randolph L. Braham. New York: World Federation of Hungarian Jews, 1966–69.

Szep, Ernő. *The Smell of Humans: A Memoir of the Holocaust in Hungary.* Translated by John Batki. Budapest: Central European University Press, 1995.

Szilágyi, Ernő, and Attila Novák. *Ismeretlen Memoár a Magyar Vészkorszakról.* Budapest: Akadémiai, 2005.

Szita, Szabolcs. *Utak a Pokolból: Magyar deportáltak az Annektált Ausztriában, 1944–1945.* Budapest: Metalon Manager Iroda, 1991.

———. *A Humánum Példái: A Magyarországi Embermentö Akciók, 1944–1945.* Budapest: Magyar Auschwitz Alapitvány, 1998.

———. *Aki Egy Embert Megment, a Világot Menti Meg: Mentőbizottság, Kasztner Rezső, ss-Embervásár, 1944–1945.* Budapest: Corvina, 2005.

Teveth, Shabtai. *Ben-Gurion and the Holocaust*. New York: Harcourt Brace Jovanovich, 1996.

Tschuy, Theo. *Dangerous Diplomacy: The Story of Carl Lutz, Rescuer of 62,000 Hungarian Jews*. Grand Rapids, MI: William Eerdmans, 2000.

Ungvary, Krisztian. *The Siege of Budapest: 100 Days in World War ii*. New Haven, CT: Yale University Press, 2006.

Varga, László. "The Losses of Hungarian Jewry." In *Studies on the Holocaust in Hungary*. Edited by Randolph L. Braham. Boulder: Social Science Monographs; New York: Csengeri Institute for Holocaust Studies of the Graduate School and University Center, City University of New York, 1990.

Vincellér, Béla. *Sötet Árny a Magyarhon Felett: Szálasi Uralma (1944 October–1945 Maju)*. Budapest: Makkabi, 2003.

Von Lang, Jochen, ed. *Eichmann Interrogated: Transcripts from the Archives of Israeli Police*. Toronto: Lester & Orpen Dennys; New York: Farrar Straus Giroux, 1983.

Vrba, Rudolf, and Alan Bestic. *Escape from Auschwitz: I Cannot Forgive*. New York: Grove Press, 1986.

Vrba, Rudolf. *I Cannot Forgive*. Vancouver, BC: Regent College, 1997.

Wasserstein, Bernard. *Britain and the Jews of Europe, 1939–1945*. London, UK: Institute of Jewish Affairs, 1979.

Weinberg, Gerhard L. *A World at Arms: A Global History of World War ii*. New ed. Cambridge: Cambridge University Press, 2005.

Weissberg, Alex. *Advocate for the Dead: The Story of Joel Brand*. Translated by Constantine Fitzgibbon and Andrew Foster-Melliar. London: Andre Deutsch, 1958.

Weitz, Yechiam. *Changing Conceptions of the Holocaust*. New York: Oxford University Press, 1994.

———. "The Man Who Was Murdered Twice." In manuscript, translated from Hebrew.

Wiesel, Elie. *Night*. New York: Hill & Wang, 1960.

Wittmann, Rebecca. *Beyond Justice: The Auschwitz Trial*. Cambridge, MA: Harvard University Press, 2005.

Wyman, David S. *The Abandonment of the Jews: America and the Holocaust*. New York: New Press, 1984.

Zsolt, Béla. *Kilenc Koffer*. Budapest: Magvető, 1980.

Zweig, Ronald W. *The Gold Train: The Destruction of the Jews and the Looting of Hungary*. New York: William Morrow / HarperCollins, 2002.

ARTICLES

Barri, Shoshana. "The Question of Kastner's Testimonies on Behalf of Nazi War Criminals." *Journal of Israeli History* 18, no. 2 (Summer 1997).

———. "The Kastner Affair: Correspondence between Kurt Becher and Dr. Chaim Posner, 1948." *Journal of Israeli History* 18, no. 3 (Autumn 1997).

Baumel, Judith Tydo. "What Did Really Happen in Hungary?" *Haaretz*, June 13, 2003.

Bilsky, Leora. "Judging Evil in the Trial of Kastner." *Law & History Review* 19, no. 1 (Spring 2001).

Breitman, Richard, and Shlomo Aronson. "The End of the Final Solution? Nazi Plans to Ransom Jews in 1944." *Central European History* 25, no. 3 (1993).

Brenner, Lenni. "Zionist Collaboration with the Nazis," *Counterpunch,* December 2002.

Deak, István. "Admiral and Regent Miklos Horthy: Some Thoughts on a Controversial Statesman." *Hungarian Quarterly* 37/143 (Autumn 1996). Reprinted in *Encounters: A Hungarian Quarterly Reader,* 1999.

Erdelyi, Lajos. "Interjúja Mauthner Gabriellával." *Mult es Jovo,* March 4, 2000.

Fischer, István. "Ki volt a Gyilkos?" *Élet es Irodalom,* no. 46 (1950).

Friling, Tuvia. "Nazi-Jewish Negotiations in Istanbul in Mid-1944." *Journal of Holocaust and Genocide Studies* 13, no. 3.

Gilroy, Harry. "Israeli Cabinet Asked to Resign." *New York Times,* June 29, 1955.

———. "Quisling Charge Stirs All Israel." *New York Times,* July 3, 1955.

Karsai, László. "Weiss Arthur Emléktáblájához," *Centropa,* 1998.

Kasztner, Rezső. "A Nagy Embervásár: Kasztner Rezső." *Haladás,* March–June 1947.

Lahav, Yehuda. "Eichmann, Becher, Kasztner." *Beszelő,* May 2001.

Laqueur, Walter. "The Kasztner Case." *Contemporary Magazine* 20, no. 6 (1965).

LeBor, Adam. "Eichmann's List: A Pact with the Devil." *Independent* (London), August 23, 2000.

Livnat, Yitzak. "Utólagos Napló." *Remeny,* no. 1 (Spring 2005).

Marrus, Michael. "Holocaust Bystanders and Humanitarian Intervention." A paper presented at a conference on Humanitarian Narratives at the University of Connecticut, October 2006.

Mayer, Egon. "Jewish Holocaust Rescuer Murdered in Tel Aviv: A Personal Memoir." *Moment: The Jewish Magazine for the '90s,* August 1995.

————. "The Rescue of Jews via Bergen-Belsen, A Workshop on Rescue Efforts Concerning Jewish Inmates of Bergen-Belsen," March 7–9, 2003.

New York Times, "Zionist Ex-Leader Accused of Perjury," July 8, 1955; "Israeli Case Revived: Perjury Trial of Dr. Kastner Moved to Jerusalem," August 1, 1955; "Israel Libel Appeal Due: Decision in Nazi Collaboration Case to Be Challenged," August 22, 1955; "Israeli Shot in Street: Kastner, Libel Case Figure," March 4, 1957; "Israeli Quisling Dead of Wounds: Dr. Kastner, Branded a Nazi Collaborator, Succumbs to Assassin's Bullets," March 16, 1957; "Kastner Cleared by Israeli Court: Supreme Tribunal Reverses Ruling He Sacrificed Jews in Hungary to Nazis," January 6, 1958.

Novák, Attila. "Egy Ismeretlen Kronikája." *Szombat*, October 2003.

Perczel, Anna. "Pest Régi Zsidónegyede." *Muemlek Vedelem*, no. 3 (2005).

Rosenblum, Jonathan. "Anatomy of a Slander." *Jewish Observer and Middle Eas Review*, August 2005.

Schmidt, Maria. "Mentés Vagy Árulas? A Budapesti Zsidó Tanacs." *Medvetanc*, nos. 2–3 (1985).

Szita, Szabolcs. "A Zsidók Üldöztetese Budapesten, 1944–1945." *Holocaust Füzetek* 4 (1994).

Új Kelet, "Kasztnernek Emlékmüvet Kellett Volna Állitani Izraelben," December 23, 1994. An unsigned article quoting Kurt Becher as saying there should have been a monument erected in Israel in honor of Kasztner.

Varnai, Paul. "Jaj a Gyermekkor Milyen Tündéri Szép Volt." *Ezredveg*, May 1, 2006.

Warburg, Gustav. "The Strange Case of Joel Brand." *Jewish Observer and Middle East Review* 3 (1954).

FILMS

Alois Brunner: The Last Nazi. Cinevision, 2000.

Auschwitz: Inside the Nazi State. KCET Television, BBC Video, Warner Home Video, 2005.

Kasztner. Brubyak Studio, 2006.

Mishpat Kastner. Israel Broadcasting Authority, 1994.

Perlasca: An Italian Hero. Rai Fiction and Focus Film.

Secret History: Last Train From Budapest. 3BM Television, for Channel Four Television, 2000.

SELECTED DOCUMENTS

I spent many hours in libraries in Toronto and New York, in the Holocaust museums in Washington and Berlin, and in the Yad Vashem Museum Archives in Jerusalem. I was ably assisted at the Zionist Archives in Jerusalem by a Hebrew-speaking researcher and in the Albert and Temmy Latner Jewish Public Library in Toronto by Steve Bergson. I spent a day at the Memorial Museum of Hungarian-Speaking Jewry in Safed, Israel, where I saw television interviews with Hansi Brand, viewed the Slovak film about the failed Europa Plan, and copied a range of documents that helped with my research. I spent many days in the Toronto Public Library's Reference Section. I received documents online from a number of helpful individuals in Hungary, Israel, the United States, and Great Britain. In particular, I would like to mention the following documents:

Bauer, Yehuda, and Ysrael Guttman. "The Negotiations between Saly Mayer and the Representatives of the ss in 1944–1945." Proceedings of the Second Yad Vashem International Historical Conference, April 1974. Yad Vashem, Jerusalem, 1977.

Dr. Gabriel Barshaked's tape-recorded interviews with Hansi Brand. Yad Vashem Archives, Jerusalem.

Dossier on the Saly Mayer Negotiations. Records of the War Refugee Board. Franklin D. Roosevelt Library, Hyde Park, NY.

Gáll, András, "Volt Egyszer Egy Huszadik Század." Available online at mek.oszk.hu/03700/03779/.

"Kasztner és Társai Akciója," prepared by Lily Ungár, Kasztner's secretary, for the Jewish Agency's Dokumentácios Osztály, 1945. I received a copy of this handwritten document via email from György Vámos.

Kasztner's diaries. Yad Vashem Archives, Jerusalem.

Kolb, Jenő. "Erőltetett Menet" (Forced March). A detailed, sixty-four-page diary of the Bergen-Belsen group's days from June 30, 1944 to December 7, 1944. Memorial Museum of Hungarian-Speaking Jewry, Safed, Israel.

Krausz, Miklós. Testimony at Grünwald trial as reported in *Új Kelet*, June 27, 1954.

Moor, Z. "Budapest 1944." A report on the selection process and the departure of the Begen-Belsen group. Yad Vashem Archives, Jerusalem.

Testimony of Hermann Krumey for the Eichmann trial, taken in Frankfurt am Main, May 27, 1961, pts. 1 and 2. Available online through The Nizkor Project, at www.nizkor.org/.

Tibori Szabó, Zoltán. "Az Erdélyi Zsidóság Identitástudatának Alakulása 1945–1948," Doktori értekezés, Kolzsvár-Cluj. Napoca, 2007.

Transcripts of the trial of Adolf Eichmann. Available online through The Nizkor Project, at www.nizkor.org/.

Trial of the Major War Criminals before the International Military Tribunal Sitting in Nuremberg, Germany . . . from the Official Transcripts. 22 vols. Published under the authority of HM Attorney-General by HM Stationary Office, 1946–1950. Available online through The Nizkor Project, at www.nizkor.org/, and in the Reference Section of the Toronto Public Library.

Index